AP
World History
Prep Plus
2018–2019

Special thanks to the following for their contributions to this text: Laura Aitcheson, Sharon Barazani, Steve Bartley, Leslie Buchanan, Matthew Callan, Lana Chiad, Lauren Claus, Jonathan Darrall, M. Dominic Eggert, Tim Eich, Mark Feery, Isabella Furth, Chris Gage, Joanna Graham, Adam Grey, Rebekah Hawthorne, Katy Haynicz-Smith, Peter Haynicz-Smith, Andre Jessee, Rebecca Knauer, Liz Laub, John Magoun, Melissa McLaughlin, Terry McMullen, Emily Moore, Jenn Moore, Kristin Murner, Amira Sa'di, Ethan Underhill, Oscar Velazquez, Lee Weiss, Dan Wittich, and Nina Zhang.

AP® is a registered trademark of the College Board, which was not involved in the production of, and does not endorse, this product.

Ha Qiongwen, *Become a red seedling*. March 1965. Poster, 77 x 53 cm. International Institute of Social History, Amsterdam, Netherlands. From: International Institute of Social History collection, https://chineseposters .net/posters/e12-474.php. Used with permission.

Than, Ker. "Massive Population Drop Found for Native Americans, DNA Shows." *National Geographic*, National Geographic Society, 5 Dec. 2011, news.nationalgeographic.com/news/2011/12/111205-native-americans-europeans-population-dna-genetics-science/. Used with permission.

"Vimala: The Former Courtesan" (Thig 5.2), translated from the *Pāli* by Ṭhānissaro Bhikkhu. *Access to Insight (Legacy Edition)*, http://www.accesstoinsight.org/tipitaka/kn/thig/thig.05.02.than.html. Used with permission.

Printed in the United States of America

10 9 8 7 6 5 4 3 2 1

ISBN-13: 978-1-5062-0337-9

Kaplan Publishing print books are available at special quantity discounts to use for sales promotions, employee premiums, or educational purposes. For more information or to purchase books, please call the Simon & Schuster special sales department at 866-506-1949.

TABLE OF CONTENTS

PART 1: GETTING STARTED

PART 2: TARGETED REVIEW AND PRACTICE

PART 3: COMPLETE TIME PERIOD REVIEW

Table of Contents

PART 4: PRACTICE EXAMS

PART 1

Getting Started

CHAPTER 1

What You Need to Know About the AP World History Exam

INTRODUCTION

Congratulations on your decision to take the Advanced Placement exam in world history! The exam is a big one: its content measures your knowledge of world history from 8000 B.C.E. to the present. In preparing for the AP exam, you certainly will have built a solid foundation of historical knowledge. While this historical knowledge is critical to your learning, keep in mind that rote memorization of facts, dates, and events alone does not ensure success! The AP exam asks you to apply what you've learned at a higher level in order to demonstrate college-level abilities.

That's where this book comes in. This guide offers much more than a review of world history. We'll show you how to marshal your knowledge of world history and put it to brilliant use on the AP exam. We'll explain the ins and outs of the exam structure and question formats, so you won't experience any surprises. We'll even give you reading and writing strategies that successful students use to score higher on the AP exam.

Are you ready for your adventure through the study and mastery of everything AP World History? Good luck!

OVERVIEW OF THE EXAM STRUCTURE

Advanced Placement exams have been around for decades. While the format and content have changed over the years, the basic goal of the AP program remains the same: to give high school students a chance to earn college credit or advanced placement. To do this, a student needs to do two things:

- Find a college that accepts AP scores.
- Score well enough on the exam.

The first part is easy because most colleges accept AP scores in some form or another. The second part requires a little more effort. If you have worked diligently all year in your course work, you've laid the groundwork. The next step is familiarizing yourself with the exam.

What's On the Exam

The main goal of the College Board (the makers of the AP World History exam) is to help students think like a historian. To that end, some skills and methods you'll be expected to demonstrate are:

- analyzing primary and secondary sources
- making historical comparisons
- using reasoning about the context, causation, and continuity over time of major historical developments
- developing historical arguments

The AP World History exam is broken down into six historical periods:

Period	Period Title	Date Range	Weight
1	Technological and Environmental Transformations	to 600 B.C.E.	5%
2	Organization and Reorganization of Human Societies	600 B.C.E. to 600 C.E.	15%
3	Regional and Interregional Interactions	600 C.E. to 1450 C.E.	20%
4	Global Interactions	1450 C.E. to 1750 C.E.	20%
5	Industrialization and Global Integration	1750 C.E. to 1900 C.E.	20%
6	Accelerating Global Change and Realignments	1900 C.E. to the present	20%

Exam Structure

The AP World History exam is 3 hours and 15 minutes long. Section I is 1 hour and 35 minutes long and consists of 55 multiple-choice questions and 3 short-answer questions. Section II is 1 hour and 40 minutes long and consists of one document-based question (DBQ) and one long essay question (LEQ).

Section	Part	Percentage of Exam	Timing
I	Part A: Multiple-Choice (55 Questions)	40%	55 minutes
	Part B: Short-Answer (3 Questions)	20%	40 minutes
II	Part A: Document Based (1 Question)	25%	100 minutes
	Part B: Long Essay (1 Question)	15%	(includes a recommended 15-minute reading period)

Question Types

Let's take a brief look at what question types you'll see on the exam. In the following chapter, we'll go into even more detail about how to approach each question type in order to earn a high score.

Multiple-Choice Questions

The 55 multiple-choice questions will be divided into sets of two to five questions based on a primary or secondary source, which could be a text excerpt, image, graph, or map. These questions assess your ability to understand and analyze historical texts and interpretations, as well as your ability to make larger historical connections. Keep in mind that even if a question set is based on a specific historical period, the individual questions may require you to make connections to other periods and events.

Short-Answer Questions

The three short-answer questions assess your ability to think like a historian by analyzing sources and interpretations, including text excerpts, images, graphs, or maps. In composing your answer, you do not need to develop and support a thesis statement, but you do need to synthesize your ideas into cohesive paragraphs. The short-answer section allows you to demonstrate what you know best since you get to choose what historical examples to discuss in relation to the prompts. Also, while two of the short-answer prompts are required, you will choose between two prompts for your final short-answer question.

Document-Based Questions

The document-based question (DBQ) assesses your ability to develop an argument based on your assessment of historical evidence. The documents on which this essay is based can vary in length and format, including written, quantitative, or visual materials. You are expected to make sophisticated connections based on the given documents; therefore, it is essential to demonstrate your knowledge of larger historical themes (rather than just events, dates, and people) in order to earn the highest scores.

Long Essay Questions

Like the document-based question, the long essay question (LEQ) also assesses your ability to develop an argument using historical evidence. This time, the emphasis is on explaining and analyzing significant issues in world history. In this section, you will answer one of three prompts, each of which focuses on different time periods. Make sure to choose the prompt that best showcases the extent of your knowledge.

HOW THE EXAM IS SCORED

Once you complete your AP exam, it will be sent away to the College Board's AP Program for grading. The multiple-choice part is handled by a machine, while qualified AP graders—a group that includes history teachers and professors—score your essay responses. Your final score is a weighted combination of your multiple-choice and free-response section scores and is reported on a 5-point scale:

> 5 = Extremely well qualified
>
> 4 = Well qualified
>
> 3 = Qualified
>
> 2 = Possibly qualified
>
> 1 = No recommendation

"Qualified" means that you have proven yourself capable of doing the work of an introductory-level world history college course. Some colleges and universities will give you credit for a score of 3 or higher, but it's much safer to get a 4 or a 5. For specific rules regarding AP scores, check out each college's websites or call their admissions offices. If you do well on the AP exam, you may even get to move straight into a more advanced class (which is where the term "advanced placement" comes from)!

CHAPTER 2

How to Get the Score You Need

BOOK FEATURES

Kaplan's *AP World History Prep Plus* contains precisely the information you need to ace the exam. There's nothing extra in here to waste your time—no pointless review of material that's not on the exam and no rah-rah speeches. We simply offer the most potent test-preparation tools available.

Customizable Study Plans

We recognize that every student is a unique individual and that there is not a single recipe for success that works for everyone. To help you get The Score You Need in the Time You Have, we developed three customizable study plans based on how much time you have to prepare. These study plans are offered as a perforated card at the front of the book so you can use, as a bookmark, the study plan that is right for you. Select your study plan, then further customize your study of each historical period using the features in the Targeted Review and Practice chapters described below.

Test-Taking Strategies

This chapter features an extended discussion of general test-taking strategies as well as strategies tailored specifically to the AP World History exam and the types of questions it contains.

Targeted Review and Practice

Chapters 3 through 7 cover all of the AP World History time periods and are designed to help you assess your current AP World History knowledge, customize your study of the periods, and, depending on your results, conduct a Rapid Review of the periods before doing more practice.

Each chapter starts with the Test What You Already Know section, which includes two parts. Part A is a 10-question multiple-choice quiz, and Part B is a list of key topics you will check off if you can answer "yes" to at least three of the following questions:

- Can I describe this key topic?
- Can I discuss this key topic in the context of other events?
- Could I correctly answer a multiple-choice question about this key topic?
- Could I correctly answer a free-response question about this key topic?

Based on your Test What You Already Know section results, you will be given specific next steps for customized study, which each chapter outlines in a chart similar to the one below:

Your Results			Next Steps
Quiz		Key Topics	
You answered 8+ questions correctly	AND	You checked off 80%+ of key topics	1. Review the quiz explanations at the back of the book. 2. Read the Rapid Review in this chapter. 3. Complete the Test What You Learned section in this chapter and review the quiz explanations.
You answered 5–7 questions correctly	OR	You checked off 50–79% of key topics	1. Review the quiz explanations at the back of the book. 2. Read the Rapid Review in this chapter. 3. Go to the Complete Time Period Review for this period in Part 3. Read each High-Yield section about the key topics you did not check off. If you are short on time, read as many of these High-Yield sections as you are able. 4. Complete the Test What You Learned section in this chapter and review the quiz explanations.
You answered <5 questions correctly	AND	You checked off <50% of key topics	1. Review the quiz explanations at the back of the book. 2. Read the Rapid Review in this chapter. 3. Go to the Complete Time Period Review for this period in Part 3 and: • If you have time in your study schedule, study the full chapter. • If you are short on time, focus on High-Yield sections and the key topics with which you are least familiar. 4. Complete the Test What You Learned section in this chapter and review the quiz explanations.

The Rapid Review section includes a short time period summary as well as a brief definition for each key topic. Additional information and overall context for each key topic is provided in the corresponding Complete Time Period Review chapter.

At the end of each Targeted Review and Practice chapter, the Test What You Learned section features a 10-question multiple-choice quiz as well as the same key topics checklist provided at the beginning of the chapter. You will be able to gauge your progress based on how much you have improved since you completed the Test What You Already Know activities.

Complete Time Period Review

Chapters 8 through 12 feature the same time periods as Chapters 3 through 7 but are designed to cover every concept tested on the AP World History exam. Unlike the textbook you might have used in class, this book focuses exclusively on the material you are required to know for the exam. Throughout the text key topics are highlighted in bold. The most commonly tested topics are identified with High-Yield icons to help you recognize when information is absolutely essential to know. You'll be directed to these chapters, for studying either High-Yield topics or the complete chapter, based on your results on the Test What You Already Know activities in the corresponding Targeted Review & Practice chapter.

Full-Length Practice Exams

In addition to all of the questions included in each Targeted Review and Practice chapter, this book includes three full-length practice exams. We generally advise you take at least one practice exam near the beginning of your test preparation and at least one other closer to your actual AP exam. Your selected study plan will give you guidance based on the time you have until your exam. Practice exams give you the opportunity to test and refine your skills as well as a chance to find out what topics you should spend additional time studying. And the best part is that mistakes you make on our practice exams are mistakes you won't make on the real AP exam.

Practice tests and the answer keys are printed in this book. You can access complete explanations for every question and score your tests to see how you would have scored 0–5 on the official exam in your online resources; register your book at kaptest.com/booksonline for free access.

Online Quizzes

For even more practice, there are two additional quizzes for each time period as part of your online resources. Make sure to register your book at kaptest.com/booksonline to gain access to these valuable resources, which are free with the purchase of this book!

CHOOSING THE BEST STUDY PLAN FOR YOU

There's a lot of material to review before the AP exam, so it's essential to have a solid game plan that optimizes your available study time. To that end, we developed three study plan options that provide content review recommendations whether you have 2 months, 1 month, or 2 weeks to prepare for the exam. Check out the perforated study plan card at the front of the book for full details of each; the highlights are listed below:

2-MONTH STUDY PLAN	1-MONTH STUDY PLAN	2-WEEK STUDY PLAN
3–9 hours each week	7–10 hours each week	4–15 hours each week
3 Practice Exams	2 Practice Exams	1 Practice Exam
10 Online Quizzes	5 Online Quizzes	

2-Month Study Plan

The 2-Month Study Plan is ideal if you have at least eight weeks to study for the AP World History exam. This plan offers the most comprehensive practice, recommending you complete all three full-length practice exams in addition to all 100 online quiz questions. To help you streamline your practice, use your performance in each Test What You Already Know section to determine how much material you will cover in the Complete Time Period Review chapters. If you have more than eight weeks to study, simply spread out the activities listed to fit the time you have.

1-Month Study Plan

The 1-Month Study Plan is for you if you have at least a month to study. During the four weeks, we suggest you complete two practice exams and half (about 50) of the online quiz questions in addition to the Targeted Review and Practice chapters. Furthermore, your performance in each Test What You Already Know section will determine how much material you will cover in the Complete Time Period Review chapters. If you have a few additional weeks to prepare, feel free to give yourself more time to complete the activities listed to fit the time you have.

2-Week Study Plan

The 2-Week Study Plan is your best option if you have less than one month to study. To make the most of your time, we suggest completing one practice exam in addition to the Targeted Review and Practice chapters. Your performance in each Test What You Already Know section as well as how much time you have before the official exam will determine how much material you will cover in the Complete Time Period Review chapters. If you have a little more than two weeks to study, spend more time on—or add to—the list of activities to fit the time you have.

After you've made your selection, tear out the perforated study plan page, separate the bookmark that contains your choice of plan, and use it to keep track of both your place in the book and your progress in the plan. You can further customize any of the study plans by skipping over chapters or sections that you've already mastered or by adjusting the recommended time to better suit your schedule.

STRATEGIES FOR EACH QUESTION TYPE

The AP World History exam can be challenging, but with the right strategic mindset, you can get yourself on track for earning the 4 or 5 that you need to qualify for college credit or advanced placement. Before diving into strategies specific to the exam, let's review some general strategies that will aid you on any standardized test.

> **✔ AP Expert Note**
>
> **General Test-Taking Strategies**
>
> 1. **Pacing.** Because many tests are timed, proper pacing allows someone to attempt every question in the time allotted. Poor pacing causes students to spend too much time on some questions to the point where they run out of time before completing all of the questions.
>
> 2. **Process of Elimination.** On every multiple-choice test you ever take, the answer is given to you. If you can eliminate answer choices you know are incorrect and only one choice remains, then that must be the correct answer.
>
> 3. **Knowing When to Guess.** The AP World History exam does not deduct points for wrong answers, while questions left unanswered receive zero points. That means you should always make an educated guess on a question you can't answer any other way.
>
> 4. **Taking the Right Approach.** Having the right mindset plays a large part in how well people do on a test. Those students who are nervous about the exam and hesitant to make guesses often fare much worse than students with an aggressive, confident attitude.

These points are generally valid for standardized tests, but they are broad in scope. The rest of this section will discuss how these general ideas can be modified to apply specifically to the AP World History exam. These specific strategies and the factual information reviewed in this book's content chapters are the potent combination that will help you succeed on the exam.

Multiple-Choice Questions

The AP World History multiple-choice section consists of 55 questions, each with four answer choices, to be completed in 55 minutes. There is no penalty for incorrect answers, so guessing is encouraged. A primary or secondary document is provided for each question set, which will contain two to five questions. Question sets come from all six periods and can deal with specific countries and regions, global situations, or a single topic, such as the basic knowledge of a religion. Question sets are often comparative both within and across time frames.

The questions range from easy and medium to difficult with no distinct pattern to their appearance. A basic strategy for scoring well on this exam is to NOT do it linearly; in other words, do not take each question set one at a time, answering each one in order. The best strategy is to do the following:

- Answer all of the questions that you know and are sure about first.
- If you can eliminate at least two answer choices and the topic is familiar, mark the question by circling the question number in your exam booklet and move on.
- If you look at the question and do not remember the topic, mark the question with an X in your exam booklet and move on.
- Go back through the exam and answer the questions you marked with a circle. Try to eliminate at least two choices, then take your best educated guess as to the answer.
- Go back through the exam for a third time to answer the questions you marked with an X. Again, try to eliminate at least two choices, and take an educated guess.

Here are some more tips for doing well on the multiple-choice section:

- The easiest question may be the last one. Go through all of the exam questions!
- Move quickly but thoroughly through the exam. Don't linger on any one question for more than 30 seconds or so.
- If you skip a question, make sure that you skip that line on the answer grid.
- If you finish with time left, go back and check your answers, and make sure you have marked all responses correctly on the grid.
- DO NOT change an answer you have made unless you are absolutely sure that your initial attempt is incorrect. Research shows that your first answer is usually the correct one.
- When eliminating tempting wrong choices, look for choices that are out of the given time period or region or are not related to specific categories (e.g., the question asked for economic factors, and the answer choice mentions law codes).

Short-Answer Questions

On the AP World History exam, you have 40 minutes to answer three short-answer questions, each of which will have two to three parts. Aim to spend about 10 to 12 minutes on each question depending on how many parts it contains. Apply any extra time you have at the end of the section to reread your responses, looking for quick errors to fix (such as missing punctuation or wording).

Use the first minute to identify all of the parts of the question. Then, before you begin writing your answer, create a plan of which historical examples you will be using for each part. Your responses to each part should be between three and six sentences long.

You will have plenty of opportunities to practice writing responses to short-answer questions in the practice exams, so be sure to complete those sections to the best of your ability for the most exam-like experience.

Scoring

According to the College Board, a high-scoring response to a short-answer question will accomplish all tasks outlined in the question. You must answer each part of the question with complete sentences and provide specific historical examples in order to receive full credit. Make sure you go beyond simply quoting or paraphrasing historical evidence and really explain its meaning or significance.

Depending on the question, a high-scoring short-answer response may:

- explain a historical interpretation, compare two interpretations, and/or explain how evidence relates to an interpretation.

- address causes and effects, similarities and differences, or continuities and changes over time for different historical issues.

The Document-Based Question

The first part of Section II is the document-based question (DBQ). This essay **asks you to think like a historian**; it will ask a specific question and present 4 to 10 related documents. Essentially, you are the historian who will take these sources and draw conclusions based on your analytical skills. The DBQ evaluates historical understanding at its purest: the task is not to remember facts but to organize information in an analytical manner.

If the DBQ prompt and accompanying documents cover something well outside the mainstream, don't panic! The exam writers do this on purpose. The other essay on the exam—the long essay question—will evaluate your knowledge of history, but the DBQ evaluates your ability to work with historical material, even material with which you're less familiar. Writing the DBQ is a skill that can be learned much like any other skill, and this book will help you hone that skill.

Organizing Your Response

The 100 minutes for Section II of the exam is divided into two parts: the first 15 minutes is the suggested reading and organizing time, and the last 85 minutes is the suggested essay writing time. The proctor will make timing announcements, and it is recommended that you spend 45 minutes writing the document-based question, and 40 minutes writing the long essay question. However, you will not be forced to move from reading to writing, or from the DBQ to the long essay, if you're not yet ready.

You will want to spend the first 10 minutes of the suggested reading period on the DBQ since this essay requires the most preparation time. Use the remaining five minutes to read and prep for the long essay question.

First, read the DBQ prompt. Underline the words that are most relevant to your task. Let's look at a sample question:

> Using the following documents, analyze how the Ottoman government viewed ethnic and religious groups within its empire for the period 1876–1908. Identify an additional document and explain how it would help you analyze the views of the Ottoman government.

All of the documents that follow will relate to the time period and the place, so you do not need to underline 1876–1908 or Ottoman government. You are being asked how the Ottoman government **viewed ethnic and religious groups** within its empire. An essay that dealt with how the groups viewed the Ottoman Empire would miss the point.

> ✔ **AP Expert Note**
>
> Take a couple of seconds to read the instructions for the DBQ and each of the other essays. These list the tasks that you must accomplish to score well. Use these instructions as a checklist.

Second, read the documents. Most of the first 10 minutes of the suggested reading period will be used to review the documents and organize them into groups for analysis. Each of the 4 to 10 documents will have a number above a box. Inside the box will be information about the source of the document, which is very important as you will see later, and the document itself.

Documents can be of many different sorts. They can be pictures, photographs, maps, charts, graphs, or text. Written documents are usually excerpts of much longer pieces that have been edited specifically for the exam. They could be from personal letters, private journals, official decrees, public speeches, or propaganda posters. Obviously, the nature of the source should guide you in how you analyze the document. Often, students have a harder time analyzing the visual and graphic sources than the written sources. Even so, use all of the documents in your essay, treating the non-written sources with the same attention as the written ones.

All of the essay questions will be presented in a booklet. Feel free to write notes in this booklet as you read the documents and to underline important words in both the source line and the document itself. Nothing in the booklet is read as part of the essay scoring. Use the generous margins for notes that will help you group the documents together and discuss their points of view.

Jot down notes about the background of the authors in the margins. Information about the authors' social class, education, occupation, and gender may be important in the essay. At the bottom of the document, write a short phrase that summarizes the basic meaning of the document, its purpose (why it was written), and a missing piece of evidence that could relate to the document. If the document is a speech, the missing evidence could be the perception of those listening to the speech. If the document is a government declaration, the missing evidence could be information about how effectively the declaration was carried out.

It is also helpful to pause after reading all of the documents to consider evidence that would provide a more complete understanding of the issue. Then you can suggest an additional document.

> **✔ AP Expert Note**
>
> You will have to use black or blue ink to write your essays. If you are used to writing in pencil or typing, practice writing in ballpoint pen. Use a comfortable pen—one with a finger cushion and a wide diameter.

Once you have finished reading and have made short notes of all of the documents, **reread the question.** Again, note what the question asks. If you have not done so already, mark which documents address the different issues that the question includes. Group the documents by their similarities. At this point, you should be able to draw enough conclusions to organize a strong, analytical thesis.

At the end of the 15 minutes, the proctor will announce that the time is up for the suggested reading period. If you have not yet finished reading and organizing your essays, take a few more minutes to finish up. A few students might be ready to write before the end of the reading period, but most find that the given time is just about right.

Scoring

According to the College Board, a high-scoring DBQ response will:

- *respond to the question with an evaluative thesis that makes a historically defensible claim. The thesis must consist of one or more sentences located in one place—either in the introduction or the conclusion. Neither the introduction nor the conclusion is necessarily limited to a single paragraph.*

- *describe a broader historical context immediately relevant to the question that relates the topic of the question to historical events, developments, or processes that occur before, during, or after the time frame of the question. This description should consist of more than merely a phrase or a reference.*

- *explain how at least one additional piece of specific historical evidence (beyond those found in the documents) relates to an argument about the question. This example must be different from the evidence used to earn credit for contextualization, and the explanation should consist of more than merely a phrase or a reference.*

- *use historical reasoning to explain relationships among the pieces of evidence provided in the response and how they corroborate, qualify, or modify the argument made in the thesis. In addition, a good response should utilize the content of at least six documents to support an argument based on the question.*

- *explain how the documents' point of view, purpose, historical situation, and/or audience is relevant to the argument for at least four of the documents.*

To effectively prepare for the DBQ, it is important to understand what components are needed for a high-scoring response. The AP World History exam readers will be looking for proficiency in four reporting categories: Thesis/Claim, Contextualization, Evidence, and Analyzing and Reasoning. The readers use a rubric similar to the following to determine your raw score, which can range from 0-7.

Reporting Category	Scoring Criteria	Decision Rules
Thesis/Claim (0–1 pt)	Responds to the prompt with a historically defensible thesis/claim that establishes a line of reasoning. **(1 pt)**	To earn this point, the thesis must make a claim that responds to the prompt rather than restating or rephrasing the prompt. The thesis must consist of one or more sentences located in one place, either in the introduction or the conclusion.
Contextualization (0–1 pt)	Describes a broader historical context relevant to the prompt. **(1 pt)**	To earn this point, the response must relate the topic of the prompt to broader historical events, developments, or processes that occur before, during, or continue after the time frame of the question. This point is not awarded for merely a phrase or reference.
Evidence (0–3 pts)	Evidence from the Documents: Uses the content of at least **three** documents to address the **topic** of the prompt. **(1 pt)** OR Supports an **argument** in response to the prompt using at least **six** documents. **(2 pts)**	To earn one point, the response must accurately describe — rather than simply quote — the content from at least three of the documents. To earn two points, the response must accurately describe — rather than simply quote — the content from at least six documents. In addition, the response must use the content of the documents to support an argument in response to the prompt.
	Evidence Beyond the Documents: Uses at least one additional piece of the specific historical evidence (beyond that found in the documents) relevant to an argument about the prompt. **(1 pt)**	To earn this point, the response must describe the evidence and must use more than a phrase or reference. This additional piece of evidence must be different from the evidence used to earn the point for contextualization.

(Continued)

Reporting Category	Scoring Criteria	Decision Rules
Analysis and Reasoning (0–2 pts)	For at least **three** documents, explains how or why the document's point of view, purpose, historical situation, and/or audience is relevant to an argument. **(1 pt)**	To earn this point, the response must explain how or why (rather than simply identifying) the document's point of view, purpose, historical situation, or audience is relevant to an argument about the prompt for each of the three documents sourced.
	Demonstrates a complex understanding of the historical development that is the focus of the prompt, using evidence to corroborate, qualify, or modify an argument that addresses the question. **(1 pt)**	A response may demonstrate a complex understanding in a variety of ways, such as: • Explaining nuance of an issue by analyzing multiple variables • Explaining both similarity and difference, or explaining both continuity and change, or explaining multiple causes, or explaining both cause and effect • Explaining relevant and insightful connections within and across periods • Confirming the validity of an argument by corroborating multiple perspectives across themes • Qualifying or modifying an argument by considering diverse or alternative views or evidence This understanding must be part of the argument, not merely a phrase or reference.

Sample DBQ

Let's look at an example of a DBQ before learning how to earn the highest score possible.

Using the following documents, analyze how the Ottoman government viewed ethnic and religious groups within its empire for the period 1876–1908. Identify an additional document and explain how it would help you analyze the views of the Ottoman Empire.

Document 1

Source: Adapted from Abdolonyme Ubicini and Pavet de Courteille, *The Present State of the Ottoman Empire*, a guide concerning the Ottoman Empire published in Western Europe, 1876.

FIGURES ON NATIONALITIES WITHIN THE OTTOMAN EMPIRE		
Ethnic Group (Total population) Percentage of Empire	**Subgroup**	**Subgroup Population**
Turkish group (14,020,000) 49.1%	Ottoman Turks	13,500,000
	Turkomans	300,000
	Tatars	220,000
Greco-Latin group (3,520,000) 12.3%	Greeks	2,100,000
	Kutzo-Vlachs	220,000
	Albanians	1,200,000
Slavic group (4,550,000) 15.9%	Serbo-Croatians	1,500,000
	Bulgarians	3,000,000
	Cossacks	32,000
	Lipovans	18,000
Persian group (3,620,000) 12.7%	Armenians	2,500,000
	Kurds	1,000,000
	Other Persians	120,000
Semites (1,611,000) 5.6%	Jews	158,000
	Arabs	1,000,000
	Other Semites	453,000
Other groups (1,232,000) 4.3%		
Total Population of the Ottoman Empire: 28,553,000		

Document 2

Source: The Ottoman Constitution, 23 December 1876.

Art. 1. The Ottoman Empire comprises present territory and possessions, and semidependent provinces. It forms an indivisible whole, from which no portion can be detached under any pretext whatever.

Art. 4. His Majesty the Sultan, under the title of "Supreme Caliph," is the protector of the Muslim religion. He is the sovereign and emperor of all the Ottomans.

Art. 8. All subjects of the empire are called Ottomans, without distinction, whatever faith they profess; the status of an Ottoman is acquired and lost according to conditions specified by law.

Art. 9. Every Ottoman enjoys personal liberty on condition of noninterfering with the liberty of others.

Art. 11. Islam is the state religion. But, while maintaining this principle, the state will protect the free exercise of faiths professed in the Empire, and uphold the religious privileges granted to various bodies, on condition of public order and morality not being interfered with.

Document 3

Source: Mr. Owen Davis, from a lecture at a British Congregational Church "Those Dear Turks," 1st November 1876.

Unfortunately for the peace of mankind, it has happened that the Turk is placed in a position where it is impossible to ignore him, and almost equally impossible to endure him; while by his origin, habits, and religion, he is an Asiatic of Asiatics, he is by irony of fate established in a position where his presence is a ceaseless cause of misery to millions of Christian people.

Document 4

Source: Hagop Mintzuri, an Armenian baker's apprentice, from his book *Istanbul Memoirs 1897–1940*, commenting about the military guards accompanying the sultan's arrival at a mosque for ceremonial prayers at the end of the fast of Ramadan.

First the Albanian guards, dressed in violet knee-breeches, who were not soldiers or police and did not speak Turkish, would fill the upper part of our market square. Then would come the Arab guards of the sultan, dressed in red salvar and adorned with green turbans. These too, did not speak Turkish and they would fill the road. Finally the Palace Guard of the sultan, chosen exclusively from Turks who were tall, sporting their decorations on their chests, would take up their positions as an inner ring in front of the Albanians and Arabs.

Document 5

Source: Süleyman Hüsnü Pasha (Pasha is a title of distinction within the Ottoman Empire), former high adviser to the sultan, commenting on the ethnic and religious diversity in Iraq, 7 April 1892.

The elements belonging to the official faith and language of the state are in a clear minority whereas the majority falls to the hordes of the opposition.

Document 6

Source: Ahmed Cevdet Pasha, respected Ottoman statesman and historian, undated official memorandum.

The Sublime State rests on four principles. That is to say, the ruler is Ottoman, the government is Turkish, the religion is Islam, and the capital is Istanbul. If any of these four principles were to be weakened, this would mean a weakening of one of the four pillars of the state structure. . . . The Sublime State is a great structure made up of various peoples and strata; all of these constituent elements are held together by the sacred power of the Caliphate. Because the only thing uniting Arab, Kurd, Albanian, and Bosnian is the unity of Islam. Yet, the real strength of the Sublime State lies with the Turks. It is an obligation of their national character and religion to sacrifice their lives for the House of Osman until the last one is destroyed. Therefore it is natural that they be accorded more worth than other peoples of the Sublime State.

Document 7

Source: Proclamation by the Young Turks, 1908.

3. It will be demanded that all Ottoman subjects having completed their twentieth year, regardless of whether they possess property or fortune, shall have the right to vote.

9. Every citizen will enjoy complete liberty and equality, regardless of nationality or religion, and be submitted to the same obligations. All Ottomans, being equal before the law as regards rights and duties relative to the State, are eligible for government posts, according to their individual capacity and their education. Non-Muslims will be equally liable to the military law.

Crafting a Solid Thesis Statement

You have one chance to make a good first impression. Usually, an AP reader can tell within the first few sentences whether or not an essay is going to be strong. A few essays can recover after a poor start, but first impressions matter. Consequently, nothing is more important in the first paragraph than the clear statement of an analytical thesis.

Different kinds of writings demand different types of opening paragraphs. In English class, you may learn a style of essay writing that asks for general background information in a first paragraph. On a DBQ, however, you do not have much time. The reader is most interested in seeing a strong thesis as soon as possible.

Your thesis can be more than just one sentence. With the compound questions often asked by the DBQ, two sentences might be needed to complete the idea. To score well, the thesis needs to include specific information that responds to the question. Many students think they have written a thesis when, in actuality, they have not; their opening paragraphs are just too general and unspecific.

> ✔ **AP Expert Note**
>
> **Your thesis can be in the first or last paragraph of your essay, but it cannot be split between the two. Many times, your original thesis is too simple to gain the point. A good idea is to write a concluding paragraph that might extend your original thesis. Think of a way to restate your thesis, adding information from your analysis of the documents.**

The thesis is that part of your essay that 1) specifically addresses the terms of the question and 2) sets up the structure for the rest of your essay.

Let's take a look at thesis statement samples based on the prompt from earlier in the chapter.

"For the period 1876–1908, analyze how the Ottoman government viewed ethnic and religious groups within its empire."

Thesis Statements That Don't Work

The following statement is not an acceptable thesis; it is far too vague. It says very little about how the essay is structured.

> There were many ways in which the Ottoman government viewed ethnic and religious groups.

The next statement paraphrases the historical background and does not address the question. It would not receive credit for being a thesis.

> The Ottoman government brought reforms in the Constitution of 1876. The empire had a number of different groups of people living in it, including Christians and Muslims who did not practice the official form of Islam. By 1908 a new government was created by the Young Turks and the sultan was soon out of his job.

This next sentence gets the question backward: you are being asked for the government's view of religious and ethnic groups, not the groups' view of the government. Though the point-of-view issue is very important, this statement would not receive POV credit.

> People of different nationalities reacted differently to the Ottoman government depending on their religion.

The following paragraph says a great deal about history, but it does not address the substance of the question. It would not receive credit because of its irrelevancy.

> Throughout history, people around the world have struggled with the issue of political power and freedom. From the harbor of Boston during the first stages of the American Revolution to the plantations of Haiti during the struggle to end slavery, people have battled for power. Even in places like China with the Boxer Rebellion, people were responding against the issue of Westernization. Imperialism made the demand for change even more important, as European powers circled the globe and stretched their influences to the far reaches of the known world. In the Ottoman Empire too, people demanded change.

✔ **AP Expert Note**

Remember, if you ADD another paragraph or statement after writing a conclusion—that becomes your conclusion. Draw a line from any information added after the conclusion with an arrow to just before your conclusion. This keeps your conclusion valid.

Thesis Statements That DO Work

Now we turn to thesis statements that do work. These two sentences address both the religious and ethnic aspects of the question. They describe *how* these groups were viewed.

> The Ottoman government took the same position on religious diversity as it did on ethnic diversity. Minorities were servants of the Ottoman Turks, and religious diversity was allowed as long as Islam remained supreme.

This statement answers the question in a different way but is equally successful.

> Government officials in the Ottoman Empire sent out the message that all people in the empire were equal regardless of religion or ethnicity, yet the reality was that the Turks and their version of Islam were superior.

Analyzing the Documents

The readers award credit based on what the essays accomplish. They do not remove points if an essay is off-task, written poorly, or wrong. There is one exception, however. In the DBQ, you must demonstrate that you understand the documents being used. If your essay makes more than one major misinterpretation, credit cannot be earned.

A major misinterpretation is one that misses the basic intent of the document. If you wrote that the Proclamation of the Young Turks (document 7) was a movement away from ethnic and religious equality, that misinterpretation would be a major error.

If, instead, you wrote that the Ottoman Empire survived for decades after the Proclamation of the Young Turks in 1908, the statement would be wrong (the Ottoman Empire collapsed after World War I) but would not be a misinterpretation of the document. All of the documents could still count as being understood properly. Be careful—especially with visual and graphic documents. Students tend to misinterpret these non-written documents more than they misinterpret traditional written documents.

> ✔ **AP Expert Note**
>
> **For charts and graphs, pay particular attention to the title and to the factors delineating the information in the visual. This will help you interpret the document. For pictures, remember that all pictures are taken for a reason and reflect the point of view of the photographer and/or the subject. Notice details in the background or foreground that can help you interpret them.**

Using Evidence to Support Your Thesis

Your ability to use the documents provided to answer the question is the focus of the essay. Use the documents to analyze, and you will earn credit for doing so.

If the essay supports the thesis with appropriate evidence from all, or all but one, of the documents, then the essay earns full credit. If it uses evidence from all but two of the documents, then partial credit is earned.

As you are writing your essay, check off each document in your booklet as you use it. When writing under the pressure of time, you may forget to mention one or two. Remember to include the documents that are in graphic or visual formats. Students often forget to analyze these to the same degree that they do written sources.

To receive full credit, the documents need to be used as part of the analysis. In other words, do you mention something about a document that helps to answer the question? If a document is mentioned only in a list, it will not count. For example, "The Ottoman Empire looked down on ethnic and religious minorities, as seen in documents 3, 4, and 5." If documents 3, 4, and 5 were not analyzed further, this essay would not receive full credit for supporting the thesis with appropriate evidence.

How should essays refer to the documents? Any of the following ways could count for supporting your thesis with evidence. Your essay could:

1. Refer to the document number directly in the sentence: "As shown by document 7, the Young Turks believed that all ethnic and religious groups should be treated equally."

2. Refer to the document within parentheses at the end of the sentence: "The Young Turks believed that all ethnic and religious groups should be treated equally (document 7)."

3. Refer to information presented in the line of source attribution: "As shown by The Proclamation of the Young Turks in 1908, the Young Turks believed that all ethnic and religious groups should be treated equally."

4. Combine the last two techniques: "As shown by The Proclamation of the Young Turks in 1908, the Young Turks believed that all ethnic and religious groups should be treated equally (document 7)." **(best option)**

5. Give no attribution: "The Young Turks believed that all ethnic and religious groups should be treated equally." **(worst option)**

Merely summarizing the documents is the easiest way to miss out on scoring well. You must link the document to the question, not just repeat what the document says. For example, the following paragraph might not count as evidence in support of the thesis:

> Document 1 is a chart with numbers for the different nationalities within the Ottoman Empire. Turks are 49.1% of the population. There are a lot of other groups listed too. The total population is about 28 million people. In document 2 the constitution says that the sultan is the religious authority and the sovereign. It also says that Islam is the state religion and that 'the state will protect the free exercise of faiths professed in the Empire, and uphold the religious privileges granted to various bodies.'

This summary does not provide any analysis. It states simply *what* the documents say; it does not describe *how* the documents show government views toward ethnic and religious groups. The task of the essay is to answer the question by analyzing.

The following paragraph would help earn full credit for evidence in support of the thesis:

> Document 1 is a chart that clearly demonstrates the ethnic diversity of the Ottoman Empire at the time of the new constitution. The Turks were a minority at 49.1% of the population, even though they controlled the government of the Ottoman Empire. The Constitution of 1876 (document 2) also reinforces the idea that the empire was formed of various ethnicities and religions. It formally states that all people are granted equality, and that all religions answer to the same law. However, this document reflects the law from the point of view of high government officials. It therefore demonstrates only the legal rules, rather than the day-to-day reality in the empire.

Another easy way to miss out on scoring well is by not having a strong thesis. How can you use document evidence to support the thesis if the thesis itself is weak? Your essay should be organized enough so that the reader can see how each document fits into the analysis presented in the thesis. Using the same terms that are mentioned in the thesis is a good way to make the links between the evidence and the thesis more apparent.

Discussing Point of View

Properly discussing the point of view (POV) of the documents is another important, and sometimes difficult, task. It separates the mediocre essays from those that score very well. Your essay will need to mention aspects of POV for at least two documents in order to receive POV credit.

So what is point of view? Essentially, POV is the analysis of why a certain person composed the material for the document. What is the author's (or the document's) "angle"? Comments in your essay that explore the motivations for the documents often count as POV. In addition, comments relating to the reliability of a source relate to that source's POV.

You cannot just say that an author is biased or prejudiced to receive the point for POV. You must state why or indicate an impact or desired effect of the document.

Ask these questions in order to earn the full credit for POV:

1. Does the occupation of the author give the document more or less reliability? For example, government officials may overstate or exaggerate information for political, state, or personal reasons.
2. Does the social class, religion, national background, or gender of the author influence what is mentioned in the document?

3. Does the type of document influence the content of what is said? A journal entry or private letter might be more candid about a topic than a public address that is meant to be persuasive. A political cartoon by definition is exaggerated and meant to convey a certain message, whereas a photograph may accurately represent what was in front of the camera for a shot, but could be staged and framed to capture only a certain perspective.

4. Does the timing of the document influence the message? Recollections and memoirs written long after an event may not have the same reliability as first-hand materials done immediately afterward.

5. Does the intended audience skew the message of a source? If a document is meant to be read by the sultan, it has a different POV than one written for a European audience.

6. Describing the tone of the document can also count for POV if the document is sarcastic, triumphant, haughty, etc. Using tone for POV can be more subtle and is best used with other descriptions of POV.

Merely attributing the document's source by repeating the source material from the document is not enough to earn the POV point. The source material, however, gives you clues as to what you could say relating to POV.

Using our sample DBQ on the Ottoman government's view of ethnic and religious groups, let's examine different examples of POV. You may want to go back to review the documents in the sample DBQ. The following statements may all count for point of view:

For document 1:

- "The census of national groups within the Ottoman Empire was compiled for Western European readers, which may make it more reliable in counting ethnic minorities than one published for a Turkish distribution." (intended audience and reliability)

- "The figures on nationalities provide a detailed picture of the population at the beginning of the sultan's reign but do not show how the population groups changed over time." (timing of the document)

- "The numbers in these census figures might be inexact because of the difficulty of counting widely dispersed people over a hundred years ago. The numbers seem rounded and may be educated guesses." (reliability)

For document 2:

- "The Constitution of 1876 reflects the official governmental laws and may not accurately represent the reality within the empire." (type of document)

- "The Constitution was most likely written by high government officials, who may have wanted the Ottoman Empire to seem more enlightened than it actually was." (background of the authorship)

- "The Constitution's protection of rights may have been an attempt to calm the masses during a sensitive time of transition." (timing)

For document 3:

- "Mr. Davis's speech may demonstrate anti-Muslim feelings that Europeans held at that time." (background of author and tone)

- "This speech given to a Christian group far away from the Ottoman Empire may be biased against the Ottoman government since the Ottomans were not in the mainstream of Western European society." (audience and reliability)

- "As a speech given in a British church, this document may have exaggerated the problems of the Ottoman government's treatment of Christians for dramatic effect." (type of document)

For document 4:

- "As an Armenian, Mintzuri was very aware of the different ethnic groups representing the sultan's guard." (background of the author)

- "Since this recollection was published in Mintzuri's memoirs years after the event, the details may be inexact." (type of document)

- "As a lower-class baker's apprentice, Mintzuri may have had strong feelings about his low position in society and consequently recorded the arrangement of guards as a ranking based on status." (occupation of author)

For document 5:

- "Süleyman Hüsnü Pasha, who had a title of distinction, was a former advisor to the sultan. Hüsnü's occupation had an effect on his opinion since he probably knew more about the conditions of the empire." (occupation of the author)

- "Since Süleyman Hüsnü Pasha was in political exile at the time of this document, he may have been more open about the situation in Iraq since he was not officially a part of the government." (background of the author)

- "Süleyman Hüsnü Pasha seems to hold a bias against the ethnic and religious minorities in Iraq, calling them 'hordes of the opposition.' This bias may have come from Hüsnü's loyalty to the official version of Islam and the Turkish language." (tone and background of author)

For document 6:

- "As a respected Ottoman statesman, Ahmed Cevdet Pasha was representing the official government views toward the different ethnic groups in the empire." (occupation of the author)

- "Since Cevdet's comments were in the form of an official memo, this document reveals the view of someone close to the power center of the Ottoman Empire." (type of document)

- "Most likely Ahmed Cevdet Pasha was a Turk and a Muslim and therefore would look more favorably on the role of Muslims and Turks within the Ottoman Empire." (background of author)

For document 7:

- "The Young Turks, as a revolutionary group of reformers, wanted the support of ethnic minorities. Consequently, they demanded complete liberty and equality in this proclamation to the people." (type of document, intended audience, and authorship)

- "The Young Turks wanted a new style of government. As a result they called on values different from those that had been practiced by the Ottoman officials." (background of authors)

- "Because this proclamation came in 1908 at the end of the sultan's rule, the message is more democratic and progressive than seen previously." (timing of document)

Some of the statements seem more sophisticated than others, and some of the statements may actually contradict each other. Even so, describing point of view is a skill that must be demonstrated for at least two documents.

Essays that use POV in a sophisticated manner and use it consistently are rewarded with very high scores, as long as every other basic component has been addressed.

Grouping Documents Together in Your Analysis

Historians analyze material by pulling together similar pieces of evidence, and, in writing your DBQ, so should you. The documents naturally come together into groups for analysis. Within each of your body paragraphs, group the documents. Essays that successfully have two or three groupings, depending on the question, often earn high scores.

Do not work with documents in isolation since a group cannot have just one document. A common mistake is for students to describe each document in order by paraphrasing what it says. This "listing" format is deadly to good performance on the DBQ.

Two earlier paragraphs served as examples of how to use and how not to use evidence to support your thesis. Let's look at these paragraphs again to see how effectively they group documents.

- "Document 1 is a chart with numbers for the different nationalities within the Ottoman Empire. Turks are 49.1% of the population. There are a lot of other groups listed too. The total population is about 28 million people. In document 2 the constitution says that the sultan is the religious authority and the sovereign. It also says that Islam is the state religion and that 'the state will protect the free exercise of faiths professed in the Empire, and uphold the religious privileges granted to various bodies.'"

- "Document 1 is a chart that clearly demonstrates the ethnic diversity of the Ottoman Empire at the time of the new constitution. The Turks were a minority at 49.1% of the population, even though they controlled the government of the Ottoman Empire. The Constitution of 1876 (document 2) also reinforces the idea that the empire was formed of various ethnicities and religions. It formally states that all people are granted equality, and that all religions answer to the same law. However, this document reflects the law from the point of view of high government officials. It therefore demonstrates only the legal rules, rather than the day-to-day reality in the empire."

In the first example, the documents are discussed independently. In the second example, they are discussed together, which creates a stronger paragraph.

Types of Groupings

How you group documents is a matter of personal opinion. Typical groupings include:

- chronological timing of the documents
- class, gender, occupation, and ethnicity of the documents' authors
- purpose or intended audience of the documents
- attitude and tone of the documents
- aspects covered by the documents (economic, political, social, or religious, etc.)
- geographic areas represented by the documents
- type of documents (pictures, charts, written documents, transcripts of speeches, etc.)

> **✔ AP Expert Note**
>
> Notice that a comparison is used to indicate that the documents are related and, thus, demonstrates a grouping. Using comparisons tells the reader that you are analyzing documents, not just listing them. Other ways to group your documents include by type, period, point of view, gender, social status, nationality, religion, location, and ideology.

For example, you could group the documents in the following ways:

By document type and intended audience:

- official proclamations/constitutions (documents 2 and 7)
- Ottoman internal correspondence (documents 4 and 5)
- documents intended for non-Ottoman audiences (documents 1 and 3)

By attitudes toward ethnic and religious minorities:

- documents that show inclusion (documents 2, 4, and 7)
- documents that show division (documents 3, 4, 5, and 6)

By focus on types of groups:

- documents that focus on religious groups (documents 2, 3, 5, 6, and 7)

- documents that focus on ethnic groups (documents 1, 4, 6, and 7)

You can group documents in a variety of ways. A single document can even be used in more than one group within an essay. You are encouraged to group documents in as many appropriate ways as possible.

Organizing Your Documents

A straightforward way to organize your grouping is to indicate why you are grouping documents together in your topic sentence. For example: "The Ottoman Constitution of 1876 (document 2) and the Proclamation of the Young Turks (document 6) both indicate that the Ottoman rulers wanted to ensure that all of their subjects understood that they were equal before the law. In the Ottoman Constitution, subjects are _____, while in the Proclamation of the Young Turks, subjects are _____."

Make sure to address each document when you list two or more documents in a grouping sentence. If you forget to actually use the document, it will cost you points for not using all of the listed documents.

Using Additional Historical Evidence

When doing research, historians continuously ask themselves where else they could find valuable information on a topic. Historians are in constant search of new areas of inquiry and new sources to explain the past. Since the DBQ is the essay that asks you to be a historian, your essay needs to provide suggestions for additional documents that could be useful in answering the question. These suggestions should not be types of documents that are already present in the DBQ, but rather the "missing voice" not already included in the list of documents.

For this task, you do not need to be very specific; you do not even need to mention a specific document. All you need to do is mention a type of document that could be useful in answering the question asked. The readers of the AP essay do not expect that high-school students would have knowledge of hidden documents in some archive that might shed light on this topic. General statements involving hypothetical types of documents would be fine *even if* they do not really exist.

Just as important as mentioning a potentially useful type of document is describing *why* it would be useful. To earn credit, you need to include both: mention of an additional document and an explanation about why it would be useful in analyzing the question. Unfortunately, students frequently mention a type of additional document without describing why.

For our sample DBQ, examples of additional documents could be:

- a document from the sultan himself since he represents the central power of the Ottoman Empire

- official orders from the Ottoman government on how to treat different ethnic and religious subjects since such a document could show how the government implemented its policies

- a chart showing statistics of religious diversity within the empire that would help describe the position of the official faith within the empire

- a speech or an article from a Young Turk on his attitude toward the Ottoman government that would help show the differences in thought between reformers and officials

- a document from a religious leader within the Ottoman Empire that would provide a sense of how official religious policies were perceived by the religious communities themselves

- a map showing the distribution of different ethnic groups within the Ottoman Empire, which would help illustrate the divisions faced by this multi-ethnic country

Any of these responses, or any combination of these, would receive credit as additional document(s). Other potential responses would also be counted if their importance could be explained.

Be careful: mentioning a type of document that you have already been given disqualifies the statement. For our sample DBQ, mentioning a document from a person outside of the Ottoman Empire would not count because document 3 is written from a British perspective. Nor would mentioning a document from an ethnic or religious minority within the Ottoman Empire count because document 4 is written by an Armenian in Istanbul. To make sure that you earn credit, you may want to mention two or three different types of additional documents and why each would be useful.

Students often mention an additional document at the end of the essay. However, discussion of the additional document can take place anywhere in the essay, and the most sophisticated essays will place this discussion of the additional documents as part of the body of the essay.

Going Beyond the Basic Requirements

Your goal for the DBQ is to earn the highest score possible. To earn a stellar score, several indicators of excellence may be considered. A high-scoring essay will likely:

- have a highly sophisticated thesis

- show deep analysis of the documents

- use documents persuasively in broad conceptual ways

- analyze point of view thoughtfully and consistently

- identify multiple additional documents with sophisticated explanations of their usefulness

- bring in relevant outside information beyond the historical background provided

Final Notes on How to Write the DBQ

Do:

- Take notes in the margins during the reading period relating to the background of the speaker and his/her possible point of view.

- Assume that each document provides only a snapshot of the topic—just one perspective.

- Look for connections between documents for grouping.

- In the documents booklet, mark off documents that you use so that you do not forget to mention them.

- As you are writing, refer to the authorship of the documents, not just the document numbers.

- Mention additional documents and the reasons why they would help further analyze the question.

- Mark off each part of the instructions for the essay as you accomplish them.

- Use visual and graphic information in documents that are not text-based.

Don't:

- Repeat information from the historical background in your essay.

- Assume that the documents are universally valid rather than presenting a single perspective.

- Spend too much time on the DBQ rather than moving on to the other essay.

- Write the first paragraph before you have a clear idea of what your thesis will be.

- Ignore part of the question.

- Structure the essay with just one paragraph.

- Underline or highlight the thesis. (This may be done as an exercise for class, but it looks juvenile on the exam.)

The Long Essay Question

The long essay question on the AP World History exam assesses your ability to apply knowledge of history in a complex, analytical manner. In other words, you are expected to treat history and historical questions as a historian would. This process is called historiography—the skills and strategies historians use to analyze and interpret historical evidence to reach a conclusion. Thus, when writing an effective essay, you must be able to write a strong, clearly developed thesis and supply a substantial amount of relevant evidence to support your thesis.

Scoring

According to the College Board, a high-scoring long essay question response will:

- *respond to the question with an evaluative thesis that makes a historically defensible claim. The thesis must consist of one or more sentences located in one place—either in the introduction or the conclusion. Neither the introduction nor the conclusion is necessarily limited to a single paragraph.*

- *explain how a relevant historical context influenced the topic addressed in the question. It should also relate the topic of the question to broader historical events, developments, or processes that occur before, during, or after the time frame of the question. This explanation should consist of more than merely a phrase or a reference.*

- *use historical reasoning to explain relationships among the pieces of evidence provided in the response and how they corroborate, qualify, or modify the argument made in the thesis.*

The AP World History exam readers will be looking for proficiency in the same four reporting categories they use to assess your DBQ response: Thesis/Claim, Contextualization, Evidence, and Analyzing and Reasoning. The readers use a rubric similar to the following to determine your raw score, which can range from 0-6.

Reporting Category	Scoring Criteria	Decision Rules
Thesis/Claim (0–1 pt)	Responds to the prompt with a historically defensible thesis/claim that establishes a line of reasoning. **(1 pt)**	To earn this point, the thesis must make a claim that responds to the prompt rather than restating or rephrasing the prompt. The thesis must consist of one or more sentences located in one place, either in the introduction or the conclusion.
Contextualization (0–1 pt)	Describes a broader historical context relevant to the prompt. **(1 pt)**	To earn this point, the response must relate the topic of the prompt to broader historical events, developments, or processes that occur before, during, or continue after the time frame of the question. This point is not awarded for merely a phrase or reference.
Evidence (0–2 pts)	Provides specific examples of evidence relevant to the topic of the prompt. **(1 pt)** OR Supports an argument in response to the prompt using specific and relevant examples of evidence. **(2 pts)**	To earn one point, the response must identify specific historical examples of evidence relevant to the topic of the prompt.\n\nTo earn two points the response must use specific historical evidence to support an argument in response to the prompt.
Analysis and Reasoning (0–2 pts)	Uses historical reasoning (e.g. comparison, causation, continuity and change over time) to frame or structure an argument that addresses the prompt. **(1 pt)** OR Demonstrates a complex understanding of the historical development that is the focus of the prompt, using evidence to corroborate, qualify, or modify an argument that addresses the question. **(2 pts)**	To earn the first point, the response must demonstrate the use of historical reasoning to frame or structure an argument, although the reasoning might be uneven or imbalanced.\n\nTo earn the second point, the response must demonstrate a complex understanding. This can be accomplished in a variety of ways, such as:\n\n• Explaining nuance of an issue by analyzing multiple variables\n\n• Explaining both similarity and difference, or explaining both continuity and change, or explaining multiple causes, or explaining both causes and effects\n\n• Explaining relevant and insightful connections within and across periods\n\n• Confirming the validity of an argument by corroborating multiple perspectives across themes\n\n• Qualifying or modifying an argument by considering diverse or alternative views or evidence\n\nThis understanding must be part of the argument, not merely a phrase or reference.

Success on the long essay section of the exam starts with breaking down the task of essay writing into specific steps.

Step 1: Dissect the Question

Always keep in mind that the AP World History exam is written to be challenging and rigorous. Thus, the questions will require you to identify specific and important information prior to constructing a response. When given an essay prompt, first take some of your time to slow down and understand exactly what the question is asking you to do. The key here is to understand how to answer all parts of the question. Circle directive words, such as *analyze*, *compare*, *contrast*, or *assess the extent to which*. Commonly, prompts will ask you to validate or refute a statement or to explain the impact of one event on another or the degree of impact. List these directives as pieces of the puzzle that you will attempt to put together with your history knowledge.

> ✔ **AP Expert Note**
>
> ### There Is No *U* In History
>
> Don't include personal opinions in the essay. The reader is looking for your grasp of the history itself and your ability to write about it.

Step 2: Formulate a Thesis

A major area of concern each year for the AP exam readers is that students do not take the time to understand all parts of the question and plan their responses. We have already dissected the question; now it is time to plan a thesis. The thesis is your way of telling the reader why he or she should care about reading your essay. If you have a weak thesis, the reader will not be convinced that you understand the question. He or she will not trust that you have the depth of knowledge necessary to answer the question. Therefore, you must have a thesis that takes a stand, answers the entire question, and shows the reader the path you will take in your essay answer. It is not enough to merely restate the question as your thesis. One of the most important things to do is to take a position. Don't be afraid of taking a strong stand for or against a prompt as long as you can provide proper and relevant evidence to support your assertions.

> ✔ **AP Expert Note**
>
> ### Think Ahead
>
> During the planning time, make a short outline of all of the outside information you're planning to use in your essay; you will have the info handy while you're writing.

Think of your thesis as the "road map" to your essay. It will provide the reader with the stops along the way to the final destination—the conclusion. Only through a thorough study of world history can you construct a strong thesis.

> ✔ **AP Expert Note**
>
> **Organize Your Writing Strategically**
>
> When composing your essay, start with your most important information. If you run out of time when you're writing, your key points are already in the essay.

Step 3: Plan Your Evidence

Now that you have a "road map," you need to brainstorm all of the relevant evidence you can recall that relates to the question. There are several ways to do this: a cluster or web diagram, a bulleted list, or a quick outline. Whatever you prefer, this is a step you *cannot* skip! Students who do not take the time to plan their evidence often find themselves scratching out irrelevant information during the exam, thus wasting valuable time. Also, you must learn to brainstorm efficiently—you should use only about five minutes to complete the first three steps of essay writing. Use abbreviations, pictures, or other cues that are efficient for you.

> ✔ **AP Expert Note**
>
> **Stick to the Subject**
>
> In your long essay, giving historical information before or after the time period in the essay topic will not get you any extra points.

Once you have a list, you can move to the next (and most important) step—writing!

Step 4: Write Your Essay

As you practice writing essays using the strategies in this chapter, you will have the luxury of taking time to write topic sentences, list evidence, and construct "mini-conclusions" for each prompt. However, on the AP exam, time is of the essence! You will have 40 minutes to construct a coherent essay response for the LEQ if you use 60 minutes (including the 15-minute reading period) for the DBQ. If you practice the prewriting strategies from the previously outlined steps 1 through 3, you will find it easy to write a developed paper in a short time.

There is no "standard" number of paragraphs you must have. A good rule to keep in mind is one body paragraph for each portion of the essay prompt. Some AP World History exam questions will be structured to fit a five-paragraph essay, while others may need more and others less. You will not be penalized for writing a strong four-paragraph response. Likewise, you will not be rewarded for constructing a weak six-paragraph response. AP readers look for quality, not quantity.

Your first paragraph should always introduce your essay. Your thesis from step 2 is only part of your introduction. The first paragraph of your essay should include your thesis and any other organizational cues you can give your reader. Ask yourself, "Could a complete stranger understand where my essay is going from just my first paragraph?" If your answer is no, then you must rework the introduction. Do not spend time creating a "hook" or flashy statement for your first sentence. Do not use rhetorical questions. AP graders are reading for the items that are listed on the scoring guide. You will notice that creativity in language and structure is not a listed item. However, a well-written and developed argument is a desired item.

Your body paragraphs should follow the "road map" you set in your introduction and thesis. Don't stray from your plan, or you will find yourself straying from the question. You have taken the time to plan, so follow it! Do not merely list facts and events in a "laundry list" fashion. You must have some element of analysis between each set of evidence you provide. Using transition words, such as *however*, *therefore*, and *thus*, to show a shift in thought can make creating analytical sentences quick and easy. You should practice stringing facts and thoughts together using these "qualifying transitions" in your sentences.

> ✔ **AP Expert Note**
>
> ### Know the Lingo
>
> Whenever possible, use historical terms or phrases instead of general ones. For example, instead of saying that the South established laws against an owner freeing slaves, say that the South established laws against *manumission*. This shows the reader that you really know your stuff.

Beware of telling a story rather than answering the question. Readers are looking for analysis, not a revised version of your textbook. Do not attempt to shower the reader with extra factoids and showy language. Say what you need to say cleanly and simply. Readers will be impressed with your ability to write clearly and concisely in a way that showcases your historical knowledge, rather than your ability to write creatively.

Because this is a formal essay, you should avoid using personal pronouns, such as *you*, *I*, or *we*. Also, avoid the use of terms that could be "loaded" unless you intend on explaining them to the reader. For instance, you would not want to use the term *liberal* to describe Thomas Jefferson unless you were prepared to explain your use of the word *liberal* in the historical context. Do not use slang in any part of your essay. Because your essay is about history, write your essay in the past tense. Do not write about Franklin D. Roosevelt as if he were still alive today.

You should end each body paragraph with a "mini-conclusion" that ties the paragraph back to the thesis. It can serve as a transition sentence into the next paragraph or stand alone. In either case, the reader should be able to tell easily that you are shifting gears into another part of the essay.

Lastly, write your conclusion. Many students have learned that they should simply restate their thesis in the conclusion; these students may recopy what they wrote in the introduction word for word. This is incorrect. Yes, you should restate your thesis, but in a new way. Instead of rewriting it word for word, explain why your thesis is significant to the question. Do not introduce new evidence in your conclusion. The conclusion should tie all of the "mini-conclusion" sentences together and leave the reader with a sense of completion. If you are running out of time when you reach the conclusion, you may leave it off without incurring a specific penalty on the scoring guide. However, if you practice writing timed essays, you will learn the proper timing it takes to write a complete essay (conclusion included).

COUNTDOWN TO THE EXAM

Make Sure You're Registered

You can register for the exam by contacting your guidance counselor or AP coordinator. If your school doesn't administer the exam, contact the Advanced Placement Program for a list of schools in your area that do. Keep in mind that College Board's deadlines for registration are often at least two months before the actual exam.

There is a fee for taking AP exams, and the current cost can be found at the official exam website listed below. For students with acute financial need, the College Board offers a fee reduction that is usually equal to about one-third of the cost of the exam. In addition, most states offer exam subsidies to cover all or part of the remaining cost for eligible students.

For more information on all things AP, contact the Advanced Placement Program:

Phone: (888) 225-5427 or (212) 632-1780

Email: apstudents@info.collegeboard.org

Website: https://apstudent.collegeboard.org/home

Three Days Before the Exam

Take a full-length practice exam under timed conditions. Use the techniques and strategies you've learned in this book. Approach the exam strategically, actively, and confidently.

> ✔ **AP Expert Note**
>
> **Do NOT take a full-length practice exam fewer than 48 hours before the actual AP exam. Doing so will probably exhaust you and hurt your official score.**

Two Days Before the Exam

Review the results of your practice exam. Don't worry too much about your score or agonize over whether you got a particular question right or wrong. The practice exam doesn't count; what's important is reviewing your performance with an eye for how you might get through each section faster and better on the exam to come.

> ✔ **AP Expert Note**
>
> **Don't just score your exam and move on! It's important to go over all of the answers and explanations, which can also serve as a quick review of important history material.**

The Night Before the Exam

DO NOT STUDY. Gather together an "AP World History Exam Kit" containing the following items:

- A few No. 2 pencils (Pencils with slightly dull points fill the ovals better; mechanical pencils are NOT permitted)

- Erasers

- A pen with black or dark blue ink (for the free-response questions)

- Your 6-digit school code (Home-schooled students will be provided with their state's or country's home-school code at the time of the exam)

- A watch (as long as it does not have internet access, have an alarm, or make noise)

- Photo ID card

- Your AP Student Pack

- If applicable, your Student Accommodation Letter, which verifies that you have been approved for a testing accommodation (such as braille or large-type exams)

Know exactly where you're going, how you're getting there, and how long it takes to get there. It's probably a good idea to visit your test center sometime before the day of the exam so that you know what the rooms are like, how the desks are set up, and so on.

Relax the night before the exam: read a book, take a hot shower, watch something you enjoy. Go to bed early to get a good night's sleep, and leave yourself extra time in the morning.

The Morning of the Exam

First, wake up on time. After that:

- Eat breakfast. Make it something substantial, but not anything too heavy or greasy.

- Don't drink a lot of caffeinated beverages, especially if you're not used to them. Bathroom breaks cut into your time, and too much caffeine is a bad idea in general.

- Dress in layers so that you can adjust to the temperature of the testing room.

- Read something. Warm up your brain with a newspaper, a magazine, or an online article. You shouldn't let the exam be the first thing you read that day.

- Be sure to get there early. Allow yourself extra time for traffic, mass transit delays, and/or detours.

During the Exam

Don't be shaken. If you find your confidence slipping, remind yourself how well you've prepared. You know the structure of the exam; you know the instructions; and you've had practice with—and have learned strategies for—every question type.

If something goes really wrong, don't panic. If you accidentally misgrid your answer page or put the answers in the wrong section, raise your hand and tell the proctor. He or she may be able to arrange for you to regrid your test after it's over when it won't cost you any time.

After the Exam

You might walk out of the AP World History exam thinking that you blew it. This is a normal reaction. Lots of people—even the highest scorers—feel that way. You tend to remember the questions that stumped you, not the ones that you knew. We're positive that you will have performed well and scored your best on the exam because you followed the Kaplan strategies. Be confident in your preparation, and celebrate the fact that the AP World History exam is soon to be a distant memory.

PART 2

Targeted Review and Practice

CHAPTER 3

Periods 1 and 2: Up to 600 C.E. – Targeted Review and Practice

LEARNING OBJECTIVES

After studying these time periods, you will be able to:

- Describe the interrelationship between various societies and their environment.

- Describe cultural and technological diffusion resulting from interactions between cultures.

- Compare major world religions and belief systems.

- Explain how different governing forms are built and maintained over time.

- Describe how various societies' economic systems arise, and what they in turn cause.

- Describe the impact of environment and disease on migration and settlement.

- Explain how different governing forms are built and maintained over time.

- Explain the effects of society, culture, and environment on nation-states.

- Describe the impact of the environment on economic and industrial development.

CHAPTER OUTLINE

TIMELINE

Date	Region	Event
8000 B.C.E.	Mid East	Neolithic Revolution
5000 B.C.E.	Mid East	Sumer civilization in the Fertile Crescent
5000 B.C.E.	Africa	Agriculture begins in Nile River Valley
3500 B.C.E.	Mid East	Bronze Age
3000 B.C.E.	Africa	Pharaohs rule Egypt
3000 B.C.E.	Mid East	Indus River Valley civilization
1600 B.C.E.	East Asia	Huang He (Yellow River) civilization
550 B.C.E.	Mid East	Persian empire
600–501 B.C.E.	East Asia & South Asia	Buddhism, Confucianism, Daoism begin
500–401 B.C.E.	Europe	Greek Golden Age
403–221 B.C.E.	East Asia	Era of Warring States in China
321–185 B.C.E.	South Asia	Mauryan empire
221 B.C.E.	East Asia	Qin dynasty unifies China
32 C.E.	Mid East	Christianity begins
206–220 C.E.	East Asia	Han dynasty
320–550 C.E.	South Asia	Gupta Golden Age
476 C.E.	Europe	Fall of Rome
518–527 C.E.	Europe & Mid East	Justinian rules the Byzantine Empire

TEST WHAT YOU ALREADY KNOW

Part A: Quiz

Questions 1–3 refer to the map below.

ANCIENT RIVER VALLEY CIVILIZATIONS

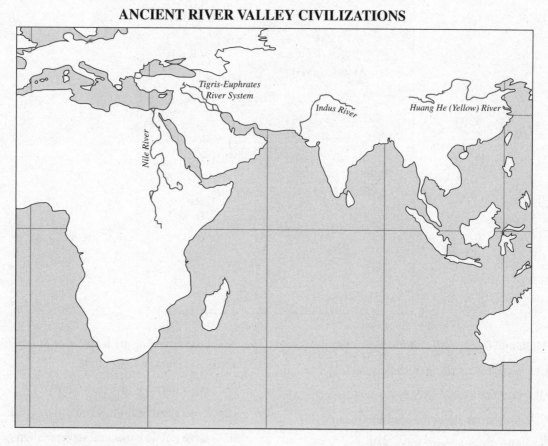

1. Which of the following correctly matches the river to the civilization that developed around it?

   (A) Nile: Indian civilization

   (B) Huang He (Yellow): Egyptian civilization

   (C) Tigris and Euphrates: Mesopotamian civilization

   (D) Indus: Chinese civilization

2. One society <u>differs</u> from the other three river valley civilizations pictured above in that it lacked

   (A) polytheistic religion

   (B) bronze tools and weapons

   (C) pictographic writing

   (D) social stratification

3. Which of the following statements correctly describes a consequence of establishing a society along a river?

   (A) In China, the annual flooding cycles were quite predictable.

   (B) In India, the Ganges River's proximity allowed civilization to spread.

   (C) In Mesopotamia, rivers confined trade to the Fertile Crescent.

   (D) In Egypt, the river served as a natural barrier against invaders.

45 | K

Up to 600 C.E.

Questions 4–5 refer to the map below.

MOHENJO-DARO AND HARAPPA

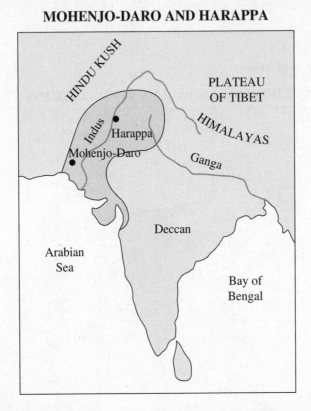

4. Mohenjo-Daro and Harappa were examples of

   (A) oasis towns along the Silk Road

   (B) dominant city-states in Ancient Greece

   (C) port cities along the Mediterranean

   (D) cities in the Indus River Valley

5. All of the following are featured at Mohenjo-Daro and Harappa <u>except</u> for

   (A) repositories of deciphered texts

   (B) streets and buildings laid out in grids

   (C) large public baths and sewer systems

   (D) expansive granaries for storing grain

Questions 6–8 refer to the passages below: Passage 1 is an excerpt from the Twelve Tables of Rome, circa 450 B.C.E., and Passage 2 is an excerpt from Hammurabi's Code, circa 1750 B.C.E.

Passage 1

"Table III.

1. One who has confessed a debt, or against whom judgment has been pronounced, shall have thirty days to pay it in. After that forcible seizure of his person is allowed. . . .

Table V.

1. Females should remain in guardianship even when they have attained their majority. . . .

Table VIII.

2. If one has maimed a limb and does not compromise with the injured person, let there be retaliation. If one has broken a bone of a freeman with his hand or with a cudgel, let him pay a penalty of three hundred coins. If he has broken the bone of a slave, let him have one hundred and fifty coins. If one is guilty of insult, the penalty shall be twenty-five coins.

3. If one is slain while committing theft by night, he is rightly slain."

Passage 2

"196. If a man put out the eye of another man, his eye shall be put out.

197. If he break another man's bone, his bone shall be broken.

198. If he put out the eye of a freed man, or break the bone of a freed man, he shall pay one gold mina."

6. The ideas expressed in the passages above most strongly represent which of the following historical trends?

(A) The formal stratification of society

(B) The development of religious morality

(C) The idea that a republic's leaders were not above the law

(D) An attempt to halt ongoing societal collapse

7. Which of the following did the Twelve Tables and Hammurabi's Code have in common?

(A) Accusers could confront the accused in court.

(B) Punishments were written to fit the crime.

(C) Lower classes and higher classes were treated equally.

(D) Men and women were treated equally.

8. Both of these documents were intended to

(A) be flexible and change with the circumstances

(B) protect the lower classes from the abuse of upper classes

(C) provide democracy to their territories

(D) unify the diverse customs of diverse populations

Questions 9–10 refer to the following religious texts: Passage 1 is an excerpt from the New Testament's Book of First Corinthians, Chapter 7; Passage 2 is a Buddhist poem translated by Thanissaro Bhikkhu, as written in the _Therigatha_.

Passage 1

"I would like you to be free from concern. An unmarried man is concerned about the Lord's affairs—how he can please the Lord. But a married man is concerned about the affairs of this world—how he can please his wife—and his interests are divided. An unmarried woman or virgin is concerned about the Lord's affairs: Her aim is to be devoted to the Lord in both body and spirit. But a married woman is concerned about the affairs of this world—how she can please her husband. I am saying this for your own good, not to restrict you, but that you may live in a right way in undivided devotion to the Lord."

Passage 2

"_Vimala: The Former Courtesan_

Intoxicated with my complexion,
figure, beauty, & fame;
haughty with youth,
I despised other women.
Adorning this body
embellished to delude foolish men,
I stood at the door to the brothel:
a hunter with snare laid out.
I showed off my ornaments,
and revealed many a private part.
I worked my manifold magic,
laughing out loud at the crowd.

Today, wrapped in a double cloak,
my head shaven,
having wandered for alms,
I sit at the foot of a tree
and attain the state of no-thought.
All ties—human & divine—have been cut.
Having cast off all effluents,
cooled am I, unbound."

9. Which of the following statements most accurately compares the role of women in Christianity and Buddhism?

(A) In both religions, women could follow an alternative life in the monastery.

(B) In both religions, men were considered spiritually superior.

(C) Christianity attracted many female converts initially, while Buddhism attracted very few.

(D) Buddhist women could not read sacred texts, but Christian women could read the Bible.

10. Which of the following is a similarity between Buddhism and Christianity?

(A) Both religions have salvation as their ultimate goal.

(B) Both religions are monotheistic in nature.

(C) Both see their founders as fully human and fully divine.

(D) Both had several variations early in their history. - coptic
- nastorian

Part B: Key Topics

The following is a list of the major people, places, and events for Periods 1 and 2: up to 600 C.E. You will very likely see many of these on the AP World History exam.

For each key topic, ask yourself the following questions:

- Can I describe this key topic?
- Can I discuss this key topic in the context of other events?
- Could I correctly answer a multiple-choice question about this key topic?
- Could I correctly answer a free-response question about this key topic? (600- 600)

Check off the key topics if you can answer "yes" to at least three of these questions.

Early Humans

- [x] Paleolithic MC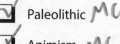
- [x] Animism MC

Development of Agriculture

- [x] Neolithic Revolution
- [ ] Pastoralism
- [x] Job specialization
- [x] Patriarchy

Development of Agriculture (cont.)

- [ ] Metallurgy
- [x] Mesopotamia

The First Civilizations

- [ ] Assyria
- [x] Shang
- [x] Cuneiform
- [ ] Ziggurats

Up to 600 C.E.

The First Civilizations (cont.)

- [✓] Hammurabi's Code
- [✓] Phoenicians
- [✓] Egypt
- [✓] Pictographs
- [✓] Roman empire
- [✓] Hebrews
- [✓] Harappa and Mohenjo-daro
- [✓] Vedas
- [✓] Hinduism
- [✓] Caste system
- [✓] Mandate of Heaven *Dynastic cycle*
- [ ] Qin dynasty
- [ ] Olmecs
- [ ] Chavin
- [✓] Maya empire

Classical Societies

- [ ] Persia
- [✓] Alexander the Great
- [✓] Hellenistic
- [ ] Mauryan empire

Classical Societies (cont.)

- [ ] Ashoka
- [✓] Gupta empire
- [✓] Daoism
- [ ] Han dynasty
- [✓] Silk Road
- [ ] Filial piety
- [ ] Republic
- [ ] Phoenicia
- [ ] Diaspora
- [✓] Christianity
- [✓] Monsoon winds
- [✓] Indian Ocean trade

Development and Spread of Religion

- [ ] Shamanism
- [✓] Ancestor veneration
- [✓] Brahma
- [ ] Buddha
- [✓] Confucius
- [✓] Islam
- [ ] Zoroastrianism

Tally Your Results For Part A and Part B

Part A: Check your answers and count the number of questions you got correct.

1. C
2. A
3. D
4. D
5. A

6. A
7. B
8. B
9. A
10. D

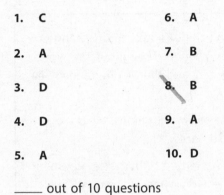

_____ out of 10 questions

Detailed explanations can be found in the back of the book.

Part B: Count the number of key topics you checked off.

_____ out of 50 key topics

Your Results		Next Steps
Quiz	**Key Topics**	
You answered 8+ questions correctly	AND — You checked off 40+ (80%+) key topics	1. Review the quiz explanations at the back of the book. 2. Read the Rapid Review in this chapter. 3. Complete the Test What You Learned section in this chapter and review the quiz explanations.
You answered 5–7 questions correctly	OR — You checked off 25–39 (50–79%) key topics	1. Review the quiz explanations at the back of the book. 2. Read the Rapid Review in this chapter. 3. Go to the Complete Time Period Review for this period in Part 3. Read each High-Yield section about the key topics you did not check off. If you are short on time, read as many of these High-Yield sections as you are able. 4. Complete the Test What You Learned section in this chapter and review the quiz explanations.

You answered <5 questions correctly	AND — You checked off <25 (<50%) key topics	1. Review the quiz explanations at the back of the book.
		2. Read the Rapid Review in this chapter.
		3. Go to the Complete Time Period Review for this period in Part 3 and:
		  • If you have time in your study schedule, study the full chapter.
		  • If you are short on time, focus on High-Yield sections and the key topics with which you are least familiar.
		4. Complete the Test What You Learned section in this chapter and review the quiz explanations.

RAPID REVIEW

Summary—Periods 1 and 2: Up to 600 C.E.

1. From the simplest barter system to long journeys along trade routes, the exchange of goods and ideas shaped this period and led to further change throughout the world. Important trade routes like the Silk Road, the Indian Ocean, and the Mediterranean Sea shaped development.

2. Once people began to settle and gradually organize into early civilizations, the discovery of agriculture began to change their lives at a more rapid pace.

3. As humans organized themselves in families, gender roles emerged. With the development of agriculture, the division of labor further deepened these divisions. These gender roles were reinforced by religious systems and governmental systems.

4. During this period, major world religions developed and spread, shaping the civilizations they encountered. Religions and belief systems, such as Hinduism, Buddhism, Confucianism, and Daoism (Asia), and Christianity and Judaism (Europe, Asia), influenced large numbers of people throughout the period.

5. Civilizations emerged that had organized governments, complex religions, social structures, job specialization, public works, systems of writing, and arts and architecture. These civilizations grew into larger and more complicated governmental organizations, such as empires (e.g., Rome, Han, and Gupta).

Key Topics—Periods 1 and 2: Up to 600 C.E.

Remember that the AP World History exam tests you on the depth of your knowledge, not just your ability to recall facts. While we have provided brief definitions here, you will need to know these terms in even more depth for the AP exam, including how terms connect to broader historical themes and understandings.

Early Humans

- **Paleolithic**: Literally, "old stone." The period from the appearance of the first hominids (human-like creatures) to approximately 8000 B.C.E.

- **Animism**: Often found in primitive tribes, the belief that spirits can possess and control natural things and forces.

Development of Agriculture

- **Neolithic Revolution**: Starting around 7000 B.C.E., this period marked the beginnings of permanent settlements and sedentary farming, leading to longer lives and higher populations.

- **Pastoralism**: The agricultural practice of domesticating animals for food or other uses, beginning around 4000 B.C.E.

- **Job specialization**: As civilizations progressed and not everyone needed to farm to live, skilled laborers like artisans were allowed to craft things that had value. The trade that followed led to the growth of cities.

- **Patriarchy**: A society in which men hold power within the family, in governance, and/or in economics.

- **Metallurgy**: The crafting of metallic ores into functional and/or valuable items, beginning around 4500 B.C.E.

- **Mesopotamia**: Literally, "The Land Between the Rivers." Geographic region centered on the Tigris and Euphrates Rivers, located in modern-day Iraq. Considered one of the four major "cradles of civilization."

The First Civilizations

- **Assyria**: Region in Southwest Asia spanning from modern-day Egypt to Iraq, this region was founded by a Semitic people around 2000 B.C.E. and lasted into the 600s B.C.E. Known for their fierce warrior spirit, the Assyrians were also great builders, creating cities like Nineveh and Ashur.

- **Shang**: A people speaking a Sino-Tibetan language, they developed an ancient civilization along the Huang He (Yellow) River in modern-day China. Along with Mesopotamia, South Asia, and Egypt, it is a "cradle of civilization."

- **Cuneiform**: The Sumerian system of writing and one of the oldest forms of writing. Completed by pressing a wedge-shaped stylus into clay.

- **Ziggurats**: The hallmark of Sumerian architecture, these multitiered pyramids served as temples to the gods.

- **Hammurabi's Code**: Oldest known code of law. Issued by Hammurabi around 1800–1700 B.C.E. to unify his empire in Babylon, this code emphasized retaliation as punishment—"an eye for an eye, and a tooth for a tooth."

- **Phoenicians**: Phoenicia was founded around 2000 B.C.E. in modern-day Lebanon, and this civilization based its livelihood on the sea. Skilled mariners, the Phoenicians traded their famed murex shells (used for "royal purple" dye) and red cedar trees. Their alphabet inspired the Greek alphabet. Collapsed around 600 B.C.E. with an Assyrian invasion.

- **Egypt**: Located in Northeast Africa on the fringe of the Sahara Desert and centered on the Nile River, this nation is considered another one of the "cradles of civilization."

- **Pictographs**: Many forms of ancient writing were based on symbols that represented a sound or a concept. Pictographic languages from this period include Egyptian hieroglyphics, Sumerian cuneiform, the text of the Harappan seals, and the text of the Chinese oracle bones.

- **Roman Empire**: The largest of the ancient world's empires, it spanned across the European continent and around the Mediterranean basin. Previously a republic, the empire was noted for its strong military, achievements in academics, and the spread of Christianity. Its peak was a 200-year period (about 20 B.C.E.–180 C.E.) known as the Pax Romana, or Roman Peace.

- **Hebrews**: Descendants of Abraham, considered the founder of Judaism, the first monotheistic religion. They settled in modern-day Israel c. 1500 B.C.E., then moved to Egypt.

- **Harappa and Mohenjo-daro**: The two key cities of the Indus River Valley Civilization. Located in modern-day Pakistan, they represent another one of the "cradles of civilization."

- **Vedas**: A collection of hymns and chants, which would form the basis of Hinduism. The Vedas were some of the few artifacts left behind by the Aryans, nomads who took over the Indus Valley civilization c. 1500 B.C.E.

- **Hinduism**: The majority religion of India today and the spiritual successor of Vedic thought. It emphasizes a cycle of reincarnation (rebirth), which can be improved or even broken by acquiring good karma for following the dharma, or rules, of one's caste.

- **Caste system**: The system of social class division in Hinduism. From highest to lowest were the priests, warriors, skilled workers and free men, bonded serfs, and pariahs (untouchables).

- **Mandate of Heaven**: Ancient Chinese concept stating that the right to rule was granted by the heavens. Used to explain the rise of every Chinese dynasty from the Zhou in 1122 B.C.E. to the Qing in 1644 C.E.

- **Qin dynasty**: One of the earliest empires in Chinese history. From 221 to 206 B.C.E., the Qin dynasty was known for its use of iron and bronze, along with the beginning of the Great Wall.

- **Olmecs**: Oldest known civilization in the Americas (c. 1000 B.C.E.). Centered in modern-day Mexico, they were known for their active trade, scientific developments, and giant stone heads.

- **Chavin**: Earliest known civilization in modern-day South America (c. 800 B.C.E.). Their mountain-based trade system helped the Andes Mountains become a cradle of Mesoamerican Civilization.

- **Maya empire:** Peaking from about 250–900 C.E., the Maya empire, centered on the Yucatan Peninsula of modern-day Mexico, was known for its massive cities of Tikal and Chichen Itza. Trade in stone, shells, and cacao helped them thrive. Collapsed c. 900 C.E. under mysterious circumstances.

Classical Societies

- **Persia**: Centered in modern-day Iran, they thrived around 500 B.C.E.–500 C.E. Their greatest kings, Cyrus, Darius, and Xerxes, helped expand the empire into Greece. In addition to being a great military power, Persia was remarkably well-managed, with its Royal Road.

- **Alexander the Great**: Macedonian king of the fourth century B.C.E. whose legendary conquests created an empire that included Greece, Persia, Southwest Asia, and parts of India. Responsible for the creation of Hellenistic culture.

- **Hellenistic**: Culture that fused the ideas of Greece and Persia, particularly after the conquests of Alexander the Great.

- **Mauryan Empire**: One of the first two empires of a unified India. The Mauryan Dynasty (321–185 B.C.E.) saw the rise of Chandragupta and Ashoka, the spread of Buddhism, and a well-organized economy.

- **Ashoka**: Great leader of the Mauryan Empire in India, he ruled around 250 B.C.E. Known for spreading Buddhism throughout India by sponsoring missionaries and encouraging vegetarianism.

- **Gupta Empire**: One of the first two empires of a unified India. The Gupta Dynasty (320–550 C.E.) revived Hinduism in India, delineated clear roles for men and women, and made great contributions in both the arts and sciences.

- **Daoism**: Beliefs of Chinese philosopher Laozi (Lao Tsu), based on the Dao, or "the Way," in which people live in harmony with nature and believe in "less government."

- **Han dynasty**: One of the earliest empires in Chinese history. From 206 B.C.E. to 220 C.E., the Han dynasty was known for its strong central government, thriving Silk Road trade, state-sponsored education, and general peace and prosperity.

- **Silk Road**: Network of land and sea routes facilitating trade between the Roman Empire, the Persian Empires, and the Chinese Empires. In addition to valuables, cultural ideas and new technologies traveled and spread along the routes.

- **Filial piety**: Confucian virtue emphasizing respect toward one's elders.

- **Republic**: First formed in Rome in 509 B.C.E., a government system in which the people elect their leaders and help create the laws. About 50 years later, the Twelve Tables helped to formalize Roman law.

- **Phoenicia**: Founded around 2000 B.C.E. in modern-day Lebanon, this civilization based its livelihood on the sea. Skilled mariners, the Phoenicians traded their famed murex shells (used for "royal purple" dye) and red cedar trees. Their alphabet inspired the Greek alphabet. Collapsed around 600 B.C.E. with an Assyrian invasion.

- **Diaspora**: The mass spreading of the Ten Northern Tribes of Israel in 722 B.C.E., following an Assyrian invasion. This caused the loss of Hebrews' cultural identity. In the present, it can refer to the mass scattering of any group of people.

- **Christianity**: Emerging in the first century C.E., this system of religion taught simplicity, love, compassion, and equality under one God. Based on the teachings of Jesus Christ, which are recorded in the New Testament. Quickly spread throughout the Mediterranean basin thanks to missionary activity, it is now the world's dominant religion.

- **Monsoon winds**: Seasonal winds that affect weather patterns (and therefore, agriculture) in South Asia. Ancient mariners used these winds to carry them to India, allowing for a thriving trade throughout the Indian Ocean.

- **Indian Ocean trade**: Archaeological evidence confirms that Egyptians, Mesopotamians, Malays, Gupta Indians, and others utilized advanced marine innovations to trade valuable goods across the Indian Ocean.

Development and Spread of Religion

- **Shamanism**: Often associated with indigenous tribes around the world, this system of belief involves a shaman, or spiritual medium, treating the ill by communicating with an unknown, unseen spirit world.

- **Ancestor veneration**: Often associated with the Chinese, this is the worship of the spirits of one's ancestors.

- **Brahma**: One of the three primary gods of Hinduism, he is regarded as the creator.

- **Buddha**: Born Siddhartha Gautama, this Indian prince founded Buddhism as an attempt to explain why there was suffering in the world. Buddhists today believe in the Four Noble Truths: that life contains suffering, that suffering is caused by desire, that desire can be rejected and nirvana (perfect peace) achieved, and that nirvana can be achieved through the Eightfold Path (a system of right forms of living).

- **Confucius**: Greatest of the Chinese philosophers (551–479 B.C.E.), his philosophy of reverence of ancestors, good education, and wise governance shaped the culture of China well into the twentieth century.

- **Islam**: The second most practiced religion in the world today. Founded in 622 C.E. by the Prophet Muhammad, it teaches the belief in Allah as the only god and Muhammad as the only prophet. A core tenet is the Five Pillars of Islam: declaration of faith, daily prayer, fasting during Ramadan, alms to the poor, and pilgrimage to Mecca (hajj).

- **Zoroastrianism**: The religion of the Ancient Persians. Based on the teachings of Zoroaster in the Avesta, it teaches that life is a constant struggle of good versus evil in which good would always prevail.

TEST WHAT YOU LEARNED

Part A: Quiz

Questions 1–3 refer to the following passage.

"Popular usage defines 'civilization' along these lines: 'an advanced state of human society, in which a high level of culture, science, industry and government have been reached.' This definition is problematic for archeologists, anthropologists, and historians, because it contains an overt value judgment. . . .

Yet we know that some aspects of civilization seem in our judgment quite negative; large-scale warfare, slavery, coerced tribute, epidemic disease, and the subordination of women may come to mind. . . .

Serious students of archaeology, anthropology, and history use a technical definition of civilization that describes without conveying value judgments. Civilizations, in this technical sense, are a specific type of human community: large, complex societies based on domestication of plants, animals, and people, plus other typical characteristics. (Culture is everything about a human community, its knowledge, beliefs, and practices; civilizations are a particular kind of culture.)"

Excerpt from Cynthia Stokes Brown's "What Is a Civilization, Anyway?", 2009

1. Which of the following statements does <u>not</u> describe an important global development during the time period 8000 B.C.E. to 500 C.E.?

   (A) The formation of nomadic confederations led to an increase in trade along the Silk Road.

   (B) Metallurgy allowed people to make stronger and more efficient weapons and tools.

   (C) Systems of paper currency were developed in response to the growth in trade.

   (D) Writing developed in response to the need for record-keeping as civilizations developed and grew.

2. Which of these is an example of a civilization that collapsed internally?

   (A) The Phoenicians

   (B) The Minoans

   (C) The Gupta Empire

   (D) The Western Roman Empire

3. Which of the following <u>incorrectly</u> pairs a contribution to modern society with the location credited with its creation?

   (A) Direct democracy: Rome

   (B) Paper: China

   (C) Bronze: Mesopotamia

   (D) Solar calendar: Egypt

Questions 4–5 refer to the passage below.

"Chi K'ang asked how to cause the people to reverence their ruler, to be faithful to him, and to go on to nerve themselves to virtue. The Master said, 'Let him preside over them with gravity; then they will reverence him. Let him be final and kind to all; then they will be faithful to him. Let him advance the good and teach the incompetent; then they will eagerly seek to be virtuous.'"

Excerpt from Confucius' *The Analects*, circa 500 B.C.E.

4. Under Confucianism, all of the following are considered fundamental relationships <u>except</u> for

   (A) parent and child

   (B) husband and wife

   (C) ruler and subject

   (D) God and disciple

5. The social hierarchies of both Confucianism and Hinduism emphasized the value of

   (A) peasants

   (B) artisans

   (C) government officials

   (D) scholars

Questions 6–7 refer to the passage below.

"Beloved-of-the-Gods, King Piyadasi, speaks thus: To do good is difficult. One who does good first does something hard to do. I have done many good deeds, and, if my sons, grandsons and their descendants up to the end of the world act in like manner, they too will do much good. But whoever amongst them neglects this, they will do evil. Truly, it is easy to do evil.

In the past there were no Dhamma Mahamatras but such officers were appointed by me thirteen years after my coronation. Now they work among all religions for the establishment of Dhamma, for the promotion of Dhamma, and for the welfare and happiness of all who are devoted to Dhamma.... They work here, in outlying towns, in the women's quarters belonging to my brothers and sisters, and among my other relatives. They are occupied everywhere. These Dhamma Mahamatras are occupied in my domain among people devoted to Dhamma to determine who is devoted to Dhamma, who is established in Dhamma, and who is generous."

Excerpt from Ashoka's *Fourteen Rock Edicts*, circa 250 B.C.E.

6. The Mauryan Emperor Ashoka influenced the spread of

   (A) Sikhism

   (B) Hinduism

   (C) Zoroastrianism

   (D) Buddhism

7. Ashoka helped spread his religious policies in all of the following ways <u>except</u> for

   (A) encouraging vegetarianism and banning animal slaughtering

   (B) engraving edicts and building shrines throughout his empire

   (C) adapting the existing caste system to recognize middle castes

   (D) sponsoring missionary activity to the outer regions of his empire

Questions 8–10 refer to the passage below.

"The succession of emperors became a matter of dexterous manipulation designed to preserve the advantages of interested parties. The weakness of the throne can be judged from the fact that, of the 14 emperors of Dong Han, no less than 8 took the throne as boys aged between 100 days and 15 years."

"China," section on Han dynasty, *Encyclopaedia Britannica*

8. The Western Roman Empire's collapse had a greater negative effect in Europe than the Han dynasty's collapse had in China because

   (A) only Rome lost political control of its empire

   (B) continual waves of nomadic invasions made recovery difficult

   (C) the increase in Rome's population made feeding the population difficult

   (D) the Han dynasty in China was able to recover power

9. Which of the following can be inferred from the information about the ages of many Han emperors?

   (A) Influential parties at court were maneuvering young emperors to the throne while exercising real power in their name.

   (B) Han power grew when young emperors reigned, as the government was in the hands of capable regents.

   (C) The dynastic line was uninterrupted from father to son.

   (D) The Chinese people wanted a young emperor for religious reasons.

10. Which of the following Chinese imperial dynasties was overthrown by the Yellow Turban Rebellion?

    (A) Tang

    (B) Qin

    (C) Han

    (D) Sui

Part B: Key Topics

This key topics list is the same as the list in the Test What You Already Know section earlier in this chapter. Based on what you have now learned, ask yourself the following questions:

- Can I describe this key topic?
- Can I discuss this key topic in the context of other events?
- Could I correctly answer a multiple-choice question about this key topic?
- Could I correctly answer a free-response question about this key topic?

Check off the key topics if you can answer "yes" to at least three of these questions.

Early Humans

☐ Paleolithic

☐ Animism

Development of Agriculture

☐ Neolithic Revolution

☐ Pastoralism

☐ Job specialization

☐ Patriarchy

☐ Metallurgy

☐ Mesopotamia

The First Civilizations

☐ Assyria

☐ Shang

☐ Cuneiform

☐ Ziggurats

☐ Hammurabi's Code

☐ Phoenicians

☐ Egypt

☐ Pictographs

The First Civilizations (cont.)

☐ Roman Empire

☐ Hebrews

☐ Harappa and Mohenjo-daro

☐ Vedas

☐ Hinduism

☐ Caste system

☐ Mandate of Heaven

☐ Qin dynasty

☐ Olmecs

☐ Chavin

☐ Maya empire

Classical Societies

☐ Persia

☐ Alexander the Great

☐ Hellenistic

☐ Mauryan empire

☐ Ashoka

☐ Gupta empire

☐ Daoism

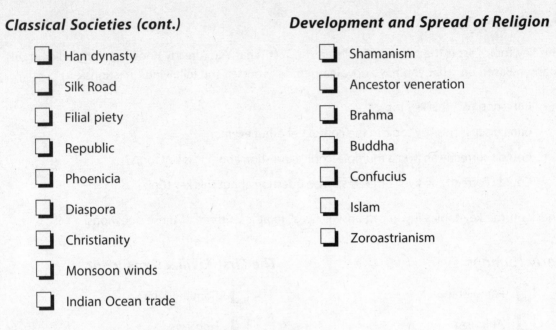

Classical Societies (cont.)

- ☐ Han dynasty
- ☐ Silk Road
- ☐ Filial piety
- ☐ Republic
- ☐ Phoenicia
- ☐ Diaspora
- ☐ Christianity
- ☐ Monsoon winds
- ☐ Indian Ocean trade

Development and Spread of Religion

- ☐ Shamanism
- ☐ Ancestor veneration
- ☐ Brahma
- ☐ Buddha
- ☐ Confucius
- ☐ Islam
- ☐ Zoroastrianism

Tally Your Results for Part A and Part B

Part A: Check your answers and count the number of questions you got correct.

1. C
2. D
3. A
4. D
5. D

6. D
7. C
8. B
9. A
10. C

_____ out of 10 questions

Detailed explanations can be found in the back of the book.

Part B: Count the number of key topics you checked off.

_____ out of 50 key topics

Next Step: Compare your Test What You Already Know results to these Test What You Learned results to see how exam-ready you are for AP World History Periods 1 and 2: Up to 600 C.E.

FOR MORE PRACTICE

Complete more practice online at kaptest.com. Haven't registered your book yet? Go to kaptest.com/booksonline to begin.

CHAPTER 4

Period 3: 600 to 1450 C.E. – Targeted Review and Practice

LEARNING OBJECTIVES

After studying this time period, you will be able to:

- Explain how states interact with peoples who do not identify with a state.

- Analyze the influence of politics on how states come into being, grow, and falter.

- Describe interactions between states and stateless societies.

- Describe the role of the arts in both changing and reflecting society.

- Describe the effects, both positive and negative, of legal systems and independence movements on race, class, and gender.

CHAPTER OUTLINE

TIMELINE

Date	Region	Event
570–632 C.E.	Mid East	Muhammad, founder of Islam
618–907 C.E.	East Asia	Tang Dynasty in China
711–1492 C.E.	Europe	Muslim occupation of Spain
750–1258 C.E.	Mid East	Abbasid Dynasty
750–1279 C.E.	East Asia	Song Dynasty in China
1096 C.E.	Mid East	First Crusade
1000–1200 C.E.	Africa	Kingdom of Ghana
1200–1400 C.E.	Africa	Empire of Mali
1211 C.E.	East Asia	Mongol conquests begin
1271–1295 C.E.	East Asia	Marco Polo's expeditions to China
1279–1368 C.E.	East Asia	Yuan Dynasty in China
1289 C.E.	Mid East	Ottoman Empire begins
1304–1369 C.E.	Africa	Ibn Battuta
1330 C.E.	East Asia	Bubonic Plague
1368–1644 C.E.	East Asia	Ming Dynasty in China
1300–1600 C.E.	Africa	Kingdom of Kongo
1405–1433 C.E.	East Asia	Zheng He exploration in the Indian Ocean
1441 C.E.	Africa	Beginning of the Portuguese slave trade

TEST WHAT YOU ALREADY KNOW

Part A: Quiz

Questions 1–3 refer to the passage below.

"Genghis Khan ordained that the army should be organized in such a way that over ten men should beset one man and he is what we call a captain of ten; over ten of these should be placed one, named a captain of a hundred; at the head of ten captains of a hundred is placed a solider known as a captain of a thousand, and over ten captains of a thousand is one man, and the word they use for this number (is tuman). Two or three chiefs are in command of the whole army, yet in such a way that one holds the supreme command.

When they are in battle, if one or two or three or even more out of a group of ten run away, all are put to death; and if a whole group of ten flees, the rest of the group of a hundred are all put to death, if they do not flee too. In a word, unless they retreat in a body, all who take flight are put to death. Likewise if one or two or more go forward boldly to the fight, then the rest of the ten are put to death if they do not follow and, if one or more of the ten are captured, their companions are put to death if they do not rescue them."

Excerpt from Franciscan emissary John of Plano Carpini's letter to Pope Innocent IV, circa 1245 C.E.

1. Which of the following statements best describes the similarity between the impact of the Roman and Mongol empires?

   (A) They both brought all of Eurasia under one rule.

   (B) They both created a large economic market.

   (C) They both established large naval forces.

   (D) They both spread a common language.

2. Which of the following statements is true of the Turks and the Mongols?

   (A) Both conquered and ruled Korea.

   (B) Both were skilled administrators and bureaucrats.

   (C) Both had written languages based on Arabic.

   (D) Both were pastoral nomads originally from the Central Asian steppes.

3. The Mongol empire declined because of

   (A) religious differences with the native peoples

   (B) succession issues

   (C) feeble rulers after Genghis Khan

   (D) the Red Turban Rebellion

Questions 4–5 refer to the following passages.

"*Kingdom of Mali*

From the beginning of my coming to stay in Egypt I heard talk of the arrival of this sultan Musa on his Pilgrimage and found the Cairenes eager to recount what they had seen of the Africans' prodigal spending. I asked the emir Abu . . . and he told me of the opulence, manly virtues, and piety of his sultan. . . . Then he forwarded to the royal treasury many loads of unworked native gold and other valuables. I tried to persuade him to go up to the Citadel to meet the sultan, but he refused persistently saying: 'I came for the Pilgrimage and nothing else. I do not wish to mix anything else with my Pilgrimage.' . . .

This man [Mansa Musa] flooded Cairo with his benefactions. He left no court emir nor holder of a royal office without the gift of a load of gold. . . . They exchanged gold until they depressed its value in Egypt and caused its price to fall."

Al-Umari, circa 1324 C.E.

"*Islam and Pilgrimage to Mecca*

[T]he faithful . . . had the same objective to worship together at the most sacred shrine of Islam, the Kaaba in Mecca. One such traveler was Mansa Musa, Sultan of Mali in Western Africa. Mansa Musa had prepared carefully for the long journey he and his attendants would take. He was determined to travel not only for his own religious fulfillment, but also for recruiting teachers and leaders, so that his realms could learn more of the Prophet's teachings."

Mahmud Kati, *Chronicle of the Seeker*, circa 1330 C.E.

4. The sources about the travels of King Mansa Musa of Mali suggest which of the following about this West African kingdom?

    (A) Its centralized government made possible the development of an effective military.

    (B) Its people practiced diverse traditional religions and a nomadic agrarian economic system.

    (C) Its wealth came partly from gold resources, and the religion of Islam had spread to Mali.

    (D) Its wealth made possible the building of many mosques and a large university library.

5. After the expansion of Islam into West Africa,

    (A) the economy slowed

    (B) a decentralized government developed

    (C) civil war broke out

    (D) trade increased

Questions 6–8 refer to the passage below.

"[Novelist] Amin Maalouf . . . asks the question, 'Can we go so far as to claim that the Crusades marked the beginning of the rise of Western Europe—which would gradually come to dominate the world—and sounded the death knell of Arab civilization?'

[This is] a conclusion that is perfectly in keeping with the modern popular consensus in both the Middle East and the West. Popular it may be, yet it is nonetheless wrong. Scholars have long argued that the Crusades had no beneficial effect on Europe's economy. . . . Rather than decadent or 'assaulted on all sides' the Muslim world was growing to ever new heights of power and prosperity after the destruction of the crusader states in 1291. . . . Indeed, they are evidence of the decline of the Christian West, which was forced to mount these desperate expeditions to defend against ever expanding Muslim empires."

Thomas Madden, *The New Concise History of the Crusades,* 2005

6. Which of the following describes the major impact of the Crusades on Western Europe?

(A) European political dominance in the Levant aided their development of shipping technology.

(B) The exposure to Eastern goods and technology helped increase trade and foster a global outlook.

(C) The feudal system was strengthened as peasants encountered the cruelties of the West Asian labor systems.

(D) The failure of the Crusades set Western Europe back economically hundreds of years.

7. How did the Crusades most strongly affect the Byzantine Empire?

(A) Faced with Western hostility, the Byzantines made a temporary alliance with the Seljuk Turks.

(B) Aided by Western troops and financing, the empire retook much of Anatolia, Syria, and Jerusalem from the Muslims.

(C) They directly caused the Great Schism in Christianity, which isolated it in the face of later Turkish advances.

(D) Latin Christians were alienated from Western Europe, which isolated them in the face of later Turkish advances.

8. In the era of the Crusades, another instance of warfare leading to cultural transfers was

(A) the Columbian Exchange between the Western and Eastern hemispheres

(B) introduction of Christian thought to West Africa due to Portuguese and English conquests

(C) interchange of ideas and techniques between China and the Muslim world under the Mongol empire

(D) spread of Jewish philosophy and ritual to Prussia and Scandinavia during the Baltic Crusades

Questions 9–10 refer to the following map.

ZHENG HE'S VOYAGES

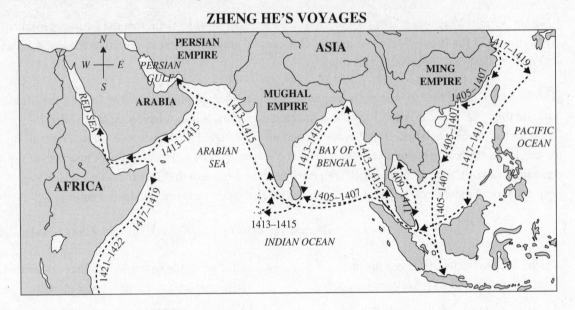

9. The map directly supports the statement that

   (A) the Ming made several voyages across the Indian Ocean

   (B) the Silk Route included a maritime path

   (C) Christopher Columbus and Ferdinand Magellan could not have accomplished what they did without East Asian navigators

   (D) the Chinese were already aware that the Philippines held nothing of value

10. Based on your knowledge of world history, the fears expressed in ending the voyages depicted on the map are best reflected in

    (A) Kublai Khan's conquest of China

    (B) the rise of the Umayyad dynasty

    (C) the sack of Constantinople

    (D) the downfall of the Mali Empire

Part B: Key Topics

The following is a list of the major people, places, and events for Period 3: 600 to 1450 C.E. You will very likely see many of these on the AP World History exam.

For each key topic, ask yourself the following questions:

- Can I describe this key topic?

- Can I discuss this key topic in the context of other events?

- Could I correctly answer a multiple-choice question about this key topic?

- Could I correctly answer a free-response question about this key topic?

Check off the key topics if you can answer "yes" to at least three of these questions.

"New" Empires

- [ ] Byzantine empire
- [ ] Islamic Caliphates

Chinese Empire

- [ ] Grand Canal
- [ ] Neo-Confucianism
- [ ] Fast-ripening rice

Korea

- [ ] Mongols

Islamic Caliphates

- [ ] Mecca
- [ ] Muhammad
- [ ] Shi'a
- [ ] Sunni
- [ ] Al-Andalus
- [ ] Umayyads
- [ ] Astrolabe
- [ ] Trans-Saharan trade

Decentralized States

- [ ] Charlemagne
- [ ] Feudalism

Western Europe and the Crusades

- [ ] Crusades

Europe during the High Middle Ages

- [ ] Bills of exchange
- [ ] Hanseatic League

Nomadic Empires

- [ ] Polynesians
- [ ] Vikings
- [ ] Seljuk Turks

Mongols

- [ ] Genghis Khan

West African Kingdoms

- [ ] Mansa Musa
- [ ] Bantu
- [ ] Swahili city-states

Long-Distance Trade

- [ ] Melaka

Travelers

- [ ] Ibn Battuta
- [ ] Marco Polo

Spread of Disease

- [ ] Bubonic Plague

European Developments

- [ ] Renaissance

Tally Your Results for Part A and Part B

Part A: Check your answers and count the number of questions you got correct.

1.	B	6.	B
2.	D	7.	D
3.	B	8.	C
4.	C	9.	A
5.	D	10.	D

_____ out of 10 questions

Detailed explanations can be found at the back of the book.

Part B: Count the number of key topics you checked off.

_____ out of 31 key topics

Your Results			Next Steps
Quiz		**Key Topics**	
You answered 8+ questions correctly	AND	You checked off 25+ (80%+) key topics	1. Review the quiz explanations at the back of the book. 2. Read the Rapid Review in this chapter. 3. Complete the Test What You Learned section in this chapter and review the quiz explanations.
You answered 5–7 questions correctly	OR	You checked off 16–24 (50–79%) key topics	1. Review the quiz explanations at the back of the book. 2. Read the Rapid Review in this chapter. 3. Go to the Complete Time Period Review for this period in Part 3. Read each High-Yield section about the key topics you did not check off. If you are short on time, read as many of these High-Yield sections as you are able. 4. Complete the Test What You Learned section in this chapter and review the quiz explanations.

You answered <5 questions correctly	AND	You checked off <16 (<50%) key topics	1. Review the quiz explanations at the back of the book.
			2. Read the Rapid Review in this chapter.
			3. Go to the Complete Time Period Review for this period in Part 3 and:
			  • If you have time in your study schedule, study the full chapter.
			  • If you are short on time, focus on High-Yield sections and the key topics with which you are least familiar.
			4. Complete the Test What You Learned section in this chapter and review the quiz explanations.

RAPID REVIEW

Summary—Period 3: 600 to 1450 C.E.

1. Similar to Periods 1 and 2 (up to 600 C.E.), Period 3 (600 to 1450 C.E.) witnessed a tremendous growth in long-distance trade due to improvements in technology. Trade through the Silk Road, the Indian Ocean, the Trans-Saharan routes, and the Mediterranean Sea led to the spread of ideas, religions, and technology.

2. Major technological developments such as the compass, improved shipbuilding technology, and gunpowder shaped the development of the world.

3. The movement of people greatly altered our world. Nomadic groups such as the Turks, Mongols, and Vikings, for instance, interacted with settled people—often because of settled people's technology—leading to further change and development.

4. Religions such as Islam, Christianity, and Buddhism preached the equality of all believers in the eyes of God. And though patriarchal values continued to dominate, the monastic life of Buddhism and Christianity offered an alternative path for women.

5. The spread of religion, aided by the increase in trade, often acted as a unifying force, though it sometimes caused conflict. Christianity and the Church served as the centralizing force in Western Europe, and throughout East Asia, the spread of Confucianism and Buddhism solidified a cultural identity. The new religion of Islam created a new cultural world known as Dar al-Islam, which transcended political boundaries.

6. The political structures of many areas adapted and changed to the new conditions of the world. Centralized empires like the Byzantine Empire, the Arab Caliphates, and the Tang and Song dynasties built on the successful models of the past, while decentralized areas (Western Europe and Japan) developed political organization that more effectively dealt with their unique issues. The movements of the Mongols altered much of Asia's political structure for a time, and the recovery from the Mongol period introduced political structures that defined many areas for centuries to follow.

Key Topics—Period 3: 600 to 1450 C.E.

Remember that the AP World History exam tests you on the depth of your knowledge, not just your ability to recall facts. While we have provided brief definitions here, you will need to know these terms in even more depth for the AP exam, including how terms connect to broader historical themes and understandings.

"New" Empires

- **Byzantine empire:** Formerly the eastern half of the Roman Empire, this Christian (Eastern Orthodox) empire controlled the Eastern Mediterranean Basin from the Fall of Rome to the Ottoman takeover nearly 1,000 years later (474–1453 C.E.).

- **Islamic Caliphates:** In the Islamic world, the states controlled by caliphs, or successors of Muhammad.

Chinese Empire

- **Grand Canal:** Begun in the fourth century B.C.E., construction resumed in 605 C.E. in China. This canal, the world's longest, connected the fertile Huang He River to the highly-populated cities in the north, allowing grain to be shipped easily.

- **Neo-Confucianism:** As trade expanded into China, Buddhism was introduced. Neo-Confucianism, popular during the Tang Dynasty, fused elements of Buddhism and Confucianism.

- **Fast-ripening rice:** Introduced to China from Vietnam during the Tang Dynasty, this crop allowed the Chinese to have two harvests per year, dramatically improving output; combined with an improved infrastructure, this crop led to a significant growth of the Chinese population.

Korea

- **Mongols:** Group of Central Asian nomads from Mongolia who, under the leadership of Genghis Khan, conquered large portions of the Asian continent. Their four empires, centered on Russia, China, Persia, and the Central Asian steppes, were led by Khan's successors, ensuring a century of peace from approximately 1250–1350 C.E.

Islamic Caliphates

- **Mecca:** Located in Saudi Arabia, it is considered the holiest city in Islam, as it is the birthplace of the Prophet Muhammad. A relic known as the Ka'ba ("Black Stone") made it a pilgrimage site before the emergence of Islam. Today, it is the focal point of the hajj, a trip to Mecca that every Muslim must make during his or her lifetime.

- **Muhammad:** An Arabian merchant (570–632 C.E.) who, after a revelation from the archangel Gabriel, began preaching a new religion called Islam. His followers quickly spread the new faith throughout Arabia during the last 10 years of his life.

- **Shi'a:** One of the two main branches of Islam. Shi'a rejects the first three Sunni caliphs and regards Ali, the fourth caliph, as Muhammad's first true successor.

- **Sunni:** One of the two main branches of Islam, commonly described as orthodox, and differing from Shi'a in its understanding of the Sunnah and in its acceptance of the first three caliphs.

- **Al-Andalus:** Located in modern-day Spain, this Islamic state thrived in the 700s C.E. Led by the Berbers, this state was renowned for its achievements in science, mathematics, and trade.

- **Umayyads:** Royal clan who took control of the first caliphate in 661 C.E. Their rule was hereditary. Under their rule, a dominant military rapidly expanded the empire, an efficient bureaucracy governed each territory, and subjected peoples were tolerated. The Umayyads' love of money, though, caused the Abbasids to overthrow them in 750 C.E.

- **Astrolabe:** Introduced to the Islamic world in the 700s C.E., where it was perfected by mathematicians. Used by astronomers and navigators to determine latitude through inclination.

- **Trans-Saharan trade:** Starting in the 400s and 500s C.E., trade across North Africa thrived thanks to an organized network of camel caravans carrying gold, salt, cloth, slaves, and other valuables. This allowed the kingdoms of Ghana and Mali to thrive, and as Islam spread to Africa, allowed its teachings to impact the lives of kings and traders.

Decentralized States

- **Charlemagne:** Ninth-century king of the Franks who ruled over the Holy Roman Empire. Despite his best efforts, his attempts to unify large territories failed, and the feudal system allowed lords and vassals to struggle for power.

- **Feudalism:** Developed in response to Viking invasions, this system allowed medieval Western Europeans to create a political system based on loyalty. A lord, usually a nobleman, would protect his vassal in exchange for mandatory labor or military service. In return, the vassal would receive a fief, or grant of land.

Western Europe and the Crusades

- **Crusades:** Launched by Pope Urban II in 1095 C.E., these holy wars were called in an attempt for Christians to reclaim the Holy Land of Israel from Muslim "infidels." The four campaigns, lasting over 100 years, were unsuccessful but did stimulate European-Muslim trade and reintroduce Europeans to wisdom that had been last taught during the Classical period.

Europe during the High Middle Ages

- **Bills of exchange:** Known as *sakk* in the Islamic world and also used in China during this period, these forerunners of modern-day bank checks were written guarantees of payment; these helped facilitate trade.

- **Hanseatic League:** Collaborative organization of trade guilds founded in Germany in the 1200s C.E., it dominated Northern European trade for the next two centuries.

Nomadic Empires

- **Polynesians:** Indigenous to the distant islands of the Southwest Pacific Ocean, Polynesians used their geographic isolation to their advantage: they raised domesticated pigs and dogs, grew tropical fruit, and mastered seafaring to travel between islands.

- **Vikings:** Starting in the 800s C.E., these people from Scandinavia used their seafaring skill to terrorize Western Europe and settle in regions as far away as North America.

- **Seljuk Turks:** Central Asian nomads who converted to Islam around the year 1000 C.E. By 1055, they had overtaken the Abbasid Empire, and they overtook the Byzantine Empire in 1071, laying the foundation for Muslim rule in modern-day Turkey.

Mongols

- **Genghis Khan:** A Mongol clan leader who united the clans and made them the most feared force in Asia. Under his leadership, the Mongol Empire expanded greatly into China, Persia, Central Asia, and Tibet. His sons ruled the Four Khanates that followed, and his grandson, Kublai Khan, became leader of Yuan Dynasty China in 1279 C.E.

West African Kingdoms

- **Mansa Musa:** Ruling from 1312 to 1337 C.E., he is the most famous of the Mali emperors. His capital, Timbuktu, was a center of trade, culture, and education. He is most famous, though, for going on hajj to Mecca (a practice that few Muslims in his time actually did) carrying a large caravan with satchels of gold, which he used to fund schools and mosques across his empire.

- **Bantu:** Ancient peoples of West Africa who, starting around 2000 B.C.E., began a great migration to East and Central Africa. By encountering other Africans and Muslims, they adapted to their new surroundings and sustained their increasing population with the banana. Their language fused with Arabic to create Swahili, still spoken by many East Africans.

- **Swahili city-states:** As the Trans-Saharan trade dominated North and West Africa, East African trade was dominated by interchanges between Bantu and Arab mariners. Cities in present-day Somalia, Kenya, and Tanzania became bustling ports, and in an effort to facilitate trade, the Bantus created a hybrid language that allowed them to communicate with the Arabs. This language, Swahili, is still spoken by over 80 million East Africans.

Long-Distance Trade

- **Melaka:** Located in modern-day Malaysia, this port city became a waystation for sea traders from China and India in the fourteenth century.

Travelers

- **Ibn Battuta:** Islamic traveler who, in the fourteenth century, visited the kingdom of Mansa Musa in the Mali Empire. His writings stimulated an interest in African trade.

- **Marco Polo:** Venetian merchant who spent over 20 years travelling the Silk Roads through the Mongol Empire, where he actually served on the court of its ruler, Kublai Khan. His efforts, which were compiled in a book, stimulated interest in trade with China.

Spread of Disease

Bubonic Plague: Also known as the Black Plague, this disease spread from China to Europe through rats. By decimating Europe's population, the plague ended the feudal system and led many to question religion.

European Developments

Renaissance: Although Christian soldiers were unsuccessful in reclaiming the Holy Land, their exposure to Muslim advances in math, science, and the arts stimulated an interest in relearning Classical wisdom. In an age when the unexplained was attributed to God, this caused people to begin questioning the true nature of phenomena, leading Europe out of the "Dark Ages" and into a period of artistic and scientific self-discovery, particularly from the fourteenth through the sixteenth centuries.

TEST WHAT YOU LEARNED

Part A: Quiz

Questions 1–2 refer to the following excerpt.

" . . . Another and perhaps more interesting issue is the obvious parallelism between what Buddhism and Islam imagined themselves to be: a cosmopolitan religion of the merchant elite. Both religions were therefore speaking to the issues and concerns of the same audience; and while such a situation may not be by definition untenable, in this case it turned out to be so and ultimately the 'Islamic international' beat out the 'Buddhist international.'

Islam was thus the first religion to be able to successfully challenge the entire support system that had sustained Buddhism for over a millennium.... At the ideological level it influenced the reinvestment of wealth in trading ventures by lay devotees; at the social level, donations to Buddhist monasteries provided status to traders; at the economic level, Buddhist monasteries were repositories of records and skills such as writing; and at the community level, participation in the fortnightly uposatha ceremony instilled an identity among the lay worshippers.

Islam with its prosperity theology, its mosques, and the larger networks of the Islamic community within the Caliphate clearly offered a viable alternative to all four of these structural components."

J. Elverskog, *Buddhism and Islam on the Silk Road*, 2010

1. Islam and Buddhism came into direct contact with each other during the time period 600 to 1450 C.E. in the region of

   (A) Western Europe

   (B) East Africa

   (C) Central Asia

   (D) Eastern Europe

2. What was the result of the cross-cultural exchange described by the historian in this passage?

   (A) A long-term tradition of hostility and competition between neighboring peoples

   (B) Borrowing of major elements of devotional practice and ritual over time

   (C) Synthesis and convergence between two world religions

   (D) Displacement of one ideology by another due to greater practicality or efficiency

Questions 3–6 refer to the following illustration.

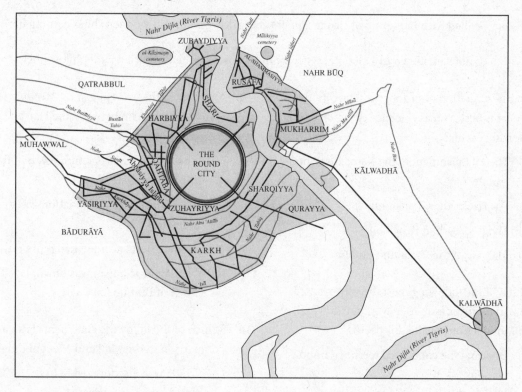

3. The city depicted in the map was an urban center along which of the following trade routes?

   (A) Mediterranean Sea

   (B) Silk Road

   (C) Trans-Saharan

   (D) Indian Ocean basin

4. The map suggests which aspect of commercial exchange between the years 600 C.E. and 1450 C.E.?

   (A) The Eastern Hemisphere was connected through both land routes and water routes.

   (B) Disease pathogens spread along trade routes, decreasing empires' populations.

   (C) Religious beliefs transformed as they diffused along trade routes.

   (D) Technologies such as printing and gunpowder were exchanged alongside goods.

5. Which of the following was the least significant consequence of commercial exchange in the city depicted in the map?

   (A) The spread of a plague

   (B) The introduction of porcelain

   (C) The writings of Marco Polo

   (D) The diffusion of Christian beliefs

6. All of the following facilitated commercial growth in the years 600 C.E. to 1450 C.E. except for

   (A) the minting of coins

   (B) government support of industry

   (C) the establishment of trade organizations

   (D) state-sponsored infrastructure projects

Questions 7–10 refer to the following excerpt.

"History is filled with the sound of silken slippers going downstairs and wooden shoes coming up."

Quote attributed to Voltaire, French Enlightenment writer, historian, and philosopher, circa 1740

7. The interpretation of history presented in the excerpt is best seen as evidence of which of the following events?

(A) The establishment of the Kamakura Shogunate

(B) The rise of the Ghana Empire

(C) The Red Turban Rebellion

(D) The rise of the Byzantine Empire

8. Which of the following most directly resulted from Temujin's desire to prevent the downfall of the Mongol Empire after his death?

(A) Dividing the conquered territory amongst his sons

(B) The widespread adoption of Buddhism by the Mongols

(C) Signing a peace treaty with Tang China

(D) Establishing the *Pax Mongolica*

9. The view in the excerpt is most strongly reflected in which reform between the Han and Tang dynasties?

(A) The military was deemphasized in favor of the tribute system.

(B) The civil service examination was open to all males.

(C) Higher-status women had more rights.

(D) Neo-Confucianism was downplayed in favor of Buddhism.

10. Which of the following statements is an accurate comparison of the Mali and Mongol Empires?

(A) Trade was discouraged in both the Mali and Mongol Empires.

(B) The Mali collected taxes from their people, while the Mongols only demanded corvée.

(C) The Mongol built their empire by conquering neighbors, while the Mali expanded their empire by sharing wealth.

(D) Neither forced the conversion of their subjects.

Part B: Key Topics

This key topics list is the same as the list in the Test What You Already Know section earlier in this chapter. Based on what you have now learned, ask yourself the following questions:

- Can I describe this key topic?
- Can I discuss this key topic in the context of other events?
- Could I correctly answer a multiple-choice question about this key topic?
- Could I correctly answer a free-response question about this key topic?

Check off the key topics if you can answer "yes" to at least three of these questions.

"New" Empires

- ☐ Byzantine empire
- ☐ Islamic Caliphates

Chinese Empire

- ☐ Grand Canal
- ☐ Neo-Confucianism
- ☐ Fast-ripening rice

Korea

- ☐ Mongols

Islamic Caliphates

- ☐ Mecca
- ☐ Muhammad
- ☐ Shi'a
- ☐ Sunni
- ☐ Al-Andalus
- ☐ Umayyads
- ☐ Astrolabe
- ☐ Trans-Saharan trade

Decentralized States

- ☐ Charlemagne
- ☐ Feudalism

Western Europe and the Crusades

- ☐ Crusades

Europe during the High Middle Ages

- ☐ Bills of exchange
- ☐ Hanseatic League

Nomadic Empires

- ☐ Polynesians
- ☐ Vikings
- ☐ Seljuk Turks

Mongols

- ☐ Genghis Khan

600 to 1450 C.E.

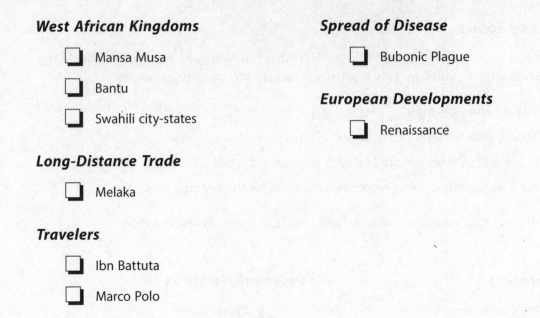

West African Kingdoms

☐ Mansa Musa

☐ Bantu

☐ Swahili city-states

Long-Distance Trade

☐ Melaka

Travelers

☐ Ibn Battuta

☐ Marco Polo

Spread of Disease

☐ Bubonic Plague

European Developments

☐ Renaissance

Tally Your Results for Part A and Part B

Part A: Check your answers and count the number of questions you got correct.

1. C   6. B

2. D   7. C

3. B   8. A

4. A   9. B

5. D   10. D

_____ out of 10 questions

Part B: Count the number of key topics you checked off.

_____ out of 31 key topics

Next Step: Compare your Test What You Already Know results to these Test What You Learned results to see how exam-ready you are for AP World History Period 3: 600 to 1450 C.E.

🖥 FOR MORE PRACTICE

Complete more practice online at kaptest.com. Haven't registered your book yet? Go to kaptest.com/booksonline to begin.

CHAPTER 5

Period 4: 1450 to 1750 C.E. – Targeted Review and Practice

LEARNING OBJECTIVES

After studying this time period, you will be able to:

- Describe the interrelationships between various economic exchange networks.

- Explain changes in the way governments work and are structured.

- Analyze the effects of labor reform movements, including changes in labor systems.

- Describe the impact of technological and scientific progress on populations.

- Describe the effect of exchange networks on culture across regions.

- Explain how industrialization and globalization were shaped by technology.

CHAPTER OUTLINE

TIMELINE

Date	Region	Event
1450 C.E.	Europe	Renaissance continues; Fall of Constantinople
1453 C.E.	Mid East	Ottomans capture Constantinople
1464 C.E.	Africa	Kingdom of Songhai is established
1492 C.E.	Americas	European explorers reach the New World
1517 C.E.	Europe	Protestant Reformation begins
1521 C.E.	Americas	Cortez defeats the Aztecs
1533 C.E.	Americas	Pizarro conquers the Inca
1588 C.E.	Europe	England defeats the Spanish Armada
1600 C.E.	East Asia	Beginning of Tokugawa shogunate
1618–1648 C.E.	Europe	Thirty Years' War between Protestants and Catholics
1652 C.E.	Africa	Cape Town Colony is established
1650–1800 C.E.	Europe	Enlightenment

1450 to 1750 C.E.

TEST WHAT YOU ALREADY KNOW

Part A: Quiz

Questions 1–2 refer to the image below.

WORLD SILVER TRADE: PRODUCTION, EXPORTS, AND IMPORTS

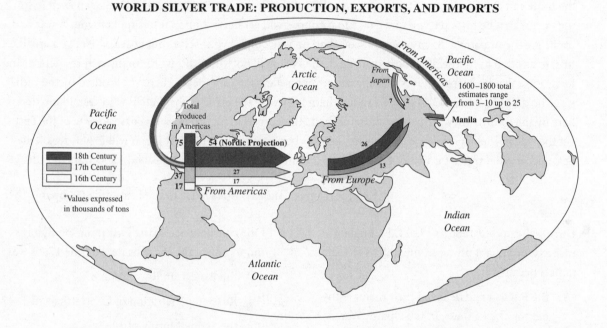

1. Which of the following statements most accurately describes the silver trade in the period from 1450 to 1750 C.E.?

   (A) Chinese demand for silver drove the trade.

   (B) Spain was unable to attain the needed supply of silver.

   (C) The Ottoman empire served as the middle-man in the trade.

   (D) The Ming dynasty was strengthened due to the inflation caused by silver.

2. What was one consequence of the silver trade in this period?

   (A) The Spanish empire used its great wealth to modernize its feudal economy.

   (B) A global trade system developed, the first between all major centers of civilization.

   (C) Britain waged the Opium War to force China off the silver standard.

   (D) Gold declined in value, increasing the volume of the Atlantic slave trade.

Questions 3–4 refer to the passage below.

"My Honourable Friends,

. . . For a Fort, at my first arrival I received it as very Necessary; but experience teaches me we are refused it to our advantage. If [the King] would offer me ten, I would not accept one. . . . the Charge is greater than the trade can bear; for to maintain a garrison will eat the Profit. It is not an hundred men can keep it; for the Portugal, if he once see you undertake that course, will set his rest upon it to supplant you. A war and traffic are incompatible. By my consent, you shall no way engage your selves but at sea, where you are like to gain as often as to lose. It is the beggaring of the Portugal, notwithstanding his many rich residences and territories, that he keeps soldiers that spends it; yet his garrisons are mean. He never Profited by the Indies, since he defended them. Observe this well. It hath been also the error of the Dutch, who seek Plantation here by the Sword. They turned a wonderful stock, they prowl in all Places, they Possess some of the best; yet their dead [fields] consume all the gain. Let this be received as a rule that if you will Profit, seek it at Sea, and in quiet trade; for without controversy it is an error to affect Garrisons and Land wars in India."

Excerpt from Sir Thomas Roe's letter to the East India Company, 1616

3. During the period 1450 to 1750 C.E., England rose as a dominant power in the Indian Ocean in part because

   (A) the English had defeated their major competitor, the Chinese, in the Opium War

   (B) it used joint-stock companies of private investors, who traded flexibly for profit rather than for royal prestige

   (C) the Ottoman empire had great difficulty retaining its position as the dominant power in the Indian Ocean

   (D) the Portuguese voluntarily withdrew their economic interests in the region

4. One consequence of the East India Company's monopoly of the India trade after the 1760s was

   (A) the American Revolution of 1776

   (B) Russian penetration of Central Asia in 1847

   (C) the Sepoy Mutiny of 1857

   (D) the settlement of Australia in 1788

Questions 5–6 refer to the passage below.

"Why, I asked, should we not admire the angels themselves and the beatific choirs more? At long last, however, I feel that I have come to some understanding of why man is the most fortunate of living things and, consequently, deserving of all admiration; of what may be the condition in the hierarchy of beings assigned to him, which draws upon him the envy, not of the brutes alone, but of the astral beings and of the very intelligences which dwell beyond the confines of the world. . . .

God the Father, the Mightiest Architect, had already raised, according to the precepts of His hidden wisdom, this world we see, the cosmic dwelling of divinity, a temple most august. He had already adorned the supercelestial region with Intelligences, infused the heavenly globes with the life of immortal souls and set the fermenting dung-heap of the inferior world teeming with every form of animal life. But when this work was done, the Divine Artificer still longed for some creature which might comprehend the meaning of so vast an achievement, which might be moved with love at its beauty and smitten with awe at its grandeur. When, consequently, all else had been completed (as both Moses and Timaeus testify), in the very last place, He bethought Himself of bringing forth man. Truth was, however, that there remained no archetype according to which He might fashion a new offspring, nor in His treasure-houses the wherewithal to endow a new son with a fitting inheritance, nor any place, among the seats of the universe, where this new creature might dispose himself to contemplate the world. All space was already filled; all things had been distributed in the highest, the middle and the lowest orders. Still, it was not in the nature of the power of the Father to fail in this last creative élan; nor was it in the nature of that supreme Wisdom to hesitate through lack of counsel in so crucial a matter; nor, finally, in the nature of His beneficent love to compel the creature destined to praise the divine generosity in all other things to find it wanting in himself."

Giovanni Pico della Mirandola, *Oration on the Dignity of Man*, 1486

5. Which of the following was one of the hallmarks of the Renaissance?

   (A) A new view of man as a creative and rational being

   (B) A celebration of Chinese and Islamic art and rejection of Greco-Roman styles

   (C) A declining interest in international travel

   (D) A growing acceptance of atheism

6. Which of the following describes a reason the Renaissance began in Italy?

   (A) Italian city-states were geographically isolated from most of Europe.

   (B) The Protestant Reformation weakened the Church's control over society.

   (C) Northern Italy helped supply and transport goods during the Crusades.

   (D) Political power in Italy was highly centralized.

Questions 7–8 refer to the image below.

Cortés Greets Xicotencatl, by indigenous Mexican artist, circa 1550

7. All of the following aspects of the Colombian Exchange are depicted in the above image <u>except</u> for

 (A) novel methods of transportation

 (B) military conquest

 (C) political alliances

 (D) disease pathogens

8. Based on your knowledge of world history, which of the following statements accurately describes an unusual aspect of the Aztec social structure?

 (A) Its ruler claimed his authority derived from divine sources.

 (B) Women could become property owners.

 (C) In Aztec society, slavery was outlawed.

 (D) Most Aztec commoners were artisans.

Questions 9–10 refer to the passage below.

"*Exclusion of the Portuguese, 1639*

1. The matter relating to the proscription of Christianity is known [to the Portuguese]. However, heretofore they have secretly transported those who are going to propagate that religion.

2. If those who believe in that religion band together in an attempt to do evil things, they must be subjected to punishment.

3. While those who believe in the preaching of padres are in hiding, there are incidents in which that country [Portugal] has sent gifts to them for their sustenance.

In view of the above, hereafter entry by the Portuguese *galeota* is forbidden. If they insist on coming [to Japan], the ships must be destroyed and anyone aboard those ships must be beheaded. We have received the above order and are thus transmitting it to you accordingly."

David John Lu, *Japan: A Documentary History*, 1997

9. What is an example of an early effort by a government to sustainably manage natural resources during the period 1450 to 1750 C.E.?

   (A) The Tokugawa Shogunate's laws to restrict timbering operations

   (B) The British government's emissions restrictions to fight air pollution

   (C) The Ottoman Empire's efforts to reduce overfishing in the Mediterranean region

   (D) The United States' designation of protected lands such as Yellowstone National Park

10. Which of the following correctly describes Japan's foreign relations during the Tokugawa shogunate?

   (A) The Tokugawa shogunate became more interested in expansionist policies resulting in the colonization of Korea.

   (B) The Tokugawa shogunate implemented strict isolationist policies that halted all overseas trade routes entirely.

   (C) The Tokugawa shogunate banned Christianity to prevent Spanish and Portuguese colonization attempts.

   (D) The Tokugawa shogunate's contact with the West allowed for an influx of ideas and ushered in Japan's Industrial Revolution.

Part B: Key Topics

The following is a list of the major people, places, and events for Period 4: 1450 to 1750 C.E. You will very likely see many of these on the AP World History exam.

For each key topic, ask yourself the following questions:

- Can I describe this key topic?
- Can I discuss this key topic in the context of other events?
- Could I correctly answer a multiple-choice question about this key topic?
- Could I correctly answer a free-response question about this key topic?

Check off the key topics if you can answer "yes" to at least three of these questions.

European Exploration

- ☐ Ottoman
- ☐ Conquest of Constantinople
- ☐ Caravel
- ☐ Columbus

Trading-Post Empires

- ☐ Joint-stock companies

Columbian Exchange

- ☐ Columbian Exchange

Mercantilism: The Role and Impact of Silver

- ☐ Mercantilism

The Role and Impact of Sugar

- ☐ Sugar cultivation

State-Building

- ☐ Gunpowder
- ☐ Mughal empire
- ☐ Songhai
- ☐ Creoles
- ☐ *Mestizos*
- ☐ Mulattoes
- ☐ Manchu
- ☐ Peter the Great
- ☐ Tokugawa shogunate
- ☐ *Daimyos*
- ☐ Triangular trade
- ☐ *Encomienda*
- ☐ *Haciendas*

Cultural and Intellectual Changes

- ☐ Printing press
- ☐ Protestant Reformation
- ☐ Scientific Revolution

The Environment

- ☐ Little Ice Age

Tally Your Results for Part A and Part B

Part A: Check your answers and count the number of questions you got correct.

1.	A	6.	C
2.	B	7.	D
3.	B	8.	B
4.	C	9.	A
5.	A	10.	C

_____ out of 10 questions

Detailed explanations can be found at the back of the book.

Part B: Count the number of key topics you checked off.

_____ out of 25 key topics

Your Results			Next Steps
Quiz		**Key Topics**	
You answered 8+ questions correctly	AND	You checked off 20+ (80%+) key topics	1. Review the quiz explanations at the back of the book. 2. Read the Rapid Review in this chapter. 3. Complete the Test What You Learned section in this chapter and review the quiz explanations.
You answered 5–7 questions correctly	OR	You checked off 13–19 (50–79%) key topics	1. Review the quiz explanations at the back of the book. 2. Read the Rapid Review in this chapter. 3. Go to the Complete Time Period Review for this period in Part 3. Read each High-Yield section about the key topics you did not check off. <u>If you are short on time</u>, read as many of these High-Yield sections as you are able. 4. Complete the Test What You Learned section in this chapter and review the quiz explanations.
You answered <5 questions correctly	AND	You checked off <13 (<50%) key topics	1. Review the quiz explanations at the back of the book. 2. Read the Rapid Review in this chapter. 3. Go to the Complete Time Period Review for this period in Part 3 and: • <u>If you have time in your study schedule</u>, study the full chapter. • <u>If you are short on time</u>, focus on High-Yield sections and the key topics with which you are least familiar. 4. Complete the Test What You Learned section in this chapter and review the quiz explanations.

RAPID REVIEW

Summary—Period 4: 1450 to 1750 C.E.

> **If you take away only 6 things from this chapter:**
>
> 1. As a result of the search for a faster way to the trade routes of the Indian Ocean, the Americas became part of the global trade network, and the process of true globalization began. This encounter set off the Columbian Exchange of goods, disease, and cultures, which spread throughout the world.
>
> 2. Improvements in and the spread of shipping technologies and gunpowder weapons allowed European countries to begin to exercise a more prominent role in world affairs.
>
> 3. Native American people died by the millions due to their exposure to previously unknown European diseases. African people were forcibly transported across the Atlantic Ocean to fill the need for forced labor on plantations.
>
> 4. New social structures emerged like those in the Americas based on race. While few women exerted power publicly, women of the harem in the Ottoman empire wielded considerable power behind the scenes.
>
> 5. In Europe, the Renaissance and Reformation challenged previously accepted beliefs and the power of the Roman Catholic Church. In other parts of the world such as China, the reaffirmation of more traditional beliefs was viewed as the key to stability.
>
> 6. European empires, such as Spain and Portugal, stretched their power overseas to conquer and control the newly encountered Americas. At the same time, dominant land-based empires such as the Ottoman, Mughal, and Qing grew powerful.

Key Topics—Period 4: 1450 to 1750 C.E.

Remember that the AP World History exam tests you on the depth of your knowledge, not just your ability to recall facts. While we have provided brief definitions here, you will need to know these terms in even more depth for the AP exam, including how terms connect to broader historical themes and understandings.

European Exploration

- **Ottoman:** Group of Anatolian Turks who, in their dedication to Islam, attacked the weakening Byzantine Empire beginning in 1281. With their capture of Constantinople in 1453, this group created an empire in Southwest Asia and Southeast Europe until its collapse in 1923.

- **Conquest of Constantinople:** In 1453, the Byzantine Empire was brought to an end when the Ottomans conquered its capital in Constantinople (now Istanbul, Turkey) and converted its famous church, the Hagia Sophia, to a mosque. Muslim control of overland trade in the region gave Europeans the impetus to begin sea exploration at the end of the century.

- **Caravel:** The ship of the European explorers during the Age of Exploration. Inspired by the Arab dhow, these compact ships of Portuguese origin featured triangular sails and a sternpost rudder, making them capable of crossing vast oceans.

- **Columbus:** Italian navigator who, under the sponsorship of Spain's Ferdinand and Isabella, attempted to sail a westward route to Asia. In so doing, his four voyages started a wave of Spanish colonization of the Americas and an exchange of new goods and ideas.

Trading-Post Empires

- **Joint-stock companies:** Predecessors of modern-day corporations, these large, investor-backed companies sponsored European exploration and colonization in the seventeenth and eighteenth centuries. One of the most famous ones was the British East India Company, which sponsored trade excursions to South and Southeast Asia.

Columbian Exchange

- **Columbian Exchange:** Beginning with the explorations of Columbus, this was the exchange of plants, animals, pathogens, and people between the Old World and the New World.

Mercantilism: The Role and Impact of Silver

- **Mercantilism:** The belief that one nation's power was based on its material wealth, particularly in gold and silver. This form of "economic nationalism" motivated European exploration.

The Role and Impact of Sugar

- **Sugar cultivation:** This land- and labor-intensive process was the impetus for the African slave trade, since diseases spread in the Columbian Exchange had decimated native populations. Further, the use of specialized labor and equipment was the predecessor of the First Industrial Revolution, which began by the year 1800 in the English textile industry.

State-Building

- **Gunpowder:** The first known chemical explosive. Created by the Chinese around 900 C.E., this chemical (and the weapons in which it was used) spread to the Islamic World and Europe via the Silk Road. In the fifteenth and sixteenth centuries, Europeans perfected the manufacture of a slow-burning propellant to maximize the potential of explosive-based weapons.

- **Mughal empire:** Islamic empire that reunified India in 1526 under Babur. His grandson, Akbar, advocated religious tolerance and sponsored great art and architecture projects. Under Aurangzeb, however, the large kingdom collapsed due to discord between Muslims and Hindus.

- **Songhai:** Successor of the great Mali Empire in West Africa, this empire thrived for over 100 years in the fifteenth and sixteenth centuries, thanks to the capable leadership, bureaucracy, and military of Emperor Sunni Ali.

- *Creoles:* In the Spanish colonies, a term for a person of Spanish blood who was born in the Americas. Socially, they were second only to the peninsulares, those of Spanish blood who were born in Spain. Despite their relative wealth, they were treated as second-class. Consequently, the Creoles would serve as leaders of many of the independence revolts in South America in the nineteenth century.

- *Mestizos* and *mulattos*: Terms for new mixed races that emerged in the Americas in the wake of colonization. *Mestizos* were half-European and half-Native American, while *mulattos* are half-European and half-African. Both were treated as lower class.

- **Manchu:** A nomadic group from Northeast China, they were the principal rulers of the Qing Dynasty, which saw a drastically increasing population and agricultural innovation, along with foreign intervention. The Qing was the last Chinese dynasty, lasting from 1644 to 1912 C.E.

- **Peter the Great:** Tsar of Russia from 1682 to 1725. His fascination with Western arts and sciences led him to rapidly modernize Russia under autocratic rule. The city of St. Petersburg, which was designed in a grid pattern like a Western European city, is named for and was built by him.

- **Tokugawa shogunate:** Ruling Japan from 1600 to 1867, this was a period of relative stability. Under Tokugawa Ieyasu and his successors, the daimyo had less power, and Western Christian merchants were forbidden from doing any trade, with the exception of the Dutch, who weren't interested in spreading Christianity.

- *Daimyos:* As feudalism was taking hold in Europe, a feudal system emerged in Japan. The system centered on the relationship between lord and warrior or peasant; the daimyo, or lord, controlled his land and his peasants. In exchange, the warriors, or samurai, provided protection. After a civil war in 1477, many of the daimyo became rulers of their own tiny kingdoms.

- **Triangular trade:** As Europeans began colonizing the Caribbean Islands and other tropical regions of the Americas, a complex trading network emerged: Europeans exchanged their manufactured goods with Africans, who exchanged their slaves with the American colonists, who exchanged their tropical crops (including sugar and its byproducts, rum and molasses) with Europeans.

- *Encomienda:* Spanish system of land grants that allowed colonists in the Americas to exploit the land and indigenous labor.

- *Haciendas:* Spanish system of landed estates. Originally, these were government-granted and allowed the use of exploited labor. Over time, though, the Spanish Crown phased out the *encomienda* system, allowing private ownership and free recruitment of labor. This system continued into the twentieth century.

Cultural and Intellectual Changes

- **Printing press:** Although movable type had been used in China since at least 1100 C.E., Johannes Gutenberg of Germany perfected the printing press and made mass printing possible in Europe in 1456. Due to the relative cheapness of printing books, knowledge and literacy became more accessible to the masses. For this reason, some historians consider it the greatest invention of the past millennium.

- **Protestant Reformation:** As the Catholic Church grew more powerful in Europe, people began to question its true authority, especially with the humanistic spirit of the Renaissance. In response to the corrupt practice of indulgences ("selling salvation"), Martin Luther, an excommunicated priest, traveled around Germany sharing a simple message that "the just shall live by faith alone." His words inspired other Protestant reformers, including John Calvin and John Wesley.

- **Scientific Revolution:** A product of both Renaissance and Enlightenment thinking, this was a period of scientific observation and exploration in which people attempted to explain what was previously unexplainable or attributed to God. Although its proponents, including Copernicus and Galileo, taught things that directly went against Church doctrine, their work inspired the modern scientific method.

The Environment

- **Little Ice Age:** Climatic period of cooling from the fourteenth through the nineteenth centuries in the Northern Hemisphere. In Europe, this devastated farms close to mountain glaciers, causing frequent famines. In North America, this caused the collapse of Norse settlements by isolating them from other mainland territories, due to increased storm activity and ocean ice.

1450 to 1750 C.E.

TEST WHAT YOU LEARNED

Part A: Quiz

Questions 1–2 refer to the passage below.

"*The Status of Jews and Christians in Muslim Lands*

What do you say, O scholars of Islam, shining luminaries who dispel the darkness (may God lengthen your days!)? What do you say of the innovations introduced by the cursed unbelievers [Jewish and Christian] into Cairo, into the city of al-Muizz [founder of Cairo, 969] which by its splendor in legal and philosophic studies sparkles in the first rank of Muslim cities?

Ought one to allow these things to the unbelievers, to the enemies of the faith? Ought one to allow them to dwell among believers under such conditions? Or, indeed, is it not the duty of every Muslim prince and of every magistrate to ask the scholars of the holy law to express their legal opinion, and to call for the advice of wise and enlightened men in order to put an end to these revolting innovations and to these reprehensible acts? Ought one not compel the unbelievers to stick to their pact [of Umar]; ought one not keep them in servitude and prevent them from going beyond the bounds and the limits of their tolerated status in order that there may result from this the greatest glory of God, of His Prophet, and of all Muslims, and likewise of that which is said in the Qu'ran?"

Jacob Marcus, *The Jew in the Medieval World: A Sourcebook, 315–1791,* 1938

1. The Ottoman, Safavid, and Mughal empires had all of the following in common <u>except</u>

   (A) utilization of firearms

   (B) political support of Islam

   (C) artistic innovations and achievements

   (D) economic dependence on oil

2. Which of the following is a difference between the early Islamic empires (1450–1750 C.E.)?

   (A) Only the Mughal empire contained a substantial number of non-Muslims.

   (B) The Ottoman empire was mostly Sunni while the Safavid was mostly Shi'ite.

   (C) Only the Ottoman empire had a military-based society.

   (D) Not all experienced problems of succession from one ruler to the next.

Questions 3–4 refer to the passage below.

"Yesterday your ambassador petitioned my ministers to memorialize me regarding your trade with China, but his proposal is not consistent with our dynastic usage and cannot be entertained. Hitherto, all European nations, including your own country's barbarian merchants, have carried on their trade with our Celestial Empire at Guangzhou. Such has been the procedure for many years, although our Celestial Empire possesses all things in prolific abundance and lacks no product within its own borders. There was therefore no need to import the manufactures of outside barbarians in exchange for our own produce."

Excerpt from a letter Chinese emperor Qianlong wrote to King George III of England, 1793

3. Which of the following regions was least affected by maritime reconnaissance voyages in the period 1450–1750 C.E.?

    (A) The Indian Ocean region

    (B) West Africa

    (C) South America

    (D) Oceania and Polynesia

4. All of the following are reasons why China stopped its global exploration during the fifteenth century except for

    (A) political leaders fearing an influx of new technological innovations would lead to social instability

    (B) Confucian values denouncing mercantilism and instead stressing the importance of frugality over expensive voyages

    (C) threats of Mongol invasions forcing rulers to concentrate attention and resources on the country's borders

    (D) rulers fearing colonization by the European empires and wanting to ensure China's safety and sovereignty

Questions 5–6 refer to the passage below.

"With the successive losses of two Ming capitals [to the invading Qing], locally prominent families and minor officials in Kiangnan had been sorely pressed to contain a rash of uprisings by various discontented and lawless elements—mainly tenants, indentured persons, and underground groups—and they now welcomed any authority that could restore the social order to which they were accustomed. Consequently, the first appearance of Han Chinese Qing officials in most locales was relatively uneventful, as social leaders adopted a cooperative, wait-and-see attitude. However, . . . it became clearer that 'barbarians' were really in charge, a common cause to oppose the Qing was forged among social elements that otherwise would have been at odds."

Excerpt from L. A. Struve's *The Southern Ming, 1644-1662*, 1984

5. Which of the following policies of the Manchus was most effective in unifying southern Ming resistance to the new foreign dynasty?

    (A) Chinese were forbidden from engaging in trade with the outside world.

    (B) Chinese men were forced to wear their hair in a queue (ponytail).

    (C) Chinese women were encouraged to marry Manchus.

    (D) Confucian scholars were removed from government positions.

6. A historical analogy to the Manchu treatment of Han Chinese is

    (A) Elizabeth I's sumptuary laws dictating styles of dress by social class

    (B) medieval European laws that Jews wear distinctive hats and badges

    (C) the Turkish policy in the early nineteenth century of replacing the turban with the fez hat

    (D) detailed Spanish-American classifications of Native, African, and Spanish ancestry

1450 to 1750 C.E.

Questions 7–8 refer to the passage below.

"Those that arriv'd at these Islands from the remotest parts of Spain, and who pride themselves in the Name of Christians, steer'd Two courses principally, in order to the Extirpation, and Exterminating of this [Native] People from the face of the Earth. The first whereof was raising an unjust, sanguinolent, cruel War. The other, by putting them to death, who hitherto, thirsted after their Liberty…: For they being taken off in War, none but Women and Children were permitted to enjoy the benefit of that Country-Air, on whom they did in succeeding times lay such a heavy Yoak, that the very Brutes were more happy than they:

Finally, in one word, their Ambition and Avarice, than which the heart of Man never entertained greater, and the vast Wealth of those Regions; the Humility and Patience of the Inhabitants (which made their approach to these Lands more facil and easie) did much promote the business: Whom they so despicably contemned, that they treated them (I speak of things which I was an Eye Witness of, without the least fallacy) not as Beasts, which I cordially wished they would, but as the most abject dung and filth of the Earth … "

Excerpt from Bartolome de las Casas's *A Brief Account of the Destruction of the Indies*, 1552

7. The purpose of the *encomienda* system was to

   (A) eliminate the Native American population

   (B) prevent the Atlantic slave trade from increasing

   (C) supply Europeans with a steady supply of labor

   (D) give Native Americans economic opportunities

8. Which of the following best describes the historical effect of de las Casas's report?

   (A) It showed that the inhumanity of the colonial system was recognized at the time.

   (B) The King decreed that African slavery should replace the *encomienda* system.

   (C) Responsibility for Native employment was transferred to the Church.

   (D) Colonial elites decided to introduce a more humane labor system.

Questions 9–10 refer to the image below.

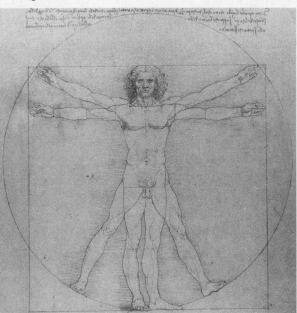

Leonardo DaVinci, *Vitruvian Man*, 1490 C.E.

9. The picture above and the three statements below refer to which of the following?

- Works of Leonardo da Vinci
- Importance of the Medici family
- Wealth of Mediterranean Sea trade

(A) Northern Renaissance

(B) Protestant Reformation

(C) Enlightenment

(D) Italian Renaissance

10. Art and literature created during the Italian Renaissance

(A) reflected a shift toward realism, scientific study, and humanist thought

(B) successfully reinforced the widespread religious devotion and faith in the Catholic Church of the time

(C) shows how women enjoyed more freedom than during the Middle Ages

(D) drew sole influence from the current time, not from other cultures nor time periods

Part B: Key Topics

This key topics list is the same as the list in the Test What You Already Know section earlier in this chapter. Based on what you have now learned, ask yourself the following questions:

- Can I describe this key topic?
- Can I discuss this key topic in the context of other events?
- Could I correctly answer a multiple-choice question about this key topic?
- Could I correctly answer a free-response question about this key topic?

Check off the key topics if you can answer "yes" to at least three of these questions.

European Exploration

- ☐ Ottoman
- ☐ Conquest of Constantinople
- ☐ Caravel
- ☐ Columbus

Trading-Post Empires

- ☐ Joint-stock companies

Columbian Exchange

- ☐ Columbian Exchange

Mercantilism: The Role and Impact of Silver

- ☐ Mercantilism

The Role and Impact of Sugar

- ☐ Sugar cultivation

State-Building

- ☐ Gunpowder
- ☐ Mughal empire
- ☐ Songhai
- ☐ Creoles
- ☐ *Mestizos*
- ☐ Mulattoes
- ☐ Manchu
- ☐ Peter the Great
- ☐ Tokugawa shogunate
- ☐ *Daimyos*
- ☐ Triangular trade
- ☐ *Encomienda*
- ☐ *Haciendas*

Cultural and Intellectual Changes

- ☐ Printing press
- ☐ Protestant Reformation
- ☐ Scientific Revolution

The Environment

- ☐ Little Ice Age

Tally Your Results for Part A and Part B

Part A: Check your answers and count the number of questions you got correct.

1.	A	6.	C
2.	B	7.	C
3.	D	8.	B
4.	D	9.	D
5.	B	10.	A

_____ out of 10 questions

Part B: Count the number of key topics you checked off.

_____ out of 25 key topics

Next Step: Compare your Test What You Already Know results to these Test What You Learned results to see how exam-ready you are for AP World History Period 4: 1450 to 1750 C.E.

⊠ FOR MORE PRACTICE

Complete more practice online at kaptest.com. Haven't registered your book yet? Go to kaptest.com/booksonline to begin.

CHAPTER 6

Period 5: 1750 to 1900 C.E. – Targeted Review and Practice

LEARNING OBJECTIVES

After studying this time period, you will be able to:

- Describe the effects, both positive and negative, of legal systems and independence movements on race, class, and gender.

- Describe the interaction of specialized labor systems and social hierarchies.

- Demonstrate ways in which economic systems, and values and ideologies, have influenced each other.

- Explain how production and commerce develop and change.

- Explain how societies can be changed or challenged over time.

- Describe the impact of ideology and belief on populations.

- Assess the impact of technology and exchange networks on the environment.

CHAPTER OUTLINE

TIMELINE

Date	Region	Event
1756–1763	Americas & Europe	French and Indian War & Seven Years' War
1776	Americas	American Revolution
1789	Europe	French Revolution
1804	Americas	Haitian independence
1820	Americas	Independence in Latin America
1839	East Asia	First Opium War in China
1848	Europe	European Revolutions
1853	East Asia	Commodore Perry opens Japan
1857	South Asia	Sepoy Mutiny
1863	Americas	Emancipation Proclamation
1871	Europe	German unification
1898	Americas	Spanish-American War
1899–1902	Africa	Boer War

TEST WHAT YOU ALREADY KNOW

Part A: Quiz

Questions 1–3 refer to the map below.

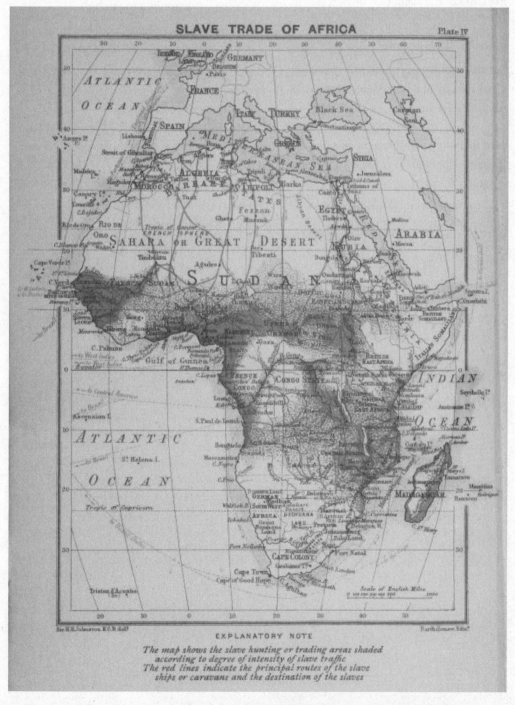

"Slave Trade of Africa," author Harry Hamilton Johnston and cartographer
John George Bartholomew, 1899

1. Based on the map, which of the following was a consequence of the transatlantic slave trade?

   (A) Christianity became the dominant religion in North Africa.

   (B) Trading routes in West Africa moved towards coastal regions.

   (C) The majority of African slaves were transported to India and other Asian regions.

   (D) Permanent European settlements, such as Cape Colony in South Africa, formed to support slave traders.

2. Which of the following developments of this period least supported the trade demonstrated on the map?

   (A) The diffusion of Islam through Africa

   (B) Improvements in maritime technology

   (C) The production of gunpowder in Europe

   (D) The establishment of colonies in the Americas

3. Which of the following most strongly contributed to the increase of the trade demonstrated on the map during the eighteenth century?

   (A) Industrialization

   (B) Sugar plantations

   (C) Absolute monarchies

   (D) Laissez-faire capitalism

Questions 4–6 refer to the following passage.

"Where the money is to come from which will defray this enormous annual expense of three millions sterling, and all those other debts, I know not; unless the author of Common Sense, or some other ingenious projector, can discover the Philosopher's Stone, by which iron and other base metals may be transmuted into gold. Certain I am that our commerce and agriculture, the two principal sources of our wealth, will not support such an expense. The whole of our exports from the Thirteen United Colonies, in the year 1769, amounted only to £2,887,898 sterling; which is not so much, by near half a million, as our annual expense would be were we independent of Great Britain."

Charles Inglis, Anglican clergyman of Trinity Church in New York City, New York, 1776

4. Based on this passage and your knowledge of world history, what were the primary motivations of proponents of the American Revolution, such as Thomas Paine?

   (A) Concerns that Great Britain would not allow the colonies to share the economic developments of the Industrial Revolution

   (B) Aspirations to expand industries such as metalwork in the colonies

   (C) Abstract ideals, as described by philosophers such as Montesquieu and Locke

   (D) Desires to attain freedom from the Anglican church and practice their faith with simplicity instead of ornamentation

5. In contrast to the American Revolution, the French Revolution

   (A) was caused by tensions in a colonial relationship with a distant imperial power

   (B) saw the wealthiest members of society be the main proponents of political change

   (C) was fueled by widespread discontent over feudal obligations to nobles and to the crown

   (D) based much of its revolutionary rhetoric on Enlightenment ideas and philosophies

6. Which of the following economic models contributed to the financial hardships described in the passage?

   (A) Mercantilism

   (B) Feudalism

   (C) Monarchism

   (D) Liberalism

1750 to 1900 C.E.

Questions 7–10 refer to the following passage.

"I anticipate an excellent effect by and by from the impressions which the yet wilder envoys and Sirdars of Chitral and Yassin will carry with them from Delhi, and propagate throughout that important part of our frontier where the very existence of the British Government has hitherto been almost unrealised, except as that of a very weak power, popularly supposed in Kafirstan to be exceedingly afraid of Russia. Two Burmese noblemen, from the remotest part of Burmah, said to me: 'The King of Burmah fancies he is the greatest prince upon earth. When we go back, we shall tell all his people that he is nobody. Never since the world began has there been in it such a power as we have witnessed here.' These Burmese are writing a journal or memoir of their impressions and experiences at Delhi, of which they have promised me a copy. I have no doubt it will be very curious and amusing. Kashmir and some other native princes have expressed a wish to present your Majesty with an imperial crown of great value; but as each insists upon it that the crown shall be exclusively his own gift, I have discouraged an idea which, if carried out, would embarrass your Majesty with the gift of half a dozen different crowns, and probably provoke bitter heart-burnings amongst the donors. The Rajpootana Chiefs talk of erecting a marble statue of the Empress on the spot where the assemblage was held; and several native noblemen have already intimated to me their intention of building bridges, or other public works, and founding charities, to be called after your Majesty in commemoration of the event."

Excerpt from Lady Betty Balfour's *The History of Lord Lytton's Indian Administration*, 1899

7. The Indian National Congress and the Pan-African Congress were important examples of

   (A) economic alliances between countries in the developing world

   (B) nationalist organizations aimed at removing European control

   (C) international organizations with the goal of preventing Cold War conflicts

   (D) nongovernment organizations aimed at bringing industrialization to Asian and African countries

8. Toussaint L'Ouverture, Simón Bolívar, and Miguel Hidalgo y Costilla

   (A) supported the Reconquista

   (B) led independence movements

   (C) advocated against the abolishment of slavery

   (D) believed in communist-inspired revolutions

9. One result of the revolt in Saint-Domingue in the 1790s was that

   (A) the United States lost some of its Latin American territory

   (B) Haiti established an absolute monarchy

   (C) Saint-Domingue imported more slaves from West Africa

   (D) the largest West Indies colony abolished slavery

10. Which of the following statements correctly describes the Sepoy Mutiny of 1857?

   (A) It began after a rumor spread that British gunpowder cartridges contained pork and beef fat.

   (B) It had early beginnings during discussions in the Indian National Congress.

   (C) It was characterized by bitter warfare between Muslim and Hindu sepoys.

   (D) It resulted in 300 million Indians ruled under the British East India Company.

Part B: Key Topics

The following is a list of the major people, places, and events for Period 5: 1750 to 1900 C.E. You will very likely see many of these on the AP World History exam.

For each key topic, ask yourself the following questions:

- Can I describe this key topic?
- Can I discuss this key topic in the context of other events?
- Could I correctly answer a multiple-choice question about this key topic?
- Could I correctly answer a free-response question about this key topic?

Check off the key topics if you can answer "yes" to at least three of these questions.

Revolutions and Independence Movements

- ☐ Enlightenment
- ☐ American Revolution
- ☐ French Revolution
- ☐ Maroon
- ☐ Haitian Revolution
- ☐ Latin American independence movements

Nationalism and the Nation State

- ☐ Nationalism

Industrialization

- ☐ Adam Smith
- ☐ Factory system
- ☐ Global division of labor
- ☐ Imperialism
- ☐ Second Industrial Revolution
- ☐ Railroads

Reactions to Industrialization

- ☐ Socialism
- ☐ Communism
- ☐ Liberalism

Reform

- ☐ Tanzimât Movement
- ☐ First Opium War
- ☐ Second Opium War
- ☐ Self-Strengthening Movement
- ☐ Taiping Rebellion
- ☐ Boxer Rebellion
- ☐ Meiji

Imperialism and Its Impact

- ☐ Social Darwinism
- ☐ Sepoy Mutiny of 1857
- ☐ Congo Free State

Legacies of Imperialism

☐ Indentured servants

☐ Chinese Exclusion Act

Emancipation

☐ Emancipation of slaves

☐ Feminism

Tally Your Results for Part A and Part B

Part A: Check your answers and count the number of questions you got correct.

1.	B	6.	A
2.	A	7.	B
3.	B	8.	B
4.	C	9.	D
5.	C	10.	A

_____ out of 10 questions

Part B: Count the number of key topics you checked off.

_____ out of 30 key topics

Your Results			Next Steps
Quiz		**Key Topics**	
You answered 8+ questions correctly	AND	You checked off 24+ (80%+) key topics	1. Review the quiz explanations at the back of the book. 2. Read the Rapid Review in this chapter. 3. Complete the Test What You Learned section in this chapter and review the quiz explanations.
You answered 5–7 questions correctly	OR	You checked off 15–23 (50–79%) key topics	1. Review the quiz explanations at the back of the book. 2. Read the Rapid Review in this chapter. 3. Go to the Complete Time Period Review for this period in Part 3. Read each High-Yield section about the key topics you did not check off. If you are short on time, read as many of these High-Yield sections as you are able. 4. Complete the Test What You Learned section in this chapter and review the quiz explanations.

You answered <5 questions correctly	AND	You checked off <15 (<50%) key topics	1. Review the quiz explanations at the back of the book.
			2. Read the Rapid Review in this chapter.
			3. Go to the Complete Time Period Review for this period in Part 3 and:
			  • If you have time in your study schedule, study the full chapter.
			  • If you are short on time, focus on High-Yield sections and the key topics with which you are least familiar.
			4. Complete the Test What You Learned section in this chapter and review the quiz explanations.

RAPID REVIEW

Summary—Period 5: 1750 to 1900 C.E.

If you take away only 6 things from this chapter:

1. Industrialization led the world to become truly interdependent. Industrialized nations in search of raw materials and new markets often colonized areas to advance their economic interests.

2. Populations grew, and many people migrated to cities in search of work in factories. Free-wage laborers were more desirable than forced labor in this new market-driven economy. As a result, slaves and serfs were emancipated.

3. Women gained some economic opportunities in the factories but were paid considerably less than their male counterparts. These new economic opportunities and Enlightenment ideals pushed women to fight for political rights as well.

4. The working class emerged as a force for change. Through organization into unions, these workers were able to advocate for improving their dangerous and oppressive working conditions.

5. Western culture strongly influenced many Asian and African areas through colonization. At the same time, Asian and African culture and art strongly influenced European intellectuals and artists. Enlightenment ideals such as equality, freedom of speech, and freedom of religion became very influential in many parts of the world, yet in other parts, traditional organized religion maintained power and influence.

6. The ideas of the Enlightenment said that the government was responsible to its people, inspiring revolutions and independence movements and pushing some governments to experiment with democratic values. This democracy, however, proved to extend to a limited class of people. "The nation" and nationalism became the new concepts of identity in the nineteenth century and would soon spread to many parts of the world.

Key Topics—Period 5: 1750 to 1900 C.E.

Remember that the AP World History exam tests you on the depth of your knowledge, not just your ability to recall facts. While we have provided brief definitions here, you will need to know these terms in even more depth for the AP exam, including how terms connect to broader historical themes and understandings.

Revolutions and Independence Movements

- **Enlightenment:** Post-Renaissance period in European history devoted to the study and exploration of new ideas in science, politics, the arts, and philosophy.

- **American Revolution:** After American colonists served alongside the British in the French and Indian War, the Crown issued a series of taxes to recover the war debt. The colonists, angered that they were being taxed without representation, protested the taxes and began fighting for independence. Although the Revolutionary War itself lasted from 1775–1781, the signing of the Declaration of Independence in 1776 was significant in that it laid the foundations for the first large-scale democracy since Ancient Greece.

- **French Revolution:** Inspired by America's victory in its own revolution, the "commoners" of eighteenth-century France sought to create a new political and social order free from royal control. The Third Estate, who vastly outnumbered the First and Second Estates (clergy and nobility, respectively), created the National Assembly and issued the Declaration of the Rights of Man and of the Citizen. In response, the French faced war with the other European powers, in which they emerged victorious thanks to the leadership of Napoleon Bonaparte.

- **Maroon:** Term for a nineteenth-century escaped slave in the Americas who settled in his or her own settlement away from plantations. They caused tensions with the colonial authorities. This term can also be used to describe their present-day descendants.

- **Haitian Revolution:** Led by Toussaint L'Ouverture, this slave revolt lasted from 1791–1804, after which the former French colony of Saint-Domingue became the independent nation of Haiti, the second independent nation in the Western Hemisphere and the world's first black republic.

- **Latin American independence movements:** Inspired by the success of the Haitian Revolution, these movements against Spanish colonial rule in Central and South America in the 1810s and 1820s led to the independence of every nation in those areas. Key leaders were Simon Bolívar, José de San Martín, and Bernardo O'Higgins.

Nationalism and the Nation State

- **Nationalism:** As European empires began growing, the people in those empires began to see themselves as part of a group with common heritages, cultures, languages, and religions. This sense of national identity and pride fueled the expansion of empires and led to the unification of nations.

Industrialization

- **Adam Smith:** English economist whose 1776 work *The Wealth of Nations* advocated a laissez-faire policy toward economics (minimal government interference), making him one of the fathers of modern capitalism.

- **Factory system:** System of labor used in the Industrial Revolution. This involved rigorous mechanization and large numbers of unskilled workers to mass-produce goods that were once made skillfully by hand. In the nineteenth century, the use of interchangeable parts simplified assembly but made work repetitive.

1750 to 1900 C.E.

- **Global division of labor:** With the Industrial Revolution underway, the European powers began devoting themselves to large-scale manufacturing and transportation, requiring raw materials like cotton from India, rubber from Brazil, and metals from Central Africa. As a result, industrialized societies grew at the expense of less industrial societies, providing an impetus for imperialist conquests later in the nineteenth century.

- **Imperialism:** As the nations of Europe began to industrialize in the nineteenth century, they needed sources of raw materials and markets for their goods. To prevent warfare among them, the European powers called the Berlin Conference in 1884 to divide the African continent into colonies and forge their new industrial empires. This has had significant effects, both positive and negative, on Africa ever since.

- **Second Industrial Revolution:** In the late nineteenth century, revolutionary new methods of producing steel, chemicals, and electrical power changed society in Western Europe, Japan, and the United States by introducing new ways of working and living.

- **Railroads:** With the invention of the steam-powered locomotive in England in the 1820s, a "transportation revolution" began in which mass-produced goods could be transported overland more quickly and inexpensively than ever before. By 1900, virtually every industrialized nation had a well-developed railroad system.

Reactions to Industrialization

- **Socialism:** A utopian ideal in response to the poor conditions of factories and factory workers. In this radical form of society, the workers would run the economy in a self-sufficient manner and share everything equally, thereby overthrowing the moneyed classes.

- **Communism:** An extreme form of socialism in which governments make economic decisions for the people. Envisioned by Karl Marx and Friedrich Engels in 1848's *Communist Manifesto*, this system advocated the overthrow of the bourgeoisie (capitalists) by the proletariat (workers).

- **Liberalism:** As industry led to the growth of a middle class, philosophers and political scientists advocated systems of government based on constitutions, separation of powers, and natural rights. Based on the philosophies of the Enlightenment.

Reform

- **Tanzimât Movement:** From 1839–1879, as the rest of the great empires were industrializing, the Ottoman Empire attempted this period of reform with a modernized infrastructure, a French legal code, and religious equality under the law.

- **First Opium War:** Instigated in 1839 after Chinese customs officials refused British imports of Indian opium (due to the addictive effects it had on Chinese workers), these wars weakened the Qing Dynasty and opened up China to commercial domination by the West for the next century.

- **Second Opium War:** Lasting from 1856–1860, this war resulted from the Western European desire to further weaken Chinese sovereignty over trade, to legalize the opium trade, and to expand the export of indentured workers whose situations closely resembled slavery.

- **Self-Strengthening Movement:** An attempt by China, in the 1860s and 1870s, to modernize its military and economy under its own terms. Changes were minimal due to imperial resistance.

- **Taiping Rebellion:** In the 1850s and 1860s, Chinese scholar Hong Xiuquan led a Christian-based revolutionary movement to reform China's society. The violent reaction by the imperial court left China financially strained and caused the bloodiest civil war in world history.

- **Boxer Rebellion:** In response to the growth of Western economic privilege in China, a secret society of Chinese, backed by the anti-Western Empress Cixi, attacked Western soldiers and workers in 1900. A Western coalition defeated the Boxers and undermined the legitimacy of the Qing Dynasty.

- **Meiji:** After witnessing the arrival of American commodore Matthew Perry in Edo Bay (Tokyo Bay) in 1854 by steamship, young reform-minded Japanese sought to overthrow the isolationist Tokugawa shogunate. They were successful and in 1868 installed Emperor Meiji, who led Japan through a period of rapid, Western-guided industrialization.

Imperialism and Its Impact

- **Social Darwinism:** Popular nineteenth-century theory used to justify the rich getting richer and the poor getting poorer in industrial societies. It drew on evolutionary theorist Charles Darwin's view of "survival of the fittest."

- **Sepoy Mutiny of 1857:** Fought in India between the British and the sepoys (Indian soldiers in British service) after rumors spread that the cartridges for their rifles were sealed in pork and beef tallow, thereby violating Hindu and Muslim religious taboos. The British victory strengthened the legitimacy of the Crown's rule, and the British went so far as to declare Queen Victoria "Empress of India."

- **Congo Free State:** Established in 1885 by Belgium's King Leopold II as his "Free State," in reality, this Central African colony was a series of large rubber plantations worked by forced labor. Brutal weather and working conditions made this one of the most heinous examples of imperialist power. In the 1960s, it declared independence and became Zaire; now, it goes by the name Democratic Republic of the Congo.

Legacies of Imperialism

- **Indentured servants:** As the nations of the Americas and the European colonies began to emancipate African slaves, this system of labor became much more prevalent. Poorer laborers came to the Americas, where they lived and worked for a small wage in exchange for a promise of several years of work.

- **Chinese Exclusion Act:** Instituted in the United States in 1882, these acts severely limited Chinese immigration, which had been prevalent earlier in the century, as many Chinese came to California and other western states for the Gold Rush and to build the Transcontinental Railroad.

Emancipation

- **Emancipation of slaves:** With the emergence of a new liberal political spirit came the idea that slavery was incompatible with Enlightenment ideals of freedom. As industry made field work and slavery less profitable, wage labor became more profitable, since it made sense to reward harder workers with higher wages. From the 1830s to the 1880s, every industrialized nation and their colonies gradually abolished slavery.

- **Feminism:** As new economic systems emerged and more professional jobs emerged, women started pushing for political and economic rights, in a challenge to the Enlightenment's conservative views of women.

TEST WHAT YOU LEARNED

Part A: Quiz

Questions 1–3 refer to the following excerpt.

"When in the Course of human events it becomes necessary for one people to dissolve the political bands which have connected them with another and to assume among the Powers of the earth, the separate and equal station to which the Laws of Nature and of Nature's God entitle them, a decent respect to the opinions of mankind requires that they should declare the causes which impel them to the separation.

We hold these truths to be self-evident, that all men are created equal, that they are endowed by their Creator with certain unalienable Rights, that among these are Life, Liberty and the pursuit of Happiness. — That to secure these rights, Governments are instituted among Men, deriving their just powers from the consent of the governed, — That whenever any Form of Government becomes destructive of these ends, it is the Right of the People to alter or to abolish it, and to institute new Government, laying its foundation on such principles and organizing its powers in such form, as to them shall seem most likely to affect their Safety and Happiness. Prudence, indeed, will dictate that Governments long established should not be changed for light and transient causes; and accordingly, all experience hath shewn that mankind are more disposed to suffer, while evils are sufferable than to right themselves by abolishing the forms to which they are accustomed. But when a long train of abuses and usurpations, pursuing invariably the same Object evinces a design to reduce them under absolute Despotism, it is their right, it is their duty, to throw off such Government, and to provide new Guards for their future security. — Such has been the patient sufferance of these Colonies; and such is now the necessity which constrains them to alter their former Systems of Government. The history of the present King of Great Britain is a history of repeated injuries and usurpations, all having in direct object the establishment of an absolute Tyranny over these States. To prove this, let Facts be submitted to a candid world."

United States of America's Declaration of Independence, 1776

1. John Locke argued that

    (A) the Church should play a role in governmental affairs

    (B) humans are born with innate knowledge of moral truths

    (C) people have the right to revolt when the government violates their natural rights

    (D) the government should own the means of production

2. The American colonists successfully won their independence from Great Britain for all of the following reasons <u>except</u> that

    (A) the French decided to support the colonists against the British and provided military support

    (B) the geographic vastness of the colonies was a hindrance to the British effort

    (C) the use of conventional military tactics by Americans proved superior to British military strategies

    (D) Americans were more motivated because they were fighting for a cause they believed in

3. Which of the following correctly describes a consequence of the Seven Years' War?

(A) Britain raised and imposed new taxes on the American colonies, angering colonists.

(B) France gained significant North American territory, including what became known as Quebec.

(C) The English government became less able to enforce laws within the American colonies.

(D) Native American tribes experienced new peaceful, friendly relations with Anglo-American fur traders.

Questions 4–6 refer to the following image.

4. Built in 1883 in Tokyo, this building is an example of

    (A) Westernization in Japan during the Meiji era

    (B) architecture constructed in Japanese cities controlled by European trading companies

    (C) palace buildings designed for Tokugawa shoguns

    (D) Shōwa-era department store architecture

5. All of the following occurred during the Meiji Restoration <u>except</u>

    (A) the overthrow of the shogun and consolidation of power under the emperor

    (B) modern technology was created entirely independently

    (C) the feudal system of labor and land ownership was eliminated

    (D) a powerful army and navy were created

6. Japan was opened to trade with the West primarily as a result of which of the following?

    (A) Commodore Matthew Perry's diplomacy

    (B) Japan's desire to avoid being colonized

    (C) Demand for Western goods and technology

    (D) The leadership of the shogun

Questions 7–10 refer to the following passage.

"You, O King, live beyond the confines of many seas, nevertheless, impelled by your humble desire to partake of the benefits of our civilisation, you have dispatched a mission respectfully bearing your memorial [message of goodwill]. Your envoy has crossed the seas and paid his respects at my court on the anniversary of my birthday. To show your devotion, you have also sent offerings of your country's produce.

I have perused your memorial. The earnest terms in which it is couched reveal a respectful humility on your part, which is highly praiseworthy. In consideration of the fact that your ambassador and his deputy have come a long way with your memorial and tribute, I have shown them high favour and have allowed them to be introduced into my presence. To manifest my indulgence, I have entertained them at a banquet and made them numerous gifts. I have also caused presents to be forwarded to the naval commander and 600 of his officers and men, although they did not come to Peking, so that they too may share in my all-embracing kindness.

As to your entreaty to send one of your nationals to be accredited to my Celestial Court, and to be in control of your country's trade with China, this request is contrary to all usage of my dynasty. It cannot possibly be entertained. It is true that Europeans, in the service of the dynasty, have been permitted to live at Peking—but they are compelled to adopt Chinese dress, they are strictly confined to their own precincts and are never permitted to return home. You are presumably familiar with our dynastic regulations.

It behoves you, O King, to respect my sentiments and to display even greater devotion and loyalty in future, so that, by perpetual submission to our Throne, you may secure peace and prosperity for your country hereafter."

Letter from Qing Emperor to King George III of England, 1793

7. The Opium Wars of the nineteenth century resulted in

    (A) the outbreak of the Taiping Rebellion

    (B) the restoration of the emperor, the downfall of the shogunate, and an industrialization program

    (C) China adopting the French legal code and, eventually, a group of young reformers installing a "puppet" emperor

    (D) China's sovereignty being weakened in order to facilitate free trade with both European empires and the United States

8. In the letter above, the Qing emperor

    (A) welcomed foreign investment

    (B) reaffirmed British trading rights

    (C) declined an offer to increase trade

    (D) declared his submission to George III

9. Which term fits best with the Chinese policy pursued at the time the letter to George III was written?

    (A) Laissez-faire

    (B) Isolationism

    (C) Communism

    (D) Democracy

10. The Revolution of 1911 that overthrew the Qing dynasty is most comparable to which of the following events?

    (A) The French Revolution

    (B) The Paris Commune

    (C) The American Revolution

    (D) The Young Turk Revolution

Part B: Key Topics

This key topics list is the same as the list in the Test What You Already Know section earlier in this chapter. Based on what you have now learned, ask yourself the following questions:

- Can I describe this key topic?
- Can I discuss this key topic in the context of other events?
- Could I correctly answer a multiple-choice question about this key topic?
- Could I correctly answer a free-response question about this key topic?

Check off the key topics if you can answer "yes" to at least three of these questions.

Revolutions and Independence Movements

- ☐ Enlightenment
- ☐ American Revolution
- ☐ French Revolution
- ☐ Maroon
- ☐ Haitian Revolution
- ☐ Latin American independence movements

Nationalism and the Nation State

- ☐ Nationalism

Industrialization

- ☐ Adam Smith
- ☐ Factory system
- ☐ Global division of labor
- ☐ Imperialism
- ☐ Second Industrial Revolution
- ☐ Railroads

Reactions to Industrialization

- ☐ Socialism
- ☐ Communism
- ☐ Liberalism

Reform

- ☐ Tanzimât Movement
- ☐ First Opium War
- ☐ Second Opium War
- ☐ Self-Strengthening Movement
- ☐ Taiping Rebellion
- ☐ Boxer Rebellion
- ☐ Meiji

Imperialism and Its Impact

- ☐ Social Darwinism
- ☐ Sepoy Mutiny of 1857
- ☐ Congo Free State

Legacies of Imperialism

- ☐ Indentured servants
- ☐ Chinese Exclusion Act

Emancipation

- ☐ Emancipation of slaves
- ☐ Feminism

Tally Your Results for Part A and Part B

Part A: Check your answers and count the number of questions you got correct.

1.	C	6.	B
2.	C	7.	D
3.	A	8.	C
4.	A	9.	B
5.	B	10.	A

_____ out of 10 questions

Part B: Count the number of key topics you checked off.

_____ out of 30 key topics

Next Step: Compare your Test What You Already Know results to these Test What You Learned results to see how exam-ready you are for AP World History Period 5: 1750 to 1900 C.E.

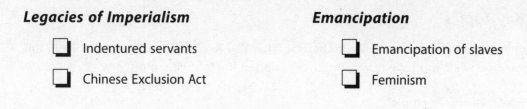 **FOR MORE PRACTICE**

Complete more practice online at kaptest.com. Haven't registered your book yet? Go to kaptest.com/booksonline to begin.

CHAPTER 7

Period 6: 1900 C.E. to the Present – Targeted Review and Practice

LEARNING OBJECTIVES

After studying this time period, you will be able to:

- Analyze the influence of politics on states.

- Describe how societies rise and change because of race, class, and gender.

- Describe the impact of ideologies and beliefs on social hierarchies.

- Explain changes in social structures over time.

- Describe the role of the arts in both changing and reflecting society.

CHAPTER OUTLINE

TIMELINE

Date	Region	Event
1904–1905	Europe & East Asia	Russo-Japanese War
1908–1918	Mid East	Young Turk Era
1910–1920	Americas	Mexican Revolution
1911–1912	East Asia	Chinese Revolution
1914–1918	Europe	World War I
1917	Europe	Bolshevik Revolution
1918–1920	Europe	Russian Civil War
1919	Europe	Treaty of Versailles
1921–1928	Europe	Lenin's New Economic Policy
1923	Mid East	Republic of Turkey is established; end of the Ottoman Empire
1928–1932	Europe	First of Stalin's Five-Year Plans
1929	Americas	Great Depression begins
1931	East Asia	Japanese invade Manchuria
1933	Europe	Hitler's rise to power
1935	South Asia	Government of India Act
1937	East Asia	Japanese invasion of China
1939	Europe	German invasion of Poland
1945	Europe	End of World War II
1947	South Asia	Partition of India
1948	Europe	Marshall Plan
1948	Mid East	Creation of Israel
1948	Africa	Apartheid established in South Africa
1949	Europe	Division of Germany
1949	East Asia	People's Republic of China established
1950–1953	East Asia	Korean War
1958–1961	East Asia	China's Great Leap Forward
1959	Americas	Cuban Revolution
1962	Americas	Cuban Missile Crisis
1973	Mid East	Arab-Israeli War
1975	East Asia	Fall of Vietnam
1979	Mid East	Iranian Revolution
1980–1988	Mid East	Iran-Iraq War
1989	Europe	Fall of Berlin Wall
1990–1991	Mid East	Gulf War
1991	Europe	Fall of Soviet Union; end of the Cold War
2003	Mid East	Iraq War
2008–2010	Global	Economic crisis

1900 C.E. to Present

TEST WHAT YOU ALREADY KNOW

Part A: Quiz

Questions 1–2 refer to the passage below.

"The fanatical sermon delivered by Gapon, who had entirely forgotten his priestly dignity, and the criminal propaganda of his assistants belonging to the local revolutionary groups, excited the working population to such an extent that on January 9th enormous masses of people began to direct their course from all the suburbs of the city toward its center. And at the time that Gapon, continuing to influence the religious sentiment and loyalty of the people to their sovereign, previous to the beginning of the procession held religious service in the chapel of the Putilov Works for the welfare of their Majesties and distributed to the leaders icons, holy banners, and portraits of the sovereigns so as to give the demonstration the character of a religious procession, at the other end of the city a small group of workmen, led by true revolutionists, was erecting a barricade of telegraph-posts and wire and hoisted a red flag over it. Such a spectacle was so foreign to the general sentiment of the workmen that from the enormous crowd going toward the center of the city were heard the words: 'These are not our people, this does not concern us. These are students who are rioting.'

Notwithstanding this the crowds, electrified by the agitation, did not give way to the general police measures and even at the attacks of the cavalry. Excited by the opposition they met with, they began to attack the military forces, endeavoring to break through to the Winter Palace square, so that it was found necessary for the purpose of dispersing the crowds to use firearms, avoiding, as far as possible, making useless victims. This latter measure explains the comparatively small losses experienced by the enormous mass of people marching to the Winter Palace square. The military forces were obliged to shoot on the Schlusselburg Road, at the Narva Gate, near the Tritzky Bridge, on Fourth Street and the Little Perspective of the St. Basil Island, near the Alexander Garden, at the corner of the Nevsky Perspective and the Gogol Street, near the Police Bridge and on the Kasan Square."

Excerpt from Arthur Cassini's "Revolution in Russia: Bloody Sunday and the Constitution," 1914

1. The protesters described in this passage likely contributed to which of the following social movements?

    (A) Tanzimât

    (B) Socialism

    (C) Anti-nationalism

    (D) Self-Strengthening

2. Which of the following was a long-term consequence of the events depicted in the passage?

    (A) The Duma was permanently established.

    (B) Tsarist rule was ended.

    (C) Socialism was largely replaced by nationalism among the working class.

    (D) Russian revolutionary efforts further developed.

1900 C.E. to Present

123 | **K**

Questions 3–4 refer to the image below.

A Chinese elementary-school textbook shows a group of Red Guards, 1971

3. The image above best demonstrates Chinese efforts to

    (A) counter anti-communist propaganda in Taiwan

    (B) eliminate distinctions between rural and urban youth

    (C) imitate Lenin's vision for the education of Soviet youth

    (D) promote gender equality resulting from the Chinese Cultural Revolution

4. Which of the following best describes the impact of the Cultural Revolution?

    (A) Literature, historical monuments, and cultural and religious sites were destroyed.

    (B) China was transformed from an agrarian to an industrial economy.

    (C) It created a climate more tolerant to diverse political ideology.

    (D) It resulted in a return to traditional values, culture, and customs.

Questions 5–7 refer to the passage below.

"The Purposes of the United Nations are:

1. To maintain international peace and security, and to that end: to take effective collective measures for the prevention and removal of threats to the peace, and for the suppression of acts of aggression or other breaches of the peace, and to bring about by peaceful means, and in conformity with the principles of justice and international law, adjustment or settlement of international disputes or situations which might lead to a breach of the peace;

2. To develop friendly relations among nations based on respect for the principle of equal rights and self-determination of peoples, and to take other appropriate measures to strengthen universal peace;

3. To achieve international co-operation in solving international problems of an economic, social, cultural, or humanitarian character, and in promoting and encouraging respect for human rights and for fundamental freedoms for all without distinction as to race, sex, language, or religion; and

4. To be a centre for harmonizing the actions of nations in the attainment of these common ends."

Charter of the United Nations, 1945

5. Which of the following conflicts motivated the international community to form the United Nations?

(A) The Korean War

(B) The Cold War

(C) World War I

(D) World War II

6. Which of the following was a primary reason for the failure of the League of Nations?

(A) The refusal of the United States and Soviet Union to join as members

(B) Global economic fallout from the Great Depression

(C) Multiple conflicts which overtaxed the League's joint military forces

(D) The rising global threat of communism

7. The United Nations is committed to all of the following except

(A) personal freedoms

(B) diplomacy

(C) international trade

(D) self-governance

Questions 8–10 refer to the passage below.

"Over the following years much of Latin America saw an upsurge of rural guerrilla conflict and urban terrorism, in response to the persistence of stark social inequality and political repression. But this upsurge drew additional inspiration from the Cuban example, and in many cases Cuba provided training and material support to guerrillas."

"History of Latin America," *Encyclopaedia Britannica*

8. Over the last four decades of the twentieth century, the political structure of most Latin American countries changed

   (A) from democracy to communism

   (B) from communism to military dictatorship

   (C) from European colonial rule to independence

   (D) from dictatorship to democracy

9. The Sandinista National Liberation Front successfully overthrew Anastasio Somoza DeBayle in which country?

   (A) Cuba

   (B) Honduras

   (C) Nicaragua

   (D) Guatemala

10. While Cuba provided support to various guerrilla rebellions in Latin America after the Cuban Revolution, which country provided the most economic and military support to Cuba?

   (A) Soviet Union

   (B) Brazil

   (C) United States

   (D) Spain

Part B: Key Topics

The following is a list of the major people, places, and events for Period 6: 1900 C.E. to the Present. You will very likely see many of these on the AP World History exam.

For each key topic, ask yourself the following questions:

- Can I describe this key topic?
- Can I discuss this key topic in the context of other events?
- Could I correctly answer a multiple-choice question about this key topic?
- Could I correctly answer a free-response question about this key topic?

Check off the key topics if you can answer "yes" to at least three of these questions.

World War I

- [ ] World War I
- [ ] Total war
- [ ] League of Nations
- [ ] Mohandas Gandhi

Global Depression

- [ ] World War II
- [ ] Great Depression

Rise of Fascist and Totalitarian States

- [ ] Benito Mussolini
- [ ] Adolf Hitler
- [ ] Fascism
- [ ] Joseph Stalin

World War II

- [ ] Firebombing
- [ ] Nuclear bomb
- [ ] United Nations
- [ ] Cold War

The Cold War

- [ ] Proxy wars
- [ ] Vietnam
- [ ] Warsaw Pact
- [ ] Non-Aligned Movement
- [ ] European Union

Revolutions

- [ ] Vladimir Lenin
- [ ] Mao Zedong
- [ ] Great Leap Forward
- [ ] Fidel Castro

Independence and Nationalist Movements

- [ ] Indian National Congress
- [ ] Muhammad Ali Jinnah
- [ ] Indian/Pakistan Partition
- [ ] Algeria
- [ ] Ho Chi Minh

Political Reform and Economic Changes

- [ ] Deng Xiaoping
- [ ] Tiananmen Square
- [ ] NATO

Technology, Populations, and the Environment

- [ ] Green Revolution
- [ ] Cholera
- [ ] HIV/AIDS

Social and Cultural Changes

- [ ] Pan-Africanism
- [ ] Liberation theology in Latin America

Tally Your Results for Part A and Part B

Part A: Check your answers and count the number of questions you got correct.

1.	B	6.	A
2.	D	7.	C
3.	D	8.	D
4.	A	9.	C
5.	D	10.	A

_____ out of 10 questions

Part B: Count the number of key topics you checked off.

_____ out of 36 key topics

Your Results			Next Steps
Quiz		Key Topics	
You answered 8+ questions correctly	AND	You checked off 29+ (80%+) key topics	1. Review the quiz explanations at the back of the book. 2. Read the Rapid Review in this chapter. 3. Complete the Test What You Learned section in this chapter and review the quiz explanations.
You answered 5–7 questions correctly	OR	You checked off 18–28 (50–79%) key topics	1. Review the quiz explanations at the back of the book. 2. Read the Rapid Review in this chapter. 3. Go to the Complete Time Period Review for this period in Part 3. Read each High-Yield section about the key topics you did not check off. If you are short on time, read as many of these High-Yield sections as you are able. 4. Complete the Test What You Learned section in this chapter and review the quiz explanations.
You answered <5 questions correctly	AND	You checked off <18 (<50%) key topics	1. Review the quiz explanations at the back of the book. 2. Read the Rapid Review in this chapter. 3. Go to the Complete Time Period Review for this period in Part 3 and: • If you have time in your study schedule, study the full chapter. • If you are short on time, focus on High-Yield sections and the key topics with which you are least familiar. 4. Complete the Test What You Learned section in this chapter and review the quiz explanations.

RAPID REVIEW

Summary—Period 6: 1900 C.E. to the Present

If you take away only 6 things from this chapter:

1. Due to improvements in health care and the decrease of the death rate, the world population went from 1 billion people in 1900 to over 6 billion. The movement of people has also increased throughout the world, with many in search of better economic opportunities. Some refugees, too, are being forced to leave their homelands.

2. Traditional social structures have been challenged as a result of movements that have attempted to empower the working class, such as the introduction of communist governments in various parts of the world.

3. Women gained the right to vote in many parts of the world, as well as access to new economic opportunities and education. The development of the birth control pill empowered women by allowing them to control their own reproductive systems.

4. The world became more and more integrated through technology, cultures have blended, and some came to dominate. At the same time, religious fundamentalism has developed in some regions, possibly to combat Western-dominated global culture.

5. The rise in the nation-state and nationalism has led to the adoption of political systems from totalitarianism to democracy. At the same time, the rise of a more globally connected world may blur the lines of the nation-state.

6. The world wars demonstrated the influence of technology on warfare, but also indicated the decline of Europe as the dominant global power. Colonial areas asserted themselves and fought for independence, but were later faced with a new global conflict called the Cold War. Since the end of the Cold War, nations have made attempts at both economic and political reforms, and international and multinational organizations have made attempts to establish a new world order.

Key Topics—Period 6: 1900 C.E. to the Present

Remember that the AP World History exam tests you on the depth of your knowledge, not just your ability to recall facts. While we have provided brief definitions here, you will need to know these terms in even more depth for the AP exam, including how terms connect to broader historical themes and understandings.

World War I

- **World War I:** Initially known as the Great War, this total war officially began in 1914 with the assassination of Austrian Archduke Franz Ferdinand, but it was rooted in secret alliances, nationalism, and militarism among the European powers. Its end in 1918 left Europe with many unresolved issues that would be settled in World War II.

- **Total war:** Warfare in which the entire nation devotes its efforts to large-scale war, usually with the aim to completely eliminate an enemy threat. The two world wars are well-known examples.

- **League of Nations:** As part of U.S. President Woodrow Wilson's plans for postwar peace (the Fourteen Points), a multinational coalition was created to prevent further war through open negotiations. Ironically, the United States never became a member. The power of the League was delegitimized in the 1930s with the Japanese invasion of Manchuria, the Spanish Civil War, and the Italian invasion of Ethiopia.

- **Mohandas Gandhi:** Regarded as the most influential leader of the Indian Independence movement, the Mahatma ("Great Soul") was known for his grassroots approach to protest. Using a combination of religious ideals, Gandhi and his followers used civil disobedience and nonviolence to help India gain its independence. Although Gandhi was murdered just five months after independence, his legacy influenced such leaders as Dr. Martin Luther King and the Dalai Lama.

Global Depression

- **World War II:** Officially taking place from 1939–1945 (though some historians argue it started as far back as 1931), this total war pitted the Axis powers (Germany, Italy, and Japan) against the Allied powers (Britain, France, the Soviet Union, and the United States) in a truly global war that attempted to resolve post-World War I issues. The outcome of this war changed the world's political and economic history.

- **Great Depression:** Generally considered to have happened from 1929–1939, this global economic recession was caused by a variety of factors, including Europe's relative inability to recover economically from World War I and the collapse of the American stock market in the wake of increased investment. Politically, this caused many around the world to favor government intervention in the economy.

Rise of Fascist and Totalitarian States

- **Benito Mussolini:** Leader of Italy's "Blackshirts" and key proponent of fascism as an anti-communist movement. In 1922, he and his followers successfully deposed King Vittorio Emmanuel II and established Italy as a military dictatorship.

- **Adolf Hitler:** Austrian-born leader who, after witnessing Germany's humiliating defeat in World War I, vowed to restore Germany to its former glory through militarism, ultranationalism, extreme violence, and anti-Semitism. Using propaganda and indoctrination, Hitler led the Nazi Party and became chancellor of Germany in 1933.

- **Fascism:** In response to the rise of communism in Eastern Europe after World War I, this political and economic system emerged in Italy in the 1920s under the leadership of Benito Mussolini. Key ideas of fascism include extreme nationalism, militarism, dictatorship, and the "corporate state," in which governments ally with big businesses to build themselves up economically.

- **Joseph Stalin:** Successor to V. I. Lenin, this dictator solidified his rule and used an extreme form of communism (Stalinism) to rule the U.S.S.R. from 1927 to his death in 1953. His political ideology included centralized planning of the economy, collective farms, and purging of all dissent.

World War II

- **Firebombing:** Use of incendiary bombs during warfare, particularly from airplanes. The bombs, filled with either thermite or napalm, cause massive burning of large areas at any given time and were particularly used in World War II and the Vietnam War.

- **Nuclear bomb:** Developed in the United States in the 1940s, this weapon ended World War II when it was dropped on the Japanese cities of Hiroshima and Nagasaki. Although it killed over 150,000 people, historians argue that it saved lives by forcing Japan's immediate surrender. Although the following decades were marked by a race for nuclear supremacy, it should be noted that the bombings of Hiroshima and Nagasaki were the only times that nuclear bombs were used in warfare.

- **United Nations:** Founded in 1945 with the intent of settling postwar concerns and recovering war-torn nations, this international organization is responsible for peacekeeping tasks around the world, with the cooperation of its member nations.

- **Cold War:** Ideological struggle pitting the United States and the Soviet Union against each other for global political hegemony, 1949–1993.

The Cold War

- **Proxy wars:** Particularly common during the Cold War, these are wars that are instigated or supported by a major power, but not fought by them. Instead, these are fought by proxy, or by another power in an attempt to help the major power achieve its aims.

- **Vietnam:** Nation in Southeast Asia that, in the wake of France's defeat at Dien Bien Phu in 1954, was divided into two. The rise of Ho Chi Minh, a Marxist leader of nationalist forces, led to one of the longest, bloodiest military engagements of the Cold War: the Vietnam War. Ho's victory caused Vietnam to turn communist.

- **Warsaw Pact:** Formed in 1955 by the Soviet Union and seven Eastern Bloc countries, this defensive alliance sought to counteract the growing influence of NATO.

- **Non-Aligned Movement:** In the wake of the Cold War, the nations of Africa, Asia, and Latin America were ushered into alliances with the United States and the Soviet Union. Some nations chose not to ally. The first formal conference took place in 1955 and was led by Nehru of India and Nasser of Egypt. By the end of the Cold War, over 100 nations had announced that they would remain neutral in the context of the Cold War.

- **European Union:** First formed in 1993, a continent-wide alliance of economic regulation that now has over 25 members, including several formerly communist countries. Originally formed as the European Economic Community by six European nations in 1957 as an economic alliance designed to eliminate trade barriers, end reliance on the United States, and ease tensions between former rivals.

Revolutions

- **Vladimir Lenin:** Leader of the Bolsheviks in Russia during World War I, a society of radical communists whose aim was to overthrow the tsar. With his return to Russia in 1917 and the Russian Civil War in the years following, Lenin and his Bolsheviks seized power and transformed Russia into the Communist Union of Soviet Socialist Republics.

- **Mao Zedong:** Leader of the Chinese Communist Party in the 1920s and 1930s, he reemerged in the 1940s as he and his followers fought the Nationalists (Kuomintang). In 1949, Mao declared victory and made himself leader of the People's Republic of China, a position he held until his death in 1976. He was also known for radical national initiatives like the Great Leap Forward and the Cultural Revolution.

- **Great Leap Forward:** Mao Zedong's ambitious plan, starting in 1958, to collectivize all aspects of the economy, most notably by having communal houses with backyard furnaces for steel production. After just five years and the deaths of millions of Chinese, the program was declared a failure, and Mao laid the groundwork for his Cultural Revolution in the 1960s.

- **Fidel Castro:** Guerrilla leader of Cuba who, in 1959, deposed the dictatorship of Fulgencio Batista in an attempt to resolve income inequities. By 1961, he had made Cuba into a Soviet ally and caused great tensions between Cuba and its nearby neighbor, the United States. He led Cuba until he resigned in 2008, citing health concerns and handing over rule to his brother Raul.

Independence and Nationalist Movements

- **Indian National Congress:** Founded in 1885 by British-educated Hindu leaders, this political party gained traction in 1919 when the failure of the Rowlatt Acts gave them more power. In the decades that followed, they became the political wing of the movement for Indian Independence and to this day, still play an influential role in India's government.

- **Muhammad Ali Jinnah:** Prior to 1920, this political leader had favored an alliance of Hindus and Muslims in the creation of one unified, independent India. However, in response to the popular rise of Mahatma Gandhi, Jinnah became leader of the Muslim League, a party devoted to the creation of a Muslim-led state in South Asia to prevent domination by the Hindu majority. In 1947, he became the first leader of his new nation, Pakistan, and led it for the last year of his life.

- **Indian/Pakistan Partition:** In 1947, the nations of India and Pakistan both became independent from Great Britain. India was dominated by the Hindus, and Pakistan, divided into West and East Pakistan (modern-day Bangladesh), was Muslim dominated. Tensions between Hindus and Muslims in South Asia continue to this day, as evidenced by the continued conflict over the disputed region of Kashmir.

- **Algeria:** Largest nation in Northwest Africa, this former French colony gained its independence in 1962 after a long war, in which nationalist troops fought against French leaders and their broken promises of better lives and freedom during the Anglo-American occupation of North Africa.

- **Ho Chi Minh:** Vietnamese nationalist leader who fought against the Japanese during the Axis occupation of French Vietnam in World War II and then fought against the French after the war. When the Soviets and communist Chinese offered support to him and North Vietnam during the Vietnam War, the Americans responded by supporting anti-communist South Vietnam. The resulting war led to Ho's leadership of North Vietnam.

Political Reform and Economic Changes

- **Deng Xiaoping:** Premier of communist China from Mao Zedong's death in 1976 to his own death in 1997, he instituted the Four Modernizations in an attempt to introduce capitalist reform in China. His non-democratic policies, though, drew the ire of educated Chinese, culminating in the Tiananmen Square uprising of 1989.

- **Tiananmen Square:** Large public square in Beijing, China. Site of a 1989 conflict between students, protesting for democratic reform, and the Chinese military, defending the leadership of Deng Xiaoping.

- **NATO:** North Atlantic Treaty Organization. Founded in 1949 by the nations of North America and Europe, this defensive alliance sought to contain the spread of communism in Eastern Europe.

Technology, Populations, and the Environment

- **Green Revolution:** Beginning in the 1960s, this movement introduced new technologies and high-yield seed strains in an attempt to boost food production in developing countries. Initially successful in Mexico and India, its terminology has been called into question due to the increased use of chemical fertilizers that pollute the environment.

- **Cholera:** Acute bacterial infection of the small intestine that was pandemic in the nineteenth century. Generally speaking, it affects people in developing nations more, since it spreads easily through contaminated drinking water.

- **HIV/AIDS:** Human Immunodeficiency Virus and Acquired Immunodeficiency Syndrome. The virus attacks the human body's immune system, leaving patients susceptible to lethal diseases that slowly kill them. First reported in the United States in 1981, its unknown origins and rapid spread have made it one of the most recent epidemics and a symbol of the interconnected nature of today's world.

Social and Cultural Changes

- **Pan-Africanism:** The idea that people of the African continent have a shared heritage and should unify in that regard, despite the fact that they live in different nations. This attitude was the basis of many African independence movements after World War II.

- **Liberation theology in Latin America:** A movement led by the Catholic Church beginning in the 1950s, this new religious movement emphasizes that the teachings of Christ can help liberate people from the political and economic injustices of poverty.

TEST WHAT YOU LEARNED

Part A: Quiz

Questions 1–2 refer to the map below.

THE VOYAGES OF HMS ORVIETO 1915–1918

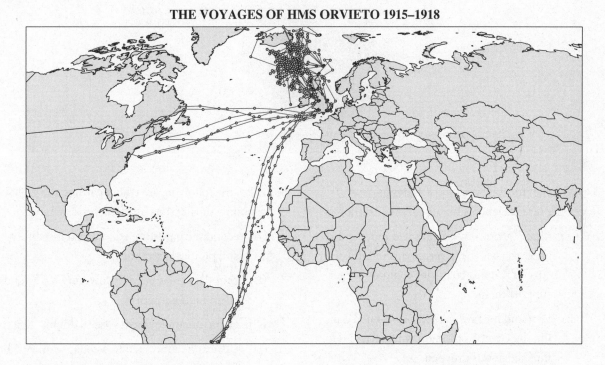

1. The travels of the *H.M.S. Orvieto* best illustrate

    (A) the success of the German U-boat campaign

    (B) the role of Atlantic trade in the Allied victory during World War I

    (C) the vast reach of British imperial territory

    (D) the superiority of newly invented ironclad ships

2. A major impact of World War I in Latin America was

    (A) a population explosion as Americans migrated to Latin America to avoid the draft

    (B) a population decline as many people volunteered to fight in the conflict, prompted by ideological sympathy

    (C) a temporary economic boom because of demand for wartime products such as Chilean nitrate

    (D) a temporary economic decline because of low international demand for luxury goods during World War I

Questions 3–4 refer to the image below.

CONTRACTION OF WORLD TRADE, 1929–1933

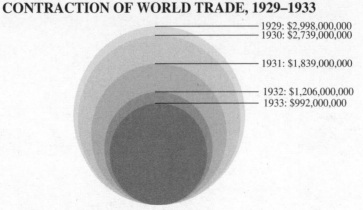

1929: $2,998,000,000
1930: $2,739,000,000
1931: $1,839,000,000
1932: $1,206,000,000
1933: $992,000,000

SOURCE: Charles P. Kindleberger, The world in Depression 1929–1933

3. Which of the following was a major impact of the Great Depression on colonial territories?

   (A) Many territories were granted independence because the governments of industrialized capitalist countries could no longer support them.

   (B) Demand for raw materials continued during the Great Depression while demand for finished goods dropped.

   (C) Local economies were devastated because many colonies relied on exports like rubber and cocoa, which were vulnerable to fluctuations in the world market.

   (D) Economic and social tensions caused many colonies to revolt and establish independent communist governments.

4. All of the following are true regarding the global economy during the Great Depression except

   (A) economic hardship led to social instability and political extremism

   (B) countries responded by lowering tariffs and encouraging imports

   (C) global unemployment rose to double digits

   (D) U.S. bank failures led to a collapse of world financial centers

Questions 5–6 refer to the passage below.

"Study the Soviet Union's merits and support all the Soviet Union's correct positions. There are two good things about the reactionaries' anti-Chinese [activities]: one is that they have revealed the reactionaries, reducing their prestige among the people; the second is that they have stimulated the consciousness of the majority of the peoples in the world, who can then see that reactionary imperialism, nationalism, and revisionism are enemies, swindlers, and contraband, whereas the Chinese flag is bright red.

The whole world is very bright. The darker the clouds, the greater the light.

Marxism and Leninism will get the greatest development in China. There is no doubt of this.

Khrushchev and his group are very naïve. He does not understand Marxism-Leninism and is easily fooled by imperialism.

He does not understand China, to an extreme extent. He doesn't research [China] and believes a whole bunch of incorrect information. He gives irresponsible talks. If he doesn't correct [his mistakes], in a few years he'll be completely bankrupt (after 8 years).

He panics over China. The panic has reached its extreme.

He has two main fears: imperialism and Chinese Communism.

He fears that Eastern European or other Communist parties will believe us and not them. His world view is pragmatism. This is an extreme kind of subjective idealism. He lacks a workable agenda and will follow gain wherever it goes.

The Soviet people are good as is the [Soviet] party. There is something not good about the style of the party and people, a somewhat metaphysical style, a kind of capitalist-liberalism inherited from history. Lenin died early and didn't have time to reform it."

Mao Zedong, "An Outline for a Speech on the International Situation," 1959

5. Which of the following was true of the Russian communist revolution, but was <u>not</u> true of China's communist revolution?

   (A) The government instituted a Five-Year Plan.

   (B) The government struggled to apply Marxist ideals to a largely agricultural economy.

   (C) The government derived support for communism mainly from the cities.

   (D) The government used totalitarian methods to eliminate opposition.

6. Which of the following best describes a cause for the Sino-Soviet split?

   (A) Diverging ideology and national interests

   (B) Competition over colonial territory

   (C) Personality clashes between Soviet and Chinese leadership

   (D) Détente between the United States and the Soviet Union

Questions 7–8 refer to the passage below.

"Are these the beginnings of profound changes in the Soviet state? Or are they token gestures, intended to raise false hopes in the West, or to strengthen the Soviet system without changing it? We welcome change and openness; for we believe that freedom and security go together, that the advance of human liberty can only strengthen the cause of world peace. There is one sign the Soviets can make that would be unmistakable, that would advance dramatically the cause of freedom and peace.

General Secretary Gorbachev, if you seek peace, if you seek prosperity for the Soviet Union and Eastern Europe, if you seek liberalization: Come here to this gate! Mr. Gorbachev, open this gate! Mr. Gorbachev, tear down this wall!"

Ronald Reagan, "Tear Down This Wall," 1987

7. Which of the following regimes is most associated with policies of "openness" and "restructuring?"

   (A) The People's Republic of China under Mao Zedong

   (B) The Soviet Union under Gorbachev

   (C) The Soviet Union under Stalin

   (D) Cuba under Fidel Castro

8. Which of the following did <u>not</u> lead to the collapse of the Soviet Union?

   (A) The reunification of Germany

   (B) The Soviet invasion of Afghanistan

   (C) The Polish Solidarity movement

   (D) The implementation of *glasnost* and *perestroika*

Questions 9–10 refer to the passage below.

"One of the last countries to return to democracy was Chile, where the Pinochet dictatorship had been more successful than most... After first imposing harsh readjustments and committing its share of mistakes, it had launched the country on a steady course...that made it a much-admired model in Latin America and continued even after the dictator finally turned over the presidency (though not control of the armed forces) to an elected Christian Democrat in 1990."

"History of Latin America," *Encyclopaedia Britannica*

9. Since the 1980s, many countries in Latin America have moved politically toward

   (A) communism

   (B) representative democracy

   (C) nationalistic fundamentalism

   (D) totalitarianism

10. Pinochet's dictatorship persisted in Chile longer than many Latin American countries because

    (A) the people were satisfied with the economic situation

    (B) the communist regime punished dissension severely

    (C) the Sandinista party remained very popular

    (D) the government had financial backing from the Soviet Union

Part B: Key Topics

This key topics list is the same as the list in the Test What You Already Know section earlier in this chapter. Based on what you have now learned, ask yourself the following questions:

- Can I describe this key topic?
- Can I discuss this key topic in the context of other events?
- Could I correctly answer a multiple-choice question about this key topic?
- Could I correctly answer a free-response question about this key topic?

Check off the key topics if you can answer "yes" to at least three of these questions.

World War I

☐ World War I

☐ Total war

☐ League of Nations

☐ Mohandas Gandhi

Global Depression

☐ World War II

☐ Great Depression

Rise of Fascist and Totalitarian States

- [ ] Benito Mussolini
- [ ] Adolf Hitler
- [ ] Fascism
- [ ] Joseph Stalin

World War II

- [ ] Firebombing
- [ ] Nuclear bomb
- [ ] United Nations
- [ ] Cold War

The Cold War

- [ ] Proxy wars
- [ ] Vietnam
- [ ] Warsaw Pact
- [ ] Non-Aligned Movement
- [ ] European Union

Revolutions

- [ ] Vladimir Lenin
- [ ] Mao Zedong
- [ ] Great Leap Forward
- [ ] Fidel Castro

Independence and Nationalist Movements

- [ ] Indian National Congress
- [ ] Muhammad Ali Jinnah
- [ ] Indian/Pakistan Partition
- [ ] Algeria
- [ ] Ho Chi Minh

Political Reform and Economic Changes

- [ ] Deng Xiaoping
- [ ] Tiananmen Square
- [ ] NATO

Technology, Populations, and the Environment

- [ ] Green Revolution
- [ ] Cholera
- [ ] HIV/AIDS

Social and Cultural Changes

- [ ] Pan-Africanism
- [ ] Liberation theology in Latin America

1900 C.E. to Present

Tally Your Results for Part A and Part B

Part A: Check your answers and count the number of questions you got correct.

1. B   6. A

2. C   7. B

3. C   8. A

4. B   9. B

5. C   10. A

_____ out of 10 questions

Part B: Count the number of key topics you checked off.

_____ out of 36 key topics

Next Step: Compare your Test What You Already Know results to these Test What You Learned results to see how exam-ready you are for AP World History Period 6: 1900 to the Present.

FOR MORE PRACTICE

Complete more practice online at kaptest.com. Haven't registered your book yet? Go to kaptest.com/booksonline to begin.

PART 3

Complete Time Period Review

CHAPTER 8

Periods 1 and 2: Up to 600 C.E. – Complete Time Period Review

EARLY HUMANS

Human Migrations out of Africa

The longest period of human history was the **Paleolithic**, or Early Stone Age. All humans lived as hunter-gatherers in small bands of 20 to 60 people. Almost everything that we know of these first humans comes to us from archaeological evidence. By examining their bones and the remains of their campsites, we find clues to how our distant ancestors lived. These people are marked by stone tool-making—the first recognizable cultural activity.

Homo sapiens evolved in East Africa, and then spread out of Africa in two great waves: the first 100,000–125,000 years ago, the second 60,000–75,000 years ago. Humans migrated to Europe and Asia through the Middle East. When sea levels were lower due to the Ice Age, a land bridge connected Siberia and modern-day Alaska, which humans used to cross over into the Americas. About 15,000 years ago, humans lived in almost all of the world's habitable regions.

Tools of Paleolithic Humans

In addition to stone tool-making, early humans developed other tools made from a variety of materials including bone, wood, and skin. Projectile points, for spears and arrows, and bladed tools, such as axes and knives, helped our ancestors take advantage of various resources. Other tools, such as harpoons and needles for sewing clothes, were adapted to the different environmental regions. Paleolithic humans also used fire as a tool. Fire protected people against dangerous animals at night and helped keep people warm, especially when used with clothing made of animal fur and hides. It also made cooking more efficient and effective.

Although no physical evidence exists, historians believe that spoken language first developed in these Paleolithic humans. The coordination of a band of people for hunting big game, such as mastodons, would likely have required communication via language. Where early humans spread, megafauna (large animals) such as woolly mammoths died out. The end of the last Ice Age is also believed to have contributed to the extinction of most megafauna outside of Africa, where such animals evolved alongside early humans and adapted to their presence.

Paleolithic Society

Early humans traveled in nomadic groups of a few dozen hunter-gatherers. These groups likely formed based on kinship and were fairly self-sufficient. Although the evidence is scarce, historians believe that these small bands of people exchanged ideas and valuable possessions, as well as mating with each other.

A few planned burial sites of Paleolithic peoples have been excavated. The items buried with the dead, as well as the elaborate artwork of cave paintings, indicate that Paleolithic people put a great deal of importance on the natural world. Most likely they believed in **animism**, which is the belief that spirits living in the natural world influence human events.

DEVELOPMENT OF AGRICULTURE High-Yield

The Neolithic Revolution: An Experiment with Seeds Leads to Farming

Early humans lived for thousands of years hunting animals and gathering roots and plants. Beginning about 10,000 years ago, the Earth's climate began to warm as the last Ice Age ended. Possibly as a result of climatic change, permanent agricultural villages began emerging, signaling the start of the agricultural revolution. This event is often called the **Neolithic Revolution**. It might have been called the Neolithic *Transition* though, because it took hundreds, if not thousands, of years of change before an agricultural economy took hold.

The discovery of agriculture, most likely made by women who were experimenting with gathered seeds, allowed people to change the way they lived. In order to create a new field out of a forested area, the first farmers used slash-and-burn agriculture, in which they would slash the bark and burn the trees to the ground. However, despite this land being fertile initially, after a few years it grew barren and the field would be abandoned to grow fallow. This forced people to migrate to neighboring areas, helping facilitate the spread of agriculture. A second great discovery was the domestication and breeding of animals. This gave rise to **pastoralism**, a type of agriculture reliant on raising livestock. Overtime, agriculture and pastoralism replaced hunting and gathering. With these skills, people could now remain in one place.

Different crops were domesticated in different regions of the world depending on the plants that were available. Agriculture emerged at very different times according to region. Grains such as wheat and barley were first grown in what is called the fertile crescent of Southwest Asia. Rice and soybeans were first grown in East Asia along the Yangzi and Huang He rivers. Yams and sorghum grew in sub-Saharan Africa. People in Southeast Asia farmed taro and bananas. Maize, beans, and potatoes were grown in the Americas.

More Stability Equals More People

Now that humans had settled, many changes could occur. Early farmers began to organize themselves in a more permanent way through the formation of villages. This permanence allowed for the development of new technologies. Farming tools, such as the hoe, emerged during this period. Even though farming required more work than hunting and gathering (the average hunter and gatherer worked only four hours a day to find food), it was much more stable.

With food stability came population growth, as fewer people starved to death. Increasing life spans meant more reproduction, and more children contributed to a greater labor force to work the land. Consider these numbers:

Time	World Population
10,000 B.C.E.	4 million
5000 B.C.E.	5 million
3000 B.C.E.	14 million
2000 B.C.E.	27 million
1000 B.C.E.	50 million
500 B.C.E.	100 million

Life in a Neolithic Village

As farmers began to develop a surplus of food, **job specialization** followed. With fewer people needed to till the land, new jobs could be developed including occupations such as metal smiths, millers, brewers, traders, and priests. With the beginning of privately owned land, a wealthier class emerged. The ownership of this land equaled economic power. This land was kept in the families' hands and passed down from generation to generation; with this, social classes emerged.

For Neolithic people, nature meant life or death. They had to learn the changes of the seasons based on the positions of the sun, moon, and stars. Religious beliefs centered on the life cycle of birth, growth, death, and regenerated life. Clay figurines of gods and goddesses have been unearthed that reflect these beliefs. Construction of megaliths—"big stones"—seemed to have religious significance, and include the famous Stonehenge, as well as others around the world.

The Neolithic Revolution also had consequences for gender roles. Men were working in the fields and herding animals, which required them to be outside the home. Women, on the other hand, performed jobs such as caring for the children, weaving cloth, and making cheese from milk, all of which required them to be in the home. Over time, the work outside the home was perceived as more important, and men began to take a more dominant role in the gender relationship, creating a **patriarchy** with men holding power in the family, government, and economy.

Early Inventions in Metal and Transportation

In Neolithic villages, three main craft industries developed and became essential elements of almost all human agricultural societies: pottery, **metallurgy**, and textiles. The earliest metal used was copper for jewelry and simple tools. Later, it was heated to become more malleable and was made into knives, axes, hoes, and weapons. Copper was the foundation for the later developments of tools and weapons made from bronze and iron.

Around 3000 B.C.E., metalworkers in **Mesopotamia** discovered a mixture, or alloy, of copper and tin that was much stronger than copper alone. This alloy—bronze—significantly changed warfare and agriculture. Bronze was made into weapons such as swords, spears, axes, shields, and armor, and tools such as bronze-tipped plows.

Sometime around 1000 B.C.E., iron tools and weapons were first developed. Metalworkers discovered that when carbon was added to iron, it became much stronger. As iron is much more common than tin, it was more affordable to lower classes. Knowledge of metalworking spread throughout Mesopotamia and from there to the rest of the Old World.

The wheel was developed sometime between 3500 B.C.E. and 3000 B.C.E., and knowledge of it spread rapidly enough that the wheel's exact origin is unknown. The wheel allowed for the transport of heavier loads and much longer-distance travel and trade. It became the standard means of overland transport everywhere except the Americas, where the wheel had no economic value due to the absence of suitable draft animals.

An Alternative Way of Life—Not Everyone Becomes a Farmer

Pastoral nomadism was another lifestyle that developed during this time. Pastoral nomads depended on their herd for survival and traveled to find grassland or steppe land required for their herds to graze. The steppe regions of Central Asia did not receive much rainfall, so the grass was better suited for grazing animals than for farming crops. Pastoralists, however, may have adversely affected the environment when they allowed their animals to overgraze these fragile grasslands.

Pastoral nomadism was not a step toward a life of farming; it was quite unique. It was a complicated and advanced lifestyle in which nomads literally lived off their animals. Geography usually determined who would be a pastoralist and who would be a farmer.

Life could be quite difficult for these early pastoralists, and in response, they developed fighting skills, using both offensive and defensive military tactics to defend their herds. It was the interaction between the pastoralists and the settled people that caused much of the development in this and other time periods.

THE FIRST CIVILIZATIONS

Farming communities often developed along river banks. As the river banks flooded and carried silt onto the land, the land became more fertile. The river also allowed for transportation and communication.

However, living near large rivers required a larger amount of cooperation amongst villagers because the flooding had to be controlled. Flood control techniques and irrigation projects were soon developed. Such cooperation among these first civilizations led to the development of the first urban centers, or city-states. Like the development of farming, the development of cities was a gradual process. Early cities were larger than Neolithic towns and villages, with a large economic center called the marketplace, which was extremely influential to the surrounding regions. The marketplace became the center of political, military, and economic control. These cities often led to the growth of more complex societies, which had the following in common:

- Food surplus, such as storable grain crops

- Specialization of labor, such as artisans and scribes

- Trade, such as that between Mesopotamia and the Indus Valley

- Social stratification, such as between elites and lower classes

- Organized government, such as the **Assyria** and **Shang** dynasties, based on defined territory

- Complex religions, such as polytheistic religious belief

- Written language, such as **cuneiform** and hieroglyphs

- Architecture, such as **ziggurats** in Mesopotamia

- Arts/Science, such as sculptures and irrigation technologies

However, despite many advantages afforded by cities, there were disadvantages as well. Social stratification led to social oppression of some people. Over-cultivation of land caused soil degradation. Because of the wealth in cities, centers were often attacked by outsiders, such as the pastoral nomads from the steppe. Additionally, crowded conditions created life-threatening sanitation problems.

Mesopotamia

High-Yield

Mesopotamia means the "land between rivers," referring to the Tigris and Euphrates rivers in the Middle East. The rivers formed part of the Fertile Crescent, an area of arable land extending from modern-day Iraq west to the Mediterranean coastline, and south from there along the Nile River. The earliest farming communities were located in the Fertile Crescent. Small-scale irrigation started in Mesopotamia around 6000 B.C.E. By 3000 B.C.E., an area that came to be known as Sumer had a population of 100,000. Cities grew as irrigation systems expanded, eventually developing into city-states.

> ✔ **AP Expert Note**
>
> ### The *Epic of Gilgamesh*
>
> One the earliest surviving works of literature, the *Epic of Gilgamesh*, is a Mesopotamian epic poem. A demigod and bored king, Gilgamesh, torments his subjects. They beg the gods for help. The gods send Enkidu, a wild man. After a great battle, the two men become best friends and go on many adventures. When the human Enkidu dies, a heartbroken Gilgamesh seeks the sage Utnapishtim, who built a ship that saved mankind from a great flood. Gilgamesh soon learns to accept mortality and to be a good king, because his city-state will outlive even him.

A city-state is a sovereign city (i.e., one that makes its own laws and is not ruled by anyone else) that has a countryside or adjoining lands that support it with agricultural goods. Although sharing a similar culture (language, writing, and religion), each city-state had its own monarch and special god or goddess that watched over it. Often warring over lands and goods, city-states built walls for defense. They also built ziggurats—distinctive step-shaped pyramids that functioned as temples. Over time, these city-states were conquered and united into a single empire which was ruled over by many different societies in succession: the Akkadians, Babylonians, Assyrians, Macedonians, Persians, and more.

A city-state's hereditary monarch was at the top of the social order, followed closely by the priests and priestesses who were often younger relatives of the rulers. A noble class of warriors and judges advised the monarch. A fourth group were the free commoners, who worked as farmers, builders, craftsmen, or professionals such as scribes. The dependent clients, a subgroup of commoners, owned no property and worked only on the estates of others. All commoners paid taxes with surplus food or labor. At the bottom of the social pyramid were the slaves, who were often either prisoners of war or debtors. Slaves were used for agricultural labor or domestic service.

Sumer illustrates the development of a patriarchal system at the dawn of civilization. For example, Enheduanna, a high priestess in the Sumerian city-state of Ur in the 2200s B.C.E., is history's earliest known poet and among history's earliest known women. Her elite background and the depictions of a scribe goddess in Ur's temples suggest that literacy was not uncommon among high-status women. However, while early Sumer was somewhat egalitarian about gender among the upper classes, later Sumerian women faced far more restrictions. Women as a whole became viewed as second-class citizens and were treated that way by the law. The reason why is still debated. One theory is that the increasing wealth of civilization led to a focus on keeping a family's property safe as it passed between generations. Since the mother of a child was always certain but the father was not necessarily so, laws and social customs increasing control over women developed.

Hammurabi and His Code

One of the most famous emperors of Mesopotamia was the Babylonian Hammurabi, who ruled from 1792 B.C.E. to 1750 B.C.E. Hammurabi used an organized central bureaucracy and implemented regular taxation. He is most famous for his code of laws, which he promulgated on stone columns. The Law Code of Hammurabi was among the first documented attempts in ancient history to ascribe specific punishments to crimes.

Hammurabi's Code of laws had three main principles. The first was the principle of retribution, whereby a crime was punished by a comparable sentence: "an eye for an eye." The second principle was about social status. The severity of a punishment correlated with a person's social standing. A commoner poking out the eye of a noble in a fight would be put to death, whereas in the reverse situation, the noble would just have to pay a fine. Hammurabi's Code was patriarchal—men were clearly the head of the household and had authority to sell their wives and children into slavery to pay off a debt. Women had rights of divorce and could own businesses, but it was clear that their first responsibility was to their husbands and homes. The third principle was that government had a responsibility to its citizens. If one's home was robbed and the thief was not caught, the local government would reimburse citizens for their loss.

Phoenicians

The **Phoenicians** established city-states along the Mediterranean coast. Though militarily not powerful, these people dominated maritime trade networks. In addition to naval prowess, the Phoenicians developed the first alphabet, consisting of 22 letters. This alphabet was later adopted by the Greeks, and eventually the Romans adopted it from the Greeks. English and many other modern-day languages inherited variations of this alphabet thanks to its use in both Greek and Rome's Latin language.

Egypt

The Nile River gave **Egypt** the lifeblood of its civilizations. Around 5000 B.C.E., agriculture began in this region. People learned to plant crops such as barley and wheat after the annual floods had receded. They soon built dikes to regulate the floods, watering their fields and enriching them with the fertile silt left behind by the Nile's water. By 4000 B.C.E., villages had developed irrigation systems.

✔ **AP Expert Note**

Be able to explain how environmental factors influence early civilizations

One example of how environmental factors influenced early civilizations is ancient Egypt, which was protected by its geography. Invaders could not attack from most approaches: the Red Sea to the east, the Mediterranean Sea to the north, the Sahara Desert around it, and the white water rapids of the Nile itself. All four were challenging barriers.

Ancient Egyptian society was ruled by pharaohs, who ordered the construction of some of the most beautiful and enduring architectural works of human history. The most famous are the pyramids of Giza, which were built as tombs for three successive pharaohs. The Egyptians excelled in bronze metallurgy, mathematics, medicine, and astronomy. The solar calendar of 365 days used today was first devised in ancient Egypt. Around 3200 B.C.E., the Egyptians developed their own written language made up of **pictographs**, or hieroglyphics.

The polytheistic Egyptians believed that the gods judged a person's life and that if found worthy, a person's spirit lived on in an afterlife. Additionally, Egyptians believed earthly belongings could be taken to the afterlife, and the dead could use their bodies. This led to the practices of mummification, a process of preserving dead bodies, and the building of elaborate tombs, such as the pyramids, in whose walls the hieroglyphic accounts of the pharaoh's life were documented. Tombs built underground in the Valley of the Kings were filled with earthly treasures, and were usually looted for them over the millennia.

As a ruler, the pharaoh was at the top of the social class structure, followed by priests, commoners, and slaves. Egypt had professional military forces and a bureaucracy of administrators and tax collectors. The way to get ahead in society was to be close to the pharaoh. Service to him meant higher status.

Unlike in Mesopotamia, Egyptian women who were literate could often take on jobs as administrators. While only one female pharaoh existed, Egyptian women enjoyed rights and freedoms that their counterparts in other civilizations of the era, like Ancient Greece, did not. Women could own property and land, hold jobs, and travel. Divorce was easy. Priestesses held great power and influence. Egyptian religion viewed its gods and goddesses as co-equal. These freedoms would largely endure until Egypt became politically and culturally dominated by the **Roman Empire**.

Ancient Egyptian art attained a high level in painting and sculpture. Much that has survived comes from tombs of the pharaohs and therefore has an emphasis on life after death. These paintings and sculptures provide detailed depictions of gods, human beings, heroic battles, and nature, and were meant to provide comfort to the dead in the afterlife.

Late Bronze Age Collapse

Between 1200 and 1150 B.C.E., the civilizations bordering the eastern Mediterranean Sea suffered a violent societal collapse known as the Late Bronze Age collapse. Nearly every city in the region was destroyed in quick succession. It led to a dark age for the area. The exact causes of this cataclysm are still a mystery. Traditional speculation revolves around a mysterious group termed the "Sea Peoples," seafaring raiders of unknown origin. Modern theories also debate other contributing factors: famine resulting from drought, the breakdown of regional trade networks, natural disasters, and internal rebellions.

Hebrews

Due to the Late Bronze Age collapse, the Canaanite city-state system in the Levant (the eastern coast of the Mediterranean Sea) broke down. Neighboring groups, like the Phoenicians, incorporated the remnants of this system into their own cultures. One such group lived in highland settlements neighboring those city-states: the **Hebrews**, speakers of the ancient Hebrew language. The Hebrews lived in the south Levant. Over the next two hundred years, their population soared thanks to favorable conditions, and they created a complex web of cities and trade.

The Hebrews trace their origin to the patriarch Abraham, whom they believe God called to found a new nation in Canaan. Although the Hebrews were sporadically conquered by neighboring empires such as the Assyrians, Babylonians, and Romans, they maintained their cultural identity through their religion—Judaism, notably a monotheistic faith.

Indus

The Indus Valley civilization existed between 3300 B.C.E. and 1300 B.C.E., and mostly remains a mystery. Discovered during the early twentieth century, its language is still not understood. However, we do know that its polytheistic religious belief system centered on a strong concern for fertility. The Indus Valley's entire area was approximately 500,000 square miles, larger than both Mesopotamia and Egypt. It lay along the Indus River in what today is northwestern India.

Large Indus cities have been uncovered in recent years, with the two largest ones named **Harappa and Mohenjo-daro**. These walled cities, designed in a grid pattern, featured broad streets, marketplaces, temples, assembly halls, baths, and uniform housing with rich and poor sections of town. The wealthiest people even had private bathrooms with showers and toilets that drained into city sewage systems. Such sophisticated and planned cities suggest a strong central government, most likely led by a priest or a king.

Technologically and economically speaking, Indus had numerous advantages: it traded pottery, tools, and decorative items; it obtained gold, silver, and copper from Persia; and it obtained wool, leather, and olive oil from Mesopotamia. Metal tools of bronze and copper have been found, as well as jewelry made of precious stones. Cotton was cultivated in this area before 5000 B.C.E. The writing system, however, has yet to be deciphered. We do know that it used approximately 400 symbols to represent sounds and words. These symbols have been found on clay seals and copper tablets.

Sometime after 2000 B.C.E., the Indus civilization began to decline, possibly due to the arrival of the Aryans combined with a number of environmental factors. By 1500 B.C.E., the civilization had collapsed.

Aryans

The Aryans, a nomadic group of Indo-Europeans, entered the Indian subcontinent through the Khyber Pass around 1500 B.C.E. and quickly dominated the inhabitants of the Indus Valley. This migration established a racial mix on the Indian subcontinent, in what is modern-day Bangladesh, India, Nepal, and Pakistan.

Few artifacts were left behind by the Aryans, so much about them is unknown. What we do know is from a collection of sacred hymns, songs, prayers, and rituals known as the **Vedas**. The Vedas reveal a hierarchical, male-dominated society. The Aryans were polytheistic with many gods connected to nature. These early Aryan religious beliefs provided the basis for **Hinduism**. The Aryan social structure had probably the largest impact on India. It developed gradually, and later became the basis for the strict **caste system**. People were divided into four *varnas* based on occupation and purity: Brahmins (priests and scholars), Kshatriyas (rulers, administrators, warriors), Vaisyas (artisans, farmers, merchants), and Shudras (servants). This system later incorporated a lower class of untouchables (outcastes).

> ✔ **AP Expert Note**
>
> **The Indo-European migrations**
>
> From Spain in the west to Iran and India in the southeast, many modern-day peoples can trace their history back to the migration of the Indo-Europeans. They were several nomadic tribes from the Pontic–Caspian steppe, a region stretching from modern-day Ukraine east to Kazakhstan. Genetic studies suggest the horse was domesticated there, helping the migration of the Indo-Europeans.

Shang and Zhou

The first river valley civilization in China developed along the Huang He, or Yellow River. This river got its name from the light-colored loess soil that caused the river to appear yellow. Despite its fertile land, the river's devastating floods earned it the nickname "China's Sorrow." It was in this river valley that China's earliest civilization developed: the Shang dynasty. With the possible exception of the Indus Valley, the Shang were geographically separated from other civilizations during this time.

The Shang ruled a northern territory from approximately 1600 B.C.E. to 1046 B.C.E. in what today is China. Major archeological evidence used to prove the existence of the Shang dynasty is found in "oracle bones." Questions about—and predictions of—the future were written on these bones, so a type of written record exists. The development of written Chinese (pictograph) characters is traced back to the Shang. These pictures evolved into symbols, or ideographs. Additionally, the Shang developed bronze metallurgy, which aided in its rise as a military state.

The next and longer dynasty, the Zhou (1122–256 B.C.E.), further cemented important Chinese cultural foundations. The most notable tradition was the concept of the **Mandate of Heaven**, meaning that power to rule was granted from heaven. Because this power was divinely given, there was a direct connection between ruler and god. This power could be taken away, however, if justice and order were not maintained. Events such as floods, earthquakes, and peasant rebellions were indications from the gods that the end neared for a dynasty. The Zhou also introduced a feudal system to China. Because the empire was far too vast to be ruled by a single emperor, the king gave nobles power over smaller regions within the empire. They often ruled from walled cities.

Culturally and religiously, the Zhou placed great emphasis on the veneration of ancestors, as the family unit was the most important social structure. The belief was that if everyone honored their responsibilities toward the family, society would function smoothly. The Zhou had a strong elite ruling class, reinforced by hereditary aristocrats. A small class of free artisans and craftsmen, a large class of peasants, and slaves completed the social class structure. Additionally, during the Zhou period, iron metallurgy spread to China.

Even with all this structure, the Zhou lost control of the western half of the empire to noble families as early as 771 B.C.E. Complete control was lost in the fifth century and was followed by the Warring States period, a time in which various noble families fought among each other for control of China. This period ended in 221 B.C.E. with the rise of the **Qin dynasty**.

Mesoamerica and South America

In the Americas, agriculture developed around the same time as elsewhere, but not all of these societies were valley civilizations.

Olmecs

Around 1500 B.C.E., the **Olmecs** settled in the coastal plain near the Gulf of Mexico along river banks. The periodic flooding left the land fertile for agriculture. The first important settlement was San Lorenzo Tenochtitlán, which was the religious, political, and economic center for the large population. Later, La Venta served as an important center; with its abundant rainfall, there was no need to build an extensive irrigation system. Similar to other early civilizations, the Olmec built large-scale buildings, exhibited polytheistic religious beliefs, and developed a writing system and calendar. Olmec artisans carved masks and human figurines out of jade, which they imported from a neighboring area.

One of the great mysteries of the Olmecs is the colossal heads they sculpted out of stone. These heads vary between 5 and 11 feet high and weigh among 6 to 25 tons each. It is believed that they are carvings of the leadership, but no one knows for sure. What we do know is that it took a great deal of organization and labor to construct such monuments, suggesting that society was most likely authoritarian, in which the lower class performed the bidding of the upper class. The decline and fall of the Olmecs is mysterious as well. Its ceremonial centers were destroyed and abandoned, but it is unknown why.

Chavin

In South America, urban centers developed in isolation from those in Mesoamerica, but at about the same time. By around 2500 B.C.E., crops such as beans, peanuts, and potatoes were cultivated in the Andean heartland. A complex society known as the **Chavin** (900–200 B.C.E.) gained influence. Chavin de Huantar, in modern-day Peru, was their most important ceremonial center. It had several large temple platforms, suggesting that priests held the highest social status. Artisans worked with ceramics, textiles, and gold. Societies in both Mesoamerica and South America constructed religious shrine centers and had polytheistic beliefs. These early American civilizations would influence the civilizations and empires that developed later.

Maya Empire

From approximately 250 B.C.E. to 900 C.E., the **Maya empire** occupied territory in modern day Belize, Guatemala, Honduras, and southern Mexico. The Maya cosmos was divided into three parts: the heavens above, humans at the center, and the underworld below. Similar to the Egyptians, the Maya people built impressive pyramids, meant to be portals to the heavens above. Warfare was also imbued with religious significance, as religious rituals would precede battle. The Mayas also made huge contributions to mathematics and astronomy, particularly the concept of zero, as well as a modern calendar with 365 days.

CLASSICAL SOCIETIES

The political and cultural beginnings in the five classical societies of Persia, Greece, India, Rome, and China laid the foundations for future development. Classical Greek and Indian societies created the foundations for the development of future decentralized governments, while classical Roman and Chinese societies created the blueprint for later centralized states.

Persia

Political Development

Ancient **Persia** was centered in present-day Iran but grew to include Egypt, Mesopotamia, Anatolia, and Assyria. People first migrated to this area around 1000 B.C.E. and established a number of small kingdoms.

Around 550 B.C.E., the Persian king Cyrus II began to conquer neighboring kingdoms. By 539 B.C.E., he controlled an empire that extended 2,000 miles from the Indus River to Anatolia (present-day Turkey). Cyrus's legacy is the method of his rule. Unlike most conquerors of this period, Cyrus honored local customs and religions of conquered peoples. He ended the Babylonian captivity of the Jews, allowing them to return to Jerusalem in 538 B.C.E. and rebuild their holiest temple; Cyrus would be mentioned 23 times in the Bible for this act, and described with the highest praise.

The Persian emperor Darius I, whose 36-year rule began in 522 B.C.E., is noted for his administrative genius. He divided the empire into 20 provinces, each of which closely resembled the homelands of the different peoples who lived in the empire. Each province was ruled by a *satrap*, who allowed the people under his jurisdiction to practice their own religion, speak their own language, and follow their own laws. *Satraps* collected tribute taxes, maintained roads, and performed other administrative duties.

Economic Development

Darius used other tools to maintain his empire, which also brought economic benefits. The Persians created an excellent road system that included the 1,677-mile Royal Road, which facilitated communication and trade within the empire. Darius also manufactured metal coins of standard value that were used throughout the empire. This network of roads and standardized coins stimulated trade.

Society

Society was divided into three categories: warriors (the dominant element of society), priests (called Magi), and peasant farmers. Although family organization was patriarchal, women in the Persian elite were politically influential, possessed substantial property, and traveled.

Greece

Political Development

Greece's political identity revolved around the concept of the *polis* (city-state). Greece's mountainous geography helped in the development of this decentralized political structure. Although different city-states emerged independently, they still shared a common language and somewhat similar cultural practices. A few city-states functioned as monarchies, but most were based on some form of collaborative rule.

It is worth noting that Athens did not start out as a democracy. Rather, political tyrants were overthrown in favor of an oligarchy, and then ultimately, a democracy. It was under Pericles that democracy was established. Over time, population pressures led to the establishment of colonies along the Mediterranean Sea, yet a centralized state was not created. These colonies relied on their own resources and took their own course. They did, however, facilitate trade throughout the region.

Greek cities in Anatolia (modern-day Turkey) resented what they viewed as the oppressive rule of the Persian Empire and revolted, starting the Persian War (499–449 B.C.E.). Athenians, too, sent their own troops in support. In two separate wars occurring a decade apart, the Persians attacked the Greek mainland. During the first war, the important victory at Marathon by the Athenians led to the Golden Age of Athens. During the second war, the Athenian-led naval victory at Salamis and the Spartan-led army victory at Plataea stopped the Persian attempts to conquer the Greek city-states. The Greeks also developed a new kind of warfare, waged by hoplites—citizen-soldiers who were heavily armored, carried spears and shields, and fought in a phalanx formation.

> ✔ **AP Expert Note**
>
> ### Be able to define important terms and compare historical examples.
>
> The city-state is a common form of government throughout history. Sumer, Greece, the Maya civilization, medieval Germany, that East African Swahili states, and modern-day Singapore are all examples of city-states. Knowing the characteristics of this form of government and comparing historical instances of it are examples of the types of knowledge the AP exam may ask you to demonstrate.

The alliance of the Greeks against the Persians led to the formation of the Delian League, of which Athens served as the leader. However, the heavy-handed leadership of Athens spurred resentment within the league. This unrest led to the Peloponnesian War (431–404 B.C.E.). Sparta and Athens led the two opposing camps. Though Sparta was victorious, the conflict weakened Greece, leaving it vulnerable to domination by a stronger power—Macedonia, a frontier state north of the Greek peninsula.

King Philip II of Macedonia, who ruled from 359–336 B.C.E., consolidated control of his kingdom and moved into Greece, and by 338 B.C.E., the region was under his control. His next goal was to conquer Persia, but that job would be left to his son, **Alexander the Great**.

Alexander, a skilled military commander and strategist, successfully conquered Persia by 330 B.C.E. and went on to conquer most of the northwestern regions of the Indian subcontinent. At that point his troops refused to go any further. By 323 B.C.E., at the age of 33, Alexander the Great was dead. What he left behind was the creation of a **Hellenistic** Empire and Era. The empire was divided among three of his generals who were the namesakes for these areas: Antigonid (Greece and Macedonia), Ptolemaic (Egypt), and Seleucid (Persia).

Economic Developments

The Greek world relied heavily on trade as the cornerstone of its economy. The Mediterranean Sea linked its communities through trade and created a larger Greek community. During the Hellenistic Era, caravan trade flourished from Persia to the West, and sea lanes were widely traveled throughout the Mediterranean Sea, Persian Gulf, and Arabian Sea. This trade created a cosmopolitan culture.

Social Structure and Gender Roles

Overall, Greece was a patriarchal society with fairly strict social divisions. Women were under the authority of their fathers, husbands, and then, sons. Most women owned no land and they often wore veils in public. Their one public position could be that of a priestess of a religious cult. Literacy, however, was common among upper-class Greek women, and Spartan women took part in athletic competitions.

The two most famous city-states were Athens and Sparta. Athens used democratic principles to negotiate order, while Sparta used military strength to impose order. Athens' government was a direct democracy that relied on its small size and the intense participation of its citizens. However, those citizens were restricted to free adult males, and excluded women, foreigners, and slaves. The Spartans, on the other hand, lived life with no luxuries. Distinction was earned through discipline and military talent. Boys began their rigorous military training at age seven, and girls received physical education to promote the birth of strong children.

Slaves comprised about 30 percent of Greek society and were acquired because they had debts they could not repay, were prisoners of war, or were traded. The treatment of slaves varied widely, depending of their assigned task and the temperament of the owner.

Culture, Arts, Science, and Technology

The Hellenistic Era greatly contributed to cultural diffusion. It was particularly facilitated by the conquests of Alexander the Great. Culturally, the Greeks stressed a central importance on human life and a growing appreciation of human beauty. This is seen through Greek religion, philosophy, art, architecture, literature, athletics, and science.

Polytheistic, the Greeks believed that their gods were personifications of nature. Each city-state had its own patron god or goddess for whom rituals were performed. One of the greatest legacies of classical Greek civilization is philosophy. The great philosopher Socrates, who posed questions and encouraged reflection, is credited as saying, "The unexamined life is not worth living." His student Plato wrote *The Republic*, in which he described his ideal state ruled by a philosopher king. Plato's student Aristotle wrote on biology, physics, astronomy, politics, and ethics. Aristotle is considered the father of logic; his system of deductive reasoning was an important element in the development of political systems, scientific advancements, and religion up to the modern era.

In literature, the great epic poems attributed to Homer, the *Iliad* and the *Odyssey*, convey the value of the hero in Greek culture. In architecture, the Greeks built temples using pillars or columns, and they developed a realistic approach to human sculpture. The Olympic games were held regularly to demonstrate athletic excellence. The Greeks also made great strides in anatomy, astronomy, and math including the medical writings of Galen and the mathematics of Archimedes, Pythagoras, and Euclid. Greek drama also flourished in its comedies and tragedies, with notable playwrights such as Euripides. Lastly, the Greek writer, Herodotus, is credited as being the father of modern history.

India

Political Development

Following the invasions of the Aryans, by the sixth century B.C.E., India developed into small regional kingdoms that often fought each other. Though there were periods of centralized rule, the subcontinent remained decentralized through most of its early history.

One significant example of centralized rule was that of the **Mauryan Empire**. In the 320s B.C.E., Chandragupta Maurya made his move to fill the power vacuum left after Alexander of Macedonia (Alexander the Great) withdrew from the region. Maurya successfully dominated the area and set up a bureaucratic administrative system to rule his empire.

His grandson, **Ashoka**, continued his grandfather's conquering ways until the bloody campaign to conquer Kalinga. This bloodbath convinced Ashoka to stop using a conquering approach and instead rule by moral example. He used his Rock Edicts (announcements carved into cliffs and in caves) to get his message out to the people. During his reign, Ashoka set up a tightly-organized bureaucracy that collected taxes and was made up of officials, accountants, and soldiers. He built roads, hospitals, and rest houses, and helped facilitate trade. After Ashoka's death, the Mauryan Empire declined and India returned to a land of large regional kingdoms; however, order, stability, and a prosperous trade were maintained.

> ✔ **AP Expert Note**
>
> Ashoka converted to Buddhism and later used Buddhist monks to spread Buddhism across Central Asia and into Southeast Asia. Knowing causes and effects for the spread of religion is a type of knowledge commonly asked for on the AP World History exam.

It was not until 320 C.E. that India would again be united under a centralized rule. Chandra Gupta established the **Gupta empire** and conquered many of the regional kingdoms. The south, however, remained outside his control. Instead of setting up an organized bureaucracy, the Gupta left the local government and administration in power. The Gupta empire is an example of a theater-state: a political structure acquiring its prestige and power by developing attractive cultural, public works. Under the Gupta, Hinduism emerged as the primary religion of Indian culture, while Buddhism mostly disappeared from the Indian subcontinent. Their rule continued until the invasion of the Huns severely weakened the empire and India subsequently returned to regional rule.

Economic Development

India's economy benefited from the expansion of agriculture and the increase in trade throughout the classical period. Ashoka encouraged agricultural development through irrigation and encouraged trade by building roads, wells, and inns along those roads. Agricultural surplus led to an increase in the number of towns; these towns maintained marketplaces and encouraged trade. Long-distance trade increased with China, Southeast Asia, and the Mediterranean basin.

> ✔ **AP Expert Note**
>
> Centralized rule means the emperor rules directly through governors, military leaders, or scholars. Decentralized rule means the emperor lets local rulers preside over their own people, although they must collect and pay taxes and/or tribute to the emperor. Centralized rule was often more stable and resistant to outside invaders.

Social Structure and Gender Roles

Like Greece, India developed into a patriarchal society with a strict social structure. Women were forbidden from reading the sacred prayers (the Vedas), and under Hindu law, they were legally subject to the supervision of their fathers, husbands, and then sons. In order to marry well, a woman's family needed a large dowry. Women were not allowed to inherit property, and a widow was not permitted to remarry. If their husbands passed away, widows were expected to burn themselves at their husbands' funeral pyre in a ritual known as *sati*.

The Brahmins and the caste system dominated the social structure. Caste—something that could not be changed—determined one's job, diet, and marriage. These restrictions were reinforced by the ruling class. As the Brahmins became more powerful, especially during the rule of the Guptas, caste distinctions grew more prominent.

Culture, Arts, Science, and Technology

During this period, India's culture thrived, including its advancements in the arts, math, and science. The Mauryan emperor Ashoka became a devout Buddhist around 260 B.C.E. after the battle at Kalinga; he changed the way he ruled his empire. He rewarded Buddhists with land and encouraged their spread by building monasteries and *stupas* (mound-like structures that contained Buddhist relics and served as places of worship). He even sent out missionaries, who facilitated the spread of Buddhism to Central Asia, East Asia, and Southeast Asia. Still, Hinduism gradually eclipsed the influence of Buddhism. The Guptas gave land grants to Brahmins, promoted Hindu values through education, and built great temples in urban centers.

Unlike Greek art, Indian art during this time stressed symbolism rather than accurate representation. Science and math, such as geometry and algebra, flourished. The circumference of the Earth and the value of pi were calculated. Additionally, the concept of zero, the decimal system, and the base 10 number system we use today were developed.

China

Political Development

China's political development during this time period laid the foundation for what would endure over two millennia. It began during a period referred to as the Warring States period (403–221 B.C.E.). During this time of turmoil and warfare, three important philosophies emerged to address the problems of the day and attempt to end the fighting: Confucianism, **Daoism**, and Legalism. These three philosophies were part of a larger intellectual flowering known as the Hundred Schools of Thought. Legalism offered the firmest solution to China's problems, preaching a practical and ruthless approach to state rule. The foundation of a state's strength, it proposed, was in its agricultural production and its military, and strict laws and punishments were required to maintain order.

> ✔ **AP Expert Note**
>
> Knowing the Chinese dynasties in the correct order is essential for proper chronological understanding of much of world history. Memorizing the dynasties, their start and end dates, and their key cultural and technological innovations will greatly assist you in both the multiple-choice and essay portions of the exam.

China's first emperor, Qin Shi Huang, believed Legalist ideas might be the solution to the country's problems. In 221 B.C.E., the emperor ended the Era of Warring States and started China's tradition of centralized rule. The Qin dynasty created a centralized bureaucracy and divided the land into administrative provinces. For protection, he sponsored the building of defensive walls, which were the predecessor to China's Great Wall. Laws, currencies, weights, measures, and the Chinese script were standardized. As Emperor Qin did not approve of Confucianism, he had Confucian books burnt. Many books of history, poetry, and philosophy were also burned to stifle dissent and to unify political thought. He also had 460 scholars buried alive.

Emperor Qin ruled only 14 years, but he established the precedent for centralized rule in China, which would last for the next 2,000 years. When the emperor died in 207 B.C.E., revolts broke out and a new dynasty—the Han—was established. In 1974 C.E., a vast mausoleum built for Emperor Qin was unearthed, including a large army of terracotta soldiers.

The **Han dynasty** (206 B.C.E.–220 C.E.) lasted much longer than the Qin dynasty and its emperors learned from the Qins' mistakes. The Han used what worked—such as centralized rule and a strong bureaucracy—but lessened the stricter aspects of the Legalist rule. As in the Zhou dynasty, the Han emperors used the "Mandate of Heaven" to justify their rule. It wasn't until the Yellow Turban Rebellion, a peasant revolt that lasted from 184 to 205 C.E., that the Han dynasty began to seriously decline.

The most prominent Han emperor, Wu (141–87 B.C.E.), built roads and canals, and established an imperial university with Confucianism as the basis for the curriculum. The university prepared students for civil service exams, which became the entry test for government jobs. Though in theory any young man could take the exams, bureaucratic appointments were made by the recommendation of existing officials. This allowed the landed gentry to promote their sons and entrench their own interests. The Han emperors still exerted absolute control, applying Confucian ideas on rigid, family structure to their authority over the empire. During the Han dynasty, a foreign policy of expansion was pursued, and Korea, northern Vietnam, and portions of Central Asia came under its control.

Economic Development

China's economy was based on agriculture, and it flourished during this period with increases in long-distance trade. Iron metallurgy was introduced during the Warring States period, which led to an increase in agriculture. That, in turn, allowed for an increase in trade and in the military strength of the empire. With the military expansion of the Han, peace and order allowed overland trade to increase. It was during the Han dynasty that the trade route known as the **Silk Road** began to flourish. The route consisted of a series of roads that connected the Han Empire with Central Asia, India, and the Roman Empire through trade.

The Han also followed a tributary system of trade. Officially, the policy stated the Han did not need to trade with their inferior neighbors, so instead, they demanded tribute from neighboring groups. These neighboring groups would visit the court, bringing tribute, and the Chinese would give trade goods in return. In addition, the Han often sent gifts to nomad groups so as to prevent any possible invasion.

Social Structure and Gender Roles

China, like the other classical civilizations, had a patriarchal society with a set social structure. A woman's most important role was to make a proper marriage that would strengthen the family's alliances. Widowed women were, however, permitted to remarry. Upper-class women were often tutored in writing, arts, and music, but overall, women were legally subordinate to their fathers and husbands.

Socially, the highest class was that of the scholar-gentry. These landlord families were often the only ones able to take the civil service exam, because preparation was very expensive. Most Chinese were peasants who worked the land. Merchants, who gained great wealth during this period with the increase in trade, did not enjoy high social status because they did not produce anything, but rather lived off the labor of others.

Culture, Arts, Science, and Technology

In China, the family became the most important cultural and organizational unit in society. The family consisted both of its living members and its ancestors. Confucianism's emphasis on **filial piety**, respect or reverence for one's parents, was also very influential. The family always provided for its own members.

Daoism's emphasis on being close to nature also had a lasting impact on China. This reverence for nature became a central value of the Han people. This was also a time of great invention and innovation. For many centuries, horses could not be efficiently used as draft animals. The solution, developed in China by the fifth century C.E., was to provide a collar around the neck and shoulders of the animal to distribute the weight. Collars of this kind reached Europe by the ninth century C.E. This development enabled the horse to become the main draft animal of Eurasia for both plowing and hauling. Agriculture was also aided by the wheelbarrow, while watermills were created to grind grain. The sternpost rudder and compass aided sea travel. Possibly most important was the invention of paper, which increased the availability of the written word.

Rome

High-Yield

Political Development

Rome's political history is one of change and evolution. In 509 B.C.E., the Roman nobility overthrew a tyrannical king, and what had been a monarchy became a **republic**—a government in which the people elect their representatives. The Roman Republic consisted of two consuls who were elected by an assembly that was dominated by the patricians, or wealthy class. The Senate, made up of patricians, advised these consuls. This system of leadership created tension between the patricians and the common people, known as the plebeians. Eventually, after a revolt, the patricians granted the plebeians the right to elect tribunes, who had the right of veto. When a civil or military crisis occurred, a dictator was appointed for six months.

As Rome expanded throughout the Italian peninsula and then the Mediterranean, it encountered a fierce competitor in the city of Carthage. Located in North Africa, Carthage was initially a colony in **Phoenicia**. It gained wealth through the thriving trade in the Mediterranean region. This economic competition led to the Punic Wars, a series of three wars which took place from 264 to 146 B.C.E. By the end of the conflict, Rome had sacked the city of Carthage, solidifying Rome's domination of the Mediterranean. Rome was also expanding east into Greece and the western coast of Anatolia, the former empire of Alexander the Great.

As Rome expanded, its republican system began to break down. The wealth and power resulting from conquest led to many problems, most notably the unequal distribution of land. The wealthy amassed large plantations using slave labor and the small farmers could not compete. Also, the growth of cities led to an increase in the urban lower class and an increase in poverty. Sporadic attempts by reformers to correct this inequality led to bloodshed, as the patricians and merchant classes resorted to violence to protect their wealth, defending their actions as saving the republic from would-be kings crowned by the plebeians.

Julius Caesar led a Roman army in its conquest of Gaul (present-day France). In 49 B.C.E. he seized Rome and soon made himself dictator for life. While fighting a civil war (49–45 B.C.E.) with the Senate, Caesar centralized military and political functions, undertook land reforms, and initiated large-scale building projects which gave jobs to the poor. Caesar pardoned many of his enemies in an effort to foster peace. After the end of the civil war, a group of senators feared Caesar aimed to become a king and assassinated him. His nephew Octavian took over. After another, shorter civil war, Octavian took the title of Augustus in 27 B.C.E. as the first Roman Emperor.

During Augustus's 45-year rule, Rome was a monarchy disguised as a republic. The Senate continued to exist, yet only served as a rubber stamp for Augustus, who did not call himself a king or emperor but rather the humbler *princeps civitatis* (first citizen). The continued expansion of the empire stimulated the growing economy, and new cities emerged. Economic prosperity, centralized power, and the strength of the Roman army resulted in stability throughout the empire; the next two and a half centuries were called the *Pax Romana*, or Roman Peace.

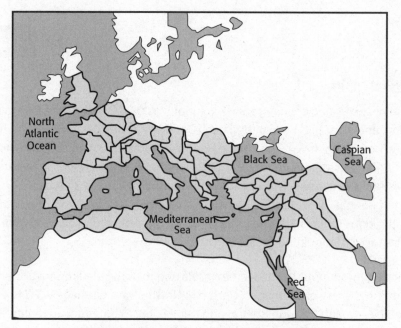

Height of the Roman Empire, 116 C.E.

Economic Development

The Roman Empire's economic success was due to two key factors: its extensive system of roads and its access to the Mediterranean Sea. The 60,000 miles of roads linked the empire's sixty million people, connecting all regions of the empire for trade and communication, and also allowing for the speedy transportation of armies. The Mediterranean Sea allowed for the transport of goods more cheaply than inland routes; the Romans kept the sea lanes clear of pirates. Taken together, these avenues of trade made the merchants very rich and created markets for the goods that the farmers produced. The resulting tax revenue strengthened the empire. A uniform currency was used, and while Latin was the language of politics and the Romans, Greek was the *lingua franca* (common language) for trade throughout the Mediterranean.

The extensive trade network made the empire very interdependent. Cities grew and so did their populations. The cities had access to fresh water through the use of aqueducts, sewers, plumbing, and public baths.

Social Structure and Gender Roles

Like other classical societies, Rome was patriarchal, where the eldest male, the *paterfamilias*, ruled as the father of the family. Roman law gave the *paterfamilias* authority to arrange marriage for the children and the right to sell them into slavery—or even execute them. Women's roles were in supervising domestic affairs, and laws put strict limits on their inheritances, though this was inconsistently enforced. As the wealth of the empire increased, new classes emerged, and these new wealthy merchants and landowners built very large homes. On the other hand, the poor were often unemployed. Slaves, one-third of the population by the second century C.E., worked on large estates in the countryside or in the cities as domestic servants. Slaves served as everything from miners, tutors, prostitutes, farm laborers, and more.

Culture, Arts, Science, and Technology

Rome's system of law had begun in 450 B.C.E. with the Twelve Tables—a series of laws that were organized into 12 sections and written down so they could be understood by all. As the empire spread, the laws spread with it. Such laws as "innocent until proven guilty" and "a defendant has the right to challenge his accuser before a judge" originated in Rome.

Much of Roman culture and achievements were inspired by Greek examples. Romans were polytheistic, like the Greeks, and believed that the gods intervened directly in their lives. The empire tolerated the cultural practices of its subjects, as long as they paid their taxes, did not rebel, and revered the emperors and Roman gods. The Jews, strict monotheists, who were scattered and generally accepted throughout the Roman Empire, were considered a problem in their homeland of Judea because rebellious groups often tried to overthrow the Roman rule. After a series of bloody rebellions in the first and second centuries, the Jews were completely defeated by the Romans and forced out of the city of Jerusalem. This was the start of the Jewish **Diaspora** (or scattering) and of the rabbinical form of Judaism.

Christianity, originally a Jewish sect, was also seen as a threat to Roman rule, and its followers were often persecuted. However, the number of Christians continued to grow throughout the empire. By 313 C.E., Emperor Constantine issued the Edict of Milan, which legalized Christianity. By 380 C.E., Emperor Theodosius proclaimed Christianity as the Roman Empire's official religion.

Rome was heavily influenced by the Greeks in art and architecture as well. Roman architecture took its inspiration from Greece, making its columns and arches more ornate. Improvements in engineering, including the invention of concrete, allowed the Romans to build stadiums, public baths, temples, aqueducts, and a system of roads.

ROLE OF TRADE IN CLASSICAL SOCIETIES

Long-distance trade expanded greatly during the classical period, allowing for the movement of goods and ideas. This long-distance trade expansion was due to a few factors: the Han Empire secured the trade routes through Central Asia; the Mauryan Empire had declined in India, but regional states were able to provide the necessary stability and security; and the Romans kept the Mediterranean Sea safe for trade and travel. This stability and security allowed long-distance trade to thrive.

Silk Road

`High-Yield`

Evidence of Chinese silks as far west as Ancient Egypt and as early as 1070 B.C.E. suggests silk has long been a highly desired commodity. However, the formal development of the Silk Road trade route originated during the Han dynasty. The Chinese were interested in Western horse breeds, which they became aware of around 130 B.C.E. thanks to diplomatic contact with Alexandria Eschate ("Alexandria the Farthest"), a Greek colony founded by Alexander the Great in Central Asia. Lucrative trade with the Parthian Empire also motivated the Han dynasty.

The Silk Road began in the east in Chang'an, went through modern-day Mongolia and Turkestan, and veered either north or south around the Taklamakan Desert. It branched southeast to India or through Central Asia and finally to the eastern end of the Roman Empire. Rarely did a merchant make the entire journey. Instead, the caravan routes were traveled in stages, from one oasis town to the next. As such, the Silk Road did not consist of a single route.

Buddhism became quite popular in such oasis towns as Samarkand, Kashgar, and Dunhuang, where merchants rested, sold their wares at market, and often built monasteries. Buddhism, as well as Christianity and Hinduism, were transformed as they moved along the Silk Road of the Classical age. Technological innovations such as yokes, special saddles, and horse stirrups helped Silk Road merchants move heavier loads across longer distances.

Goods That Traveled East to West	Goods That Traveled West to East
Silk	Glassware
Spices	Jewelry
Cotton	Bronze goods
Pearls	Wool and linen
Coral	Olive oil
Ivory	Gold and silver bullion

Indian Ocean

The Indian Ocean is sometimes referred to as the sea lanes of the Silk Road. This ocean trade went from Guangzhou in southern China through the South China Sea, through the islands of Southeast Asia, India, the Arabian Sea, and the Persian Gulf. The principal players in the trade were Malay and Indian sailors. Religion and culture spread across the seas. Some merchants spread Buddhism to Southeast Asia, while others promoted the Hindu denominations focused on Shiva and Vishnu.

✔ AP Expert Note

An important feature influencing trade in the Indian Ocean was the monsoon winds. These regular, seasonal patterns of winds facilitated maritime trade, allowing merchants to sail one way during the winter and return during the summer. Geographical and climatological features such as the monsoon winds played a tremendous role in the ability to travel throughout the ancient and pre-modern worlds. Vessels traversing the Indian ocean were notable for their sewn hulls, and for use of the lateen sail (triangular shape), which permitted sailing longer distances.

Mediterranean Sea

The Mediterranean Sea is often referred to as the Roman Lake, because the Roman Empire surrounded the sea. Sea trade flowed from Syria to Spain to North Africa. The Romans kept their "lake" safe and free from pirates, which allowed trade to thrive and enabled the transport of goods from one part of the expansive empire to the other.

Saharan Trade

The Saharan trade routes connected people south of the Sahara to the Middle East and Mediterranean. Routes were used primarily by the Berbers—nomads who traversed the desert. Camels were required to transport goods across the Sahara. Goods traded included: salt from the Sahara, gold from Western Africa, and Mediterranean commodities. However, Trans-Saharan trade was less successful than other trade routes because traversing the Saharan desert was tough, and the region was sparsely populated.

Sub-Saharan Trade

Sub-Saharan trade routes connected the regions of Africa located south and east of the Sahara desert to the **Indian Ocean trade** routes. Most likely, these trade routes were borne out of Bantu migration patterns. Similar to the Sahara, the sub-Sahara contained many geographic obstacles impeding access and movement within the region. Archaeological evidence has confirmed the trade of iron weapons and agricultural goods throughout the region.

DEVELOPMENT AND SPREAD OF RELIGION   `High-Yield`

Early civilizations were mostly polytheistic. Often, gods or goddesses were associated with nature, and sacrifices were made to these gods to ensure good fortune, such as plentiful harvests. Over time, religious practices became more complex. Even after the emergence of codified religious beliefs, **shamanism** and animism continued to be important in many people's understanding of the forces of nature. In addition, **ancestor veneration** remained a part of religious belief in East Asia, Africa, and the Mediterranean world.

Around 600 B.C.E., new religions and philosophies emerged to address some new questions or concerns that previous traditions had not sufficiently answered. Philosopher Karl Jaspers called this time period the Axial Age. The axial represents the core ideas around which a society revolves. Great philosophers emerged during this period, with new answers to difficult questions. These "axial" ideas went on to make indelible marks on the civilizations in which they developed.

Hinduism

Hinduism originated in India, but we cannot link a specific time or person to its creation. It is a belief system that evolved over time and actually refers to a wide variety of beliefs and practices that developed in South Asia. Hinduism is often described not as merely a religion but, because of the important effect it has on its followers, a way of life.

At the most basic level, Hindus believe they have a *dharma*, which roughly translates as duty, to perform in life. If all follow their *dharma*, the world works smoothly. If it is violated, the natural order falls out of sync. This *dharma* is determined by birth and one's stage in life. If one follows his or her *dharma*, then good karma (the sum of all good and bad deeds performed) will be the result. It is the accumulation of this good karma that allows someone to move up in the level of *Saṃsāra* in their next life.

Up to 600 C.E.

> **✔ AP Expert Note**
>
> The two epic poems the *Mahabharata* (with its important section called the *Bhagavad Gita*) and the *Ramayana* are key elements of Hinduism. Other epic poems such as Homer's *Iliad* and *Odyssey*, and the *Sundiata* in Mali, played important roles in defining the culture of each of their societies. Knowing the role of literature in a society and being able to compare historical examples are the types of knowledge required in an AP exam.

Hindus believe they will be reincarnated (reborn) after death. The new position they assume in the next life will depend on how well they performed their *dharma* in the past life. The ultimate goal for Hindus is to end the cycle of reincarnation by finally reaching *moksha*, or oneness with the universe. Hinduism is a polytheistic religion that believes in **Brahma**, the creator god, and his various incarnations including Vishnu, Shiva, and Devi. Bhatki is a popular practice in which followers have a personal devotion to a particular deity.

The Caste System

The social structure known as the caste system has had an enormous impact on the followers of Hinduism. The four *varnas* are the basis for the caste system (discussed previously under "Aryans") The caste system is based on the concepts of purity and pollution, including pure foods, sounds, and sights. Jobs are ranked because purity is associated with those who work with their minds, and pollution is associated with those who come in contact with polluted items such as sweat or human excrement. To ensure this purity, people have been to marry only members of their own caste.

Hinduism remains important in India and a few areas of Southeast Asia to which the religion spread. Some of the core ideas of Hinduism were reformed by Siddhartha Gautama, creating the worldwide religion of Buddhism.

Buddhism

Siddhartha Gautama, who lived from approximately 563 B.C.E. to 483 B.C.E., became an important Axial Age thinker. He was raised as a prince in a small state near present-day Nepal. After living a sheltered life, he decided to leave the palace in search of answers to questions such as: "Why is there so much suffering in the world?" and "Is there a way out of suffering?" According to Buddhist teachings, after meditating under a pipal tree, the prince reached enlightenment and became known as the **Buddha** (translated variously as "Awakened One" or "Enlightened One").

The Buddha made a crucial decision that helped transform his ideas from the thoughts of one man into a world religion: he decided to teach what he had learned to others. The Buddha taught that there were four noble truths:

1. All life is suffering.

2. Suffering is caused by desire.

3. There is a way out of suffering.

4. The way out of suffering is to follow the Eightfold Path.

The Eightfold Path includes right understanding, purpose, speech, conduct, livelihood, effort, awareness, and concentration. The idea was that if a person wants to stop suffering, he or she must stop desiring, and after the person stops desiring, he or she must live in a righteous manner by following the Eightfold Path. The ultimate goal for Buddhists is to reach *nirvana*, which is the release from the cycles of reincarnation and the achievement of union with the universe.

Buddhism took the central ideas of Hinduism such as *dharma*, karma, and *Saṃsāra*, but altered them significantly. According to Buddhism, people did not need the rituals of the Brahmins. Gods and goddesses are not necessary—everyone can seek enlightenment on his or her own, and no one is an outcast by birth. This belief challenges the very important caste system in India. There is, Buddhism espouses, complete equality among all believers.

The Mauryan emperor Ashoka actively encouraged the spread of Buddhism. Back in India, however, some Buddhist beliefs were absorbed into Hinduism, which remained the dominant religion. Buddhism spread throughout Asia along the Silk Road, where it met with great success. It greatly influenced Central Asia, China, Japan, Korea, and Southeast Asia. As it spread, it blended with the native ideas of the lands it encountered The followers of the Buddha acted as missionaries, preaching his message. These ideas particularly appealed to low-caste Hindus as well as to women. Buddhism's flexibility and message of universal acceptance helped transform it into a major world religion.

Confucianism

Confucius (551–479 B.C.E.) was a philosopher who believed that his answers to the questions of why we are here and how we should live could bring an end to the warfare that existed in his time. The key to ending the chaos and to bringing back peace, he felt, was to find the right kind of leadership to rule China.

His two most important concepts were *ren* (appropriate feelings) and *li* (correct actions), which must be used together in order to have any effect. Additionally, filial piety (respect for one's parents) was a key concept.

✔ **AP Expert Note**

Like many great religious leaders, Confucius did not write his knowledge down. Confucius's teachings were brought together by his disciples in a book called *The Analects*. Knowing the basic doctrines (e.g., books, poems) of the major religions is required by the AP exam. Be able to compare the basic concepts of religions and belief systems.

Confucius taught that order would be achieved when people knew their proper roles and relationships to others. Rulers would govern by moral example. People would learn to behave properly through the example of those superior to them. According to Confucius, there are five key relationships:

1. Ruler to ruled

2. Father to son

3. Husband to wife

4. Older brother to younger brother

5. Friend to friend

Confucianism became the most influential philosophy in China. During the Han dynasty, Confucian ideas were used (in addition to some Daoism and Legalism) to bring peace and order. These ideas left a permanent mark on China and were continually used by subsequent dynasties throughout the country's history. These ideas also spread to Korea and Japan, where they became very influential.

Daoism

Some claim that the Chinese sage Laozi founded the Daoist school of thought during the sixth century B.C.E., around the same time as Confucius; however, its ideas can be traced back further in Chinese history. The *Tao te Ching* or *Dao de Jing*, a collection of Daoist wisdom, is attributed to Laozi. Daoist ideas represent a protest movement during the troubled times of the Warring States period. Laozi gained many disciples in China, though some mixed his ideas with magic and attempted to search for immortality.

The literal translation of the Dao is *the way*. According to Daoism, all life is interdependent, and human beings should exist in harmony with nature. Its advice is to relax and be in harmony with the Dao. In order to solve the problems of the day, Daoists taught the concept of *wu wei*, which means act by not acting. Do nothing and problems will solve themselves, like in nature. Be like water—soft and yielding—but at the same time, very naturally powerful.

Daoists believe it is useless to try to build institutions to govern men, because institutions (or anything that rewards knowledge) are dangerous. Institutions lead to competition and, eventually, to fighting. The less government interference, the better; the ideal state is a small, self-sufficient town. The ultimate goal should be to cultivate the virtues of patience, selflessness, and concern for all.

In Chinese society, Daoism provided a counterpoint to the proper behavior of Confucianism—it encouraged people to take time off, relax, and just let things happen. It allowed the Chinese to be Confucian at work and Daoist while not at work. Daoism's attitude toward war was that it should be used only for defensive purposes. The Han followed this idea by stationing troops along the Great Wall to maintain the safety of trade routes.

Legalism

The philosophy of Legalism was based on the principle that man was inherently evil and needed strict laws and punishment to behave properly. Additionally, a strong central government with an absolute leader would ensure a more stable society. Legalism was adopted by the first emperor of the Qin dynasty, Qin Shi Huang, who created China's first centralized government and ended the Warring States period.

Judaism

The Hebrews believe that they are protected by YHWH (God), with whom they have a special relationship. This name was considered too holy a word to say aloud.

> **✔ AP Expert Note**
>
> You will see the Hebrews are also referred to as the Israelites and Jews. The terms are generally interchangeable up to the time of Jesus. In the Common Era, they are typically referred to only as the Jews. The people of the modern-day state of Israel are commonly referred to as Israelis rather than Israelites.

According to the Torah, the Hebrews are God's chosen people. As a result, they entered into a covenant with God; they were forbidden from worshiping any other god and were obligated to follow certain religious laws, like the Ten Commandments. Some of these commandments include a prohibition against murder, adultery, or theft. Most important, the Hebrews followed a monotheistic tradition, which claims there is only one creator (God) who made the world and all life. As a monotheistic religion, Judaism would go on to influence the development of Christianity and **Islam**.

According to religious tradition, the prophet Moses led the Hebrews back to the "Promised Land" on the eastern shores of the Mediterranean after a period of enslavement in Egypt. The kingdom of Israel was established, led by a monarchy. The height of Israelite power came during the reigns of King David and his son Solomon around 1000 B.C.E. Later, the Neo-Babylonian Empire invaded, destroyed Solomon's Temple in Jerusalem, and scattered the population. Thousands of Jews were deported to Babylon, where they would remain in captivity until their liberation in 539 B.C.E. by the Persians under King Cyrus II.

Centuries later, in 63 B.C.E., the Roman Empire would conquer the Jews. Uprisings against the Romans in 66 C.E. and 135 C.E. were violently suppressed with large military campaigns. Many Jews were killed and their holiest temple was leveled. In 135 C.E., the Romans drove the Jews out of their homeland. This scattering of the Jews is referred to as the Diaspora. Jews survived in scattered communities around the Mediterranean region, Persia, and Central Asia.

Zoroastrianism

Due to the loss of many written records over the ages, the exact founding of **Zoroastrianism** can only be narrowed to a time span of 1500–1000 B.C.E., but evidence points to it being one of the oldest religions still practiced in the modern day. A Persian prophet named Zoroaster attempted to explain the wars, conquests, and famines that had plagued the Fertile Crescent since the rise of the first Sumerian city-states. He saw Earth as a battleground between the forces of good and evil in which each person must participate.

Zoroastrianism, like Judaism, was a monotheistic religion. According to Zoroaster, each person's actions battling for the forces of good would be judged at the end of time by the one god: *Ahura Mazda* ("Wise Lord"). The influence of Zoroastrianism is found in Judaism, Christianity, and Islam; for example, in the concept of Satan, heaven and hell, and the Messiah. Historians believe Babylonian captivity of the Jews led to cross-cultural pollination of these religious ideas.

Christianity

Jesus was born to Jewish parents between 6 and 4 B.C.E. in the area known as Judea (modern-day Israel), which was part of the Roman Empire. At the time, tension existed between Rome and its Jewish subjects.

Christian teachings describe Jesus as being concerned with the growing cosmopolitan nature of Jewish society and preaching a simple message of love and compassion. The faithful would experience eternal life in heaven with God. These ideas appealed to the lower class, slaves, and women. Men and women were considered spiritually equal before God. For many, this message gave them a sense of purpose. Christian tradition attributes Jesus the power to perform miracles, such as healing the sick and raising the dead.

This message of the Kingdom of God alarmed Roman authorities, however, and to quell a potential rebellion, they had Jesus executed by crucifixion around 30 C.E. His followers believed that Jesus rose from the dead and that he was the son of God. As such, they compiled a body of writings about his life and his messages, which became the New Testament.

> ✔ **AP Expert Note**
>
> The terms *Old Testament*, *New Testament*, and *Gospels* are Christian. Although the Christian *Old Testament* contains much of the Jewish holy texts, the *Torah*, the term *Old Testament* implies to a Christian point of view.

The earliest followers of Jesus were all Jews, but in the mid first century C.E., a Roman citizen named Paul began to spread Jesus' message to non-Jews (gentiles). He and other missionaries used the Roman roads and sea lanes to spread this new religion. Disciples became known as Christians.

However, Christians, much like the Jews, refused to honor the state cults or to worship the Roman emperor as a god. As a result, they were often persecuted. Even so, the religion continued to spread throughout the empire until Emperor Constantine issued the Edict of Milan in 313 C.E., making Christianity legal in the Roman Empire. Emperor Theodosius went on to later make it the official religion of the empire.

Christianity also spread to Mesopotamia, Iran, and even parts of India. Over time, the Southwest Asian Christians and the Western (or Roman) Christians grew apart. Southwest Asian Christians followed a form of the religion called Nestorianism. This form of Christianity continued to spread across the Silk Road into Central Asia, India, and China.

Another form of Christianity developed in Northern Africa and is called Coptic Christianity based on the Coptic language its followers use. Coptic Christian kingdoms existed in Ethiopia since the sixth century, and the religion still thrives in Egypt and Ethiopia to the modern-day.

COMPARATIVE CLOSE-UP: ROLE OF WOMEN IN RELIGION	
Religion	Role of Women
Buddhism	Women could achieve *nirvana*. An alternative lifestyle was available for women as nuns in a monastery.
Christianity	Men and women were equal in the eyes of God. Women could go to heaven. Many early converts were women. Women could live in convents.
Confucianism	Men were superior to women. One of five key relationships was that of husband to wife.
Hinduism	Men were superior to women. Women were not allowed to read the sacred prayers, the Vedas. Only a male Brahmin could reach *moksha*.

SPREAD OF DISEASE

During the second and third centuries C.E., both the Han and Roman Empires suffered large-scale outbreaks of epidemic diseases. Due to the trade and interaction that had taken place, the incidence of disease increased. Diseases such as smallpox, measles, and bubonic plague had a devastating effect on the population because people did not have the immunity or the medicine to combat them. The Antonine Plague (165–180 C.E.) killed approximately 30 percent of the Roman Empire's population, and it was even worse in the cities; it is estimated that diseases caused up to 2,000 deaths per day in Rome. The effects of these diseases caused great economic and social disruptions. Trade within the empires declined, and economies became more regionally focused.

MOVEMENT OF PEOPLES

Bantu Migration

The migration of the Bantu people began around 1500 B.C.E., and by 1000 C.E. the Bantu occupied most of sub-Saharan Africa. The migration is believed to be due to overpopulation stretching resources in the Bantu homeland in modern-day Nigeria. As a result, groups of people gradually began to leave to set up new agricultural settlements. The Bantu people often intermarried with those they came in contact with, and these people often adopted the Bantu language and joined the Bantu society.

Around 1000 B.C.E. the Bantus began to produce iron tools, which enabled them to clear more land and expand agriculture. This led to an increase in both population and migration. The overall population of Africa grew from 3.5 million in 400 B.C.E. to 22 million in 1000 C.E.. Around 500 C.E. the cultivation of bananas—which had made their way to Africa via the Indian Ocean trade—enabled the Bantus to expand into heavily forested regions and to continue migrating. Today there are over 500 distinct (though related) languages that can be traced back to the Bantus.

Polynesian Migration

Humans migrated to New Guinea and Australia around 45,000 years ago via watercraft. These people developed maritime technology and agricultural expertise, and eventually established settlements on Pacific islands. Beginning around 1600 B.C.E., the movements that settled the Polynesian islands migrated to surrounding islands including Vanuatu, Fiji, Samoa, and much later, Hawaii. Long-distance voyages were taken using double canoes with large triangular sails, which carried a platform between the two hulls for shelter. Some scholars believe that the settlement was accidentally caused by sailors being blown off course, while others believe it was a planned colonization. As the migration spread, so did the cultivation of new food crops such as yams, taros, breadfruit, and bananas, as well as the introduction of domesticated animals such as dogs, pigs, and chickens.

The Polynesian islands developed into hierarchical chiefdoms in which leadership was passed down to the eldest son, and relatives served as the local aristocracy. Conflict between groups, as well as population pressure, often led to further migration to new areas. The cultures and languages of these widely dispersed islands often adapted and evolved differently.

FALL OF CLASSICAL EMPIRES

As the Foundations period, the time from 8000 B.C.E. to 600 C.E., drew to an end, the classical societies that helped to shape it were all suffering through periods of decline, for mostly similar reasons, as outlined in the following chart. The recovery from this decline shapes the beginning of our next chapter.

	Han	Western Rome	Gupta
Time of Fall	220 C.E.	476 C.E.	550 C.E.
Economic Reasons	Scholar officials were often exempt from taxes, and peasants often fled from tax collectors. As a result, a severe reduction in tax revenue financially crippled the empire. Long-distance trade decreased, but the Chinese were quite self-sufficient and were not severely hurt by this.	The rich landowning class often resisted taxation, driving away tax collectors with their private armies. Plus, the Catholic Church's land was not taxable. Inflation and the drop in tax revenue crippled Rome's economy. As the empire declined, so did trade, which relied on safe roads.	The government had great difficulty raising enough taxes to pay the army to protect its borders.
Political Reasons	The government was unable to check the power of the large private estate owners. The emperor relied heavily on the advice of his court officials and was often misinformed for the court officials' personal gain.	The government had trouble finding bureaucrats who could enforce the laws. Power struggles for the throne plagued the empire. From 235 to 284 C.E., 20 out of 23 emperors died a violent death. The division of the empire into two sections allowed the eastern portion to remain stronger, while the western portion weakened.	The regional powers of the Guptas allowed them to keep much of their administrative power. They eventually grew more powerful than the central government.
Social Reasons	The population increase led to smaller family plots and made it more difficult for the peasant class to pay taxes.	Diseases dramatically reduced the population, particularly the farming population. Germanic immigrants were mistreated, causing ill will.	Regional governors declared regional independence, further weakening the empire's control.
Role of Nomadic Invasions	The Huns invaded, but only after the empire had already fallen. Nomadic invasions took place because the empire was no longer providing nomads with what they needed.	The Roman army could not defend against nomadic groups such as the Ostrogoths, Huns, and Visigoths. The Visigoths sacked Rome in 476 C.E.	The government was too weak to defend against the nomadic invasions of the Huns.
Protection of Borders	Although the government had built the Great Wall to keep the Huns out, nomads were able to easily bypass the wall.	The Roman empire had grown to an immense size, and borders were far from administrative centers. Germanic Goths and other barbarians were hired to man the legions, as not enough Romans could be recruited. These mercenaries had no loyalty to the emperor or incentive to die for an empire that disdained them.	The Gupta Empire was not as centralized as the Mauryans under Ashoka. They remained divided into regions where local politicians made most of the laws and decisions. When the Huns attacked, the empire easily fell apart along the fault lines of the local regions.

All the classical societies entered a period of recovery, during which they were decentralized following their collapse. The western half of the Roman Empire (Western Europe) experienced the most severe collapse. A few possible reasons include:

- Rome was economically interdependent, and the decline in trade severely hurt the economy.
- Continual waves of nomadic invasions made recovery difficult.
- The spread of disease led to a decrease in population and a weakened empire.

THE ENVIRONMENT

Environmental problems such as soil depletion and deforestation, while less dramatic than the impact of diseases, were subtle factors in the collapse of many societies and empires.

Soil Depletion

As settled agriculture spread throughout Africa and Eurasia, extensive irrigation systems and slash-and-burn agriculture took a toll on the land. By 600 C.E. people had been farming the same lands for thousands of years. Crops such as wheat and barley depleted the soil of nutrients and, in some areas, led to desertification.

Deforestation

During this era, wood constituted a vital natural resource. It was used as the primary fuel source for fire and as the main building material. Over time, forests around urban and agricultural areas became denuded of large trees. The loss of ground cover resulted in loss of topsoil, mudslides in hilly areas, and challenges to local economies as the need for wood forced urban areas to import timber from further away. Although these challenges were often noted in ancient accounts, there was little that ancient and classical societies could do to avoid them.

Diseases

Agricultural societies, including pastoralists, introduced new diseases into human civilizations. Agriculture upsets the soil and allows for more standing water, spreading the breeding ground for the Anopheles mosquito, which carries malaria. Close contact with domesticated animals such as cattle and pigs allowed for the spread of viruses such as measles and smallpox that plagued mankind until the modern era. Other diseases also became more common. For example, the bubonic plague bacteria was transmitted via rats, a pest common worldwide.

CHAPTER 9

Period 3: 600 to 1450 C.E. – Complete Time Period Review

"NEW" EMPIRES

After the fall of the Han and Roman Empires, a form of political centralization eventually returned in parts of the world: China, a new empire—the **Islamic Caliphates**, the **Byzantine Empire** (formerly known as the Eastern Roman Empire).

Chinese Empire

High-Yield

Tang Dynasty

Political Development

Following the fall of the Han dynasty in 220 C.E., China returned to regional small kingdoms. It was not until 581 C.E. that the Sui dynasty reunited China proper. This short-lived but influential dynasty used Buddhism and the Confucian civil service system to establish legitimacy. In addition, Sui rulers initiated the construction of the **Grand Canal**, an economically vital series of waterways that linked the Yellow and Yangtze Rivers. They also launched numerous military campaigns to expand the Chinese Empire. Rebellions overthrew the Sui dynasty in 618 C.E., but it had laid the economic and military foundations for future dynasties.

The following Tang dynasty (618–907 C.E.), expanded China's control to Tibet and Korea. A reformed civil service examination, which the Tang used to recruit bureaucratic officials, now admitted gentry and commoners. In the middle of the eighth century C.E., Tang power began to decline. Government corruption and increased taxation increased tension among the populace. Military governors had accumulated too much power relative to the central government. Numerous rebellions led to more independent regional rule, then the final collapse of the Tang dynasty in 907 C.E., and finally an era of rule by regional warlords—the "Five Dynasties and Ten Kingdoms" period.

Economic Developments

Tang rulers had difficulty breaking the power of the large landowners. Nevertheless, China underwent an economic revolution under their rule. Farmers improved crop yields by utilizing new technologies, such as heavy iron plows and water buffaloes, and implementing elaborate irrigation practices. Farmers also took advantage of the Grand Canal's complex irrigation networks and an improved road networks. Because of these advances in agriculture and transportation, the Chinese population grew dramatically, until by 640 C.E. the Tang capital at Chang'an (modern-day Xi'an) had approximately one million inhabitants.

Trade with other countries flourished during the Tang dynasty. By establishing military garrisons as far out as western Afghanistan, trade was protected along the Silk Road. Due to trade along the Indian Ocean and the Silk Road, Chang'an became a major trading center and cosmopolitan hub; its West Market flourished with Indian, Iranian, Syrian, and Arab traders and their goods. The Chinese also invented many technologies during this period, such as the mechanical clock, gunpowder, lightweight porcelain, and steel, and they introduced such products to these systems of exchange.

Cultural Developments

Poetry flourished during the Tang dynasty, with poets such as Li Bai and Du Fu contributing to what has been dubbed a golden age. The invention of printing allowed literature to increase in popularity.

During the Sui and Yang dynasties, Buddhism and Daoism emerged as influential philosophies that challenged the traditionally dominant Confucianism. Early Tang rulers supported Buddhist monasteries and followed guidance from Buddhist advisors. However, later Tang rulers ceased to support Buddhism and even destroyed Buddhist monasteries. An anti-Buddhist campaign attacked this religion's foreign nature and its monasteries' economic and political power.

Neo-Confucianism, a remodeled form of Confucianism, developed in response to Buddhism and Daoism. It rejected mysticism in favor of a rationalist approach, emphasizing individual self-improvement and the goodness of humanity. Nevertheless, it also reworked some concepts and ideas from Buddhism. Neo-Confucianism dominated Chinese philosophy from the late Tang dynasty until the twentieth century C.E., and it spread to Japan, Vietnam, and Korea.

During the Tang dynasty, Chinese women were largely subordinate to men, and male children were preferred to female children. Women's marriages during the Tang dynasty were arranged within their own social class. However, women of higher status had comparably more rights than in most other dynasties. Some upper-class women could own property and even remarry. Princess Pingyang helped found her family's dynasty, the Tang, by personally recruiting and leading a force of 70,000 men dubbed "the Army of the Lady." They seized Chang'an, the Sui capital. One emperor's concubine, Empress Wu, even amassed her own personal power, until in 690 C.E. she took the title of Heavenly Empress. Concerned with any possible threat to her power, she had thousands of the emperor's concubines killed and had their sons banned from office. She also started a school dedicated to Buddhist and Confucian scholarship and supported Buddhist art.

Influence

Neo-Confucianism moved to the forefront of Chinese philosophy and was also very influential in Japan and Korea. Delegations from the "outside," such as Japan or Siam (present-day Thailand), had to show great deference to the Chinese emperor in his presence with the *kowtow*—a prostrate bow during which one touches one's head to the ground multiple times. This symbolized the Chinese self-perception of being superior to all foreigners.

Song Dynasty

Political Development

The founding of the Song dynasty is traditionally dated to 960 C.E., but it was not until 979 C.E. that it had reestablished centralized control over China, ending the "Five Dynasties and Ten Kingdoms" period. The civil service exam system retained great prominence during Song rule. It checked the power of the landed aristocracy and fostered the development of a powerful, moral elite known as the scholar-gentry.

The Song deemphasized a military approach to security and instead reestablished the tribute system with its nomad neighbors, in which the Chinese provided nomads with gifts in exchange for peace. Despite this system, peace did not endure. The Song's scholar-controlled army was often ineffective, and an excess of paper money in circulation caused inflation. By 1126 C.E., China had lost the northern half of the empire to the semi-nomadic Jurchen. The Southern Song continued to flourish until 1274 C.E. However, military threats from the north continued, and finally the most powerful of all northern groups invaded, absorbing the Song dynasty into the new Mongol Empire in the thirteenth century C.E.

Economic Development

The economic revolution which began under the Tang dynasty continued under Song rule. Following Vietnamese agricultural practices, Chinese farmers began to cultivate **fast-ripening rice**, which improved crop yields. The population continued to increase, until it reached 115 million people in 1200 C.E. (as compared to 45 million people in 600 C.E.).

Technological innovation continued during Song rule as well. The capital of Kaifeng became a manufacturing center for cannon, movable type printing, water-powered mills, looms, and high-quality porcelain. After the Song lost control of Northern China, the Southern Song established their capital at Hangzhou, and commerce soared there as well. Ocean trade with East Africa, Southeast Asia, India, and Persia grew, especially due to naval innovations such as cotton sails and the magnetic compass. Because trade was so successful, copper supplies dwindled; paper currency and letters of credit—known as flying cash—emerged as forms of monetary compensation.

Cultural Developments

During the Song dynasty, small feet became a beauty standard, leading to the practice of foot binding. Young girls had their toes and the arches broken, and then tightly bound in order to 'fold' each foot. These bandages were periodically changed and any necrotic tissue removed. By adult-hood, these women were unable to walk without a cane. The small feet produced were also seen as a sign of wealth and status; it was impractical for peasant and middle-class women to work with bound feet. However, eventually foot-binding spread to all social classes. Opposition to foot bind-ing would grow alongside the Taiping Rebellion (1850-1871 C.E.); the practice would be formally banned in 1912 C.E. but persist in some regions into the 1950s C.E. The last factory dedicated to making shoes for women with bound feet would close in 1999 C.E.

Landscape painting flourished during the Song dynasty. This artwork was often influenced by Dao-ist beliefs. Fireworks, originating in the Tang dynasty, became increasingly popular with the masses.

> ✔ **AP Expert Note**
>
> **Tang and Song innovations included:**
>
> - **Compass**
> - **Water-powered clock**
> - **Gunpowder**
> - **Light porcelain**
> - **Neo Confucianism**
> - **Paper money**
> - **Letters of credit (flying cash)**
> - **Printing press with movable type**

Korea

The Goguryeo–Sui War, a series of Chinese invasions of Korea that took place between 598 C.E. and 614 C.E., was pivotal in the collapse of the Sui dynasty. The war overextended the Sui dynasty dur-ing a famine. 300,000 Chinese troops died at the Battle of Salsu, history's most lethal battle in pre-modern warfare; this resulted in the perception that the Sui dynasty had lost the Mandate of Heaven.

In the seventh century C.E., China's Tang dynasty conquered the Goguryeo dynasty, which ruled the northern half of the Korean Peninsula. The Tang dynasty split the territory of the Goguryeo with Korea's Silla dynasty in the peninsula's south. The Silla were able to maintain much of their autonomy and oversaw a golden age for Korean culture.

In the tenth century C.E. the Koryo dynasty gained power in northern Korea. Its rulers modeled their kingdom after China and maintained their power until, in the thirteenth century C.E., the **Mongols** invaded.

Japan

Political Development

Japan's geography as a group of islands led to the development of small, independent communities. By the 600s C.E., the Yamato clan exerted religious and cultural influence on other clans. Its leader, the prince Shotoku Taishi, strove to copy China's model of empire-building and create a strong, stable state. Yamato rulers began to call themselves emperors of Japan. They were unsuccessful in creating a centralized state, however, and Japan remained divided by its clans.

The Fujiwara clan, which dominated during the Nara Period (710–794 C.E.), sent emissaries to China and modeled their capital, Nara, on Chang'an. They could not, however, successfully introduce a Chinese-style bureaucracy, and a strict hereditary hierarchy developed instead.

In the Heian Period (794–1185 C.E.), the Japanese emperor installed the new capital of Heian (modern-day Kyoto). During this era, the weakness of Japan's centralized government led local aristocrats to recruit samurai. These warriors followed their lord's orders and defended his interests, and they developed a strict warrior code called *bushido* ("the way of the warrior").

After several centuries of civil conflicts, a Japanese noble, Minamoto no Yoritomo, created a form of feudal military government. Under this Kamakura Shogunate (1192–1333 C.E.), the emperor became a symbolic figurehead and the shogun, the supreme military general, controlled a centralized military government. The shogun divided Japanese land into regional feudal fiefdoms based on military power. Regional military leaders called daimyo led groups of samurai warriors. When the Mongols attempted to invade Japan in the thirteenth century C.E., they encountered this military and political system.

Economic Development

Japan was a predominantly agrarian society with an artisan class of weavers, carpenters, and iron-workers. Trade, which focused on markets in larger towns and foreign exchange with Korea and China, developed during the Kamakura Period.

Most Japanese people were peasants, who worked on land owned by a lord or by a Buddhist monastery. Though their freedom was limited, peasants could keep what remained of their harvest after they paid their tax quota. Those unable to pay became landless laborers known as *genin*, who could be bought and sold with the land. As slaves, they performed jobs such as burying the dead or curing leather; eventually, these jobs would be associated with the *burakumin* outcast group.

Cultural Development

In early Japan, people believed that *kami*—spirits—were present in their natural surroundings. These beliefs coalesced into the Shinto religion. People built shrines to honor *kami*, and Japanese emperors claimed to descend from the supreme Shinto deity, the sun goddess Amaterasu.

Although Shintoism remained a significant force in Japan, its society also welcomed Chinese and Korean influences. The Japanese people adopted Confucianism and Buddhism, as well as Chinese technology and script. Japan also developed its own version of Buddhism known as Zen Buddhism, which added a strong aesthetic dimension.

In early Japanese society, women could inherit or own land. Over time, however, women lost much of their legal and social power. Many women, however, such as Murasaki Shikibu, created literary works, including her famous novel *The Tale of Genji*.

Islamic Caliphates

High-Yield

Pre-Islamic Arabia

Prior to the introduction of Islam, inhabitants of the Arabian Peninsula, or Bedouins, lived in nomadic tribes led by sheikhs. Settlements arose along trade routes, as Arabs transported products between the Mediterranean Sea and the Indian Ocean. Although patriarchy dominated Arabian social structures, women were allowed to inherit property, initiate divorce agreements, and participate in business dealings.

Most Arabs practiced a polytheistic form of religion which included a principal god, Allah, although idol worship of lesser deities was commonplace as Allah was viewed as a remote figure. This period is termed *Jahiliyyah* ("Times of Ignorance") in Islamic histories.

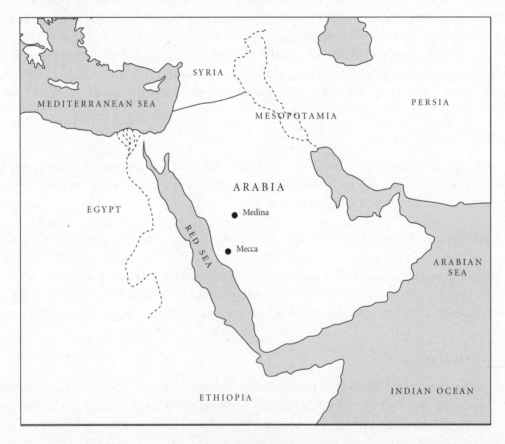

Arabia

Born in 570 C.E. in **Mecca**, **Muhammad** later married a merchant widow named Khadija. Together, they traveled on caravans and met Jews, Zoroastrians, and Christians. Muslims believe that the angel Gabriel revealed to Muhammad that he had been selected to be God's messenger.

Muhammad believed and preached that all people were to submit to one all-powerful, all-knowing God: Allah. All would face a final day of judgment; those who had submitted to God would go to a heavenly paradise, and those who had not would go to a fiery hell. He also taught that he was the last of a long line of prophets from the Jewish and Christian scriptures that included Abraham, Moses, David, and Jesus.

Muhammad's message was not met with enthusiasm in Mecca; he and his followers migrated to Medina in 622 C.E., on a journey known as the *Hegira* (or *Hijrah*). Muhammad's message proved popular in Medina, where he was viewed as a prophet and a political leader. In 630 C.E., after further organizing his new religion, he and his followers returned to Mecca, capturing the city.

After his death, Muhammad's revelations were written down by his followers in the Quran, which is believed to be the actual words of God as revealed to Muhammad. The word Islam means "submission to Allah."

Five Pillars of Islam

Islam is based on five duties—called pillars—that define the faith:

1. Statement of faith: "There is no god but Allah, and Muhammad is the messenger of Allah."
2. Pray five times a day facing Mecca.
3. Give alms (charity) to the poor.
4. Fast during the holy month of Ramadan.
5. Make a pilgrimage, or hajj, to Mecca during one's lifetime, if able.

Islam is a universal religion that promises salvation to all who believe and follow its principles. Islam appealed to women because the Quran afforded women equal status to men before God, outlawed female infanticide, and permitted wives to keep their dowries. However, the Quran also allowed inheritance to be restricted to male offspring. It also restricted women's social experiences in order to protect the legitimacy of offspring. In general, though, Islam appealed to the poor and powerless, and it fostered a strong sense of brotherhood.

Political Development

By the time of Muhammad's death in 632 C.E., much of Arabia was under Islamic control. However, Muhammad did not designate a successor, and Muslim followers disagreed over who Muhammad's successor should be. One group, the **Shi'a**, believed that the Muslim leader should be a descendant of Muhammad. The other group, the **Sunni**, believed that the wisest member of the strongest tribe should succeed Muhammad. Although Muhammad's father-in-law Abu Bakr was chosen to be the first caliph, and he served as the political and religious leader of the Arab Empire, the split between Shi'a and Sunni Muslims led to religious and political divisions in the Muslim world that endure today.

After the first four caliphs, the Umayyad dynasty took control in 661 C.E. and transformed the caliphate into a hereditary monarchy, with its government centered in Damascus. With its military expertise and the weakness of the Byzantine and Persian Empires, the Umayyad dynasty continued to conquer additional territories—including Syria, Egypt, Persia, North Africa, Spain (which became known as **Al-Andalus**), and Byzantine territory in West Asia. The Umayyad caliphates set up a bureaucratic structure in which local administrators governed the conquered areas. All cultures were tolerated as long as they obeyed the rules of Islam, paid their taxes, and did not revolt. Arabic became the language of administration, business, law, and trade, and many conquered peoples converted to Islam.

The Abbasid dynasty overthrew the **Umayyads** in 750 C.E. and moved the imperial capital to Baghdad. At the time, Baghdad was the second largest city in the world next to Chang'an. The size of the Abbasid Empire made it difficult to control. Eventually, the remaining Umayyad prince settled in Spain and established a separate caliphate there. Berber tribesmen controlled much of the northern African coast, and the Mamluks revolted and gained control over Egypt from 1250 to 1517 C.E. Thus, by the mid-ninth century, the Abbasid political authority had become mostly symbolic, and the caliphate was broken into smaller states.

Despite this, the culture of the Muslim world created a common bond from Spain to many parts of Africa, the Middle East, Central and South Asia, and Southeast Asian islands. The term *Dar al-Islam* ("the home of Islam") refers to these areas in which a Muslim traveler or trader found himself welcome regardless of his homeland.

Economic Developments

Trade flourished throughout the caliphate and beyond, as Muslim merchants relied on a common set of principles. Improved irrigation led to increased agricultural production and tax revenue. Many types of agriculture, including sugarcane, citrus fruits, and coffee, spread throughout the Islamic empire. Artisans flourished in the cities, as urban areas became centers for manufacturing pottery, fabrics, and rugs. Paper, which was introduced from China, emerged as a form of currency.

Cultural Developments

Mosques, hospitals, and schools were built throughout the empire. Scholars developed intellectual fields such as algebra and medicine, and developed innovations such as the **astrolabe** and the concepts of latitude and longitude. Muslim scholars also reexamined the works of Greek philosophers such as Plato and Aristotle. Scholars at the House of Wisdom, built in Baghdad during the rule of the fifth Abbasid caliph Harun al-Rashid, sought out Greek and Persian texts and translated them into Arabic. One fourteenth century Moroccan geographer, Ibn Khaldun, wrote an economics, ethnography, world history, and sociology text called *Muqaddimah* or *Prolegomena* ("Introduction"). Universities were established in Cordoba, Toledo, and Granada. In art and architecture, geometric shapes known as arabesques and calligraphy replaced depictions of idols.

Influence

Even though the Muslim Empire declined and ended with the Mongol invasions, the influence of Islam continued to spread throughout the period. Islam spread to West Africa through **trans-Saharan trade**, to East Africa and Southeast Asia through Indian Ocean trade, to Central Asia and China through the Silk Road trade, and to India through the migrations of the Turks. By the conclusion of this period, *Dar al-Islam* had developed into one of the most dominant influences throughout the world.

Byzantine Empire

Political Development

The Byzantine Empire, a continuation of the Eastern Roman Empire, was the only survivor from the classical age. The Roman Empire had officially been divided into east and west in 375 C.E., with the western half severely weakened because of Germanic invasions along with several other factors.

The emperor Justinian, who ruled the Byzantine Empire from 527 C.E. to 565 C.E., tried and failed to reconquer Western Rome. However, Justinian's laws were a success. His *Body of Civil Law* (*Justinian's Code*) was based on the Roman *Twelve Tables of Law* and became the foundation of the Byzantine Empire's legal system. Justinian controlled both the political and religious power in his empire, and he also replaced Latin with Greek as the official language of the empire.

The Byzantine Empire's strong central government was a hereditary monarchy. It made law, had an efficient military, oversaw effective land distribution, and maintained a bureaucracy that answered to the emperor. The emperor was considered a friend and imitator of Christ. As the head of the Eastern Orthodox Church, the Byzantine emperor appointed the church's patriarch. The empire was divided into themes—or military districts—and military generals ruled local regions. Free peasants received land in exchange for military service.

The Byzantine military was not able to face the challenge of the Seljik Turks, however, and it was largely destroyed by 1071 C.E. This defeat resulted in the loss of the empire's Asia Minor territories to the Turks.

Economic Developments

The Byzantine Empire's location on the Mediterranean Sea, along with its position as a crossroads between Asia and Europe, provided favorable avenues of trade. It developed a silk industry after silkworms were smuggled out of China. Byzantine artisans also produced glassware, linen, jewelry, gold, and silver.

Cultural Developments

Most subjects of the Byzantine Empire spoke Greek. Constantinople was the empire's intellectual center, with libraries containing Greek, Latin, Persian, and Hebrew texts. Constantinople also housed the Hagia Sophia, an elaborate cathedral which exemplified Byzantine art and architecture. Byzantine citizens theoretically had social mobility—through participation in the imperial bureaucracy, army, trade, or church—but individuals rarely changed their own social class.

The Eastern Orthodox Church continued to separate from Europe's Roman Catholic Church. The two churches disagreed over religious practices, such as the worship of idols (images of saints). The pope and patriarch excommunicated each other in 1054 C.E., and the two churches officially separated. The Eastern Orthodox form of Christianity later spread to the Slavic people and Russia.

DECENTRALIZED STATES

High-Yield

Western Europe—Early Middle Ages

Political Development

Compared to Byzantium, China, and the Islamic world, Western Europe remained politically decentralized following the decline and fall of the Western Roman Empire.

By 500 C.E., smaller German kingdoms had emerged. The Franks came closest to reestablishing imperial control, with the leadership of Clovis in the sixth century C.E. and the Carolingian Empire of **Charlemagne**, which lasted from 768 C.E. to 814 C.E. Both leaders used the Roman Catholic Church to strengthen their legitimacy, but they were unsuccessful in establishing a political structure that could outlast their reigns.

Instead, Europe developed a system of **feudalism**, in which lords gave lands to vassals in exchange for military service and loyalty. This system allowed various lords and vassals to compete for power, in the absence of central authority. The one centralizing power in this period was the Roman Catholic Church and its ruler, the pope; by the thirteenth century C.E., the Church owned approximately one-third of European land.

Economic Developments

The absence of a strong central authority led many peasants to seek protection on large estates. These peasants became serfs; they had the right to work a portion of the land and could pass that right onto their children, but they could not leave their land. Serfs could keep a portion of their harvests, but they sent the majority of their earnings to their lord. In addition, serfs paid taxes for using their lord's mill, provided labor during agricultural off-seasons, and sent gifts on holidays to their lords. Lords' estates became large, walled manors that were economically self-sufficient. They maintained mills, bakeries, and breweries. They had private armies served by knights. The introduction of the heavy plow increased agricultural production, allowing the cultivation of fertile clay soils, but the crop surplus was not substantial enough to sustain cities and towns in the early Middle Ages (the period from 500 to 1000 C.E.).

Cultural Developments

Birth largely determined one's social status. Marriage was the key to political power, and marital alliances were crucial to a family's continued social success. Women also entered convents, where some women could exercise leadership skills. Noblewomen had more power and authority than peasant women and could inherit land if they were widowed or without sons.

Beginning in the twelfth century C.E., a concept called chivalry developed. Chivalry stressed honor, modesty, loyalty, and duty. As warfare decreased, the concepts of chivalry incorporated courtly romance and knights' participation in tournaments. Chivalry, unlike its Japanese counterpart *bushido*, was more of an ideal than an actual code of conduct.

Christianity was the principal source of religious, moral, and cultural authority throughout Middle Ages, and strong papal leadership contributed to this authority. The Roman Catholic Church developed a strong hierarchy, which consisted of a pope, cardinals, archbishops, bishops, and priests. Monasteries, building complexes where monks dwelled, also developed throughout Europe. These sites often maintained large landholdings and served as refuges for individuals in need. Monks preserved classical knowledge by hand-copying great works of literature and philosophy.

COMPARATIVE CLOSE-UP: POLITICAL AND SOCIAL INSTITUTIONS IN EUROPE		
	Western Europe	**Eastern Europe**
Political Institutions	Manor lords maintained local authority. Central authority was weak, and attempts at restoring it typically failed in the long run.	The Byzantine emperor had absolute power and was the centralizing authority. The emperor was also supported by a bureaucracy.
Social Institutions	The Roman Catholic Church was the social and cultural unifier. The pope was the spiritual head and strong centralizing figure. Latin was the church's language.	The Byzantine emperor and patriarch were co-heads of the Eastern Orthodox Church. Greek was the church's language.

WESTERN EUROPE AND THE CRUSADES

The Crusades were a series of Christian holy wars conducted against infidels—non-believers. The most significant crusade was a massive expedition led by the Roman Catholic Church to recapture Palestine, the land of Christian origins, from the Muslims. Pope Urban II launched the Crusades in 1095 C.E., when he urged Christian knights to take up arms and seize the Holy Land.

After the First Crusade, the Christians captured Edessa, Antioch, and Jerusalem, and divided that territory into feudal states. However, the disorganized Muslim forces reorganized under the leadership of Saladin and retook Jerusalem in 1187 C.E. The Fourth Crusade never made it to the Holy Land. The crusaders, supported by the merchants of Venice, conquered and sacked the Byzantine capital of Constantinople in 1204 C.E. This event severely weakened the Byzantine Empire.

Though the quest for the Holy Land was a failure, it led to great economic developments in Europe; it encouraged trade with Muslim merchants and increased the European demand for Asian goods. As a result, Italian merchants from cities such as Venice and Genoa greatly profited, and Europe was reintroduced to the goods, technology, and culture of the other regions.

EUROPE DURING THE HIGH MIDDLE AGES

As Europeans interacted with other regions, they adopted new agricultural techniques, such as the three-field system of crop rotation, and foreign agricultural technologies, such as iron plows, watermills, and horse harnesses. These innovations increased crop production and population sizes in Europe.

While the traditional feudal economy was solely based on agriculture in the countryside, a new pre-modern economy was evolving by 1100 C.E. During the early medieval period, the old Roman towns decreased in size. Now, after centuries of decline, increased trade began to stimulate the growth of commercial cities in the heart of Europe. Most often located on riversides, these towns grew into marketplaces and adopted foreign financial innovations, such as banks and **bills of exchange**. Some representative examples of these new urban centers included:

Bruges: Located on a river system that connected the North Sea with Central Europe along the Rhine River, its cross-channel trade brought raw wool from England which was converted into clothing to sell.

Hamburg: A major port on the North Sea. Hamburg was part of the **Hanseatic League**, an alliance of trading cities and their merchant guilds, which controlled trade along the Northern European coast. The League regulated taxes and created rules for fair trade among the member cities.

Florence: This central Italian city controlled the flow of goods through the peninsula. Called the Republic of Florence, this city-state became a center for banking and commerce by 1300 C.E.

Service providers and craftspeople set up businesses in these towns, further stimulating growth. Among those providing services were barbers, blacksmiths, coopers (barrel makers), jewelers, leatherworkers (tanners), innkeepers, and merchants of beer and wine. These cities began to plan their growth, regulate business, and collect taxes. Wealthy towns in Italy invested in new buildings and statuary for beautification.

NOMADIC EMPIRES

Nomadic and migrating peoples and contributed to the diffusion of technologies, ideas, agricultural techniques, and diseases between 600 C.E. and 1450 C.E. For instance, as **Polynesians** migrated between the scattered islands of Oceania, they introduced new foods and domesticated animals to the various islands. The nomadic **Vikings**, Turks, and Mongols also brought social, cultural, and economic changes to the regions that they encountered and perhaps conquered.

Vikings

The Vikings were a nomadic group which settled in present-day Scandinavia (Denmark, Norway, and Sweden). In order to supplement their farm production, they conducted seasonal raids into Europe and ransacked towns. Using small and maneuverable boats, the Vikings raided and terrorized coastal communities in France, Scotland, Ireland, and England. The Vikings eventually evolved from plunderers into traders, and they established communities in Scotland, northern France, and Eastern Europe.

These outstanding seafarers also traded actively throughout the North Sea and Baltic Sea. In the 800s C.E., they colonized Iceland and Greenland, and around 1000 C.E., they established a short-lived colony in Newfoundland (modern-day Canada). The transplanted Viking settlements in France became known as Normandy.

In 1066 C.E., a Norman lord named William from northern France invaded England with his army. He defeated the Saxons and established Norman power in what became modern-day Britain. Over time, the Normans and Vikings were Christianized and absorbed into the larger European feudal order.

> ✔ **AP Expert Note**
>
> ### The Eurasian Steppe
>
> Stretching from Eastern Europe to the Pacific Ocean, the Eurasian steppe was home to many nomadic tribes who would periodically invade the settled societies bordering the steppe. Prior to the refinement of gunpowder weapons, even small groups of steppe nomads were typically a fierce military force thanks to their expert horsemanship and use of mounted archers with composite bows.

Turks

The Turks, a pastoral nomadic group from the central Asian steppes, began to gradually migrate out of the steppes at the end of the first millennium. They were often hired by Muslim leaders as mercenaries. The **Seljuk Turks**, who had converted to Islam, invaded Abbasid territory and captured Baghdad in 1055 C.E. The caliph was left as the spiritual authority of the empire, but the Seljuk Sultan became the secular monarch. By 1071 C.E., the Seljuk Turks had defeated the Byzantine Empire and conquered most of Anatolia (modern-day Turkey).

Following the collapse of the Seljuk dynasty, a new Turkic body arose at the turn of the fourteenth century C.E., when a tribal leader named Osman founded the Ottoman Empire. The Ottomans would conquer Constantinople in 1453 C.E., bringing a final end to the Eastern Roman (Byzantine) Empire.

The Afghan Turks were nomads from Afghanistan. They began a series of raids into India in the tenth century C.E. They looted cities for gold and jewels and destroyed Hindu temples. It wasn't until the twelfth century C.E. that they started to govern after invading. This created the Delhi Sultanate, which ruled northern India from 1206 C.E. to 1526 C.E. The Afghan Turks introduced a strong Muslim presence in India.

MONGOLS

The Mongols were a pastoral, nomadic group from the central Asian steppe (modern-day Mongolia). These nomadic herders' lives revolved around their camels for transportation, their horses for mobility, and their sheep, goats, and yaks for food, clothing, and shelter. Their clan-based society was organized around bloodlines. The man born Temujin, later renamed **Genghis Khan**, successfully united the various Mongol tribes and created history's largest contiguous land empire.

The Mongols' greatest strength was their mobility. During wartime, every male from 15 years old to 70 years old had to serve. Each soldier was rewarded with captured goods and slaves. The Mongols' military strategy was also extremely effective; they were masters at psychological warfare and at feigning retreats. The Mongols were also skilled at using diplomacy to play enemies off one another and to weaken anti-Mongol alliances.

Once his troops were united, Genghis Khan led them into Central Asia, Tibet, Northern China, and Persia. In 1215 C.E., the Mongols attacked and destroyed Zhongdu (modern-day Beijing). The Mongols had relatively few defeats, but they failed to invade the Delhi Sultanate and Japan.

In 1227 C.E., the Great Khan died. While regional control was divided among his four sons in the form of khanates, supreme authority passed to his son Ögedei. However, by 1259 C.E. infighting over succession to the position of Great Khan led to civil war and then fragmentation of the Mongol Empire. In total, the Mongol conquests were the fourth deadliest span of warfare in human history, with conservative estimates placing the death toll at 30 to 40 million people, roughly ten percent of the world's population at the time.

Mongol Rule in China: The Yuan Dynasty

In 1279 C.E., Genghis Khan's grandson, Kublai Khan, conquered the Southern Song dynasty. For the first time, China was under foreign rule. Kublai Khan created a Chinese-style dynasty, taking the name Yuan, and maintained a fixed and regular tax payment system and a strong central government. Foreigners, not Chinese, were employed in most bureaucratic positions and the civil service exam was no longer used. The Chinese were subject to different laws and were consciously separated from the Mongols.

In time, overland and maritime trade flourished. Though the Mongols were not directly involved in the trade, they welcomed merchants and foreigners. Merchants converted their foreign currency into paper money when they crossed into China. Under Mongol rule, China prospered and the Mongol capital Khanbaliq developed into a flourishing city.

The Mongol rulers only achieved a limited level of popularity among their Chinese subjects, due to both their discriminatory practices and high taxes. The Red Turban Rebellion (1351–1368 C.E.) would see the Chinese overthrow their Mongol conquerors. Zhu Yuanzhang, a peasant turned Red Turban commander, would found the Ming dynasty (1368–1644 C.E.).

Mongol Rule in Korea

When the Mongols conquered Korea in the thirteenth century C.E., the Koryo dynasty maintained their local rule, with Korean kings marrying Mongol princesses. However, by the 1350s, with Yuan dynasty destabilizing, the Koreans expelled Mongol garrisons.

After the Mongols were overthrown in China, the Koryo dynasty lost power in Korea and the Joseon dynasty (1392–1897 C.E.) emerged.

Mongol Rule in the Middle East: The Ilkhanate

In 1258 C.E., Kublai's brother Hülegü Khan defeated the Abbasid Caliphate, conquered Mesopotamia and Persia, and burned the city of Baghdad, destroying its famed House of Wisdom. Over time, these Mongols converted to Islam and began to mix with their conquered populations. The conquered populations' local rulers were permitted to rule, as long as they delivered tax revenue and maintained order. Though the Mongols did not support agriculture, they did facilitate trade.

As the Mongols continued west, they were defeated in 1260 C.E. by the armies of the Mamluk dynasty (also known as the Slave dynasty) in Egypt.

Mongol Rule in Russia: The Golden Horde

During the centuries before the Mongol invasion, Russia was dominated by feudalism. The princes of Kiev, which also controlled the Russian Orthodox Church, ruled according to the legal principles that the Byzantine emperor Justinian had created.

When the Mongol ruler Batu Khan conquered and ruled Russia, he created the Mongol khanate called the Golden Horde. Batu Khan allowed many local rulers to keep their power, and Russian bureaucrats collected peasants' taxes, which were heavy during this time. Batu Khan's Mongol descendants constituted the upper social classes of the Golden Horde.

The Russian rulers of Muscovy, a territory north of Kiev, gained more control during Mongol rule by closely associating themselves with their Mongol rulers. The Mongols maintained control until Prince Ivan III effectively ended their rule in 1480 C.E. and formed the Russian state.

Pax Mongolica

Although Mongol invasions initially interfered with trade and peace, a period called the Mongol Peace (or *Pax Mongolica*) lasted during the thirteenth and fourteenth centuries C.E., when vast areas of Eurasia were under Mongol rule. For about a century, Mongol rule united two continents and eliminated tariffs, which allowed for relatively safe trade and contacts between vastly different cultures.

During this period, the Silk Road trade reached its peak. Paper money—a Chinese innovation—was used in many parts of the Mongol Empire. The Mongols often adopted or converted to local religions, or at least maintained religious tolerance.

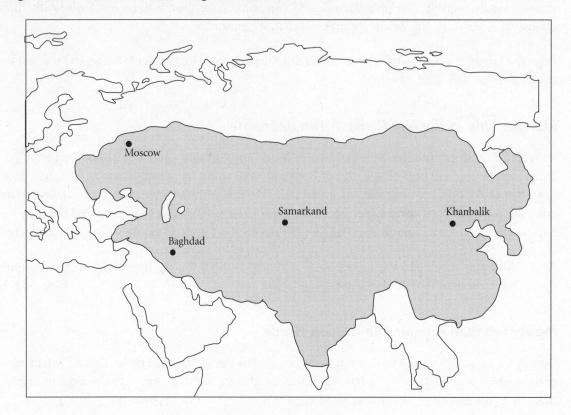

Mongol Conquests

Mongol Decline

In 1274 C.E. and 1281 C.E., the Mongols tried to expand their empire again by invading Japan. However, typhoon winds destroyed their fleets both times. The Japanese believed that the kamikaze, or "spirit winds," had protected them.

Despite great military accomplishment, the Mongol Empire lasted for only three or four generations. The Mongols were successful conquerors but poor administrators. Overspending led to inflation in different regions of the empire, and after the death of Kublai Khan, leadership was weak and ineffectual. Rivalry among the great Khan's potential successors further destabilized the empire, and the vast domain was divided among various generals. By 1350 C.E., most of the Mongols' vast territory had been reconquered by other armies and the Mongols had largely assimilated into the societies that they had invaded.

WEST AFRICAN KINGDOMS

Ghana

The Ghana Empire, or Awkar, began as a series of interconnected agricultural villages along the Niger River. It became heavily involved with trans-Saharan trade around 500 C.E., as Ghana had abundant supplies of gold that it traded for salt. Its kings controlled and taxed the gold trade. Ghana's merchants also traded with Berbers (nomadic peoples from North Africa who often used camel caravans for transportation) and Arab merchants from North Africa for Mediterranean items such as cloth, weapons, and manufactured items.

As Ghana's wealth and power increased, it built a large army funded by taxes. In the 900s C.E., the kings, elites, and traders converted to Islam, which led to improved relations with Muslim merchants. Ghana's kings did not force their people to adopt Islam, however, and traditional animistic beliefs endured among a minority.

Around 1076–77 C.E., northern Berbers and other tribal groups assaulted and weakened the Ghana Empire. Ghana was eventually absorbed by the growing West African kingdoms, especially the Mali Empire.

Mali

Sundiata Keita established the Mali Empire in 1230 C.E., but it was not until his victory at the Battle of Kirina in 1235 C.E. against the rival Sosso that he cemented his nation's place as the strongest West African state during the thirteenth and fourteenth centuries C.E. The poem known as *The Epic of Sundiata* describes how Sundiata Keita founded Mali. This poem exemplifies African oral traditions; it was composed and recited by Mali *griots* (storytellers).

Although most people in Mali were engaged in agriculture, the kingdom of Mali prospered from its participation in the trans-Saharan trade in gold and salt. The kings of Mali controlled and taxed trade within their territories. Local Mali rulers served in religious and economic roles; they honored Islam, provided protection and lodging for merchants, and ensured that the kings of Mali received their tax income. The people of Mali were encouraged, but not forced, to convert to Islam.

Mansa Musa ruled Mali from 1312 C.E. to 1337 C.E. A devout Muslim, Mansa Musa fulfilled one of the five pillars of faith and went on a pilgrimage, or *hajj*, to Mecca. He brought thousands of soldiers, attendants, subjects, and slaves with him, as well as hundreds of camels carrying satchels of gold. Mansa Musa created a period of inflation, which affected many regions along major trade routes, because he distributed so much gold to other peoples during his journey. Inspired by his travels, Mansa Musa built libraries, Islamic schools, and mosques throughout the kingdom. Timbuktu became Mali's political capital and West Africa's cultural center of Islamic scholarship and art.

Following 1350 C.E., after a series of kings that spent lavishly and misruled, provinces began to assert their independence and separate from the Mali Empire, and its power and influence declined.

Northeastern African Kingdoms

Many inhabitants of North Africa converted to Islam after 700 C.E. as Arab travelers spread their religious beliefs. Christianity also endured, however, especially in Egypt and Ethiopia. Ethiopia evolved into a kingdom with strong Christian traditions. Coptic Christianity stayed popular in Ethiopia, and in Egypt a minority of Coptic Christians remained even after the introduction of Islam.

East African City-States

East Africa was populated by peoples who spoke **Bantu** languages and had migrated centuries earlier from the Niger River territory. These Bantu peoples settled in cities along the East African coast.

Although they did not politically unite to form kingdoms, individual city-states such as Mogadishu, Kilwa, and Sofala prospered from participating in Indian Ocean trade with Muslim merchants during the seventh and eighth centuries C.E. In the 900s C.E., Islamic merchants traded gold, slaves, and ivory for pottery, glass, and textiles from Persia, India, and China. As East Africans associated with Arab traders, the Swahili language (which mixes Bantu and Arabic) developed. Because of this, East African city-states are often called **Swahili city-states**.

Much like Ghana and Mali, these powerful city-states were governed by kings. When they converted to Islam for legitimacy and alliances, the kings ruled as caliphs and taxed and controlled the trade. They built stone mosques and public buildings in their cities. The ruling elite and wealthy merchants of East Africa often converted to Islam but did not completely separate from their own religious and cultural traditions.

In Southeastern Africa, the kingdom of Zimbabwe prospered from participating in trade with East Africa's city-states. In eleventh century C.E., its inhabitants created the Great Zimbabwe, a city of stone towers, palaces, and public buildings. Zimbabwe prospered between 1300 C.E. and 1450 C.E.

LONG-DISTANCE TRADE   `High-Yield`

The volume of long-distance trade dramatically increased between 600 C.E. and 1450 C.E. Luxury items of high value, such as silk and precious stones, were typically transported over land routes. Merchants used sea routes to transport bulkier commodities, such as steel, stone, coral, and building materials.

The Silk Road trade linked the Eurasian land mass. Trans-Saharan trade connected West Africa to the Mediterranean and Islamic Empire. The Indian Ocean trade linked China, Southeast Asia, India, Arabia, and East Africa. The Mediterranean Sea trade linked Europe with goods from the Islamic Empire and Asia.

Because of this global exchange, and because of increased agricultural productivity and slightly warmer global temperatures between 800 C.E. and 1300 C.E., cities located along trade routes grew substantially. For instance, **Melaka**, a city on the coast of the Malay Peninsula in Southeast Asia, served as an important port city on the Indian Ocean. It became the Sultanate of Melaka, an Islamic state, as Muslim traders settled into the region and spread Islam in the early fifteenth century C.E. Melaka maintained a safe environment for trade, welcomed merchants, and charged reasonable fees. As a result, it thrived in this interconnected world, along with cities like Hangzhou in China, Samarkand in Central Asia, Baghdad in modern-day Iraq, Kilwa in East Africa, Venice in Italy, and Timbuktu in Mali, Africa.

Although cities generally increased in size between 600 C.E. and 1450 C.E., military invasions, diseases, and reduced agricultural productivity caused some cities to experience periods of significant economic decline.

Merchants set up their own communities, where they often influenced the dominant culture along trade routes. For example, Muslim merchants in the Indian Ocean region, Chinese merchants in Southeast Asia, and Jewish merchants in the Mediterranean settled in diaspora communities in trade cities.

MISSIONARY CAMPAIGNS

Buddhism

Along the Silk Road, Buddhism traveled to Central Asia and adapted into variants which included polytheism. In Tibet, it became popular as it combined shamanism and the importance of rituals. In East Asia, monks, merchants, and missionaries adapted Buddhism to the political ideas of Confucianism by including Daoist ideas, an emphasis on family, and ancestor worship.

Particularly during chaotic times, Buddhism appealed to people as an avenue toward personal salvation. Chinese Buddhism spread to Korea, where it received royal support, and to Japan. In Japan, Shinto leaders initially resisted Buddhism. Eventually, syncretism (the fusion of differing systems of beliefs) occurred after Buddhism blended into the worship of Shinto divinities.

Because Buddhism lacked an organized Church, it could merge with local people's ideas. However, Buddhism was often replaced by more organized religions. In Central Asia, for instance, Islam eventually replaced Buddhism as the dominant religion. In China, the Tang dynasty stopped supporting Buddhism in the ninth century C.E.

Christianity

Like Buddhism, Christianity emerged as a missionary religion. When the Western Roman Empire was declining, missionary efforts turned toward Northern Europe. The Western Church and the pope sponsored missionary campaigns aimed at converting the Germanic people. The Eastern Orthodox Church also spread Christianity to Eastern Europe and Russia.

Syncretism aided the spread of Christianity. Pagan heroes or holy figures, such as the saints, were seen as mediators between God and his people. Polytheistic holidays were incorporated into Christianity, and Christians placed Christmas on the same day as the pagan winter solstice celebration.

In Asia, Nestorian Christianity—the belief that Jesus existed as two distinct entities, mortal man and divine figure—spread to Mesopotamia and Persia, where Islamic conquerors allowed Christians to practice their religion. Merchants also spread Nestorian Christianity as far as India and China, but they received little or no support from local rulers.

Islam

Islam spread through three main avenues: military conquest, trade, and missionary activity. Once Islam was introduced through one of those avenues, the religion spread because of its tolerance for other beliefs, its simple principles, and its emphasis on charity and spiritual equality. Also, Muslim rulers often levied a special tax against non-Muslims, which provided an economic incentive for conversion.

In sub-Saharan Africa, merchants introduced Islam to the ruling class through trade, and syncretism occurred. The kings still held a divine position, and women continued to have a prominent place in society, as was the local custom. In East Africa, Islam arrived via the Indian Ocean, where it mixed Arabic and African languages to create Swahili. In India, Turks brought Islam to the region in the eleventh century when they formed the Delhi Sultanate and used Hindu stories with Muslim characters, attracting both warriors and low-caste Hindus.

The Sufis were the most active missionaries after 900 C.E., spreading Islam to Southern Europe, sub-Saharan Africa, Central Asia, India, and Southeast Asia.

AGRICULTURAL AND TECHNOLOGICAL DIFFUSION

The increase in global interaction through this time period led to the spread of agriculture and technology, and great changes throughout the world.

Origin	Diffusion	Effect
Magnetic compass from China	Europe via the Indian Ocean trade	Increase in maritime trade and exploration
Sugarcane from Southwest Asia	European Crusaders	Increases in Mediterranean island plantations and increases in slave labor
Gunpowder from China	Persia, the Middle East, and eventually Europe by the Mongols	Advances in weapon technology

Travelers

The tremendous amount of long-distance interaction in this period can be illustrated through the travels of three individuals: a Muslim scholar (**Ibn Battuta**), an Italian merchant (**Marco Polo**), and a Nestorian Christian priest (Rabban Sauma). Each traveler recorded his observations during his journeys.

	Ibn Battuta 1304–1369	Marco Polo 1253–1324	Rabban Sauma 1225–1294
Background	Muslim scholar from Morocco	Italian merchant from Venice	Nestorian Christian priest from Mongol Empire in China
Places traveled	Throughout Dar al-Islam: West Africa, India, Southeast Asia	Throughout the Silk Road to the Mongol Empire in China.	Began pilgrimage to Jerusalem in Beijing, but diverted when sent by Mongol Ilkhan of Persia to meet with kings of France and England and the pope to negotiate alliances against Muslims.
Significance	Found government positions as a *qadi*, or judge, throughout the lands he traveled. Demonstrated the widespread influence of Islam and increased European interest in Eastern goods.	Allowed by Kublai Khan to pursue mercantile and domestic missions throughout the empire. Increased European interest in goods from the East.	Did not succeed in attracting the support of Christian Europe to the Mongol cause. Europeans never conquered the Middle East, but instead went around it to reach the Indian Ocean.

600 to 1450 C.E.

Spread of Disease

In addition to religions, technologies, and goods, diseases spread along trade routes. Carried by infected rodents and fleas, the Black Death (**bubonic plague**) spread from the Yunnan region of southwest China. In the 1340s C.E., Mongols, merchants, and travelers spread the disease even farther along the trade routes west of China. Oasis towns, trading cities of Central Asia, Black Sea ports, the Mediterranean Sea, and Western Europe were all affected. Some scholars estimate that as many as 100 million people, out of a world population of 450 million, died. A third of Europe's population died in the first five years of the plague.

This seemingly apocalyptic event led to many social changes. In Western Europe, for example, the resulting labor shortage led to workers demanding higher wages. Peasants rebelled, weakening the feudal system. Antisemitism led to Jews being scapegoated for the plague, and many Jewish communities were massacred. Christians questioned their faith amid all of the death and seemingly senseless destruction. Self-flagellation (whipping oneself) became popular as a way for people to atone for their apparent sins. The Roman Catholic Church lost much of its seasoned clergy to the plague, and their replacements often lacked proper education and literacy as standards were lowered by necessity.

RECOVERY AND RENAISSANCE IN ASIA AND EUROPE

High-Yield

600 to 1450 C.E.

Chinese Developments

In 1368, the Mongol Yuan dynasty collapsed and Emperor Hongwu started the Ming dynasty. Hongwu eliminated evidence of Mongol rule, reinstated the Confucian education system and civil service exam, and tightened central authority. The Ming relied on mandarins, a class of powerful officials, to implement their policies on the local level. They also conscripted laborers to rebuild irrigation systems; as a result, agricultural production increased. Though the Ming did not actively promote trade, private merchants traded manufactured porcelain, silk, and cotton.

The Ming dynasty strongly promoted Chinese cultural traditions and established Neo-Confucian schools which stressed Confucian values such as self-discipline, filial piety, and obedience to rulers. They also funded projects that emphasized Chinese cultural traditions, such as the Yongle Encyclopedia. This encyclopedia was the largest general encyclopedia of its time, and it covered a wide array of subjects, including agriculture, art, astronomy, drama, geology, history, literature, medicine, natural sciences, religion, and technology. More than 2,000 scholars contributed to its development. Increased printing contributed to the growth of popular culture. The Ming dynasty saw three of the "Four Great Classical Novels" of Chinese literature published: The *Water Margin, Romance of the Three Kingdoms* and *Journey to the West*. The often banned yet landmark work *The Plum in the Golden Vase* also saw publication.

> ✔ **AP Expert Note**
>
> ### Romance of the Three Kingdoms
>
> *"The world under heaven, after a long period of division, tends to unite; after a long period of union, tends to divide. This has been so since antiquity."* - opening lines
>
> Perhaps the most widely-read novel in both late imperial and modern China, and culturally influential throughout East Asia, *Romance of the Three Kingdoms* is an 800,000-word epic. It has been adapted in everything from operas, to comics, to video games like *Dynasty Warriors*. The story opens with the Yellow Turban Rebellion at the twilight of the Han dynasty, and it follows a sprawling cast during the Three Kingdoms period as they battle over whose faction will reunite China.

Jesuit missionaries such as Matteo Ricci arrived in China, introducing European science and technology. However, the Jesuit goal of converting the Chinese population to Christianity proved to be unsuccessful.

European Developments

By the 1400s C.E., the regional states in Europe were developing into monarchies. These monarchies were strong enough to tax citizens directly and maintain large standing armies. Italy, Milan, Venice, and Florence benefited greatly from increased trade, which increased tax revenues and their governments' authority.

Kings in France and England began to successfully assert their authority over their feudal lords. In Spain, Fernando of Aragon and Isabella of Castile married and united Spain by reconquering the lands formerly controlled by Muslims. The competition among these states led to a refinement and improvement in weapons, ships, and technology, which prepared these regional states for future expansion.

The increased interaction with regions outside Europe ignited a major intellectual and artistic movement known as the **Renaissance**. Contact with the Islamic world, such as the Muslim territory al-Andalus in the Iberian Peninsula, reintroduced the ancient Greek and Roman texts that had been preserved and developed by Arabs. From the 1300s C.E. through the 1500s C.E., European painters, sculptors, and writers drew inspiration from the Greek and Roman classical past.

The study of these classical texts became known as Renaissance humanism or *studia humanitatis* (the "studies of humanity"). Renaissance humanism stressed the achievements of human beings. While medieval scholars and artists focused their works on revealing God, humanist scholars and artists attempted to reveal human nature. In Italy, artists such as Leonardo da Vinci and Michelangelo used perspective to create realistic masterpieces. Noble families, such as the Medici family, who had grown wealthy from lucrative trade with the Islamic and Byzantine cultures, became patrons of painters, sculptors, and scientists.

Chinese Exploration

After reestablishing authority over China, the Ming decided to refurbish their country's large navy. From 1405 to 1433 C.E., they sponsored seven massive naval expeditions, in order to reinforce Chinese presence in the Indian Ocean, impose imperial control over trade, and impress foreign peoples with the authority of the Ming dynasty.

The mariner Zheng He led these expeditions. His first trip alone involved 28,000 troops. Zheng He sailed to Southeast Asia, India, the Persian Gulf, Arabia, and East Africa. Zheng He dispensed and received gifts throughout these travels. However, Confucian officials convinced the Chinese emperor that the voyages were too expensive and unprofitable, especially because of renewed concern over the northern Mongol border. Thus, in 1433 C.E., the voyages ended, Zheng He's records were destroyed, and the ships were allowed to rot.

European Exploration

In the 1400s C.E., the ideas of the Renaissance inspired some Europeans to explore. These explorations were not diplomatic, but instead focused on profits, the spread of Christianity, and the desire for adventure. The goods from the East, such as spices, which Europeans desired were very expensive because of the long overland journey between Asia and Europe.

However, what if Europeans could find their own route to Asia by sea and cut out the Muslim middlemen's profits? The Portuguese were early leaders in exploration, under the leadership of Prince Henry the Navigator, who established Portuguese schools and sponsored expeditions along the West African coast.

Competition increased among European powers, and a race to dominate the seas began. This competition continued well into our next period, with the European involvement in the Indian Ocean trade and their encounter with the Americas.

CHAPTER 10

Period 4: 1450 to 1750 C.E. – Complete Time Period Review

IMPACT OF INTERACTION—THE DEVELOPMENT OF A GLOBAL ECONOMY

European Exploration

High-Yield

The Ming dynasty had extensively explored the Indian Ocean from 1405 to 1433, but decided to halt the voyages and destroy their ships due to pressure from conservative factions in the court. Other Easterners like Muslims, Indians, and Malays continued to use the Indian Ocean for commerce and trade, establishing effective routes and creating a vibrant trade system. When the Europeans did arrive, the world shifted from a primarily Asian-centered economy to a global economy.

Europe emerged from an age of isolation with a desire to explore. Major motivations included the search for resources and new trade routes to Asian markets, and the desire to spread Christianity. The Asian goods that Europe purchased, such as pepper, ginger, cloves, and nutmeg, were very expensive. Europeans wanted to gain direct access to these goods, increasing supply and lowering prices. Additionally, the Ottoman **conquest of Constantinople** in 1453 ended the Byzantine Empire, solidifying Muslim influence in the region and making it less friendly to European traders. The acquisition of technology from China and the Muslim world helped Europeans expand their seagoing capabilities with maritime equipment such as the sternpost rudder, triangular lateen sails, the magnetic compass, and the astrolabe. Portugal was an early leader in European exploration, aided by the development of the **caravel**, a small, highly maneuverable sailing ship.

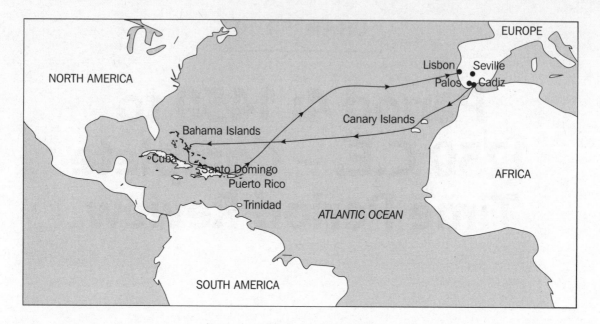

Columbus's First Voyage

Explorer	Year	Accomplishment
Bartolomeu Dias (Portugal)	1488	Rounded the Cape of Good Hope at the tip of Africa and entered the Indian Ocean
Christopher Columbus (Spain)	1492	Sailed west to reach Asia and instead reached the Bahamas. Sailed around the Caribbean, but thought he had reached an island just off the coast of Asia
Vasco da Gama (Portugal)	1497	Reached Calicut, India in 1498 by rounding Africa
Ferdinand Magellan (Spain)	1519–1522	Sailed around South America to the Philippine Islands where he was killed; his men sailed back through the Indian Ocean and were the first to circumnavigate the globe

Trading-Post Empires

The initial goal of European powers in exploring the Indian Ocean was not to conquer, but to control trade. They wanted to force merchant ships to trade in fortified trading sites and to pay duties for the privilege. By the mid-1500s, Portugal had 50 trading posts from West Africa to East Asia, but by the late 1500s its power had started to decline—the country lacked the administrative and military capabilities to keep up with other European powers. The English and Dutch quickly took Portugal's place as the dominant seafaring powers with faster, cheaper, and more powerful ships. Their imperial expansion was aided by the use of **joint-stock companies**, in which investors, rather than royal governments, funded expeditions.

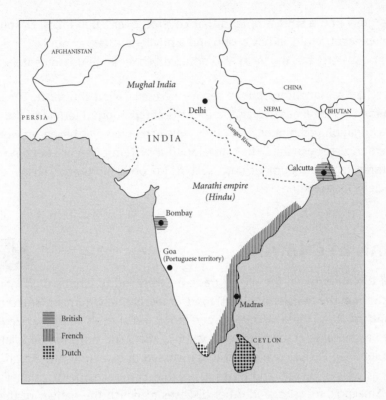

Trading Posts

AMERICAN CIVILIZATIONS

Aztec

The Aztecs occupied territory in Mesoamerica, and the capital city Tenochtitlán was located in what today is Mexico City. A militant warrior tradition characterized Aztec culture. They developed a system of feudalism which had similarities to that of Japan and Europe. The Aztecs were ruled by a single monarch, who exerted power over local rulers.

The Aztecs had an agricultural economy, with cacao beans sometimes used as currency. They practiced *chinampa* agriculture, where farmers cultivated crops in rectangular plots of land on lake beds. A priestly class oversaw polytheistic religious rituals, which sometimes included human sacrifice. Although Aztec society was patriarchal, women were able to own property and agree to business contracts.

Inca

Indigenous clans in the Andean highlands of South America developed a rich and complex culture, leading to the rise of an empire in the fifteenth century C.E. These people—the Incas—conquered a large territory and absorbed many groups in central and western South America. In ninety years, the Inca Empire grew into a stretch of land that covered over 3,000 miles. Despite its large size, the Inca Empire was centralized, led by a king and a privileged class of nobles. The capital city was Cuzco, in present-day Peru, but the Incas also occupied other large urban centers.

The Inca Empire had a mandatory public service system, called the *mit'a*. Their economy was rooted in agriculture, as the Incas had adapted to the steep, rugged terrain of the Andes with the use of extensive irrigation techniques. Their polytheistic religion was based on worship of the sun and incorporated ancestor worship. They developed a system of record-keeping called *quipu*; it used knotted strings to record numeric data, such as tax obligations and census records. Living in a patriarchal society, Inca women had few rights.

COLUMBIAN EXCHANGE

High-Yield

The inclusion of the Americas in the global trade network led to what would later be called the **Columbian Exchange**: the transfer of plants, food, crops, animals, humans, and diseases between the Old World and the New. The exchange of food crops and animals revolutionized life around the world, leading to an increase in the nutritional value of diets and boosting population worldwide. However, the Columbian Exchange also led to the spread of disease to the Americas, brought by human carriers, as well as by rats and mosquitoes that Europeans unintentionally brought with them on ships. Smallpox, measles, and other diseases to which the natives of the Americas had no immunity devastated their populations; some estimates of mortality rates for native populations are as high as ninety percent. The loss of natives due to disease played a direct role in their inability to fend off European advancement, and also led to the importation of enslaved Africans to work plantations. Relying on dwindling native populations as a labor force became economically unsustainable, and African slaves were used to meet labor demands.

Europe to the Americas	Americas to Africa, Asia, and Europe
Wheat	Maize (Corn)
Sugarcane	Potatoes
Cotton	Beans
Horses	Tomatoes
Cattle	Peppers
Pigs	Peanuts
Sheep	Avocadoes
Goats	Pineapples
Chickens	Tobacco

Mercantilism: The Role and Impact of Silver

Silver, the most abundant American precious metal, was responsible for stimulating the global trade network. Spain controlled the two areas richest in silver production, Mexico and the Potosí mines in the Andes, and made use of large numbers of indigenous forced laborers. The Spanish were driven primarily by the economic theory of **mercantilism**. The term "mercantile system" is used to describe the ways in which nation-states enrich themselves by limiting imports and encouraging exports. The goal of mercantilist policies was to achieve a favorable balance of trade that would bring wealth into the country while maintaining domestic employment. The most important objective for mercantilist policies in the sixteenth century was the growth of a nation's economic power relative to competing nation-states. Spain used silver to trade for silk and porcelain in Asia, as China used the precious metal as a primary medium of exchange, and to finance a powerful military and bureaucracy.

The Role and Impact of Sugar

Sugar was another important product at this time. Intensive labor and specialized skills were required for **sugar cultivation**. Because smallpox had wiped out so many native peoples in the Americas, enslaved Africans became the main labor force. These slaves worked under very harsh conditions—mistreatment, extreme heat, and poor nutrition—which led to a significant number of deaths from disease and abuse.

These sugar plantations were, in many aspects, proto-factories, as they were financed and organized to create a single product in a complex process, foreshadowing the organization of mechanized production in the upcoming Industrial Revolution.

STATE-BUILDING

Ottoman Empire

High-Yield

The Ottoman Empire emerged from a group of semi-nomadic Turks who migrated to northwest Anatolia in the thirteenth century. Military might and **gunpowder** weapons drove the Ottomans to power. An elite fighting force of slave troops composed of Christian males, called Janissaries, formed the professional backbone of the Ottoman military. In 1453 the Ottomans conquered Constantinople and brought an end to Byzantine rule. Sultans like Mehmed the Conqueror and Suleiman the Magnificent created an absolute monarchy. Islamic religious scholars and legal experts served administrative functions in the government. As the empire prospered, sultans grew more distant and removed themselves from government administration. The vizier headed the bureaucracy, and often had more control and actual power than the sultan. Political succession was often problematic, as many new sultans would execute their brothers to eliminate any challenge to their authority.

In the capital city of Istanbul, formerly Constantinople, the Christian cathedral Hagia Sophia was converted to a grand mosque. The city also had aqueducts, a flourishing marketplace, rest houses, religious schools, and hospitals. A large merchant and artisan class conducted business, but their work was closely regulated by the government.

The sultan's harem, consisting of wives, concubines and female servants, was influential in Ottoman politics and society. Members of the harem were often of slave origin and non-Muslim, as the enslavement of Muslims was forbidden. Wives and concubines were awarded status when they produced male heirs to the sultan's throne. They were educated in the Quran, reading, sewing, and music. The sultan's mother served as an advisor to the throne, overseeing the imperial household and engaging in diplomacy.

The empire reached its peak in the mid-1600s, but became too large to maintain. The effectiveness of the administration declined, and was plagued by corruption. In addition, the Ottomans struggled to keep up with ongoing European military and naval advancements.

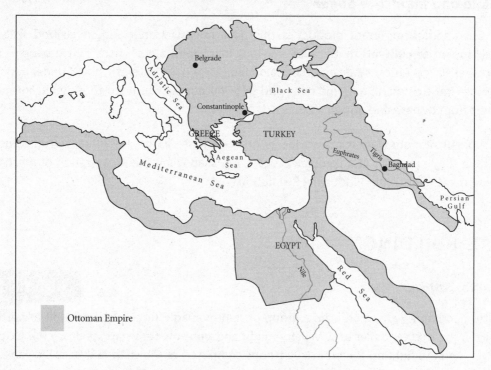

Expansion of the Ottoman Empire

Mughal India

In 1526, Babur, a descendant of Turkic nomads, began his conquest of India, unifying the subcontinent's regional kingdoms and establishing the **Mughal empire**. His grandson Akbar continued Babur's legacy and ushered in a period of economic stability and religious harmony. Akbar created a religion called the Divine Faith which combined elements of Islam and Hinduism together and legitimized his rule as head of state and religion. He initiated a policy of cooperation with Hindu rulers and the Hindu population by encouraging intermarriage. He also abolished the *jizya* (non-Muslim tax), and promoted Hindus to high-ranking government positions. Akbar and his descendants, Jahangir and Shah Jahan, were great patrons of the arts. Emperor Shah Jahan oversaw the construction of the Taj Mahal, built as a tomb for his late wife. The Taj Mahal is perhaps the greatest example of Mughal architecture's unique blend of Islamic domes, arches, and minarets with Hindu-inspired ornamentation.

Aurangzeb, Shah Jahan's son, seized the throne with a neglectful and corrupt bureaucracy and pushed to extend Muslim control of India. He sought to rid India of all Hindu influences, purify Islam, and reinstate the *jizya*. His many wars drained the treasury, and peasant uprisings and revolts by both Muslim and Hindu princes weakened the empire. At this time, India had become a major overseas destination for European traders looking to fulfill demand for cotton. With a weakened empire, those traders were able to increase their influence in the region.

Songhai

In the 1400s, the West African state of **Songhai** emerged to take power over the weakened Mali Empire. Its leader, Sunni Ali, consolidated his empire by appointing governors to oversee the provinces, building a large army, and creating an imperial navy to patrol the Niger River. The lucrative trans-Saharan trade flowed through the city of Gao, which brought salt, textiles, and metal in exchange for gold and slaves.

Songhai emperors were Muslims who supported the construction of mosques, schools, and an Islamic university at Timbuktu. Though Islam served as the cultural foundation of the empire and a key element in establishing cooperation with Muslim merchants, traditional African religious beliefs were not fully abandoned.

Just as Europeans were making inroads into Africa, the Songhai Empire began to lose control of its subjects. The empire went into decline and was defeated by the Moroccans in 1591, made easier by use of firearms by the Moroccans.

Kongo

In the fourteenth century, the Kongo emerged as a centralized state along the west coast of central Africa. In this organized state, a powerful king ruled, and officials oversaw military, judicial, and financial affairs. In 1482, a small Portuguese fleet arrived and initiated commercial relations, and within a few years the Portuguese had developed a close political and diplomatic relationship with the king. To improve relations, kings like Affonso I converted to and spread Christianity across the kingdom.

The Portuguese brought great wealth to Kongo, exchanging textiles and weapons for gold, silver, ivory, and slaves. Eventually, the Portuguese dealings undermined the king's authority and led to conflict. The Portuguese defeated the Kongo's forces in 1665, and the kingdom never fully recovered.

Spanish and Portuguese Colonies in the New World

Spanish conquistadors led the way in the conquest of the Americas. The primary Spanish settlements, New Spain (Mexico) and New Castile (Peru), were each governed by a viceroy, who reported directly to the Spanish king. In 1494, the Treaty of Tordesillas, an agreement between Spain and Portugal based on an earlier decree by Pope Alexander VI, divided control of any future American territories: the Spanish controlled the land west of the agreed upon line of demarcation, and the Portuguese controlled the territory east of the line.

Along with its goal of increasing wealth through the creation of an empire, Spain desired to expand the influence of Christianity. Catholic missionaries came to the Americas alongside the conquistadors and built mission churches to convert American Indians, many of whom adopted Christianity but blended it with their indigenous religions. For the most part, however, these Spanish missionaries forcibly imposed European culture on the natives.

The social result of the conquest of this new empire was a multicultural and ethnically-mixed population. The *peninsulares*, the highest social class, came directly from the Iberian peninsula, and their American-born descendants were called **Creoles**. Those of mixed European and American Indian descent were called ***mestizos***, and those with European and African ancestors were called ***mulattoes***. At the bottom of the social order were the American Indians, Africans, and the mixed class of *zambos*.

Qing Dynasty

By the 1640s, the Ming dynasty had declined and been taken over by a peasant army which established the short-lived Shun dynasty. The **Manchu**, a community of hunters, fishermen, and farmers from the lands to the northeast of China, soon ousted the Shun and established the Qing dynasty. Thus, China came under the rule of foreigners for the second time (the first being the Mongol-ruled Yuan dynasty).

The Manchus established and expanded their rule through military conquest. Like Genghis Khan, who reorganized the Mongol army to diminish the importance of tribal allegiances, the Manchu leader Nurhaci created a large army consisting of units called banners, which were organized on a social basis. Each banner comprised a set of military companies, but also included the families and slaves of the soldiers. Banners were led by a hereditary captain, many of whom came from Nurhaci's own lineage. When the Manchu army defeated new groups, they were incorporated into several banners to decrease their potential for insubordination.

The Manchu had adopted elements of Chinese culture generations before the conquest. Unlike the Mongols, they incorporated traditional Chinese practices into government, including using the Confucian civil service exam system to fill government positions. Like the Mongols, however, the Manchu wanted to preserve their own ethnic and cultural identity. They forbade intermarriage between Manchu and Han Chinese, barred Chinese from traveling to Manchuria and learning their language, and forced Chinese men to wear their hair in a braid called a queue as a sign of submission.

The Qing dynasty created a multiethnic empire that was larger than any earlier Chinese dynasty. It expanded into Taiwan in 1683, increased control of Mongolia throughout the 1690s, and established administrative oversight of Tibet in 1720. The final area to be annexed was Chinese Turkestan in the 1750s. The Manchus ruled Tibet and Turkestan relatively leniently. Local religious leaders, such as the Dalai Lama in Tibet, were allowed to remain in place, and men were not forced to wear the queue. By this time, the expanding Qing and Russian empires were nearing each other, which resulted in Manchu and Russian leaders approving the 1689 Treaty of Nerchinsk, which defined borders and regulated trade.

Russian Empire

After hundreds of years under Mongol tributary rule, Russia emerged as an empire in its own right. The Mongols had forced the Russian princes to submit to their rule and provide them with tribute and slaves. Russian princes collected the khan's taxes and suppressed uprisings, gaining power in the process. Eventually, the Muscovite princes were able to defeat their rivals for power. Ivan III, a grand prince of Moscow, stopped paying tribute to the Mongols and in 1480 began building his own empire. He established a strong central government, and ruled as an absolute monarch, a czar, who was also the head of the Russian Orthodox Church. The czar claimed that his authority to rule came directly from God. After a series of Muscovite princes, the Romanov family came to power in 1613, and ruled Russia for the next 300 years.

Peter the Great, who reigned from 1682 to 1725, was fascinated with Western technology and instituted a policy of rapid modernization. Needing skilled technicians and industrial experts to carry out his modernization plans, he established schools to produce them. He greatly reformed the military by strengthening the navy and introducing a system of ranks. Peter created an interlocking military-civilian bureaucracy composed of 14 hierarchical ranks which functioned as a meritocracy; even people from non-noble origins could rise through the ranks to positions of great authority. His obsession with Westernizing Russia was best demonstrated by his insistence that all Russian men wear Western clothes and shave their beards, imposing heavy taxes on those who refused to comply. His construction of a new capital city, St. Petersburg, provided better access to the West.

Japan: Tokugawa Shogunate

Tokugawa Ieyasu established the **Tokugawa shogunate** in 1600, after a period of civil war that began in 1467. Fighting had broken out among various *daimyos* (warlords) over succession of the *shogun*, the supreme military leader of Japan. Ieyasu hoped to stabilize the country and end the unrest by increasing his control over the *daimyos*. He required that they spend every other year at the capital, Edo (now Tokyo), where he could more easily monitor them and prevent rebellion.

Relationships with the outside world became closely controlled. Japanese were forbidden from going abroad and from constructing large ships. Europeans were expelled from Japan, and foreign merchants were not allowed to trade in Japanese ports—the only exception was a small number of Chinese and Dutch ships. Despite all these restrictions, the Japanese economy grew, as agricultural production increased and the population grew. In this comparatively peaceful era, the samurai warrior class took on more administrative responsibilities.

Christianity had made some important inroads in Japan by 1580, with 150,000 Japanese Christian converts, but the government ended these missions and outlawed the religion. The government even went as far as to torture and execute the missionaries who did not leave, as well as the Japanese Christians who did not renounce their religion. Dutch merchants continued to be the principal source of information about Europe during this time, keeping the Japanese up-to-date with important scientific and technological developments.

SYSTEMS OF FORCED LABOR

Atlantic Slave Trade

The forced migration of over 15 million Africans to the New World was one of the most significant components of the Columbian Exchange. The spread of Islam established new trade routes across the northern part of the African continent, bringing African slaves to the Middle East as well. Slavery had existed in Africa since ancient times; tribes often took prisoners from neighboring tribes and enslaved them. Many African societies did not recognize private land ownership, so land did not equal wealth in the way that owning slaves did.

By the time Europeans ventured into sub-Saharan Africa, the slave trade had been well-established on the continent for 500 years. The Portuguese explored the west coast of Africa in the 1500s and began exporting slaves to plantations in Brazil. The slave trade had become transoceanic, and profits from it encouraged other European powers to enter the business.

By the mid-1600s, thousands of slaves were brought across the ocean each month. This trans-Atlantic journey, known as the Middle Passage, consisted of a four-to six-week trip belowdecks in overcrowded ships. The death toll en route was considerable, with as many as half the enslaved Africans on any one ship dying from disease or brutal mistreatment. Most African slaves were sent to Brazil or sugar plantations in the Caribbean. The **triangular trade** that developed sent European manufactured goods (firearms, in particular) to Africa in exchange for slaves, slaves to the Caribbean and American mainland, and American products back to Europe. Indeed, the Atlantic slave trade and the institution of slavery had an enormous impact on the economies of the Portuguese and Spanish colonies of South America as well as on the Dutch, French, and British colonies of the Caribbean and North America. The labor of enslaved Africans produced huge profits in the extraction of gold and silver from mines, as well as in the production of cash crops such as sugar, cotton, rice, and tobacco.

As more slaves were brought to the coast, African kingdoms reoriented their economies to trade with the Europeans. Some African societies benefited economically from the trade, but several experienced severe population loss and a drastic change in male-female ratio. Also, because many slaves were traded for guns, the addition of firearms led to an increase in violent political conflict in Africa. Though many of the enslaved Africans were Christianized by the Europeans, they retained parts of their language and culture. A unique cultural synthesis occurred, as African music, dress, and mannerisms mixed with Spanish and indigenous cultures in the Americas.

Encomienda System

The early Spanish settlers in the Caribbean needed to recruit a great deal of labor. The **encomienda** system established by the Spanish crown granted colonists the right to demand labor of native peoples in the mines and fields. The laborers were worked hard and punished severely.

Conquistadors like Hernán Cortés and Francisco Pizarro brought this system to the American mainland. On the *haciendas* (large estates), natives were often abused; as a result, Spanish officials replaced the *encomienda* system with the *repartimiento* system. *Repartimiento* compelled native communities to supply labor for Spanish mines and farms as *encomienda* had, but it limited work time and mandated that wages be paid to native workers. Many communities, however, were required to send large groups of laborers to work on state projects. In Peru, for instance, the labor system called *mita* mobilized thousands of natives to work in the silver mines. They were paid wages, but there were also many abuses. The *mita* system had disastrous impacts on the American Indian populations of Peru, as it drained them of able-bodied workers at a time when their communities were experiencing huge population losses due to epidemics of Old World diseases. It also led to American Indians fleeing their communities to avoid being compelled into service. With fewer workers able to work the fields, agricultural production decreased, leading to famine and malnutrition. The demise of these systems led to the establishment of the Atlantic slave trade, and widespread use of slave labor in the Americas.

Russian Serfdom

After the Mongol rule of Russia, many free peasants fell into great debt and were forced to become serfs on large estates; serfs were legally bound to the land they worked, with extensive obligations owed to their landlords. The Russian government encouraged this process beginning in the 1500s as a way to satisfy nobility and regulate peasants at the same time. As new territories were added to the empire, serfdom extended along with it.

In 1649, an act proclaimed that serfs were born into their status, with no mechanism by which they could become free. While serfs were not technically slaves, noble landowners had nearly unlimited control of them.

CULTURAL AND INTELLECTUAL CHANGES

European Renaissance

New ways of thinking about the nature of humanity and the world emerged in the early fifteenth century, beginning on the Italian peninsula. The Crusades brought southern Europe into contact with Arab culture, increasing international contact and trade. Scholars uncovered long-forgotten Roman and Greek literature that had been preserved and studied by Islamic scholars. This intellectual revival became known as the Renaissance, or rebirth, referring to the reemergence of ancient knowledge.

> ✔ **AP Expert Note**
>
> **Hallmarks of the Renaissance:**
>
> - A new view of man as a creative and rational being
> - A rediscovery of ancient Greco–Roman knowledge
> - Unparalleled accomplishments in literature, music, and art
> - A celebration of the human individual

Renaissance Italy was a patchwork of feudal domains, with lands belonging to the Roman Catholic Church, kingdoms, and city-states. Famous noble families such as the Medicis had grown wealthy as merchants, since Italy was ideally located for receiving goods from the Middle East and Asia along Mediterranean trade routes. This lucrative trade with the Islamic and Byzantine cultures allowed wealthy Italians to become patrons of painters, sculptors, and scientists. The period was also a celebration of the Roman past; classical architecture and engineering were reexamined and relearned.

Perhaps the single most important technological and cultural development of the Renaissance was the printing revolution. In 1456, Johann Gutenberg of Germany printed a complete edition of the Bible using the first **printing press** in the West (the Chinese had been using movable type for centuries). This printing revolution brought enormous changes to Europe. Printed books were less expensive and easier to read than copied manuscripts. The increase in the availability of books led to a rapid rise in literacy. European readers gained access to a wide range of knowledge on subjects including medicine, law, mathematics, and philosophy. Along with helping to spread classical knowledge and Renaissance ideas, these new printing presses helped fuel the religious upheaval that Europe experienced during the 1500s.

Protestant Reformation

Just as the Renaissance inspired an era of exploration, it also created an atmosphere that encouraged debate and criticism of the existing order. The most powerful institution of the day was the Catholic Church, headquartered in Rome. It had held great power over kings and peasants alike for centuries, and it had grown large, wealthy, and corrupt. Practices such as selling forgiveness and salvation began to offend even those in the priesthood.

A movement to reform the Church grew out of these concerns. In 1517, in the German domain of Wittenburg, an obscure priest named Martin Luther posted a list of issues that he believed the Church should address. The main issues raised by the **Protestant Reformation** were:

- Divisions within the papacy, in which more than one pope claimed authority
- Religious traditions and rituals that were not derived from the scriptures (such as purgatory, pilgrimages, and worship of the saints)
- Corrupt practices such as the sale of religious relics and indulgences (forgiveness)
- Mismanagement of Church finances
- Lack of piety in the priesthood

Martin Luther and his fellow reformers unleashed a storm of controversy that eventually split the Catholic Church and divided Europe. Luther was excommunicated from the Church but gained the sympathy of German princes who adhered to his version of Christianity. At the time, German lands were divided in hundreds of small kingdoms and ruled by the Holy Roman Emperor, in this case Charles V of Spain, a staunch Catholic. Many of the Northern German princes resented having to support both the Church and a non-German emperor. The German kingdoms became divided into two armed camps, Catholics siding with the Church and Protestants siding with Luther. The resulting conflict devastated German lands, but ended in a treaty (the Peace of Augsburg, 1555) that enabled each prince to decide which religion—Catholic or Lutheran—would be the religion of his domain. Most states in northern Germany chose Lutheranism, while the south remained largely Catholic.

The Protestant movement spread from central Europe to the Netherlands, Switzerland, France, and Denmark. The English King Henry VIII, once a strong supporter of the Catholic Church, fell away from the Church after a dispute with the pope regarding his marriage. With the help of Parliament he created the Church of England, of which the English monarch became the head.

Enlightenment

Two English political thinkers, Thomas Hobbes and John Locke, lived through the horrors of the English Civil War and came to strikingly different conclusions about human nature and the proper form of government, providing the philosophical foundation for the Enlightenment. Hobbes believed absolute monarchy was needed to keep order, while Locke believed in self-government. According to Locke, people possess natural rights to life, liberty, and property, and government's purpose is to protect these rights. If government fails at this job, Locke reasoned, the people had the right to overthrow it. This notion later inspired revolutionary thought in Europe and the Americas. Enlightenment thinkers were reformers, putting forth ideas like the following:

John Locke (England)
Natural rights of men to life, liberty, and property

Voltaire (France)
Freedom of speech, freedom of religion, separation of church and state

Montesquieu (France)
Separation of powers within government

> ✔ **AP Expert Note**
>
> Outcomes of the Protestant Reformation:
>
> - A redrawing of the religious map of Europe, with Protestants in the north and Catholics in the south
>
> - A decline in the power of the Roman Catholic Church
>
> - Further power struggles between the citizenry and monarchs; when radical Protestants in England took over Parliament, civil war erupted and the king was arrested and publicly beheaded
>
> - A series of wars that would pit Catholics and Protestants against each other for the next 200 years

This new emphasis on free thought led to the questioning of traditional authority. Both the Church and the monarchy were challenged, and the political radicalism of the Enlightenment caused great anxiety in the courts of Europe. Though it started in England, the Enlightenment was centered in

Paris, where it reached its peak in the mid-1700s. There, intellectuals called *philosophes* gathered to discuss politics and ideas. The *philosophes* believed that reason (one of their primary areas of interest, along with nature, happiness, progress, and liberty) could be applied to all aspects of life.

As a result of the Roman Catholic mission to China, Jesuits brought back Chinese knowledge to Europe. The Confucian civil service exams influenced European rulers, and the rational morality of Confucianism appealed to Enlightenment philosophers.

Scientific Revolution

The development of modern science and Enlightenment philosophical ideals had a tremendous impact on the development of the modern world and the modern mentality. Prior to 1500, scholars relied mostly on classical texts and the Bible to answer questions about the natural world. The **scientific revolution** began as scientists challenged conventional ideas and used observation to understand the structure and composition of the universe. The Polish cleric and astronomer Nicolaus Copernicus paved the way for modern astronomy when he put forth a heliocentric theory of the universe in 1543, contradicting the Church's belief in an Earth-centered universe. Building on this revolutionary discovery, the Italian scientist Galileo Galilei constructed his own telescope in 1609 and used it to develop new theories about the universe. His findings angered both Catholic and Protestant leaders because they challenged the teachings and authority of the Christian churches. In fact, Galileo was put on trial before the Inquisition and forced to read a signed confession in which he stated that his ideas were false.

The scientific revolution led to the development of the scientific method, a logic-based approach to testing hypotheses through observation and experimentation. Use of the scientific method led to significant advances in the fields of physics, biology, medicine, and chemistry, as well as to the development of the social sciences in the late nineteenth century.

Foundation of Sikhism

In the north of the Indian subcontinent, Guru Nanak (1469–1539) founded Sikhism around the the turn of the sixteenth century. Born to Hindu parents of the merchant caste, he is reputed by Sikh tradition to have traveled extensively. Nanak's declaration that "There is no Muslim, and there is no Hindu" captures the essence of Sikhism. An example of syncretism, it bridges Hinduism and Islam, incorporating beliefs from both while maintaining an anti-sectarian stance.

Sikhism would be led by a series of gurus, who would modify its practices. For example, priestesses would be allowed, divorce legalized, and both veils and *sati* banned. Initially a pacifistic faith, it would grow militant in response to violent prosecution under the Mughal empire from the mid-sixteenth century onward, culminating in the founding of the Sikh empire (1799–1849). However, Sikhism would maintain its focus on social justice.

THE ENVIRONMENT

Perhaps the most significant environmental event of this era was the European discovery of the Americas, and the resultant Columbian Exchange of people, goods, and diseases between the New and Old Worlds. Foods like the potato, introduced to Europe from the Americas, had a huge impact on food production and population increases. In the Americas, entire landscapes were stripped to build plantations that grew cash crops like sugarcane, coffee, and tobacco. As mentioned in chapter 3, these agricultural practices degraded the topsoil and reduced vegetative cover, which led to flooding and mudslides.

The raising of cattle and pigs dramatically changed the landscape as forests were cut to provide grazing land. The introduction of feral pigs to the New World may have contributed to the transmission of diseases in the North American regions initially explored by the Spanish. The introduction of horses to the Americas had a significant impact on some American Indian tribes as they adopted more nomadic lifestyles—for example, some tribes used horses to track and hunt the massive buffalo herds which grazed on the Great Plains.

An early awareness of resource conservation can be seen in the Tokugawa Shogunate's laws which restricted timbering operations and mandated that new trees be planted when old ones were cut, and in Louis XIV's forestry program intended to manage France's timber resources. Although these programs were economically motivated, the idea that a nation's natural resources be managed by the government would play an important role in the development of environmental management programs in the future.

Climatically, the **Little Ice Age**, a multi-century period of cooling in Earth's temperature, dramatically affected human society. Although no consensus has been reached on the precise timing of the Little Ice Age, the period is conventionally considered to have lasted from the sixteenth through the nineteenth centuries. As temperatures fell, growing seasons shortened and some types of crops, particularly grains in the north, failed completely.

CHAPTER 11

Period 5: 1750 to 1900 C.E. – Complete Time Period Review

REVOLUTIONS AND INDEPENDENCE MOVEMENTS

High-Yield

North America

From 1756 to 1763, the European powers fought the Seven Years' War. As it was fought on three continents—North America, Europe, and the Indian subcontinent—the Seven Years' War can be called the first global war. The North American theater became known as the French and Indian War. This is because the British and their colonists fought an alliance of the French and their American Indian allies. Globally, the war proved disastrous for the French. They lost both their Canadian territories in North America and their trade influence in India.

Britain, in debt due to this costly war, enacted a series of laws aimed at raising tax revenues from its North American colonies. The British government felt justified in levying these taxes, as they felt the war had been partially waged in the interest of the colonists. American colonists, however, resented being subject to taxes that had been enacted by a government in which they had no representation. The colonists railed against taxation without representation and increasingly wished to govern themselves. Tensions escalated. After the Boston Tea Party, the British government retaliated against Massachusetts by passing the Intolerable Acts, which essentially took away its ability to self-govern. This outraged the other American colonies and led to the formation of the First Continental Congress in 1774.

The Continental Congress organized and coordinated colonial resistance. In 1775, British troops and American militia clashed at Lexington, Massachusetts. On July 4, 1776, the Declaration of Independence—inspired by **Enlightenment** ideas—justified independence. It listed a long list of abuses by the British crown and declared that all men were created equal. Though the British forces possessed many advantages, such as a strong centralized government, stronger military, and colonial loyalists, they were ultimately at a disadvantage. This was due to the war being fought on American soil and to the foreign support the Americans received, most notably from France. In 1781, the **American Revolution** ended with the British surrender at Yorktown to George Washington.

> ✔ **AP Expert Note**
>
> **Be Able to Explain How Different Wars Interconnect**
>
> The American Revolution wasn't fought in isolation. You can trace its origin to the Seven Years' War. The foreign support offered to the Continental Congress served as a means for those nations to undermine their rival, Great Britain. The debt France built up aiding the United States would be a major contributing factor in the French Revolution and thus the subsequent Napoleonic Wars.

In 1783, the Peace of Paris formally recognized American independence. The colonies created a federal republic with 13 states and a written constitution that guaranteed freedom of speech and religion. In reality, however, there was no legal and political equality. Only white male property owners enjoyed full rights. The women, landless men, slaves, and indigenous people did not have access to this new freedom. Yet the U.S. Constitution was still an important step in the development of a republic responsible to its people through democratic means.

France

Unlike Americans, who sought independence from British colonial rule, French revolutionaries wanted to replace the existing monarchy and political structure—called the *Ancien Régime*—with a more democratic republic. In order to understand the **French Revolution**, it is important to first understand the social structure of Revolutionary-era France. Society was divided into three classes, or estates. The First Estate was the clergy; the Second Estate was the nobility; and the Third Estate was everyone else. This third class included the *bourgeoisie*, which is roughly equivalent to the modern-day middle class. As evidenced by the chart below, the clergy and nobility controlled nearly all the political power.

Estate	Political Leaders	Numbers	% of Population	% of Land Ownership	Taxes Paid
1st Estate	Roman Catholic Clergy	100,000	<1% of pop	10% of land	No taxes
2nd Estate	Nobility	400,000	2% of pop	20% of land	No taxes
3rd Estate	Peasants, townsfolk	24 million	98% of pop	70% of land	Extensive taxes

Revolutionary sentiment brewed among the Third Estate, inspired by to the nobles' refusal to pay taxes, *bourgeois* resentment of the monarchy's power, the incompetence of Louis XVI, entrenched poverty among the peasantry, grain shortages, and the success of the American Revolution.

The Estates General convened in May 1789, but a dispute over voting created an impasse. Traditionally, each estate met and voted separately. The result from each estate was weighted equally, meaning that the First and Second estates always outvoted the Third Estate two to one. This time, the Third

Estate wanted all the estates to meet as one body and votes to be counted per delegate head. After weeks of deadlock, the Third Estate, claiming to represent the interests of all French people, unilaterally declared themselves the National Assembly.

Spurred on by the peasants storming the Bastille, a fortress in Paris which symbolized the monarchy, the National Assembly began issuing reforms. These included ending the privileged status of nobles, abolishing feudalism, and issuing the landmark Declaration of the Rights of Man and of the Citizen. The latter, like the Declaration of Independence, reflected Enlightenment-era political ideals. In 1791, the Assembly produced a new constitution that replaced the absolute monarchy with a limited monarchy. However, these reforms were both not enough for French radicals and too much for conservative monarchists. Backed by Paris crowds, the radicals took control of the Assembly and eventually beheaded the king.

The Committee for Public Safety, formed by the extremist Jacobins and led by Maximilien Robes-pierre, now governed France. It instigated a radical "Reign of Terror," executing many aristocrats. Eventually, the Jacobins were deposed, and Napoleon Bonaparte took advantage of the ensuing power vacuum by naming himself First Consul, then Consul for Life, and finally Emperor. In 1804, Napoleon issued his Civil Code, which affirmed the political and legal equality of all adult men, established a merit-based society, and protected private property. However, it also limited free speech and allowed censorship of the newspapers.

Napoleon and his army rapidly defeated many of the European powers and took control of much of the continent. The Napoleonic era lasted from 1803 to 1814, as warfare ranged from Europe to North Africa and the Middle East. At times, France found itself faced with multiple enemies. Taking on Russia in 1812 proved fatal, however, as the army did not survive the winter campaign. A "White Terror" ensued in France, so called because white was associated with royalists, as the restored monarchy of Louis XVIII imprisoned or killed many associated with Napoleon and the republic. The powers which had defeated Napoleon met at the Congress of Vienna in 1815 to set the terms for a new global balance of power.

The downfall of Napoleonic France left the British Empire as the most powerful state in the international system. From 1815 until the outbreak of World War I in 1914, the *Pax Britannica* period saw British power and influence spread to almost every corner of the globe. Only the Russian Empire rivaled it, and then only in regional terms. This led to conflicts such as the Crimean War and the "Great Game" in Central Asia, and later the Anglo-Japanese Alliance (1902–1923) to contain Russian influence.

Haiti

By the end of the eighteenth century, the Caribbean island of Hispaniola had become a major center of sugar production. The Spanish controlled the east (Santo Domingo), and the French controlled the west (Saint-Domingue). One of the richest of all the European colonies, Saint-Domingue's population consisted of three groups. There were 40,000 white French settlers, 30,000 *gens de couleur* (free people of color) of interracial ancestry, and 500,000 black slaves, most of whom had been born in Africa. These slaves worked under brutal conditions, and the mortality rate was high. Some slaves escaped and formed independent communities in remote areas. These peoples were known as **maroons**. In some cases, maroons directly assisted slave resistance movements.

When the French Revolution began in 1789, the white settlers sought the right to govern themselves, but opposed extending political and legal equality to the *gens de couleur* and slaves. The National Assembly objected to the exclusion of both groups, and only allowed the island's whites a third of the seats they sought on the basis of the colony's entire population. The Declaration of the Rights of Man undermined the island's racial hierarchy with its first article: *"Men are born and remain free and equal in rights."* Both the *gens de couleur* and slaves drew inspiration from that statement.

A slave revolt occurred in August of 1791. As a result, the whites, *gens de couleurs*, and slaves battled each other in a see-sawing multi-sided **Haitian Revolution**. French troops—and later, British and Spanish troops—invaded the island in hopes of gaining control. The slaves, however, were led by Toussaint L'Ouverture, a black military leader who built a strong and disciplined army, and, by 1797, controlled most of Saint-Domingue.

In 1803, independence was declared. By 1804, Haiti was the second independent republic in the Western Hemisphere, and the first republic that abolished slavery. However, great economic difficulty followed independence. Many nations, such as the United States, refused to recognize or conduct trade with Haiti due to its emancipation of slaves. Haiti was at a further disadvantage, as the new nation of small farmers was not as economically productive as the former large-scale plantations.

Latin America

In Latin America, the colonies controlled by the Spanish and Portuguese were comprised of a governing class of 30,000 *peninsulares* (Spanish-born Spaniards living in the New World colonies), 3.5 million Creoles (New World-born people of European descent), and 10 million less-privileged classes including black slaves, indigenous people, and those of interracial backgrounds known as mulattoes. The Roman Catholic Church also formed a major social and political force in these colonies.

Napoleon's 1807 invasion of Spain and Portugal weakened the authority of those countries in their respective colonies. By 1810, revolts had occurred in Argentina, Venezuela, and Mexico. A crucial document in the history of **Latin American independence movements** is the Jamaica Letter. Written by the Creole leader and revolutionary Simón Bolívar, it expressed his views on the independence movement in his native Venezuela and on the need for a union of the former Spanish colonies. Like the Declaration of Independence and the Declaration of the Rights of Man and of the Citizen, the Jamaica Letter is firmly rooted in Enlightenment political ideals.

In Mexico, Father Miguel de Hildalgo led a peasant rebellion, but conservative Creole forces gained control of the movement. Simón Bolívar led revolts in South America and by 1824 deposed the Spanish armies. His goal was to establish a United States of Latin America, called Gran Colombia, but it did not last. The Portuguese royal family had fled to Brazil after Napoleon's 1807 invasion. When the king returned in 1821, he left his son, Pedro, to rule as regent. Pedro agreed to the demands of Creoles and declared Brazil independent.

As a result of these independence movements, the Creoles became the dominant class, and many *peninsulares* returned to Europe. Latin American society remained economically and racially stratified. Slavery continued. The wealth and power of the Roman Catholic Church persisted. Overall, the lower classes continued to be repressed.

NATIONALISM AND THE NATION-STATE

During the nineteenth century, people came to identify themselves as part of a community called a nation. The forces that drew these people together were their common language, customs, cultural traditions, values, historical experiences, ethnicity, and sometimes religion. **Nationalism** was often a reaction against foreign rule, as mass politics resulted in the people of a country defining themselves in contrast to their ruling elite. In 1815, the Congress of Vienna sought to stifle nationalist movements in Italy and Germany that had been inspired by the ideas of the French Revolution.

The Revolutions of 1848

Sometimes called the Springtime of the Peoples, the Revolutions of 1848 saw a series of uprisings throughout Europe. Reformers were dissatisfied with rising industrialization and with the conservative consensus that had dominated Europe since the Congress of Vienna. In Italy, Germany, and the Hapsburg Empire, they sought to unify their scattered countrymen under national banners. They also shared the goals of revolutionaries elsewhere in Europe of seeking democratic reforms. The revolutions, however, failed. Rather than reform, many governments increased repression. Many ex-revolutionaries fled to places like the United States, where they would work as activists in their new homelands. For example, one-tenth of the Union Army in the American Civil War consisted of German-born immigrants politically opposed to slavery.

Unification of Italy and Germany

On the Italian peninsula, the Roman Catholic Church still exerted great influence and discouraged the growth of Italian nationalism. The pope himself personally held large estates in central Italy. Under the leadership of Garibaldi in the south, young men pushed for an Italian nation, fighting a military campaign to unite the people behind this idea. In the north, Count Camillo Benso di Cavour, the prime minister to King Victor Emmanuel II of Sardinia, aligned with France and expelled Austria from northern Italy. In 1871, the Kingdom of Italy was proclaimed, and Sardinia's king was chosen as its ruler.

Farther north, the Kingdom of Prussia became more powerful after the defeat of Napoleon. The chancellor of Prussia, Otto von Bismarck, envisioned a united Germany. So, he engineered a series of conflicts with Denmark and Austria to consolidate the territory required. Bismarck eventually manipulated France into declaring war on Prussia, and used this conflict as a pretext for gathering then-separate German domains together to fight as one. The Franco-Prussian War (1870–1871) was a resounding victory for Prussia, and Bismarck proclaimed the birth of the German nation. He did so in the French palace at Versailles, further humiliating France by taking the territory of Alsace-Lorraine on the Franco-German border. The latter would be an important factor in the outbreak of hostilities between France and Germany in World War I.

The birth of a unified Germany caused a significant shift in the balance of power in Europe. France was in decline, and Germany now rivaled Great Britain as an industrial producer and leader in technology. German military strength and diplomacy contributed to its position in Europe.

The new German nation was in many ways deeply conservative in its politics. Bismarck, however, supported a series of reforms that robbed domestic left-wing opponents of causes that might galvanize larger movements. He established state pensions and public health insurance plans that protected the social welfare of the masses.

Zionism

The existence of minority groups conflicted with the nationalist concept of a singular ethnic and religious identity. One such group was the Jewish people. They lived as a minority in many European nations as a result of the Jewish diaspora—the cultural and physical dispersion of Jews since the time of the Roman Empire. Antisemitism increased over the nineteenth century, as burgeoning nationalist identities strengthened traditional prejudice toward Jews and Judaism. In reaction to this antisemitism, the Zionist movement arose. Like other nationalist movements, it sought to establish a state for one people, in this case for the Jews. A Jewish reporter, Theodor Herzl, launched the movement in 1897. Zionism successfully created the independent state of Israel in 1948.

Latin America

By the 1830s, most of Latin America was made up of independent nations, which had been established by revolutions against their respective colonial governments. These new nations faced many problems, such as economies that had been disrupted by many years of warfare and large armies loyal to regional commanders (*caudillos*) instead of to the new national governments. Additionally, the role of the Catholic Church remained strong. Few questioned its doctrines, but many wanted to limit its role in civil life. In Mexico, for example, politics was a struggle between conservatives and liberals, and instability and financial difficulty made it a target for foreign intervention by the United States and Europe.

INDUSTRIALIZATION

`High-Yield`

Scientific discoveries and technological advancements led to the rise of modern industry in the eighteenth and nineteenth centuries. The following factors made rapid industrialization possible:

- Increased agricultural production, to support a large workforce
- Possession of natural resources like coal and iron ore
- Investment capital (money) to build factories

- A stable government that protected private property

- Technical knowledge and communication of discoveries

- Control of sea ports, rivers, and canals

The Industrial Revolution would affect human labor, consumption, family structure, and much more. Major economic and social changes that occurred in industrialized nations were:

Domestic Effects	Global Impact
Growth of urban centers	Widened gap between industrial and non-industrial nations
Creation of middle class of merchants and factory owners	Competition for colonial territory to secure natural resources
Unsafe, harsh conditions in factories	Greater economic power in Europe
Loss of traditional artisan guilds	The Revolutions of 1848
Rising standard of living	World trade increased

Preconditions for Industrialization

England was the first modern industrial economy for several reasons:

- **Geography**—England's position in the Atlantic Ocean gave it access to raw materials from around the globe as well as sea access to markets for its manufactured goods.

- **Natural resources**—Rivers, coal, and iron ore were plentiful. They provided energy to power factories and other manufacturing.

- **Labor force**—Its growing population surpassed the amount of labor needed for agricultural production, thus providing surplus workers for industrial jobs.

- **Capital**—A business class existed which had grown wealthy through commerce, especially from the transatlantic slave trade, and was able to reinvest its profits in industry.

Other nations were close behind Great Britain in developing industrial capability. The United States and Germany both surpassed Britain in terms of steel production by 1900, while Russia, Japan, and the Ottoman Empire followed behind. Spain and the rest of continental Europe were largely excluded from industrialization during this period.

An Agricultural Revolution

Though it is counterintuitive, the Industrial Revolution was partially made possible by agricultural advances. The Dutch began this process by erecting earthen walls to reclaim land from the sea and using fertilizer from livestock to renew soil nutrients. In the 1700s, British farmers began experimenting with crop rotation, and Jethro Tull invented a mechanical seed drill that sped up the planting process. Farmers began to share their knowledge and techniques through farm journals. This resulted in higher agricultural output, which in turn created the population growth so key to maintaining an industrial labor force.

Technology

Technological development was the driving force of industrialization. For example, hydropower was used to make mills more efficient. A major advancement was the steam engine, which would become the foundation of this new mechanical age. Coal was vital in the production of iron, which was used to construct machinery and steam engines. New methods for producing iron resulted in a better product produced at lower costs. Iron was a vital material during the Industrial Revolution, especially in railroad construction. Cars, ships, and factories were both products and tools of further industrialization. A second industrial revolution in steel, chemicals, and electricity transformed society in the late nineteenth century. These advancements led to innovations in scientific fields such as engineering and medicine.

Financial Institutions

New financial systems also developed to support the new industrial production. More complex corporate structures, stock markets, and insurance enabled businessmen to raise the capital they needed to begin or expand production as well as to protect their investments from loss. Large businesses often had a global reach. Transnational corporations such as the United Fruit Company had operations that affected lives in North, Central, and South America. The ideals of laissez-faire capitalism that **Adam Smith** had proposed became the inspiration for these changes.

Impact on Gender, Family, and Social Structures

Industrialization greatly affected gender roles and families. It also radically altered the traditional social structures of the day. The family, which previously had been a self-sufficient economic unit, moved economic production outside the home. Working-class women and children entered the industrial workforce as low-paid factory laborers.

A sharp distinction now existed between family life and work life. The status of men increased because industrial work and the wage were considered more important than domestic work, which was largely performed by women. Middle-class values became distinct from those of the industrial working class, which were stereotyped as promiscuous, alcohol-abusing, and immoral. Middle-class women generally did not work outside the home, but instead were pressured to conform to the new models of behavior often referred to as the "cult of domesticity"—the glorification of women as the center of the well-kept home.

The Factory System

The Industrial Revolution led to the establishment of the **factory system** in which factories employed large numbers of workers and power-driven machines to mass-produce goods. In the late 1800s, manufacturers sought to increase productivity and profits by designing products with interchangeable parts: identical components that could be used in place of each other. This process simplified assembly, but also made factory work tedious and repetitive. Factory work was also dangerous and had a negative impact on the health of laborers, both from environmental factors such as dust and chemicals and from accidents with machinery.

Global Effects of Industrialization

As a result of industrialization, a new **global division of labor** emerged. Industrial societies needed raw materials from other lands and there was a large demand for materials such as raw cotton from India and Egypt, and rubber from Brazil and the Congo. Latin America, sub-Saharan Africa, South Asia, and Southeast Asia became dependent on exporting cash crop products to the industrialized nations, but established little or no industrialization themselves. Most of the profits from these cash crops went abroad, and wealth was concentrated among the owners and investors in these corporations.

The dependency theory explains the uneven result of development as the result of **imperialism** by industrial nations. In short, the industrialization of some areas was achieved at the expense of others. Cash crop and colonial economies reinforced dependency on American and European manufactured goods.

Advances in Transportation and Communication

During the First Industrial Revolution (approximately 1760–1820), the development of the steam engine led to creation of steamships and steam-powered locomotives, which rapidly sped up transportation. The creation of canals enabled heavy loads to be transported long distances and linked previously separate waterways. The development of the telegraph revolutionized the speed at which businesses, people, and armies could communicate.

During the **Second Industrial Revolution** (1870–1914), the development of the internal combustion engine transformed how machines operated and initiated the rise of oil as a global commodity. It also saw the beginning of widespread electrification. Economic inequality within industrialized countries, spurred on by the growth of industries like steel and **railroads**, led to a sharp increase in socialist parties and unions.

REACTIONS TO INDUSTRIALIZATION

As the nineteenth century progressed, the ideals of reason and egalitarianism from the Enlightenment inspired many political movements. Some were revolutionary, while others were liberal or reformist. As the Industrial Revolution redefined both society and the economy, new tensions arose.

Socialism and Communism

The appalling conditions experienced by industrial workers in the 1800s inspired revolutionary reformers. Under the broad title of **socialism**, these movements critiqued capitalism and suggested instead an economy that was run by the *proletariat*, which is equivalent to the modern-day working class. **Communism**, which advocated an extreme form of socialism, sought to create self-sufficient communities in which property was owned in common. One of the most prominent socialist thinkers was Karl Marx, who, along with Friedrich Engels, wrote *The Communist Manifesto* in 1848. Marx and Engels advocated the overthrow of the moneyed classes which would be followed by a "workers' state."

The most notable expression of socialism in the eighteenth century was the Paris Commune, a revolutionary socialist government that ruled the city of Paris following the collapse of the French Empire in the Franco-Prussian War. It existed from March 18 to May 28 in 1871, and enacted a number of anti-clerical and pro-labor laws. The Paris Commune inspired many later socialist and communist revolutionaries, like Lenin, and it also popularized the use of the red flag as a left-wing symbol. The French Army overthrew the Commune, killing approximately 20,000 revolutionaries in the process of retaking Paris.

Unionism

The union movement advocated the organization of workers so that they could negotiate with their employers for better wages and working conditions. This led to extreme tensions and considerable bloodshed: factory owners fought to stop workers from banding together, and workers struggled to remain unified against violent oppression. As a left-wing movement, unionism was often accused of being socialistic. The lines sometimes became blurred, due to overlapping concerns about the industrialized economy and the well-being of the working class.

Liberalism

One response to industrialization was the rise of **liberalism**, which resulted from the rapid growth of the middle class. With philosophical roots in the Enlightenment, liberals wanted written constitutions based on separation of powers. They were opposed to monarchies and proponents of natural rights. Having greatly benefited from the new capitalist, industrial economy, liberals were staunch supporters of these laissez-faire economic ideas and lukewarm to unionism and socialism.

✔ **AP Expert Note**

Be Sure to Know the Definitions of Political Terms

Source documents on the AP exam will reference terms that might be unfamiliar to you or possess a different meaning from what you might expect. For example, *liberalism* in the classical sense differs from the modern-day American usage. It put a major emphasis on laissez-faire economics. Political terms can gain different nuance depending on the time period, or outright change definition. Take note of the publication date on AP source documents!

REFORM

The traditionalist nations of the Ottomans, Russia, China, and Japan were all forced to confront modernization and the social issues accompanying it during this period. Conservative forces resisted these dramatic reforms to varying degrees of success.

Ottoman Empire

By the 1700s, the once-legendary Ottoman armies had fallen behind those of Europe. As the empire's military weakened, its political power weakened too. The Ottomans suffered from economic problems, further undermining their position. In addition, nationalist revolts in the Balkans and Greece contributed to the empire's problems.

The Ottomans also experienced economic decline. Europe circumvented them and began to trade directly with India and China. Also, global trade shifted to the Atlantic Ocean, where the Ottomans had no involvement. European products flowed into the empire, and it began to depend heavily on foreign loans. Europeans were even given capitulations (special rights and privileges), such as being subject to only their own laws, not to those of the Ottomans. All of this was a great blow to the empire's prestige and sovereignty.

The empire did attempt to reform itself, beginning with the rule of Mahmud II. He organized a more effective army and a system of secondary education. The Ottomans built new roads, laid telegraph lines, and created a postal service. These reforms continued into the **Tanzimat** ("Reorganization" in Ottoman Turkish) **Movement** from 1839 to 1879, when the government used the French legal system as a guide to reform its own laws. Public trials were instituted.

However, these reforms were met with great opposition, particularly from religious conservatives and the Ottoman bureaucracy. Many saw the concept of civil liberties as a foreign one, a kind of soft imperialism in its spread through Ottoman society. The new sultan, Abdul Hamid II, adopted the first Ottoman constitution in 1876 but suspended it in 1879 and reinstituted absolute monarchy.

The Young Turks, a group of exiled Ottoman subjects, pushed for universal male suffrage, equality before the law, and the emancipation of women and non-Turkish ethnic groups. In 1908, they led a coup that overthrew Abdul Hamid II and set up a "puppet" sultan that they controlled. Though the Ottoman Empire attempted to reform, it was still in a delicate state by 1914. Ultimately, it dissolved in the aftermath of World War I, with large portions colonized by the British and French Empires or ruled by their local allies.

Russia

Much like the Ottoman Empire, the Russian Empire was autocratic, multiethnic, and multilingual. Russian czars were supported by both the Russian Orthodox Church and the noble class, which owned most of the land. The peasants were the majority of the population, but the feudal institution of serfdom essentially enslaved them. Even at the end of the nineteenth century, the country's literacy rate was below 20 percent, far beneath other European nations. Unlike the Ottomans, who were losing territory, the Russian Empire vastly expanded—east to the Pacific, south into the Caucasus and Central Asia, and southwest to the Mediterranean. Its military power and strength could not compete with that of Europe, however, as demonstrated in its defeat in the Crimean War in 1856.

The loss to the Franco-British-Ottoman alliance in the Crimean War (1853–1856) highlighted the comparative weakness of Russia's military and economy, pushing the government to modernize. A first step was the emancipation of the serfs by Czar Alexander II in 1861. He also created district assemblies (*zemstvos*) in 1864, in which all classes had elected representatives. The government also encouraged industrialization. Policies designed to stimulate economic development were issued, such as the construction of the Trans-Siberian Railroad and the remodeling of the state bank.

Anti-government protests increased through the involvement of the university students and intellectuals known as the *intelligentsia*. The more these groups were repressed by the government, the more radical they became. A member of the revolutionary "People's Will" group, which was organized in 1879 and employed terrorism in their attempt to overthrow Russia's czarist autocracy, assassinated Czar Alexander II in 1881, bringing an end to government reform. The new czars used repression—not gradual political reform—to maintain power.

Fast-paced, government-sponsored industrialization led to many peasant rebellions and industrial worker strikes. As a response, in 1897 the government limited the maximum workday to 11.5 hours, though it also prohibited trade unions and outlawed strikes. Czar Nicholas II, in an attempt to deflect attention from the growing opposition, focused on expansion through the Russo-Japanese War in 1904, but the Russians suffered an embarrassing defeat. This loss also sparked an uprising.

In January 1905, a group of workers marched to the Czar's Winter Palace to petition. They were killed by government troops. The Bloody Sunday massacre set off anger and rebellion across the empire, which as a whole was known as the Revolution of 1905. The government made concessions by creating a legislative body called the Duma, but, in reality, not much changed in Russia until the upheavals of World War I.

China

The Chinese, like the Ottomans and Russians, were forced to confront their own issues of reform and reaction in the nineteenth century. The Qing dynasty had grown increasingly ineffective as rulers. New World crops, like sweet potatoes and corn, brought about a rapid population increase. During the Qing dynasty, it is estimated that the Chinese population quadrupled to 420,000,000. This increase created great strains on the nation. Famines were increasingly common, provoking a series of rebellions which further weakened the Qing dynasty.

The Chinese military also stagnated from the mid-seventeenth century onward, as the evolution of gunpowder weapons finally ended the threat of horse-riding steppe nomads that had troubled China for millennia. The last nomadic confederation to threaten China, the Dzungar Khanate in what is the modern-day Chinese region of Xinjiang, lost a series of conflicts with the Qing dynasty. These conflicts culminated in organized genocide, as approximately eighty percent of the Dzungar people were killed under the orders of the Qing emperor and ethnic Chinese people were settled on their former lands. Without neighboring threats, China had no reason to keep pace with the military technology of the European empires, and its army lacked battlefield experience.

With its vast population and resources, China was self-sufficient and, along with its rejection of foreign influence, felt it required nothing that the outsiders produced. However, Europeans, Britain in particular, sought trade with China to acquire silks, lacquerware, and tea, the latter of which was increasing in popularity in their homelands. British merchants paid in silver bullion for Chinese goods. The amount of bullion a nation or company owned determined its wealth and its strength (mercantilism). This silver drain from Britain inspired its merchants to find something the Chinese wanted other than bullion. They found it in opium, an addictive narcotic made from the poppy plant. Despite the emperor declaring the opium trade illegal, British merchants smuggled it into the country. Chinese merchants agreed to pay for opium in silver, which the British merchants used to buy Chinese goods, making a profit on both ends of this drug trafficking. This reversed the silver drain from Britain to China but also created a large number of Chinese opium addicts.

The **First Opium War** (1839–1842) broke out over a customs dispute, but resentment over British drug trafficking played a major role as well. China suffered a major defeat, and a series of unequal treaties gave Britain and other European nations commercial entry into China. For example, Hong Kong was ceded to the British in 1841, and control over it was only transferred back to China in 1997. This began a period of Chinese history referred to as the Century of Humiliation.

The **Second Opium War** (1856–1860) resulted from the Western European desire to further weaken Chinese sovereignty over trade, to legalize the opium trade, and to expand the export of indentured workers whose situations closely resembled slavery. In October 1860, a Franco-British expeditionary force looted and burned Beijing's Old Summer Palace. British and French museums still feature its stolen art, and the palace ruins are an important landmark for China. Shock over the defeat led to the Qing's **Self-Strengthening Movement**. Drug use also became even more rampant thanks to opium flooding the country.

Uprisings such as the **Taiping Rebellion** (1850–1864) placed further stress on China. An obscure scholar named Hong Xiuquan, who believed he was the brother of Jesus Christ, founded an offshoot of Christianity. A social reform movement grew from this in the 1850s, which the government suppressed. Hong established the Taiping Tianguo (Taiping Heavenly Kingdom), and his followers created an army that, within two years of fighting, controlled a large territory in central China. Nationalism influenced this rebellion, as the majority Han ethnic group resented rule by the minority Manchus, who had conquered the native Ming dynasty but now seemed powerless against European imperialism.

Internal disputes within the Taipings finally allowed the Qing dynasty to defeat them, but it was a long struggle that exhausted the imperial treasury. Between twenty and thirty million people died in the Taiping Rebellion, making it the bloodiest civil war in history. It did, however, lead to greater inclusion of Han Chinese in the Qing dynasty's government. Both Sun Yat-sen and Mao Zedong viewed Hong Xiuquan as a spiritual predecessor, for both his anti-Manchu and his anti-imperialist stances.

The Qing did implement limited reforms. With government-sponsored grants in the 1860s and 1870s, local leaders promoted military and economic reform in China using the slogan: *"Chinese learning at the base, Western learning for use."* These leaders built modern shipyards, railroads, and weapon industries, and they founded academies for the study of science. It was a solid foundation, but the Self-Strengthening Movement brought only minimal change. It also experienced resistance from the imperial government.

The Qing's last major reform effort took place in 1898. It was known as the Hundred Days' Reform. This ambitious movement reinterpreted Confucian thought to justify radical changes to the system, with the intent to remake China into a powerful modern industrial society. The Emperor Guangzu instituted a program to change China into a constitutional monarchy, guarantee civil liberties, and build a modern education system. These proposed changes were strongly resisted by conservative officials. Particularly upset was the Empress Dowager Cixi, who cancelled the reforms and imprisoned the emperor in a coup. With that, Qing China's chance for a reformed society ended.

Another rebellion further complicated issues in China. The anti-foreign **Boxer Rebellion** (1899–1901) sought to rid China of foreigners and foreign influence. Empress Cixi supported the movement, hoping to eliminate all foreign influence. A multinational force from countries such as the United States, Russia, and Japan, however, handily defeated the Boxers and forced China to pay a large indemnity in silver for the damages. Now, Cixi belatedly supported modest reforms: the New Policies, also known as the Late Qing Reforms. In Qing China's weakened state, some provinces adopted them, others did not.

Amid all of these rebellions and attempts at reform, a revolutionary movement was slowly emerging. It was composed of young men and women who had traveled outside China—who had seen the new liberalism and modernization of both the West and Japan. They hoped to import those ideas. Cells were organized in Guangzhou and overseas in Tokyo and Honolulu, where plots to overthrow the Qing were developed.

Under the leadership of Sun Yat-sen (Sun Zhong-shan), after many attempted unsuccessful uprisings, the Qing were forced to abdicate in 1911 and the Republic of China was proclaimed. Sun dreamed of a progressive and democratic China based on his Three Principles of the People: nationalism, democracy, and socialism. His goal would never be achieved due to civil war and the Warlord Era.

Japan—The Meiji Restoration

In its radical response to the challenges of reform and reaction, Japan emerged from this period as a world power. Even as it continued to selectively isolate itself from the rest of world, it was changing from a feudal to a commercial economy.

The Japanese knew of China's humiliation at the hands of the British in the mid-1800s. After the California Gold Rush of 1849, the United States became more interested in Pacific commerce, sending a mission to conclude a trade agreement with Japan. Commodore Matthew Perry, in an example of gunboat diplomacy, arrived in Edo (Tokyo) Bay in 1853 with a modern fleet of armed steamships. For the Japanese, who had restricted its trade from much of the world for over two centuries, this was a troubling sight. Contact with Americans caused tense debate within the ruling Tokugawa Shogunate and the samurai class.

Two clans in the south—Satsuma and Choshu—supported a new policy to "revere the emperor and repel the barbarians." This was a veiled critique of the shogun in Edo, as they perceived his inability to ward off the Western "barbarians" as embarrassing. A younger generation of reform-minded samurai far from Edo made bold plans to undermine the *bakufu* (the military government led by the shogun). These "men of spirit" banded together to overthrow the shogun, restore the emperor, and advance the idea of Japanese modernization.

The rebels armed themselves with guns from the West, and a civil war broke out in 1866. When the anti-government forces demonstrated their military superiority, the momentum began to shift in favor of the rebels. The overthrow of the Tokugawa Shogunate was complete in 1868, when the victorious reformers pronounced that they had restored the emperor to his throne. His title was **Meiji**, or Enlightened One. The nation rallied around the 16-year-old emperor, and plans were made to move the imperial "presence" to the renamed capital of Tokyo (Eastern Capital).

This transition in Japanese history can be seen as both a restoration and a revolution. While the emperor was nominally restored to authority, real power was held in the hands of nobles. A national legislature called the Diet was established, but the aristocratic upper house was in primary control. They reformed Japan in radical ways. Compulsory public schools were introduced. The feudal system was abolished, and the ownership of weapons was no longer restricted to the samurai class.

Some samurai were displeased not just with the loss of their privileges, but with the mass adoption of "barbarian" ways by Japan. The resulting Satsuma Rebellion (1877) saw traditionalist samurai launch a brief civil war. Both sides fought with modern weapons, however. In the end, the government's army of peasant conscripts defeated the rebels.

The rapidity of the industrialization and modernization of Japan impressed the rest of the world. This development was driven, in part, by the *zaibatsu* ("financial cliques"), which were family-owned business conglomerates that dominated the economy. Within the first generation of the Meiji period, Japan had built a modern infrastructure and military, had defeated the Chinese and Russians in war, and had begun building an empire in the Pacific. The rise of Japan as an imperial power altered the global balance of power as the twentieth century began.

COMPARATIVE CLOSE-UP: REFORM AND REACTION IN THE NINETEENTH CENTURY			
	Political	**Economic**	**Social**
Ottoman Empire	Institutes French legal code (equality before the law, public trials) but reforms see major opposition. Empire collapses after World War I.	As trade shifts to the Atlantic Ocean, it becomes heavily reliant on loans from Europe.	Young Turks push for greater centralization, universal male suffrage, emancipation of women.
Russia	*Zemstvos* (local assemblies) are created. Duma established after Revolution of 1905, but is subject to whim of czar. Monarchy overthrown in 1917.	Government sponsors industrialization projects such as the Trans-Siberian Railroad. Unions and strikes banned by law.	Emancipates the serfs in 1861. Students and intelligentsia spread ideas of change in the countryside.
China	Hundred Days of Reform attempts to create constitutional monarchy, but is halted by Empress Cixi. Rebellions like the Taiping and Boxer weaken the empire. Qing dynasty overthrown in 1911.	After the Opium Wars, European powers gain economic and territorial concessions under the Unequal Treaties and divide China into spheres of influence.	Peasant-led Taiping Rebellion attempts to create a more egalitarian society, but is eventually defeated.
Japan	Tokugawa Shogunate is overthrown by samurai and other elites. The emperor is restored to power. A legislative body, the Diet, is formed.	Government sponsors massive industrialization and trade. Japan rises to economic prominence.	Samurai class loses power, but some transition to roles in industrial leadership. New industrial working class develops.

IMPERIALISM AND ITS IMPACT

At the turn of the twentieth century, large portions of Africa and Asia had been absorbed into foreign empires. The Belgians, British, French, German, Italians, Portuguese, and Spanish, along with the United States and Japan, were enthusiastic empire builders. Every nation in Africa except for Ethiopia and Liberia would be colonized by 1900. China would be carved into spheres of influence, Korea would be conquered by Japan, and the United States would take over the Philippines. What explains this desire for an empire? Economic, political, and cultural factors motivated it.

Economically, overseas colonies served as sources of raw materials and as markets for manufactured goods. These colonies were strategic sites with harbors and resupply stations for naval ships, commercial and military. Politically, colonial expansion spurred nationalist sentiment at home, as citizens took pride in military conquest. Lopsided wars against native peoples and second-tier powers were often justified with sensationalist journalism about supposed crimes committed in those foreign countries against Europeans, often missionaries or women.

Culturally, the motivation and justification for imperialism arose in part from the concept of **Social Darwinism**, which attempted to apply the principles of Darwinian evolution to societies and politics. According to proponents of this theory, societies either prospered or failed because, as is the case in nature, only the strong survive as they are able to dominate the weak. Therefore, the imperial powers must be better than those in Asia and Africa and had the right to impose their economic and political will on them.

The theory of scientific racism developed during this period of imperialism to explain differences between nations. These theorists assumed that humans consisted of several distinct racial groups and that European racial groups were intellectually and morally superior. These ideas were often used as justification for the exploitative and cruel treatment of colonial peoples.

James Bruce, the Eighth Earl of Elgin, who fought in the Second Opium War and ordered the looting and burning of the Summer Palace, and later served as Viceroy of India in the British Raj, wrote about the peoples he encountered. His journals were published in the 1872, and reflect the racism that underlined imperialism: *"It is a terrible business, however, this living among inferior races. . . . one moves among them with perfect indifference, treating them, not as dogs, because in that case one would whistle to them and pat them, but as machines with which one can have no communion or sympathy."*

Additionally, missionaries hoped to convert Asians and Africans to Christianity. While many missionaries served as protectors of native peoples, some saw their mission as one of bringing civilization to the uncivilized. The poem "The White Man's Burden" by Rudyard Kipling, written in 1899, illustrates this mindset well. Below is an excerpt:

Take up the White Man's burden—
Send forth the best ye breed—
Go bind your sons to exile
To serve your captives' need;
To wait in heavy harness,
On fluttered folk and wild—
Your new-caught, sullen peoples,
Half-devil and half-child.

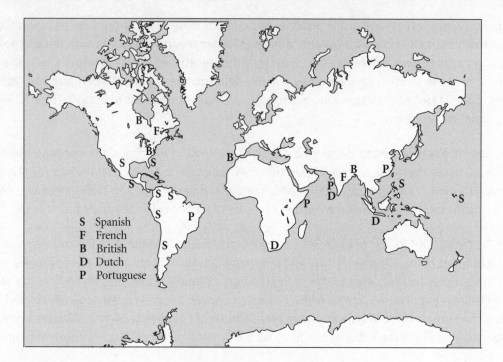

European Imperialism

India

England's involvement in India began strictly as a business venture. Founded in 1600, the British East India Company enjoyed a monopoly on English trade with India, and increasingly took advantage of the Mughal Empire's growing weakness. Expanding its trading posts, the Company petitioned the British government to outright conquer areas important to its trade in order to protect its interests. It enforced its rule with a combination of British troops and Indian troops, known as **sepoys**.

In the subcontinent's Punjab region, which overlaps modern-day eastern Pakistan and northern India, the previously pacifistic Sikhs grew militant due to persecution under the Mughal Empire. While only seven percent of the Punjab's population, the Sikh message of religious tolerance and social justice attracted many supporters from other faiths. This eventually led to the founding of the Sikh Empire (1799–1849).

Following the collapse of the Mughals, the Sikh Empire was the last rival power on the subcontinent to the British East India Company. The British sought greater control over Central Asia as part of their "Great Game" with the Russian Empire; they also saw the non-sectarian Sikhs as a potential threat to their control over the rest of India. Sepoys were often used to police areas of the Indian subcontinent that clashed with their own ethnic or religious identity. The British Empire did this to play different native groups against each other, ensuring that they stayed in overall control. Following two Anglo-Sikh wars, the British conquered the Sikhs, cementing imperial control over India.

In 1857, the sepoys mutinied after they received rifles with cartridges rumored to be greased in animal fat; beef and pork fat violate Hindu and Muslim customs, respectively. The sepoys killed British officers, escalating the conflict into a large-scale rebellion. At least 800,000 Indians would die in the ensuing war. This conflict has been called many names, such as the **Sepoy Mutiny of 1857**. By May 1858, the British government had crushed the rebellion. It went on to impose direct imperial rule on India (the "British Raj") with a viceroy represented British authority.

> ✔ **AP Expert Note**
>
> **One War Can Have Many Different Names**
>
> When studying for AP World History, please be aware that a war's name can vary depending on time and context. For example, "Sepoy Mutiny" is increasingly disfavored due to its implicit pro-British perspective, as mutiny is a crime, but the College Board still uses it for APWH. Modern-day alternatives include the "First War of Indian Independence". The standpoint of a war's participants also affects naming. What Americans call "The Vietnam War" is called "The American War" by the Vietnamese.

Under British rule, forests were cleared; tea, coffee, and opium were cultivated; and railroads, telegraphs, canals, harbors, and irrigation systems were built. English-style schools were set up for Indian elites and Indian customs were suppressed. British imperialism had a profound effect on the decline of existing Indian textile production, as British merchants desired Indian cotton, which would be shipped to England, made into textiles, and then sold in India. Severe famines became more frequent, as British laissez-faire policies focused on export agriculture rather than domestic food production, and heavy taxes to support the empire left poorer Indians unable to buy food whenever prices rose. Between the eighteenth and mid-twentieth centuries, areas under British administration would experience fourteen major famines. Over fifty-five million people would die.

Counterintuitively, the existence of British rule eventually inspired a sense of Indian national identity. The elite Indians who had been educated in British universities were inspired by Enlightenment values and began to criticize the British colonial regime. They called for political and social reform. As such, with British approval, the Indian National Congress was founded (1885) as a forum for educated Indians to communicate their views on public affairs to colonial officials. It was initially sought to reform rather than end British rule. By the end of the nineteenth century, however, the Congress sought self-rule and joined forces with the All-Indian Muslim League. In 1909, wealthy Indians were given the right to vote, but, by that time, the push for independence had become a mass movement.

Africa

With the exception of coastal colonies and trading posts, Europeans had little presence in Africa in the early nineteenth century. European territorial acquisition occurred rapidly during the imperial "Scramble for Africa." From 1875 to 1914, almost the entire continent was carved up by European empires, with Ethiopia and Liberia the only two African nations to retain their independence.

From 1879 to 1882, the Urabi Revolt (or Revolution) saw Egyptians fight against foreign domination of their country's government, army, and economy. After a naval bombardment of Alexandria, the British launched an invasion that defeated the rebels and took control of the Suez Canal, a key shipping route. In 1885, King Leopold II of Belgium established the **Congo Free State**, ostensibly as a free-trade zone. In reality, the Congo served as his personal colony, with rubber plantations supported by forced labor. The conditions were brutal; infamously, workers who did not meet their quota would have a hand hacked off. As European competition intensified, a world war seemingly loomed. In response to this rising tension, German Chancellor Otto von Bismarck called the Berlin Conference (1884–1885). Delegates—none of whom were African—were invited to establish the ground rules for the colonization of Africa. It was decided that any European state could establish an African colony after notifying the others and establishing a large enough presence.

European colonies in Africa operated under three main types of rule: direct rule, indirect rule, and settler rule. The French, Belgians, Germans, and Portuguese used direct rule. These centralized administrations, usually in urban centers, enforced assimilationist policies by forcing the adoption of Western values and customs. The British mostly used indirect rule to govern their colonies. This system used indigenous African rulers within the colonial administration, although they were often relegated to subordinate roles. Settler rule refers to the type of colonialism in which European settlers imposed direct rule on their colonies. Settler colonies differed from other African colonies in that many immigrants from Europe settled in these colonies. These settlers were not like missionaries or European colonial officials. They were more like early European settlers in the United States and Canada, who planned to make the colonies their permanent home and displace the native population.

Japan

Because Japan was so greatly strengthened by government-sponsored industrialization, it was able to compete with other imperial powers. The First Sino-Japanese War (1894–1895) was sparked by a rebellion in Korea. Japan quickly defeated the Chinese fleet and was ceded Taiwan, the Pescadores Islands, and the Liaodong peninsula. China was forced to sign unequal treaties with Japan as it had with the Western powers. In 1910, Japan annexed Korea.

Japan's victory in the Russo-Japanese War (1904) is, however, the most notable globally. The war solidified Japan's international position. As the first time a non-European people had defeated a major Western power, it inspired anti-colonial activists across the world from Vietnam to Ireland. It also offered inspiration to states under threat of foreign encroachment, such as the Ottoman Empire.

LEGACIES OF IMPERIALISM

Many economic and social changes occurred throughout the world as a result of imperialism. For one, local manufacturers were transformed into suppliers of raw materials and consumers of imported goods. In India, for instance, cotton was cultivated solely for export to England, and inexpensive English textiles were then imported. India, once the world's leading manufacturer of cotton fabrics, became a consumer of British textiles.

Migration increased as well. Europeans migrated to the United States, Canada, Argentina, Australia, and South Africa in search of cheap land and better economic opportunities. These Europeans often served as a new labor force in industrializing areas. Most traveled as free agents, though some were **indentured servants**.

Migrants from Asia and Africa, on the other hand, were most often indentured servants and went to tropical lands in the Americas, the Caribbean, Africa, and Oceania. With the decrease in slavery, planters still needed laborers to work on their plantations. Because most of the migrant laborers were men, gender roles in the home societies shifted as women took on roles that men had done previously. Indentured servants were offered free passage, food, shelter, clothing, and some compensation, in return for five to seven years of work. As a result, large communities from around the world migrated to new lands, bringing their culture and traditions.

Despite their success at creating supportive ethnic enclaves when they were allowed to immigrate, migrants were often subjected to regulations aimed at blocking their entry into a new nation. For example, the **Chinese Exclusion Act** was passed by the U.S. Congress in 1882. This act placed a ten-year moratorium on Chinese immigration. The rationale for this discriminatory law was that Chinese migrants threatened the social order.

In addition, Social Darwinists adapted Darwin's evolutionary idea of "survival of the fittest" to explain the development of human societies. These ideas were used to justify the invariably unequal and often brutal mistreatment of non-whites by European imperialists and colonizers.

EMANCIPATION

Slavery

Many nineteenth century liberals in Europe and North America supported the abolition of slavery, as the Enlightenment ideas of liberty and equality directly conflicted with the institution of slavery. Additionally, frequent slave revolts in the 1700s and 1800s were making slavery a dangerous business. Economically, it became less profitable, as protection from the revolts required an expensive military force.

As the price of sugar decreased, the profitability of sugar declined, but the price for slaves increased. Many plantation owners shifted their investments to manufacturing, where wage labor was more profitable. In turn, those laborers would buy the manufactured goods. Though smuggling of slaves continued through much of the nineteenth century, the slave trade officially ended first in Great Britain in 1807, and then in the United States in 1808. While importing slaves to the United States was illegal after 1808, the institution itself was not. The emancipation of the slaves occurred in British colonies in 1833, French colonies in 1848, the United States in 1865, and Brazil in 1888. 1888 marks the year in which slavery was finally illegal worldwide.

Freedom, however, did not bring equality. In the states of the southern United States, for example, property requirements, literacy tests, and poll taxes were implemented to prevent freed slaves from voting, and many freed slaves were trapped in low-paying jobs, such as tenant farming.

The end of the transatlantic slave trade and the eventual **emancipation of slaves** throughout the Americas led to an increase in indentured servitude. These workers signed a contract giving them transportation to the land where they would work, as well as room and board and a small wage, in return for five to seven years of labor. In the mid to late nineteenth century, these indentured servants came from Asian nations like India, Ceylon (modern-day Sri Lanka), the Philippines, Indonesia, and China. This migration led to distinct cultural changes in many Latin American and Caribbean nations.

Serfdom

The key to social change and reform in Russia was the emancipation of the serfs. Opposition to serfdom had been growing since the 1700s. While some opposed it on moral grounds, most saw it as an obstacle to economic development in Russia, as well as a source of instability due to the possibility of peasant revolt.

In 1861, Czar Alexander II abolished serfdom, and the government compensated landowners for the loss of land and serfs. The serfs gained their freedom and their labor obligations were gradually cancelled. However, they won very few political rights and had to pay a redemption tax for most of the land they received. Few former serfs prospered and most were desperately poor and uneducated. Their emancipation led to little increase in agricultural production, as peasants continued to use traditional methods of farming. It did, however, create a large urban labor force for the industrializing empire.

Changing Gender Roles

> **High-Yield**

Generally speaking, Enlightenment thinkers were fairly conservative in their view of women's roles in society. In an effort to challenge these accepted beliefs, Mary Wollstonecraft published *A Vindication of the Rights of Woman* in 1792, which argued that women should have access to a public education as they possessed the same capacity for reason as men.

In Britain, Canada, and the United States, a reform and pro-democratic women's movement became active in the nineteenth century. Women began to push for the right to vote in democratic elections. Advocates of **feminism** sought legal and economic gains for women, along with access to professions, education, and the right to vote. In 1848, an assembly of 300 women met in Seneca Falls, New York, demanding political rights, equality in marriage, and employment.

Some feminists, however, were wary of granting women the right to vote, fearing they were too conservative and religious and would thus vote accordingly. The movement continued, however, and New Zealand became the first country to grant women the right to vote (1893). Several others followed after World War I, including Great Britain and Germany (1918), followed soon by the United States (1920).

CULTURAL INFLUENCES

African and Asian Influences on European Art

During this time of seeming Western cultural dominance, European artists took note of the artistic styles of both Africa and Asia. They admired the dramatic, spare style of traditional West African sculpture, wood, and metalwork, as well as the use of color and stylized forms of design found in Japan. Based on those Japanese influences, the Impressionists focused on simple themes in nature, feeling that this type of art liberated them from the rules of classical painting. A new movement of modern art was soon launched, free of traditional constraints.

Cultural Policies of Meiji Japan

As Japan was opening up to the industrialization of the West, it was also heavily influenced by the culture of the West. Japanese literature took inspiration from European literature, and writers experimented with Western verse. Architects and artists created large buildings of steel, with Greek columns like those seen in the West, although wooden buildings would continue to predominate throughout the country until their destruction in the Allied firebombings of Japan in World War II.

Leisure and Consumption

The industrial age brought higher wages and shorter work hours. These changes gave people new opportunities. The middle class increased, leading to a new focus on the concept of leisure. The field of advertising communicated to the people the sense of needing things. The bicycle, for instance, became the "must-have item" of the 1880s and a vehicle of women's emancipation. Newspapers, theaters, and professional sports all became popular in this new era of leisure and consumption.

THE ENVIRONMENT

The Industrial Revolution had significant, long-lasting impacts on the environment. Air and water pollution affected the health of people living in the rapidly growing urban areas. Entire landscapes were destroyed as humans cut down timber for railroad ties, stripped hills and mountains for ores, and denuded areas of vegetative cover for farming. This increase in deforestation exacerbated desertification in some areas and flooding and mudslides in others. The invention of dynamite in 1867 opened the way to more effective removal of earth and stone, particularly for mines and tunnels. Mechanical methods of hunting made fishing and whaling more effective, with the result that many areas were significantly depleted even by the early twentieth century. Many whale species were in danger of becoming extinct until the discovery of petroleum products made whale oil less valuable. Improved firearms made hunting easier, often with disastrous results as animals like the bison of the North American plains were hunted almost to extinction.

Improvements in medicine, along with better diets resulting from more food production, led to a dramatic rise in population as well as to an increase in the average life expectancy. The Earth's population in 1750 was 790 million. By 1900, the population had doubled. Urbanization increased even faster than population growth because new methods of transportation (most notably railroads and steamships) led to increases in both internal migration within a country and external migration. Cities were some of the most dramatic examples of human changes to the environment during this period.

It was also during this era, however, that concern for the environment, beyond the need to conserve for a nation's resources, first began to assert itself. Many nations formed forestry services, initially based on the French and then the American model. National parks and nature preserves were created to keep areas from being developed. Western curiosity and scientific observations began to note the interconnectedness of nature and man's impact upon it. Scientific methods in medicine and chemistry began to find and then develop cures and preventative measures like sanitation systems, use of soaps and disinfectants, and vaccinations for many of the diseases that have plagued mankind throughout the centuries.

CHAPTER 12

Period 6: 1900 C.E. to the Present – Complete Time Period Review

WORLD WAR I

Long-Term Causes of WWI

- **Nationalism:** After the national unifications of Italy and Germany by 1870, other ethnic groups, such as the Poles, Czechs, and southern Slavic peoples, hoped for nations of their own. The difficulty was that these groups lived within multinational empires that would not agree to their own dissolution. The map of Europe had been redrawn before, and could be again, but this was usually done through revolution and war.

- **Alliances:** The European balance of power had long depended on alliances, defensive plans that would protect a nation in the event it was attacked. But by 1914 the major powers found themselves committed to support their allies even in conflicts that did not threaten their own interests. Germany, Austria-Hungary, and Italy had mutual agreements, and France and Russia were allied if Germany were to attack either one.

- **Imperialism:** Tensions stemmed from imperialism both in Europe and in the world at large. As the Ottoman Empire weakened and withdrew from its Balkan lands in southeastern Europe, the Austro-Hungarian and Russian Empires competed to acquire or dominate the area. At the same time Britain, France, Germany and Italy engaged in competition for overseas colonies, like those in Africa.

- **Militarism:** The belief that warfare was an honorable and even desirable way to settle conflicts, militarism led to constant threats, arms races, and ultimatums over minor disputes. For example, the naval arms race between Germany and Britain caused friction between two nations that had previously been allies.

Immediate Causes of WWI

World War I began when all four factors—nationalism, alliances, imperialism, and militarism—violently intersected. During a tour of a Balkan province in the summer of 1914, the heir to the Austro-Hungarian throne and his wife were assassinated by Slav nationalists who wanted the province united with other southern Slavic nations. Austria-Hungary accused Serbia of supporting the terrorists and declared war. Russia sided with its Slavic client Serbia, while Germany pledged support for Austria-Hungary, its close Germanic ally. When Germany declared war on Russia, France honored its alliance and joined Russia. Great Britain, with no alliances, was the last major European power to enter the war, when German forces violated Belgium's neutrality on their way to attack France.

The Great War

World War I, originally referred to as the Great War, was largely fought in Europe, but because of European economic and imperial dominion in much of the world at the time, there were secondary fronts in Africa, Asia, and on all the world's oceans. Other factors made this war the greatest and worst the world had yet seen. Industrial progress had greatly increased the killing power of weaponry; artillery, machine guns, and mass-produced ammunition led to casualties in the millions. Armies were stalemated and took to trenches to survive, leading to a long cruel war of attrition to simply exhaust the enemy. The heroic notion of war was gone, and in crucial ways that played out over the rest of the century, Europe lost its self-assurance of being the world's superior civilization.

This first **total war** mobilized entire nations. Civilians were crucial to the war effort, as industrial workers labored to provide armies with supplies. With so many men on the front lines, many women entered the workforce. Aircrafts bombed cities, and submarines tried to cut off food shipments. Governments controlled industry and agriculture and used propaganda to paint the enemy as evil.

In the end, Germany and the other Central Powers were unable to hold out against British, French, and American economic and military pressure, even after Russia had left the war and conceded eastern Europe to the Germans. Germany sued for an armistice in November, 1918.

The Treaty of Versailles

The peace conference to settle the issues stemming from the war was held near Paris at the Palace of Versailles. The leading Allied powers—Italy, Great Britain, France, and the United States—were labeled the "Big Four." The European victors looked to increase their power at the expense of the defeated enemy. In contrast, U.S. President Woodrow Wilson entered the Versailles meetings with his plan, called the Fourteen Points. In it, he called for self-determination of nationalities, peace without victory, disarmament, fair treatment of colonial peoples, and the establishment of the **League of Nations**, a multinational organization for maintaining world peace.

In the end France, supported by Britain, would not allow the generous peace that Wilson had envisioned. Instead, the treaty laid down harsh terms to which Germany had to agree: one-sided blame and heavy reparations that would cripple the entire European economy. The map of Europe was redrawn at the expense of the German, Austro-Hungarian, and Russian Empires. New nations such as Poland, Czechoslovakia, Hungary, and Yugoslavia were all created in 1919 by the peace settlement. Although most of Wilson's ideas were rejected, the League of Nations was approved. Ironically, the U.S. Congress opposed it and the United States did not join the idealistic new international order. The League was established in 1921, but without the great powers of America, Russia, or Germany (before 1926) as members it struggled to keep the peace when tensions arose.

The Treaty of Versailles was deeply flawed, as critics saw even at the time: it left many conflicts unresolved or even made worse. The imposition of war guilt and one-sided reparations on Germany, the economic powerhouse of central Europe, practically guaranteed a crippled recovery from the war's devastation. Many colonized peoples complained that Wilson's "self-determination" only applied to nations dominated by the defeated Central Powers. The worldwide British and French Empires continued to rule over millions of Africans and Asians.

Impact of the War on the Allies

- Though victorious, Great Britain was profoundly weakened by the Great War. It had lost a significant percentage of its youth, and its economy was worn out. After the war, it was in debt to the United States and its great empire became more and more of a burden. Imperial dominions like Canada and Australia became more independent, Ireland broke free, and native movements for independence in Africa and Asia grew in strength and credibility.

- France was devastated by the war. The Western Front was fought on its territory, with huge casualties and destruction of property. Also in debt to the United States and aware that it had only won with the help of its allies, France adopted a conservative and defensive outlook on the future.

- Italy was one of the leading Allied nations and had been promised large pieces of the Austro-Hungarian Empire when the Allies won. It received some, but not all it had hoped for. Postwar politicians continued to press for more concessions and to look for other imperial projects to distract the nation from its continuing weakness and internal divisions.

- The United States was elevated to world-power status by the war, but its traditional isolationism died hard. Most Americans remained detached from foreign conflicts, being repelled by Europe's vengeful peace and inability to pay its debts. Conservatives won the White House in 1920, focusing on industrial expansion and retreating from European affairs.

Impact of the War on the Central Powers

- Germany was economically, politically, and socially devastated. Although its territory was spared from battle, it had lost millions of men in the fighting and was now, by the terms of the Versailles treaty, forced to pay huge reparations to the Allies. In addition, it lost its army and navy, all of its overseas empire, and the productive provinces on its eastern and western borders. The Kaiser abdicated and out of the chaos of democratic, socialist, and communist uprisings, a weak parliamentary-style government was assembled in Weimar in 1919. Within a few years hyperinflation devastated the middle class and angry ex-soldiers promoted the myth that Germany had not been defeated militarily, but had been "stabbed in the back" by traitors on the home front.

- Austria-Hungary dissolved as the war ended, and the Versailles treaty confirmed the independence of new nations like Poland, Czechoslovakia, Yugoslavia, Hungary, and the small new German state of Austria. Each of these states was individually weaker than the old Empire had been, however. The area promised to be the seedbed of future conflicts over nationalism and renewed imperial control by greater powers for the rest of the century.

- The Ottoman Empire, which had fought with the Central Powers, collapsed in 1918. Turkey declared itself a republic and, under the leadership of Ataturk, instituted a program of modernization and Westernization. Freed from Turkish domination, Arab nationalism rose, inspired partly by Wilson's call for national self-determination and partly by Allied promises made in return for help in defeating the Ottomans. Instead, their land was carved into French and British zones of imperial control, called "mandates." Palestine was a center of tension, where Arab nationalists competed with Jewish Zionists for control of land they had both been vaguely promised by the British.

Impact of the War on Other World Powers

- Russia was in a state of complete disorder. A liberal revolution had overthrown the Czar in 1917, and a Communist coup seized power a few months later. The Communists withdrew from the war and signed a desperate peace treaty with Germany in early 1918. Civil war broke out almost immediately and for five years, the forces of the left, led by the Bolsheviks (Reds), and the right, both liberals and supporters of the czar (Whites), fought to control Russia. Bitter fighting and the deaths of as many as a million Russians ended with a Red victory and the establishment of the Union of Soviet Socialist Republics in 1922. The Bolsheviks, instinctively anti-capitalist and angered by Western intervention in the Russian civil war, withdrew from European diplomacy while promoting communist revolution wherever they could, adding to the instability of the postwar world order.

- Japan had fought with the Allies during the war and received Germany's Asian territories afterward. At Versailles it proposed a Racial Equality clause for the League of Nations, hoping to be recognized as an Asian world power fully equal to Europe and America. The Western powers refused, and Japanese resentment and nationalism were further inflamed.

- When Japan gained Germany's concessions in China through the Versailles treaty, there was a surge of nationalism in China, beginning with riots and leading to the cultural and intellectual May Fourth Movement. This marked a shift toward a more populist political base and away from the intellectual elites of the former imperial governing class. Both Chinese Nationalism in the 1920s and 30s and Chinese Communism in the latter half of the century drew on this growing populism.

- India fought loyally as part of the British Empire in World War I, in the hopes of gaining more independence after the war. When the fighting ended, Britain introduced some minor reforms and liberalization but maintained complete control. This led to a surge in Indian nationalism under the leadership of the Congress Party as well as the charismatic **Mohandas Gandhi**, who demanded full independence. As with other parts of the colonial world, Indians saw Europeans in a new light after the self-destructive maelstrom of the Great War.

GLOBAL DEPRESSION

High-Yield

The 1920s saw further modernization of the world economy and concerted efforts by Europeans and Americans to build a future free of war. This changed by the 1930s. One of the greatest causes of the long spiral downwards to **World War II** was the **Great Depression**, which struck in 1929. As the leading creditor nation, the United States was crucial to the health of world markets. After the New York stock market collapsed in October 1929, the American credit-based economy contracted. Existing loans were called in, and new loans were cancelled.

The impact was especially severe in Europe, which had depended on American loans to recover from World War I. A wave of bank failures in the United States had a ripple effect in London, Berlin, Tokyo, and other financial capitals. In the following years, global unemployment rose to double-digit levels. Countries tried to protect their economies by cutting public expenditures and limiting imports, which tended to worsen the problems. For example, the United States passed the highest tariff (a tax on imports) in its history, further limiting its trading partners' abilities to repay their American debts.

✔ **AP Expert Note**

Causes of Global Depression

- Overdependence on American loans and purchasing
- Increased tariffs and protectionism
- Industrial and farming surpluses leading to deflation
- Poor banking management

Consequences of Global Depression

The great hardships of the Depression led to social instability and a rise in political extremism in many nations. Communists on the left criticized the obvious failings of capitalism and advocated Soviet-style collectivism, while fascists on the right sought governmental control and direction of private enterprise to achieve national self-sufficiency. Britain, France, and the United States remained democracies even as they experimented with more state regulation of their economies. Japan, Italy, and Germany, on the other hand, looked to dictatorial rule to unify their divided societies, overcome economic hardships, and solidify national power and prestige through aggressions against their neighbors.

RISE OF FASCIST AND TOTALITARIAN STATES

Many countries veered towards increased state power and authoritarian regimes in the 1930s, but a few countries had a large impact on the rest of the world. These large, powerful countries took totalitarian doctrines of state control to the furthest extremes. Their ideological need to expand, conquer and control caused growing tensions with the existing Versailles world order, dominated by the imperial economics and diplomacy of Britain, France, and the United States.

Italy

By 1921, the success of Marxist revolution in Russia led to a growing fear of communism in other nations, especially those that had been destabilized by the war. It was in Italy that the first fully organized reactionary and anti-democratic movement emerged. A small group of men led by **Benito Mussolini** marched on Rome in 1922, demanding to form a government. The king consented, and Italy was soon dominated by Mussolini and his Fascists. Mussolini became the prototypical modern dictator as he accumulated more and more power. By the 1930s, his rule was unquestioned. In light of the tenuous status of the League of Nations, Italy was able to brutally invade Ethiopia in 1935, conquering one of Africa's only independent states.

Germany

After the war, Germany rebuilt its government as a parliamentary democracy. Burdened with war debts and rampant inflation, the new government tried to reestablish Germany's place in the international community. However, the 1930s Depression, with the withdrawal of American credit, caused a collapse of the economy and rising popularity for German Communists.

Opposing the Communists with street fighting and uniformed gangs was the National Socialist German Workers' Party, also known as the Nazi Party. Its charismatic leader **Adolf Hitler** railed against Communism and used traditional anti-Semitism to suggest that Communism was really a global conspiracy organized by the Jewish people. In fact, all of Germany's economic, diplomatic, and social problems were blamed on the nation's Jewish population. Hitler preached ultra-nationalism and the promise of a greater Germany, much as Mussolini had done in Italy—but Nazism's greatest difference from **Fascism**, on which it was based, was this addition of racial hatred and the promotion of "Aryan" (Germanic) racial superiority.

In 1933, with a close election victory, Hitler was appointed chancellor. He became dictator, or führer, within months by eliminating his political opponents through terror, intimidation, and forced labor camps. Jews were increasingly persecuted and driven from public life. The Nazi party and its propaganda of German revival and expansion dominated most areas of national life. Germany under the Nazis pushed to annul the Versailles treaty's restrictions on German power and to weaken the Western-led alliances among its neighbors. By 1936 the German army moved to reoccupy the demilitarized Rhineland on the French border.

Japan

In 1930s Japan, the global depression exacerbated existing trends towards an aggressive anti-Western nationalism. A militant kind of racial superiority became the national ideology, with clear links to Fascism's methods and message. Military officers increasingly replaced civilian politicians in the highest posts of government, and liberal institutions were restricted. One feature of Japanese authoritarianism was an emphasis on collective rule in the name of the divine Emperor; Japan was never ruled by a glorified dictator.

Japan's goal of economic self-sufficiency necessitated an imperial foreign policy, as the country had few natural resources of its own. Japan had already seized Taiwan and Korea in a growing overseas empire, but it now fixed its eye on the rich resources of Northeast China. Japan's invasion of Manchuria in 1931 led to protests in the League of Nations but no effective action, so the Japanese kept their new territory and withdrew from the League.

> ✔ **AP Expert Note**
>
> ### Fascism as an Ideology
>
> - Unquestioned rule by a charismatic leader, with no opposing state institutions
> - A single political party that overrides and dominates all social structures
> - Opposition to communism as a threat to tradition and private property
> - Ultra-nationalism and glorification of the state
> - Militarism and glorification of war as the ultimate expression of power
> - Domination of independent big business and destruction of independent labor unions
> - Rejection of liberalism and democracy, seen as weak and ineffective

Soviet Union

At the same time that Mussolini was consolidating his power in Italy and Hitler was beginning his rise, there was a transfer of power in Moscow. Lenin, the architect of the Bolshevik Revolution, died of a stroke seven years after the revolution. The resulting power struggle within the ruling Bolshevik party ended when **Joseph Stalin** took control in 1927.

Marx's original communism had promoted the idea of a collective leadership, effecting a "dictatorship of the people." Stalin, following Lenin's example but also in line with Russia's tradition of absolute Czarist rule, ruthlessly eliminated his colleagues and twisted communism into a one-man dictatorship. His method of rule became associated with modern Soviet-style communism, but it is also referred to as Stalinism.

Stalinist Communism as an Ideology

- Complete state ownership and centralized control of the economy through the use of a Five-Year Plan

- Forced industrialization to modernize the country and military in defense against a hostile capitalist world

- World leadership in the international communist movement to subvert capitalism and imperialism

- Forced collectivism for farming and control of food supply

- Promotion of atheism, forcing organized religion underground

- Complete control of all culture, art, media, and entertainment in service of communism

Drawing from lessons learned during the waging of total war from 1914 to 1918, Stalin, Hitler, and Mussolini represented a new form of political leadership in the twentieth century. Along with the rule of Japan's generals, their dictatorships demonstrated that political ideology, right or left, communist or anti-communist, was in some ways less important than the methods and goals used to mobilize society. Whether in Berlin or Moscow, modern totalitarianism displayed certain distinct features.

Totalitarian Regimes

- A single leader with almost unquestioned authority

- A single ideological party in charge of all government, society, and culture

- Creation of a police state to terrorize and control the populace

- Aggressive elimination of all opposition groups

ORIGINS OF WORLD WAR II

The League of Nations

The Treaty of Versailles had created the League of Nations, an organization of mostly European nations but also Ethiopia, Japan, Siam, and many Latin American states. The United States, which had reverted to an isolationist foreign policy, never joined. The League did have some successes in demonstrating the power of institutional cooperation between nations, notably with combating malaria and other diseases in Europe, stopping labor abuses, controlling the distribution of opium products, and lessening the slave trade in Africa and Asia. However, the League never succeeded with its primary purpose, that of stopping large-scale international conflicts. Dominated by Britain and France, the League promoted voluntary cooperation and anti-war policies like trade sanctions, rather than creating a global police force. In the 1930s, the League failed to react effectively to the actions of totalitarian regimes: the Japanese invasion of Manchuria, the Italian conquest of Ethiopia, and the German militarization of the Rhineland. The League's final failure was its paralysis during the drawn-out civil war in Spain.

The Spanish Civil War

Spain had a growing urban population and a poor countryside dominated by wealthy families and the Catholic Church. In 1932, the king abdicated and a republic was formed which introduced liberal reforms such as universal non-religious education, equality for women, and redistribution of farmland to the peasants. Conservative reaction and increasing social discord reached a climax in 1936, when right-wing army officers revolted, led by General Francisco Franco. The resulting civil war lasted for three years. The conflict has been called a "dress rehearsal" for the Second World War for two reasons. First, Spanish democracy and liberalism stood in between two extremes: the fascist-backed forces of Franco and the communist-dominated forces supporting the left-wing Republic. The idea of a moderate center holding firm against totalitarianism on the left and right seemed doomed. Second, the war was fought with the active participation of foreign volunteers and soldiers, especially from Fascist Italy and Nazi Germany. These powers tested new weapons and tactics that would prove effective on the global battlefronts a few years later. The most famous example of this was Germany's air raid on the undefended town of Guernica, in response to which the painter Pablo Picasso produced one of the twentieth century's most famous paintings, *Guernica*. This work of modern art stands as a continual reminder of civilian suffering in the midst of war. Franco defeated the Republican forces in 1939, but Fascist Spain, shattered by the war, played little part in the Second World War that broke out a few months later.

Hitler Claims a Greater Germany

Hitler followed his reoccupation of the Rhineland with further claims to German-inhabited territories in Eastern Europe. Traditional Great Power politics, which Wilson had hoped to end with the League, returned in force. Britain and France's policy of appeasement (trying to distinguish reasonable from unreasonable demands) allowed Germany to annex Austria, which the Versailles treaty had forbidden. In the 1938 Munich Agreement, against Czech protests, Hitler was given the Sudetenland, a German-speaking area in western Czechoslovakia. In exchange, Hitler pledged to make no more territorial demands. However, he invaded and annexed the rest of the country the next spring. With the failure of appeasement, Britain and France reluctantly guaranteed the security of Hitler's next victim, Poland, which separated eastern Prussia from the rest of Germany. The Western allies counted on the Soviet Union to oppose this German threat to its border. However, Hitler and Stalin overcame their ideological differences with a joint agreement to invade Poland in September 1939. Britain and France declared war, and fighting soon consumed the continent, just twenty-five years after the first World War began. In both cases, the immediate cause was German ambition to dominate eastern Europe.

WORLD WAR II
`High-Yield`

Many of the unresolved issues at the end of the first World War were instrumental in causing the even more devastating second World War. These conflicts were accentuated by the ideological extremism of the 1920s and 1930s, when totalitarian states sought to centralize their societies and expand their domain without regard for diplomacy or human rights. The main arenas of the war were in eastern Europe and western Russia, as well as in China and the adjacent lands of eastern Asia. Peripheral combat zones popped up in western and southern Europe, North Africa, and the island systems of the central and southwest Pacific Ocean.

Although the German invasion of Poland in 1939 is usually said to be the beginning of the Second World War, the war in Asia had been going on since the Japanese invasion of China in 1937. However, neither of these wars was particularly connected to the other; it was in 1941, with the entry of the United States and the Soviet Union, that the European and Pacific conflicts were linked into one global war. Although the campaigns on the western and eastern edges of Eurasia were widely separated, events in Europe did affect the Asian conflict and vice-versa. Japan's seizure of Europe's southeast Asian colonies was aided by the preoccupation of Britain, France, and the Netherlands with fighting Germany; the Soviet Union, fighting for its life in the west, did not intervene against Japan in the east; and America's decision to fight Germany first probably prolonged the conflict in the Pacific by several years.

The War in Europe

From 1939 to 1942, the triumph of Nazi Germany was almost entirely unchecked. The Germans took control of most of eastern and northern Europe with few casualties. After the fall of France, only Britain was left to defend itself against invasion, all while fighting to keep open its sea lanes to America and the British Empire. Repelled by British air and sea power, Hitler in 1941 turned his attention to the Mediterranean and then to his proclaimed enemy, the Soviet Union. After helping his weaker ally Italy to invade the Balkans and North Africa, he launched a massive invasion of the U.S.S.R., which nearly reached Moscow before winter set in. 1942 was the high tide of Axis power: Germany dominated all of Europe, pushed further into southern Russia and Egypt, and sank ships carrying U.S. reinforcements to Britain and Russia. The Soviet Union, however, rallied its people and drew on the immense resources provided by Stalin's single-minded industrial development of the 1930s. In a series of huge and brutal battles, notably in the sieges of Stalingrad and Leningrad, the German army was slowly destroyed and pushed back into eastern Europe. By late 1944, the Allies had effectively crushed Germany on three fronts through successive invasions of North Africa, Italy, and France. Combined with logistical support by American industry, intensive aerial bombing of German cities, and Soviet military power, the Allies turned the tide of war in Europe. The end came in 1945, when Berlin fell to the Red Army, Hitler committed suicide, and American and Russian troops shook hands at the Elbe River in the center of Germany.

The War in the Pacific

Japan's invasion of China, in pursuit of imperial rule over eastern Asia, strained relations with the United States. Gambling that it could seize the industrial resources of southeast Asia from the distracted European imperial powers and fend off the United States in a defensive war, Japan attacked American forces in Hawaii and the Philippines in late 1941. By mid-1942, just as Germany was at the peak of its power in the West, Japan too dominated its hemisphere. It controlled eastern China, southeast Asia as far west as Burma, and most of the western Pacific Ocean from New Guinea to the Aleutians. It threatened Australia, India, Hawaii and Alaska. However, alarmed by totalitarian aggression in the 1930s, the United States had been moving away from its long-standing isolationist policies and had already begun a massive rearmament program. Once it entered the war in 1941, America devoted most of its resources to defeating Germany, but its military presence in Asia was still enough to overwhelm Japan. In a series of fierce naval and air campaigns, American forces advanced on Japan, island by island. By 1944, the United States retook the Philippines, began to bomb the Japanese homeland, used submarines to blockade Japan, and prepared to launch an invasion as soon as Germany surrendered. In the summer of 1945, Berlin fell and the Soviet Union soon declared war on Japan, looking to seize Manchuria and Korea. Most of Japan's major cities had been leveled by mass **firebombing**, and America's use of atomic bombs to level Hiroshima and Nagasaki led to a level of destruction never before seen. Japan's leaders surrendered and American began to occupy the devastated country.

Impact of the War

By a broad estimate, well over 20 million soldiers died in what would be the greatest war in history. Just as the causes of the war followed on and developed from those of the first World War, so too did the methods. The most notable difference was the increase in mobility. Improved tanks, planes, and trucks provided new offensive power, and trench warfare was replaced by spread-out battlefields that devastated entire regions and cities. New weapons were born of modern science: radar to detect planes and ships, sonar to locate submarines, computers to break codes and calculate aim, aircraft carriers to sink battleships, and jet planes and rockets to deliver high-caliber explosives against tanks—and even cities. The most devastating weapon of all was the **nuclear bomb** that America used to end the war against Japan.

In addition to soldiers, 30 million civilians were killed by military action and state persecution. Wartime famine and disease laid waste to another 20 million lives. Although all the nations committed war crimes, Germany and Japan adopted the most brutal policies with explicitly racist ideologies of conquest. Millions died in both East Asia and Europe, in work camps set up to detain, torment, and murder political or racial enemies. The noncombatant death toll in Europe is estimated at 20 million, as Jews, Communists, labor leaders, prisoners of war, homosexuals, the mentally disabled, and Romani peoples were shot or gassed to death. In particular, Hitler targeted the Jews, blaming them for all of Germany's problems. Six million of Europe's 9.5 million Jews were killed in the Nazi Holocaust. Millions of East Asians, from China and Korea to Indonesia and the Philippines, were also killed as the Japanese advanced their conquests. Added to this misery were the uncountable wounded, traumatized, and separated. Beyond the human cost the destruction of wealth, by explosive and expenditure, was on the order of a trillion U.S. dollars at the time.

Outcomes of the War

There was no armistice or peace conference at the end of World War II. The Allies demanded unconditional surrender, and the devastated Axis nations had no choice but to accept. Both Japan and Germany were occupied by Allied armies. Within the framework of the occupation, the Allies purged the ruling classes, imposed extensive social reforms, and attempted to remake the countries in the image of their own (Western or Soviet) societies. They also held war trials in which top generals and government officials were charged, convicted, and sometimes executed, for crimes against humanity. This set a new precedent in international law, as making war could now be punishable in international courts.

Even more so than after World War I, the victors were in hardly better shape than the losers. France and China, and other countries of Europe and East Asia, had been devastated by their conquerors and occupiers. Great Britain, although never invaded, was crippled economically and like France was already losing control of parts of its empire.

The clearest "victor" was the United States, which had suffered smaller losses in terms of men killed, had built up its industrial power to supply much of the Allied forces, and, except for the attack on Hawaii in 1941, had not been touched by actual combat. One lesson had been learned: the United States recognized the consequences of its isolationism between the wars and took a strong position of leadership in the postwar world. At the Bretton Woods conference in 1944, the United States committed to support the economies of other develop nations by linking its strong domestic currency and undamaged economy to the international gold standard. This enabled a rapid recovery of Europe and Japan over the following decades. In short, a nation crippled by the Depression had been unified and revitalized by the war, and its outlook on world affairs was both positive and triumphant.

On the other side of the world, the Soviet Union had faced annihilation and survived to emerge as a great military power, dominating northern Eurasia, but it was not nearly as secure and strong as the United States. Its losses had been almost 27 million, and immense areas had been occupied and ruined by the war. Building on its successful alliance with the non-Communist Anglo-Americans, it participated in the founding of the **United Nations**, and in the war crimes tribunals. However, it refused to join the American-led postwar international economic system, instead following both ideological and national security imperatives by establishing a rigid Communist hegemony in Eastern Europe. Like the United States, the Soviet Union took a renewed sense of national greatness from its victory, and foresaw opportunities to spread Communism across a shattered world.

The United Nations

The victorious Allies resolved to try again with an international organization. The United Nations (UN), headquartered in New York City, attempted to fix the flaws of the failed League of Nations. The Security Council, with permanent membership for the five Allied victors of the war (United States, U.S.S.R., Great Britain, France, and the Republic of China), was specifically tasked with keeping the peace by military action if necessary, subject to veto by any of the great powers. The General Assembly of all the member nations is a forum for discussing world problems and their solutions. It cannot pass laws, but it can raise issues and suggest resolutions. Shortly after its founding, the UN was busy settling disputes in the Middle East and helping the many refugees left by World War II. It made its strongest mark in the Korean War (1950–1953), authorizing an international armed force to resist the Communist attack. In later years, as the **Cold War** split the Allies into opposition and many new nations emerged with little stake in a Western-oriented world order, the UN has proved less able to maintain world peace. Just as with the failed League, without the sovereign power of military enforcement, international organizations must mirror the actual balance of national power at the global level.

IMPACT OF THE TWO WORLD WARS

The waging of total war in the global conflicts of the twentieth century has militarized civilian life ever since, in countless ways. New media such as posters, radio, and cinema extended governments' ability to propagandize their wars. State control of the economy and direction of cultural affairs, the idea of citizens as part of the "home front" in military efforts, and endless sacrifice in the name of national defense are accepted aspects of modern life. Industrial production and technical prowess are seen as better measures of national strength than the size or training of the army. From this point forward, no conflict, no matter how small, has excluded civilians from being targets. Thus terrorism, the deliberate use of violence in social settings for political purposes, has become the norm for many non-state actors on the global stage.

Finally, the armed mobilization of the world and near-destruction of European state power from 1914 to 1945 led to a wave of national liberation struggles against imperial control in order to assert national self-determination, racial dignity, and ideological superiority. Slowly but surely, and often violently, the European-dominated world order that began roughly 400 years earlier was coming to its close.

THE COLD WAR

High-Yield

The global conflicts of the twentieth century did not end with the Second World War, but they changed thereafter. The imperial conflicts of the Great Powers of Europe, conducted since the 1600s along understood lines of diplomacy, alliances, and occasional field combat, had come to an end due to the destruction or bankruptcy of all major contenders. What followed was a bipolar and worldwide contest between two non-European superpowers, the United States and the Soviet Union. Primarily because it was between nuclear-armed states, but also because the antagonists did not share a border or past history of war with each other, the conflict was never fought out as a Third World War (which many survivors of the First and Second World Wars expected). Instead it was a "Cold War," a conflict of symbols, threats, imperial influence, trade, and local **proxy wars** between client states.

Origins of the Cold War

The irony, and tensions, of a grand alliance against Nazi Germany by the two leading capitalist democracies and the first Communist totalitarian state were obvious throughout the war. Even before the fall of Berlin, disputes about the postwar international order threatened the Allies' strategic cooperation. From 1945 on, the Soviet Union sought to control the nations on its western frontier, both to extend communism, and to create a buffer to protect itself from future invasions. The United States and Great Britain protested, as the initial cause of the war in 1939 had been to stop Germany from dominating smaller states like Poland and Czechoslovakia. The Red Army's occupation of Eastern Europe, and the Western powers' unwillingness to continue the war, led to a de facto division. In the late 1940s, Europe was divided into a capitalist and democratic West and a communist and totalitarian East. In the middle was Germany, split into two states by the Iron Curtain, its capital city divided into West and East sectors by the Berlin Wall. The competition to control Germany, still Europe's greatest industrial and military nation, was a defining feature of the Cold War from beginning to end.

✔ **AP Expert Note**

Attributes of the Competition Between the United States and the Soviet Union:

- **Military:** The U.S.S.R. tested its first nuclear bomb in 1949, and a far more powerful thermo-nuclear bomb (H-bomb) was acquired by both nations in the 1950s. However, both nations eventually realized that nuclear weapons were impractical in any war fought for political or territorial advantage. The Cuban Missile Crisis of 1962 was the closest the two countries would come to nuclear war. The crisis scared both sides into more conservative nuclear policies, including treaties to limit the proliferation and testing of nuclear weapons. In addition, the two countries spent billions on conventional arms in order to develop ever more sophisticated systems for fighting.

- **Technological:** Both nations sought advancements in missile technology in order to deliver nuclear bombs between continents, eventually leading to the launch of the first satellite by the U.S.S.R. in 1957. This began the Space Race, which culminated in the U.S. moon landing in 1969, countered by a strong Soviet space station program in the 1970s. Soviet engineering and science were world-class in state-sponsored sectors like armaments, intelligence-gathering, math and physics, and construction, but rigid ideology hampered technological development in other areas like computers, biochemistry, automobiles, and media.

- **Geopolitical:** Both superpowers vied for influence across the globe, especially in the newly independent and developing nations of Asia and Africa. The Americans and Soviets fought wars in Korea, **Vietnam**, India, Afghanistan, and Angola, and even provided combat troops to the opposing sides. Both superpowers used trade concessions, subsidies, infrastructure investments, cultural and educational exchanges, and diplomatic or military support against local adversaries to maintain and extend geopolitical control. The North Atlantic Treaty Organization (**NATO**) and the **Warsaw Pact** were the main alliances for America and the U.S.S.R, respectively. Other American-led treaty organizations and alliances in Latin America, the Middle East, and South and Southeast Asia were less effective.

- **Ideological:** Democratic capitalism and dictatorial Communism were presented to the world as the two choices available for political and economic organization. As many new nations emerged from Western imperial domination in the 1950s and 60s, they perceived that both choices originated in the European historical and cultural tradition, from which they had just freed themselves. In 1956, the **Non-Aligned Movement** was founded by the leaders of Yugoslavia, India, Indonesia, Egypt, and Ghana. Its goal was to explore a middle course between East and West for the developing nations of the world.

Progress of the Cold War

The first few decades of the Cold War were the most tense, when the atmosphere of paranoia and existential fear from the Second World War drove both sides to proxy wars in Korea and Vietnam. Domestic politics, already deadly in Stalin's Russia, became infected with fears of spies and treason in the West as well. Uprisings in the Soviet states of East Germany, Hungary, and Czechoslovakia were brutally suppressed; China was torn by its self-inflicted Cultural Revolution; and state- and corporate-influenced conformity in the West led to countercultural rebellion, antiwar riots, and political crises like Watergate.

By the 1970s, the Cold War had become more complex. The U.S. took advantage of a Sino-Soviet split and normalized relations with China in the 1970s, which inspired a détente (diplomatic warming) with the U.S.S.R. as well. Increased trade, cultural exchanges, arms agreements, and diplomatic settlements in Europe all followed.

The 1980s saw a resumption of high tension between the superpowers. This was primarily due to the Soviet Union's increasing awareness of its internal weaknesses and contradictions. The Soviet invasion of Afghanistan, American escalation of the arms race to space-based weapons, and conflicts in Angola, East Africa, and Central America were defused only after Soviet leader Mikhail Gorbachev's post-Stalinist reforms.

The Cold War ended suddenly and unexpectedly with the resulting implosion of the Soviet Union. In 1989, Gorbachev did not counter Polish, German, and other Eastern European attempts to break away from Russian domination. The Red Army withdrew peacefully and Soviet support for allies and client states ended; within a few years the Soviet Union itself broke up into numerous non-Communist republics, the largest being the new Russian Federation.

Impact of the Cold War

Although the United States and its allies had "won" the final phase of the global conflicts, the result was hardly a peaceful and unified world. America's economy, society, and culture had been distorted by decades of militarization and ideologically-driven foreign policy. Around the world, modern struggles continued between national self-determination and imperial control, as well as between personal liberty and social order. U.S. economic and cultural dominance, if not military strength, was challenged by rising powers like China, India, Japan, the **European Union**, and a revived Russia, as well as by a growing number of smaller but influential states like Iran, Brazil, South Africa, Nigeria, and Mexico.

REVOLUTIONS

Several major revolutions of historical importance occurred alongside the twentieth century's global conflicts. Ancient regimes and civilizations, which were resistant to the West's expansive imperialism and industrialism, set their own terms for modernization and Westernization in violent and original ways.

Communist Revolutions

Two of the most important Communist revolutions were in Russia and China, in response to exploitation of the laboring classes. This was in contrast to the eighteenth and nineteenth century's revolutions and reform movements in other Western European and American societies. Russia's and China's goals were to establish liberal principles of social and economic freedom for the middle classes and peasants against aristocratic and landed privilege, with little concern for the growing class of urban and industrial workers.

Russia

By 1914, Russia was far behind Western Europe economically and technologically. It was slowly building an industrial base with foreign capital and increasing agricultural production; however, it was still dominated by a small and wealthy aristocracy, imperial court and bureaucracy, and rigid censorship enforced by the state police. Despite public unrest, Czar Nicholas II retained all real executive power and had little interest in broadening the base of his government to include the rising middle classes.

The losses and fruitless sacrifices of World War I led to disorder and riots in March 1917. The czar was forced to abdicate, and a provisional republican government took power. The liberal government decided to stay in the war, resulting in food shortages, revolts, and continued strikes. The leading party of Communists, the Bolsheviks, was led by **Vladimir Lenin**. They promised the people exactly what they wanted: "Peace, Land, Bread." In November 1917, Lenin's party seized power and declared Russia the world's first Socialist state; in early 1918, it made peace with Germany, ending Russia's part in the war.

The Bolshevik government seized all private land, banks, and industries; the former owners were persecuted and their estates looted and burned. Soviets, or popular committees, ruled locally under command of the central Party. The Cheka, the secret police, spied on and arrested any who deviated from revolutionary enthusiasm. Marx had said Communism was designed for developed states like Germany and Britain, where the industrial working class would seize and freely share the capital that fueled their production. There was nothing in Marx about how to communize a society like Russia that was largely agricultural and pre-industrial. The Bolsheviks' solution, called Marxism-Leninism, called for dictatorial central direction by a single Party until industry, national wealth, and Communist thought had developed enough for the state to "wither away."

In 1924, Lenin died and Joseph Stalin came to power. Stalin instituted his Five-Year Plans with the goals of increasing industrial and agricultural productivity. Individual farms were collectivized, and over five million who resisted were killed. An intensive program of heavy industrialization was begun. Education and basic health care were universal and free, women were given equal rights under the law, and organized religion was suppressed in favor of official atheism. At the same time, civil rights were non-existent. Until the 1950s, the Communist Party used state terror and purges to enforce submission; hundreds of thousands were tried and executed, and millions were imprisoned in a vast network of deadly labor camps. For several decades this aspect of Communism was denied or minimized, and Soviet propaganda seemed to offer a glimpse of a "future that works" to Marxist true believers around the world.

China

Even more than Russia, at the beginning of the twentieth century, China struggled to reconcile its 2000-year history and imperial traditions with the challenges of the modernizing West. The declining Qing Dynasty finally succumbed to the Chinese Revolution of 1911. The last emperor abdicated and China was declared a Republic, with a program of Western-oriented idealistic reforms focused on national independence from foreign control, constitutional democracy, and popular welfare. In reality, the country was fragmented into a series of warlord-dominated zones, reflecting China's long history of chaotic regional struggles whenever the strong central government weakened.

The Kuomintang (KMT) was the ruling nationalist party founded by Sun Yixian (Sun Yat-sen), and led after his death in 1925 by Jiang Jieshi (Chiang Kai-shek). They struggled to unify and modernize China in the face of continued Western extraterritorial privileges and increasing Japanese imperialist pressure. Although the new Soviet Union helped build the KMT's military power in the 1920s, by the 1930s, the Chinese Communist Party (CCP) had emerged as a major political and military rival, with a program more oriented towards China's huge rural population than its urban middle and working classes. The growing conflict with Japan after 1931 increased national feeling and cooperation among factions, but also weakened or destroyed China's most modern and Westernized sectors. After Japan's surrender in 1945, open civil war broke out, which ended in 1949, with the KMT's defeat and withdrawal offshore to Taiwan.

The second Chinese Revolution was launched in 1949 by the Communists' leader **Mao Zedong**, who proclaimed the People's Republic of China. Similar to the Russian experience, the Chinese had to adapt the German industrial theories of Marx to a huge and almost entirely rural nation. Stalin sent advisors and aid to the newest and largest Communist state (while the United States refused to recognize the new regime and treated it as a hostile power). Following totalitarian models of the period, the Party eliminated all opposition by killing and imprisoning millions, completely controlled cultural and political expression, and elevated Mao as the supreme and perfect dictator. Mao expanded the Party's existing land reform program, whereby landlords were dispossessed and often killed, and landless peasants were given their own parcels to farm in cooperative groups. This required social adjustment as well as economic: Communist ideology was promoted as a replacement for Confucian ideals, which had worked for thousands of years to enforce Chinese class hierarchies. Businesses were nationalized and a Five-Year Plan was begun to develop heavy industry along Soviet lines.

MAO'S INITIAL CHANGES TO CHINA	
Economic	• All businesses were nationalized. • Land was distributed to peasants. • Peasants were urged to pool their land and work more efficiently on cooperative farms.
Political	• A one-party totalitarian state was established. • Communist party became supreme. • Government attacked crime and corruption.
Social	• Peasants were encouraged to "speak bitterness" against landlords (10,000 landlords were killed as a result). • Communist ideology replaced Confucian beliefs. • Schools were opened with emphasis on political education. • Health care workers were sent to remote areas. • Women won equality (but little opportunity in government and were paid less than men). • The extended family was weakened.

Mao's ideological but often impractical focus on China's huge rural population led to erratic methods of national development. Not satisfied with the technocratic Soviet model, in the late 1950s Mao decreed the **Great Leap Forward**. All life was collectivized, private property was abolished, and ancient social customs replaced by Party activities. To achieve a modern industrial capacity, backyard steel furnaces were set up, in which farmers made iron and steel from scrap metal. The Great Leap Forward was a failure. The backyard furnaces produced poor quality iron, and bad weather combined with a drop in agricultural productivity to cause a major famine and the deaths of at least 30 million Chinese.

Mao's second major initiative was the Cultural Revolution of the late 1960s. In an effort to re-revolutionize China, young students known as the Red Guards imposed Maoist orthodoxy on institutions throughout Chinese society. Middle-class and educated people were persecuted or sent to the countryside for reeducation in the ways of the peasantry. As a result, the country lost an entire generation of skilled leaders. After Mao's death in 1976, the Party promoted a more moderate and rational path to modernization.

COMPARATIVE CLOSE-UP: THE ROLE OF WOMEN DURING THE RUSSIAN AND CHINESE REVOLUTIONS	
Russia	**China**
• Women served in the Red Army. • 65% of factory workers were women. • The government ordered equal pay (though it was not enforced). • Maternity leave with full pay was established. • Women entered professions.	• A new marriage law forbade arranged marriage (was met with resistance). • Women worked alongside men in factories. • State-run nurseries were set up to care for children. • Party leadership remained male. • Efforts were made to end foot-binding.

The Rise and Fall of Communism

China's radical Communist revolution took place just as Russia's was moderating. Maoism's apparent success inspired a new generation of Communist parties in the developing world during the Cold War. Cuba's successful revolution, led by **Fidel Castro** in 1959, introduced Communism to the Western Hemisphere. This led to direct nuclear confrontation between the United States and the Soviet Union in the 1962 Cuban Missile Crisis, and to repeated struggles between U.S.-supported governments and rural rebels supported by Cuba and the U.S.S.R., across Latin America and the Caribbean basin. Limited successes in Peru, Colombia, Venezuela, the Dominican Republic, Nicaragua, and Chile were countered or crushed by the United States and the local governing classes. In Cuba and much of Latin America, the economies were primarily based on commodity exports. Communism had even less chance to overcome its contradictions than in the self-sufficient Marxist states in Eurasia.

Likewise, in Asia and Africa, uprisings, civil wars, and occasionally successful revolutions were based on anti-imperialist or nationalist forms of Communism, supported by Soviet and/or Chinese diplomacy, aid, and military supplies. Successful examples include Vietnam and North Korea, which resisted Western military pressure. More isolated Communist movements or governments arose in underdeveloped former colonies like Indonesia, Malaya, Angola, Mozambique, and the Republic of the Congo, but these states struggled. The collapse and retreat of Soviet and Chinese Communism at the end of the 1980s signaled the failure of Marxist-Leninism and Maoism as world-changing revolutionary ideologies in the twentieth century.

Populist and National Revolutions

Early in the twentieth century, before the Great War, a number of independent empires on the periphery of the European world order underwent revolutions led by middle-class elites: Russia in 1905, Ottoman Turkey in 1908, and China and Persia in 1911.

Mexico

In this period Mexico experienced a populist Revolution that lasted almost ten years and involved, far more than the others, the common people of the country fighting for increased rights and participation in national affairs.

For decades, Mexico had been ruled by the dictator Porfirio Díaz. His approach to modernization was to encourage foreign investment in land and industry. In 1910, the people rose up against Díaz in support of the liberal leader Madero. The liberal elites soon discovered they had incited a greater uprising than expected, and events spiraled out of control. Leaders from rural districts such as Pancho Villa and Emiliano Zapata advocated and fought for land reform. Power changed hands continually throughout the civil war, as leaders were assassinated or overthrown. Eventually, conservative forces won out and under Carranza an assembly wrote the historic Constitution of 1917.

The Constitution promised land reform, imposed restrictions on foreign economic control, set minimum salaries and maximum hours for workers, granted workers the right to unionize and strike, and placed restrictions on Church-owned property and schools. Since the concessions to the masses of urban laborers and rural farmers were approved by conservative elites, there was no counter-revolution; Mexico has been relatively stable and slowly developed on its own terms ever since. After its establishment in 1929, the National Revolutionary Party (later named the Party of Institutionalized Revolution, or PRI) dominated politics for the remainder of the century, instituting land redistribution and standing up to foreign companies. Although the Mexican Revolution inspired reformers and populists in Latin America, it was unique with no direct influence on events elsewhere.

The Islamic World

In contrast to Communism's emphasis on radical change, Islamism in the twentieth century has focused on tradition, including earlier history when the Caliphate, established by the Prophet, united all Muslim peoples under one rule. As the European world order collapsed in this period, Western-style nationalism proved an effective force for anti-imperialist independence movements. At the same time, it conflicted with the world's emphases on reunification and consolidation in the name of the faith.

Turkey

In 1914, the breakup of the Ottoman Empire, the last incarnation of the Caliphate, was already taking place due to European imperial pressure in Eastern Europe and Northern Africa. In fact, the Great War itself was started by competition of two Empires, Austria-Hungary and Russia, to control former Ottoman lands in the Balkans. During the Great War, the Allies mobilized Arab resentment of Turkish domination. The Young Turks, progressive modernizers who had already pressed the sultan for reforms before the war, fought to preserve Anatolian Turkey from being carved up by the victorious Allies in 1919. Under Kemal Ataturk, the Caliphate was abolished, with Islam taking a back seat to nationalism and modernization in the new Republic of Turkey. The Kemalist state has since balanced industrial development and its strategic position between West and East, against the continuing strength of Islamic faith and practice among its people. Turkish intellectuals and clerics continue to debate the possibilities and contradictions of the world's most secular Muslim state.

The Arab World

The Arabian Peninsula was largely unified by the Saud dynasty by 1932, becoming Saudi Arabia. However, the Pan-Arab advocates in the Levant saw the Ottoman Empire cynically replaced by imperial Britain and France, which divided the region up into "mandates" of the League of Nations. Iraq, the former Mesopotamian provinces of the Ottomans, rebelled and was gradually given independence by Britain by 1932; on the other hand, Jordan, Palestine, and Syria did not achieve independence until after the Second World War. Tthe Arab national states of the Middle East are still torn by competing sects and ethnic groups, but united by opposition to Israel and by their Islamic heritage. They have exchanged kings for dictators, have used their oil wealth and strategic locations in international relations, and have tried to both appease and control Islamic activism.

Iran

Persia, descended from one of the world's oldest civilizations, was still an independent empire in 1914, despite Russian and British incursions. Nationalist elites, allied with the Islamic clergy, had been engaged in a revolution against the dynastic Shahs since 1906. They created a parliament and a constitutional monarchy, and removed some of the foreign influence over their government. After the Great War, in response to Soviet and British interference to control the nation's oil resources, army leader Reza Pahlavi was declared the new Shah and the country was renamed Iran. Anti-Communist and secular, he introduced numerous modern reforms along Western lines. He also followed Turkey's example in demanding that Muslims liberalize their practices to accommodate social progress, wear modern clothing, and give more freedom to women. After he chose to back Nazi Germany in the Second World War, Pahlavi was replaced in 1941 by his son, Mohammed Reza Pahlavi.

The new Shah continued to modernize Iran in the postwar world, as U.S. influence replaced British influence and Soviet pressure remained a constant factor. In the 1960s, he began a massive land reform and industrial program to enlist peasant and working class support against the land-lords, clergy, and educated middle classes who resented his authoritarian and anti-democratic rule. Fueled by oil revenue, his regime increased in world influence in the 1970s, but he lost touch with the changing social dynamics among his people. Faced with the uncertainties of an industrial revolution, more Iranians from every class saw the traditionalist Shi'ite Muslim clergy, led by exiled Ayatollah Khomeini, as their most faithful representatives. In 1979, increasing civil resistance forced the Shah to leave Iran. Khomeini returned, and within months the nation voted to become an Islamic Republic. The Islamic Revolution put the clergy in charge and imposed a fundamentalist theocracy that was hostile to the secular and Christian West, to Israel, and to atheistic Communism. Iran remains a regional industrial and military power and an example of the power of religious, rather than political or economic, ideas in modern revolutionary history.

Cuba

From 1939 to 1959, Cuba was ruled by the dictatorship of Batista, under which a small percentage of people were very wealthy and the masses of peasants were impoverished. **Fidel Castro** organized a guerrilla movement which initially failed, but eventually captured power in 1959. Though he had promised to hold elections, Castro did not do so, and at first even denied that he was a communist. When he established close ties with the Soviet Union, the United States viewed him as a threat.

In 1961, Castro announced his communist plans for Cuba: collectivized farms, centralized control of the economy, and free education and medical services. Tensions with the United States continued when a group of Cuban exiles in 1961, supported by the United States, launched a failed invasion attempt, known as the Bay of Pigs.

In 1962, a standoff known as the Cuban Missile Crisis occurred when Soviet missiles were discovered in Cuba. The United States and the Soviet Union compromised, and a third world war was avoided.

INDEPENDENCE AND NATIONALIST MOVEMENTS

High-Yield

Throughout the twentieth century, independence movements and nationalism have risen in response to the decline or defeat of colonial powers. The primary mission of these movements has been to resist and expel foreign occupiers. In some cases, the new nations have been able to negotiate their independence with a relative lack of violence, depending on their economic, social, and historical relationship to the colonial power. Factors in the outbreak of colonial warfare included the size of European settler populations, the perceived importance of the colony to the ruling country's economy and national prestige, and the radicalism of the independence movement's ideology.

Negotiated Independence

India

India's nationalist movement under the British Empire, originating in the late nineteenth century, was led by the upper-class members of the **Indian National Congress**. From the beginning, India's nationalists were divided between Hindu and Muslim factions. The Muslim population was in the minority, over all, and its leaders often deviated from Congress' insistence that British India was destined to be a single independent federated nation. After World War I, Britain's Government of India Act of 1919 granted some domestic power to the Congress but left far more power in British hands compared to the "white" dominions of Canada and Australia, which were also agitating for more independence at this time. Britain balanced its reform effort with increased prosecutions for sedition, arousing popular resentment. At Amritsar, a British general ordered troops to fire on a protest rally, killing many hundreds of unarmed civilians. This shocking episode, and the British public's approval of it, began to push Indian opinion away from Dominion status (domestic self-rule within the Empire) and towards complete independence.

At this time, Mohandas Gandhi emerged. Gandhi focused on the peasant roots and spiritual traditions of India and helped turn the Congress Party from an elite debating society into a disciplined mass movement. His methods of *satyagraha*, civil disobedience against unjust laws, and *ahimsa*, nonviolence in the face of police action, highlighted the injustice of British rule. In the 1930s, Britain proposed a federal structure for India to protect minority Muslim rights, but the Muslim League, under **Muhammad Ali Jinnah**, countered with a demand that India be divided into two separate states, Muslim and Hindu.

When World War II began, the British offered domestic rule in return for cooperation against Germany and Japan. Despite Gandhi's "Quit India" resistance campaign and Japan's attempts to recruit an Indian liberation army as it approached the Bengali border, the Indian people again generally supported Britain in the war. After the war, the British realized they could no longer count on the Indian bureaucracy for governing and policing, but they could not afford a military campaign of suppression and conquest. On August 15, 1947, independence was granted to India.

However, increasing violence between Hindus and Muslims had persuaded the British to agree to an **India/Pakistan Partition**, which led to the creation of Hindu India and Muslim Pakistan. This division led to a mass cross-migration of Muslim and Hindu refugees amid terrible civil slaughter. Hundreds of thousands were killed, which poisoned relations between India and Pakistan going forward. The two nations fought four wars over the next fifty years. Pakistan itself was composed of western and eastern provinces, separated by India. The populations, of different ethnic groups and ancestral history, shared only their Muslim religion. In 1971, East Pakistan fought for its national independence and became Bangladesh.

Africa

By 1914, almost all of Africa had been carved up by European powers. Economically, it had been transformed by the development of monoculture plantations of cash crops for export and mines of precious materials such as gold and diamonds. The ownership of these properties was exclusively in the hands of European merchants. In the period after World War II, the largely left-wing popular European governments had little interest in subsidizing imperial enterprises. In addition, many of the African colonies saw a rise in a democratically-minded elite class, eager for independence.

As in India, Africans mobilized urban residents into mass-movement independence parties, with labor organizations, social clubs, literary circles, and youth movements all becoming vehicles for protest. These movements grew steadily in the decade after the war, with early liberation in North Africa: Morocco, Libya, Egypt, Tunisia, and Sudan. The Gold Coast, taking the name Ghana and led by Kwame Nkrumah, was the first sub-Saharan nation to achieve its independence in 1957. As Britain and France accepted their inability to maintain worldwide empires and faced pressure by the U.N., a flood of new African nations sprang up in the next ten years. Almost thirty new nations gained independence in relatively peaceful transfers of power. This was only less than a century after the infamous "Scramble for Africa" of the late nineteenth century.

The arbitrary political borders drawn by the European colonial powers created many nations that were comprised of unrelated ethnic groups. These often had a history of conflict that began long before the colonial era, and in the new states they became rivals competing for power. For example, the Republic of the Congo exploded in a five-year civil war in 1960, when Belgium abruptly withdrew in the face of nationalist demands. Secessionist movements, such as Biafra in Nigeria and Shafta in Kenya, and civil conflict, such as in Chad and the Hutu genocide in Burundi, were not uncommon in post-colonial Africa. There were also structural difficulties in development, as the colonial powers had modernized the local economies and societies solely to exploit and export national resources. More broad-based modernization efforts often stumbled over tensions between unequally developed regions and sectors, and dictatorships and military rule were characteristic aspects of Africa's political culture in the 1960s and 70s.

Zionism and Palestinian Nationalism

Following World War I, the British ruled Palestine under a League of Nations mandate, replacing the Ottoman Empire. In the Balfour Declaration of 1917, the British government supported a homeland for Jews in Palestine, in line with the European Zionist movement for Jewish nationalism. However, Arab Palestinians saw both British rule and Jewish settlements as forms of western and non-Islamic imperial control, and the British tried to control the violence between communities as the Jewish minority slowly grew in numbers and wealth.

At the end of World War II, the regional Pan-Arab movement joined the Palestinians in opposing the creation of a Jewish state, but the Holocaust had motivated the Jewish people to find a secure homeland. By 1947, the weakened British Empire turned the question over to the United Nations, which planned to divide the area into two states. Paralleling India, in that a negotiated end to colonial rule led to violence and mass migrations between rival groups, a war ensued. Jewish victories over the neighboring Arab nations led to the creation of the state of Israel on May 14, 1948. As Jews were expelled from newly independent Arab states in the region and relocated to Israel, Palestinian refugees from Israel resettled in cities and camps in neighboring Jordan and adjacent lands.

Both sides claim the ancient Holy Land as their national homeland, and fighting continues to plague this region. Israel fought three subsequent wars with its Arab neighbors, including the Six Day War in 1967, which expanded its territory into the Jordanian West Bank and Egypt's Sinai. Since then, Israel and the Arab states gradually established a local "Cold War" kind of stability in the 1970s and 80s, and the Palestinian Liberation Organization (PLO) has used terrorism to press for a Palestinian state to replace Israel in the region.

Island States

Islands have been important for expanding European empires since the Age of Exploration, either as plantation colonies or for their strategic position on the sea lanes. In the twentieth century a large number of island colonies achieved independence as national movements confronted weakened or restructured empires. The first was Cuba, which rebelled from Spain in 1898, only to come under effective political domination by the United States; it would take another sixty years for a Communist revolution to expel U.S. influence. Ireland, long dominated by nearby Great Britain, waged a guerrilla war after World War I to achieve home rule as the Irish Free State, a Dominion like Canada and Australia. Complete independence as the Irish Republic followed soon after in 1937. Britain's rule in Protestant Northern Ireland remained a source of conflict and terrorist violence for decades to come.

After the Second World War, the United States conceded independence to island colonies that were unprofitable, strategically unnecessary, or unsustainable in the face of nationalist resistance. The Philippines, Papua-New Guinea, and many Polynesian island groups in the Pacific; Jamaica and a number of smaller islands in the Caribbean; Cyprus in the Mediterranean; and Madagascar and Sri Lanka in the Indian Ocean all negotiated their national freedom in the postwar period. As with their continental counterparts, these countries were often consumed by factional or ethnic strife that had been suppressed by the colonial powers.

Armed Struggles for Independence

Africa

Several European colonies in Africa had developed relatively large settler communities. These groups, supported by the colonial governments, resisted independence movements by the native majorities, leading to armed conflicts and full-fledged wars. In Kenya, the violent Mau Mau rebellion was suppressed by the British Army, but this accelerated the movement towards full independence in 1963. Similarly, since 1848 coastal **Algeria** had been part of metropolitan France, and a large white settler community had lived there for many generations as a privileged class over the native Algerians. In the 1950s, the National Liberation Front (FLN) began a terrorist campaign to drive out the French. A large French army waged counterinsurgency war for years, and the local French government collapsed as the conflict proved unwinnable. After Algerian independence in 1962, large numbers of colonial whites departed; Algeria has since been torn between Islamic and modernizing socialist currents, leading to civil war in the 1990s.

Southeast Asia

The peninsulas and archipelagos of Southeast Asia were occupied by Japan during the war. The defeat of the Europeans by an Asian army, as well as the harsher policies of the Japanese themselves, helped rouse a generation of nationalist movements to evict the ruling empires.

In the Dutch East Indies, Sukarno declared independence for Indonesia in 1945, and the Netherlands fought a four-year colonial war before admitting defeat and withdrawing from its 350-year old possessions. Britain was challenged by a communist insurgency in Malaya in the 1950s, which it successfully defeated while preparing the colony for independence. While not directly comparable, the Malayan experience contrasts remarkably with Vietnam. Among other factors, many Malayans knew and trusted the British and were willing to fight with them against the guerrillas, and the British emphasized small-unit jungle tactics rather than massive firepower.

Vietnam

French Indochina was evacuated by Japan in 1945, and immediately a group of Vietnamese nationalists under the leadership of **Ho Chi Minh** began a guerrilla campaign against the returning French. The French-Indochina War lasted nine years before defeat at Dien Bien Phu forced France to quit. Indochina was divided into Vietnam, Laos, and Cambodia. Reflecting the communist ideology of the fighters in the north, Vietnam was split into a communist North and a nationalist South. Cold War dynamics led the United States to support South Vietnam in the name of resisting communist China's regional aggression. After 1965, the United States committed a massive army to defend South Vietnam, but the North's determination, roots in ancient Vietnamese patriotism, and greater willingness to take casualties eventually won them the war. A negotiated peace preceded full Communist victory in 1975, after thirty years of war. Vietnam was devastated by intensive combat and took years to recover. Laos and Cambodia also suffered destruction from civil conflicts, including the Cambodian revolutionary genocide of the 1970s. The nationalist character of Vietnamese communism was revealed a few years later when Vietnam fought a war to repel Chinese influence in postwar Indochina.

Failed Struggles

The story of nationalism in the twentieth century would be incomplete without reviewing the many instances of regions or peoples who failed to achieve independence. Some struggles involved violence, terrorism, and guerrilla warfare; others were tied to regional or superpower politics; and others still were expressed more through art and mobilization. Just a few of the most prominent examples were: the Basque region, Catalonia, Northern Ireland, and Turkish Cyprus in Europe; Chiapas, Quebec, and Puerto Rico in the Americas; Biafra and Darfur in Africa; Tibet, Taiwan, Okinawa, Mindanao, East Timor, Kashmir, West Papua, Kurdistan, Palestine, Tamil Sri Lanka, and Chechnya in Asia.

POLITICAL REFORM AND ECONOMIC CHANGES

In the last third of the twentieth century, new trends and patterns in global politics led to changes in many countries. The developed world's economy had recovered from the destruction and distortions of the century's global conflicts. The Cold War, already a period of relative peace compared to the world wars, had come to a peaceful end. Large sections of the underdeveloped world, freed from imperial influence, were engaged in industrial revolutions similar to the ones that had transformed Europe and America. Increasingly efficient technologies and transportation, free trade, and liberal monetary policies promoted further globalization, driven by a single world economy based on consumer and business markets. This was accompanied by the relative decline of the United States and the growth of other regional world powers. Some of these world powers were derived from the ancient empires of previous eras, such as in Europe, Russia, Western Asia, South Asia, and East Asia; some were located in new geographies due to changes in resources and populations: Brazil, North America, South Africa, and Australasia.

China

After Mao died in 1976, **Deng Xiaoping** came to power and instituted the Four Modernizations: industry, agriculture, technology, and national defense. Foreign and domestic investment was encouraged; industrialists assembled massive conglomerates and great wealth, and entire cities were redeveloped. Research and development focused on futuristic technologies, and thousands of students were sent abroad to study. As a result of these capitalist-style reforms, the economy boomed, and within a generation China had left behind its developing nation status. It was now on a path to restore, peacefully, its traditional position as a major global influencer.

This new China could not be called Communist, but the Communist Party still ruled China as a bureaucratic dictatorship. The rising middle class began to push for democratic reforms. In May of 1989, in parallel with the collapse of the Soviet Union, massive student demonstrations occurred in **Tiananmen Square**. Fearing both the Soviet outcome and the nationwide chaos that often occurred when an emperor was deposed, China's leadership sent troops and tanks to brutally crush the rebellion. Today, the government continues to promote the idea that single-party leadership and political stability are the only keys to China's success.

Africa

In the 1970s and 80s, United Nations economic sanctions and international boycotts brought global attention to the fundamental injustice of the apartheid system in South Africa. Finally, in 1989, the government began to institute racial reforms. African National Congress leader Nelson Mandela was released from jail after 26 years, and in 1994 he became the first president elected by all the people of South Africa.

Most African countries, newly independent since the 1960s and 70s, continued to struggle with growing populations, poverty, and resource mismanagement. Some long-term trends include: increasing commitments to democracy, a growing urbanized middle class, suppression of endemic diseases, and new infrastructure to promote intra-continental trade rather than commodity exports to the developed world. Countering these positive developments have been the ongoing epidemic of HIV/AIDS, numerous wars (including a major civil war in the Congo involving most of its neighboring countries), the 1994 genocide in Rwanda, emigration of skilled labor to European and Persian Gulf markets, and ongoing neo-imperial economic domination, often by the former colonial countries.

India and South Asia

After independence in 1948, India adopted a British-style parliamentary political system under the leadership of Nehru. Following Congress's socialist orientation, the state took ownership of major industries, resources, transportation, and utilities, but local and retail businesses and farmland remained private.

Unlike Gandhi, Nehru advocated industrialization, which revived Indian business traditions that the British had suppressed. India's foreign policy was one of non-alignment during the Cold War, but in fact it favored relations with the Soviet Union when its rival Pakistan aligned with China.

Pakistan's development of nuclear weapons led to India doing the same. The resulting standoff mirrored the Cold War: like the United States and the Soviet Union, each side found it could not realistically threaten the other with atomic weapons, for fear of retaliation.

Dynastic traditions in the ruling classes of South Asia produced female prime ministers when the wives or daughters of Pakistani, Indian, and Bangladeshi leaders were elected to lead their countries. Nehru's daughter, Indira Gandhi, ruled India on and off from the 1960s until her assassination in 1984; she centralized the government's power, supported the break-up of rival Pakistan, and ruled by decree at one point.

Like Pakistan and Bangladesh, which struggle with Islamic militants and ancient social traditions, secular India has been challenged by Hindu radicals who seek to suppress India's Muslims and other religious minorities. Even so, India remains democratic, and supports a vibrant commercial and media culture that is independent of Western dominance. Later leaders have attempted to liberalize India's bureaucratically inefficient economy, both to modernize and industrialize the peasant countryside, and to compete with China in offering cheap manufacturing and outsourced services to Western nations using modern shipping and telecommunications. India's common use of English from the British period is an advantage. Like China, India seeks to reestablish itself as a major regional power in production, culture, and military force.

Soviet Union/Russia

After the death of Stalin, Khrushchev took power in 1953. He publicized and criticized Stalin's faults and crimes, shocking Soviet loyalists. Khrushchev also encouraged more freedom of expression in hopes of enlisting a new generation to help rebuild the country in modern ways. He also revitalized Communist interest in promoting world revolution, supporting radical factions engaged in colonial liberation struggles. Khrushchev's exaggerated personality and apparent losses in Cold War confrontations in Cuba and Berlin led to his removal, making him the first Soviet leader to retire alive.

From 1964 to 1982, Brezhnev focused on keeping the Party in control, with a more restrictive policy toward dissidents and free expression. During this period, industrial growth declined; the primary problems were the absence of economic incentives for individuals and a self-defeating system of production quotas which lowered rather than raised the baselines of acceptable quality and quantity. Communism proved insufficient for Russia's economic needs, while capitalism was better able to promote fair working conditions via government regulation and democratic restrictions on accumulation of wealth.

The Soviet Union opened itself to more Western contact in the 1970s, but the resulting ideologies only caused more dissatisfaction. The Soviet Union's involvement in Afghanistan's guerilla war in the 1980s highlighted its own ideological and social weaknesses on the domestic front. When Gorbachev came to power in 1985, he felt that only reform could save the Communist system. He introduced his policy of *perestroika* (restructuring), with limited elements of free enterprise and private capital. His parallel policy of *glasnost* (openness) encouraged open discussion of the strengths and weaknesses of the Soviet system. As with some other pre-revolutionary settings (France in 1789, Mexico in 1910, Russia in 1917), the attempted reform of a weakening regime only hastened its decline. The most tension existed between the Russian core and the Eastern European nations, as well as the western Soviet republics, like the Baltic states, Belorussia and Ukraine. From 1989 to 1991, these blocs successively declared their independence from U.S.S.R. control, with the discredited Soviet leadership unable to reimpose the old order. The Soviet Union essentially dissolved, succeeded by independent and non-Communist republics, including Russia itself.

In the 1990s, Russia's new leader Yeltsin oversaw the liquidation of the state-controlled economy. Massive amounts of capital wealth and natural resources were taken over by oligarchs with connections to the old system, and for years the common people saw few benefits from the fall of Communism. Several challenges remained, however: Russia's military forces were weakened, the former Eastern European satellites gravitated towards the European Union and NATO, and terrorists from the Islamic southern provinces challenged domestic order.

Eastern Europe

The Soviet Union dominated its satellite states in Eastern Europe following World War II, installing Communist leaders and closely monitoring their affairs. Economic hardships, foreign domination, and lack of political liberties led to discontent that erupted at times in rebellion. For example, Communist forces had to put down extensive riots in Germany, which became known as the Uprising of 1953 in East Germany.

In 1956, Hungary rose up, much like it had in 1848 under Austrian domination, but the Red Army crushed the revolt just as the Russian Army had done a century earlier. In 1968, the Prague Spring movement for civil and economic freedoms in Czechoslovakia was likewise suppressed by Soviet tanks. As with most Communist states in this period, the people did receive more education, the urban working classes grew in size, and the aristocratic classes were dispossessed as industry supplanted agriculture. Eastern Europe's relative success at integrating with the West in recent years indicates that in many ways the two halves of Europe have progressed on separate but parallel tracks.

The decline of the U.S.S.R. in the 1980s was marked by the rise of Solidarity, a Polish union-led social movement that defied martial law and eventually elected Lech Walesa the first anti-Communist president in 1990. In Czechoslovakia, the Velvet Revolution succeeded in 1989 where earlier efforts in 1968 had failed; without Soviet interference, poet Vaclav Havel was elected president. In that same summer, mass demonstrations in East Germany led to the opening of the border to West Germany, including the dramatic televised demolition of the infamous Berlin Wall. Further negotiations solidified the unification of Germany; the country remained in the Western military alliance despite Soviet protests. Memories of Germany's aggressive role in the twentieth century's global conflicts have not faded among its neighbors, but Germany has since amicably dominated the European Union through economic, not military, power.

After two generations of peace, warfare returned to Europe in the 1990s in, once again, the Balkan region. The end of the Cold War opened a series of ethnic-based civil wars in Yugoslavia, which split apart into its pre-1919 components of Serbia and Montenegro, Bosnia, Croatia, Slovenia and

Macedonia. Led by Slobodan Milosevic, Serbia revived its nationalist dream of "Greater Serbia" with a genocidal policy of "ethnic cleansing" in largely Islamic Bosnia and Kosovo. **NATO**, the North Atlantic Treaty Organization, intervened to suppress Serbia, and Milosevic was eventually tried for war crimes at the International War Crimes Tribunal.

Japan and East Asia

For seven years following World War II, Japan was governed by a U.S.-dominated occupation that imposed a liberal constitution, land reforms, and a new education system. The goal was to make Japan more Western-oriented and economically strong, both to prevent a revival of militarism and to defend against Communism in East Asia. Rather than allow a rebuilt military capable of new aggression, the United States offered a defensive alliance under its own naval and air forces. At the same time, the European empires in southeast Asia were disappearing, along with their closed trade systems. America promoted free trade and access to other countries' resources.

With these crucial changes from the prewar world, Japan was able to develop an export economy of manufactured goods, with a strong focus on technology. By the 1970s, Japanese corporations and banks were world-class competitors with European and American enterprises, and Japan had rebuilt itself as a solidly united and wealthy member of the First World, the only country from Asia with such global influence.

In similar ways, several smaller nations used Japan's approach to build themselves into economic powerhouses. Taiwan, Singapore, Hong Kong, and South Korea lacked natural resources or large territories, but they invested in infrastructure and human capital in order to become advanced industrialized countries or city-states.

In the early 1990s, Japan's economy formed a speculative bubble that, when it burst, caused a contraction that lasted almost ten years. The "Lost Decade" was made worse by a rapidly aging demographic profile. Other East Asian economies, including not just the four above but also Australia, Thailand, Vietnam, Indonesia, the Philippines, and especially China, grew at faster rates in the 1990s; eventually, though, they too suffered a financial crisis in 1997.

Latin America

Due to gaining national independence in the nineteenth century, and being distinctly in the United States' area of influence since the beginning of the twentieth century, Latin America's struggle to develop and modernize was less affected by Europe's issues than were the colonies and former empires of Eurasia and Africa. After the Second World War, Latin America's countries began to focus more on internal economic development rather than continue their traditional emphasis on commodity exports. Growth was slower than in Europe or parts of Asia, and as countries became wealthier, old conflicts arose; populist or socialist regimes favored more redistribution, while the traditional elites argued for social stability, wealth accumulation, and capital reinvestment. Military dictatorships often controlled these conflicts, except in countries like Mexico, Colombia, Venezuela, or Costa Rica, which had achieved a long-term political consensus between the classes and their leaders. Not coincidentally, these countries, along with the continental giant Brazil, also had the highest growth rates and most successful industrial progress. Communism, as promoted by Cuba, challenged many Latin American nations in the 1960s and 1970s, but the countering forces, supported by the United States, prevailed.

In the later decades of the century, regional growth slowed under the impact of high debt incurred during the boom in credit and commodity prices in the 1970s. The world economic crunch in the 1980s led to widespread defaults on loans, negative growth, and instances of hyperinflation in Argentina and Brazil. This, along with the defeat of world Communism, led to a 1990s trend in Latin America toward electoral democracy and neoliberal economics, featuring less regulation, more private investment, the privatization of state enterprises, and freer trade policies. This evident tribute to North American ideology had mixed results: there were more private enterprise and consumer imports, but also more unemployment and exploitative low-wage jobs.

TECHNOLOGY, POPULATIONS, AND THE ENVIRONMENT

Developments in Science

Western science continued to advance in the twentieth century. New scientific theories such as Einstein's Special and General Theories of Relativity, Planck's Quantum Theory, Von Neumann's Game Theory, Shannon's Information Theory, and Wilson's Plate Tectonic Theory led to significant advances in physics and astrophysics, economics, telecommunications and computing, and earth science. Development also continued from earlier theoretical breakthroughs in subjects like genetics, evolution, probability, logic, chemistry, and statistics. This kind of work supported a vast number of more specific discoveries, many of which stemmed from a desire for knowledge but resulted in practical technological designs and production. Pure science, in conjunction with more results-oriented research and development, thus became an industry in its own right; governments, corporations, and universities supported sciences in the hope of producing another breakthrough invention or method. The Nobel Prizes, first awarded in 1901, have become a coveted worldwide marker of national and institutional prestige in the sciences.

Developments in Technology

During the early twentieth century, technological inventions stemmed from the nineteenth century's drive to improve devices that ease or replace human labor. Electric motors and internal combustion engines were more practical and portable than steam engines. Automobiles and airplanes supplemented the railroad as transportation. Radio and television continued what the telephone and telegraph had started in communications. Electric appliances in general began to replace servants in households and the workplace. Huge infrastructure investments, like power grids, highways, and communication networks, spread from wealthier areas to further parts of the world.

The second half of the century saw radical breakthroughs; the new field of Information Technology allowed exponential increases in productivity by having machines control other machines. Analog devices like mechanical computers and automated switchboards in the early decades were revolutionized by electronic circuitry developed during World War II. Digital computers and similar equipment exploded onto the technological landscape in the 1960s; these were increasingly min-iaturized, and then applied to every form of mechanical device for governments, businesses, and consumers. The internet, connecting the world's computer systems and users into a single general information-sharing entity, began the next wave of transformation of society in the 1990s.

Consequences of Development

Cheap and easily adapted technology compressed the amount of time and money it took to mod-ernize an undeveloped region. Accordingly, the industrial revolutions of the later twentieth century in Asia, Africa, and Latin America were faster and more extensive than Europe's and North America's revolutions had been a century earlier. The general trend of automated control of mechanized production led to huge shifts in the employment of the working classes in developed countries. Factory work and resource extraction, as well as farm work, now used far fewer workers, while lightweight semi-skilled and service industries expanded to provide more consumer services. Rapid transport and communication, as well as liberalized trade conditions, also allowed these industries to be located in lower-wage world regions, further stressing the prospects of the lowest classes in higher-wage nations. Mass production of goods and energy around the world, however, led to large-scale environmental issues of ecological pollution, public health, and toxic disposal. The production of the world's power supply almost entirely from carbon combustion (the burning of oil and coal) began to change the global climate itself.

Population Growth

The human population of the world has grown tremendously in the past century, from approximately 1.6 billion to 6.1 billion people. Improved public health was facilitated by the use of sewage systems, and new medicines, including vaccines; similarly, education increased the life expectancy of families. Technological advances in agriculture, known as the **Green Revolution**, introduced chemical fertil-izers and high-producing seeds to the developing world. This postwar phenomenon fed the growing world population and prevented the famines that have cut short earlier eras of peace and prosperity.

Despite increased life expectancy, birth rates actually went down in developed societies as families invested more resources in raising fewer children. Thus, the population growth in the industrialized West and Japan stabilized by the end of the century, while the increase was more dramatic in the poorer regions in Asia and to the South. China and India currently have populations over a billion, despite strict family planning policies in China and birth control programs in India.

While traditional killer diseases such as malaria, **cholera**, smallpox and tuberculosis have come under control due to international public health efforts, population growth in some areas has been affected by new epidemic diseases that have spread more easily in the increasingly interconnected twentieth-century world. The influenza pandemic of 1918 killed 75 million people, and since the 1970s, **HIV/AIDS** has killed over 30 million people. In addition, in the wealthier parts of the world, longer lives, changing diets, and toxic environments have led to increases in other types of diseases such as diabetes, heart disease, and certain kinds of cancer.

Demographic Shifts

Though migration has been a theme throughout world history, it has increased across the past century. This includes internal migration (such people moving from rural to urban areas, or fleeing urban areas due to civil strife) and external migration (such as people migrating long distances and across borders, or in search of better economic conditions). The biggest factors have been imperialism, industrialization, and war.

Cause	Effect
Imperialism	In the early twentieth century, colonial empires expanded plantation crops for a growing world market; with slavery no longer an acceptable system, contract labor was imported to work the fields. For instance, British developments in the Caribbean and Indian Ocean basins attracted millions of Chinese and Indian workers.
Industrialization	From its inception, industrialization has depended on a working class drawn from rural area. The pattern seen in nineteenth-century Europe and America has been repeated across the southern tier (Latin America, Africa, southern Asia) as well as in Soviet Russia and modern China; hundreds of millions have moved to urban areas for work. The resulting explosion of urban areas, including industrial slums and social unrest, parallels earlier history in the West.
War	The extensive wars of the twentieth century's global conflicts have produced millions of refugees and displaced persons as borders changed, populations were expelled, workers were summoned to relocated war industries, and people evacuated devastated cities. Similar movements took place in the post-colonial adjustments and wars of liberation that characterized the Cold War era.
Post-Imperialism	Some external migrations have followed from past imperialism. Communities of Algerians and Vietnamese, for example, have settled in Paris; Pakistanis and Jamaicans have settled in London; Filipinos, Cubans, and Iranians have found havens in U.S. cities. This unexpected consequence of imperialism has resulted in new cultural identities for the host nations, as well as exclusionary reactions like anti-immigration movements.

Environmental Issues

The globe's huge population growth, combined with continuing industrialization, has contributed to significant environmental problems in this century that include the overuse of natural resources, contamination by pollution, and losses of plant and animal species. Many oceanic fish species are significantly depleted to the point where governments have had to prohibit commercial fishing. Unique flora and fauna species have disappeared with the destruction of tropical forests for slash-and-burn agriculture and timber operations. Smog has polluted many city areas, which has increased lung diseases, which can kill vulnerable populations. Water pollution has restricted fresh water access for many, particularly in developing nations. The damming of rivers for power, flood control, or irrigation has also interrupted aquatic species' life cycles; in some cases, so much water is drained off for irrigation projects that the watercourse fails to reach the sea. The increased use of petroleum and heavy metals like mercury in industrial production has also contributed to the pollution of entire ecosystems. Human population growth and prosperity has led to dramatic increases in the amount of trash produced by industrialized societies. Non-degradable and often toxic, this waste ends up in landfills or is transported to less developed countries to be salvaged.

Scientists have established that the industrialized world's massive increase in carbon-based fuels and other greenhouse gases has begun a gradual rise in overall global temperatures. This climate change is projected to have worldwide effects on the ecologies and food supplies of all human habitats, from droughts in some areas to increased precipitation in others. A broadly threatening aspect is rising ocean levels from melting ice caps, which will threaten the viability of most cities that are located on seacoasts.

In reaction to these threats, environmentalism has grown in visibility and political power; this movement to protect and wisely use our natural resources first appeared in the late 19th century. Since the 1970s, when postwar development led to visible environmental degradation, most national governments in the West have set up agencies to monitor industrial use of resources and to regulate waste products. The post-Communist states and developing nations have been slower to follow, for fear that excessive regulation will slow national growth. Countries with large natural territories have created regional and national parks and wildlife refuges in order to keep such areas intact for future generations of wildlife and people. International organizations, such as Greenpeace, the Sierra Club, and the World Wildlife Fund, work to protect the environment both through direct action and by lobbying governments for legal action.

GLOBALIZATION

High-Yield

More than ever before, the twentieth century world became interconnected through trade, cultural exchange, and political interaction on a mass scale. By the end of the century there was no single system of global hierarchy, beyond the domination of advanced Western nations in the areas of finance, trade, culture, and technology. However, even the European supremacy of past centuries began to be challenged by rising regional powers like China.

The ongoing problem of establishing international law and order did not end with the creation of the League of Nations and United Nations. Regional groups and treaty organizations, with echoes of the ancient tradition of defensive leagues and alliances between nations, do much to channel and direct global exchange.

Trade Organizations

Trade organizations are tasked with regulating trade and investment.

Organization	Description
World Bank	Created by the United States to ease reconstruction at the end of World War II, the World Bank assembles and distributes loans from wealthier nations to poorer ones. It uses its power to influence development in ways that favor established patterns and parties in the world economy.
International Monetary Fund (IMF)	A postwar U.S. creation that coordinates monetary exchange rates to maintain global financial stability.
Organization for Economic Co-operation and Development (OECD)	An economic group originating in postwar Europe that expanded in 1960 to include other Western-oriented capitalist democracies.
World Trade Organization (WTO)	Replaced the postwar General Agreement of Tariffs and Trade (GATT) in 1995. WTO is a worldwide group that works to promote unrestricted global trade, following the Free Trade theory first put forth by industrial Britain in the nineteenth century. Just as in the past, free trade for competitive industries runs up against the desire for tariff protection for agricultural producers; countries are more willing to depend on trade partners for manufactured goods than they are for their food supply.
Organization of Petroleum Exporting Countries (OPEC)	The only example here which does not represent the institutional dominance of the wealthy industrialized West. OPEC was organized in 1960 by four Arab states and Venezuela, as a cartel to raise the price of oil. In 1973, to retaliate against Western support for Israel in the Yom Kippur War, the mostly Muslim OPEC declared an oil embargo against the United States, Britain, and other allies, and raised oil prices worldwide. The short-term effects on the world economy were harsh, but in the long term OPEC lost influence as oil companies found new reserves outside of the group's control.

Regional Organizations

Regional organizations have formed to protect local interests. Unlike economic associations, these groups represent less powerful and formerly colonized areas in opposition to Western pressures.

Organization	Description
Association of Southeast Asian Nations (ASEAN)	Formed in 1967 to accelerate economic progress and promote political stability in the nations of the southeast Asian archipelago. In recent years it has expanded relations with neighboring regional superpowers like India, China, Japan, and Australia.
European Union (EU)	Formed from the European Community in 1993 in an effort to strengthen European economic trade relations and balance the influence of the United States. It has worked to smooth the reabsorption of formerly Communist eastern states into a larger but still Western-oriented Europe. Part of its policy has been to form an economic superpower equal to the United States through the adoption of a single multinational currency, the Euro.
Organization of American States (OAS)	The postwar successor of Western Hemisphere conferences that go back to the 1890s. It has been torn between a sense of mutual security in the face of threats from outside the hemisphere and internal conflicts mostly involving Latin American suspicion of U.S. dominance.
North American Free Trade Agreement (NAFTA)	Involves the United States, Canada, and Mexico, working since 1994 to remove trade barriers between these countries. To some degree it is a response to the EU's greater integration since the end of the Cold War.
Arab League	Includes twenty-two Arabic-speaking Muslim nations from northwest Africa to the Persian Gulf. Since 1945, it has tried to coordinate regional responses to a continual series of crises in the Middle East and northern Africa.
Organization of African Unity (OAU)	Begun in 1963 as sub-Saharan Africa rapidly gained independence from Britain, France, and Belgium. Along with providing coordination and cooperation among member states, the OAU explicitly supported the end of white minority and colonial rule in the continent. With no military force and a policy of noninterference, the OAU was ineffective in stopping wars or human rights violations among its members. In 2002, it was replaced by the African Union (AU), which attempts to emulate the EU with tighter monetary and military bonds among member states.

International Peace and Human Rights

Before the First World War, European nations set up a permanent Court of Arbitration at the Hague in the Netherlands in order to prevent wars by giving nations a way to settle international differences. This was supplemented after the First World War by a World Court operated by the League of Nations; the United Nations restored the World Court after the Second World War. The World Court continues to administer and judge cases of international law between consenting parties, enforced primarily by the UN Security Council.

Before World War I, agreements such as the Hague and Geneva Conventions defined the laws of war and war crimes; after World War II and the Holocaust, the victors set up tribunals at Nuremberg and Tokyo to prosecute war criminals. The Cold War stopped any universal standards from being enforced as each side protected its own interests. The UN did set up tribunals for the genocides committed in former Yugoslavia and Rwanda in the 1990s.

Human rights began to gain more attention from international organizations. In 1948, the newly formed United Nations issued a Universal Declaration of Human Rights to set the standard by which totalitarian or other abusive regimes could be judged and sanctioned. The conflict between the West's most modern conceptions of human rights (religious tolerance, political freedom, and women's liberation) and the conventional social and political practices of numerous non-Western member states has yet to be fully resolved. In addition, Western individualism and capitalism continues to conflict with collectivist notions that human rights include basic needs like food, health care, and income.

Finally, nongovernmental organizations (NGOs) such as CARE, Red Cross, Doctors Without Borders, and Greenpeace are rooted in citizen activism and have roots going back to Britain's Anti-Slavery Society in the early 1800s. NGOs work to tackle problems that reach beyond national boundaries and governments. These groups operate like nonprofits, in contrast to influential multinational corporations like Wal-Mart, General Motors, China Petro-Chemical, Hitachi, and Siemens, whose operations are at the heart of globalization, affecting hundreds of millions of people.

SOCIAL AND CULTURAL CHANGES   High-Yield

Racial Rebalancing

In 1900, W. E. B. Du Bois declared that "the world problem of the twentieth century is the problem of the color line," and his analysis has stood the test of time. The vast majority of inhabitants in colonies controlled by the white nations of Europe and America were people of color. They received varying degrees of civil and social rights, depending on class and situation, but in almost no cases were they held to be equal in status or ability to the white population. Added to this was the oppression of black and brown minority populations in white settler colonies in the Americas and Australasia. Much of the global fight for independence and national identity can be examined in a racial context, where racial inequality is overthrown along with imperialism. Some important examples of the struggle for racial equality include:

- The negritude movement among Francophone African intellectuals in the 1930s, rejecting assimilation and advocating solidarity among black Africans around the world.

- Afrocentrism among African-Americans in the United States during the Civil Rights era, seeking to correct the Eurocentrism in history, literature, and social studies produced by dominant European and American culture.

- **Pan-Africanism**, a conscious appeal to all people of African descent to see themselves as one nation, becoming a more practical proposition as African colonies achieved mass independence in the 1960s.

- The Civil Rights Act of 1965 in the United States, culminating in a mass movement by American blacks and liberal whites to repeal Southern segregation and white supremacy laws.

- The Brazilian Constitution of 1988, emphasizing civil liberties and criminalizing racial prejudice and speech against minorities, including the large Afro-Brazilian population.

Changing Gender Roles

Before 1914, there were few professional opportunities for women in the Western world. Most educated women were relegated to childrearing, nursing, or teaching, while working class women had long been employed in home production or light industry. The fight for female suffrage in the West saw its first successes in New Zealand, Australia, and Finland at the turn of the century. Women's participation in the industrial and professional labor forces during the First World War changed more minds, and in most of Europe and the United States women became voters between the 1920s and 1940s. In the prosperous 1920s, fashion and popular culture helped create a new image of the modern middle-class woman—free from some of the constraints of traditional gender roles. The Second World War further advanced women's image as workers, citizens, and even soldiers, but peacetime saw a backlash as women were expected to return homemaking and low-prestige, part-time jobs in the service economy. In less developed parts of the world only the most adventurous or high-status women were visible in public life, even as industrialism and urbanization offered up more opportunities to work outside the home.

In the 1960s and 70s, the Western world experienced a sexual revolution, challenging traditional gender norms, marriage as an institution, and the nuclear family. Related factors included greater access to convenient birth control, liberalized divorce and property laws, countercultural rebellion, and the availability of more lucrative service-sector jobs. Since the 1970s, issues of accessible and affordable child care and equal pay for equal work have been debated but not fully resolved. The realms of politics, law, and medicine have become more open to women in the last half of the twentieth century, while successful female leaders, such as in Israel and Great Britain, have demonstrated that national-level politics is no longer an all-male domain.

In parts of the developing world, changes to gender roles have varied. Some socialist and Communist societies instituted important legal reforms for women, such as the 1950 marriage law in China which granted free choice of partners. In reality, many traditional customs still prevail there as in other largely rural and pre-modern areas. China's one-child policy of the 1980s and 1990s overlapped with rapid industrialization, lowering birth rates and freeing women to work in more long-term positions.

Religious Development

Traditional religious devotion declined in much of the developed world during the twentieth century, leading to a rise in secular agnosticism and humanism, as well as liberal Christianity and Judaism. New forms of spirituality also developed from blending Eastern and Western traditions. **Liberation theology in Latin America** reinterpreted Catholicism as an aggressive social reform movement, to the disapproval of the Vatican. However, many communities of faith have turned to fundamentalist forms of religion as a result of globalization, reacting against the changes to traditional beliefs and customs. The shift toward fundamentalism has occurred in factions of all the major religions throughout the world.

Internationalization

As the world becomes more and more connected, distinctions and barriers between cultures have become blurred and weakened. Western entertainment companies (in particular movie and music producers) have spread worldwide, carrying Western cultural ideas along with them. American fast food brands like McDonald's, Coca-Cola, and Kentucky Fried Chicken can be found in most parts of the world today. Western vendors of finance, technology, scholarship, business expertise, architecture and engineering have helped spread ideas about individualism, consumption, self-fulfillment, and family roles to areas with sometimes radically different approaches to life. This trend has been characterized as cultural imperialism, replacing the political and physical imperialism of the past with something more insidious and destructive.

Globalization, on the other hand, has enabled cultural diffusion to take place in the other direction. Through tourism and immigration, Western consumers have opportunities to appreciate non-Western arts, foods, and other cultural markers. Sports have also become more internationalized, with the Olympics and the World Cup Soccer competitions enjoying popularity in all regions of the world. In addition, the rise of the use of the English language is an indication of a developing global culture. The English language has spread worldwide, transmitted through international business and diplomacy, as well as through movies, music, and the Internet.

PART 4

Practice Exams

Practice Exam 1

HOW TO TAKE THE PRACTICE EXAMS

The next section of this book consists of three full-length practice exams. Taking a practice AP exam gives you an idea of what it's like to answer AP questions under conditions that approximate those of the real exam. You'll find out which areas you're strong in and where additional review may be required. Any mistakes you make now are ones you won't make on the actual exam, as long as you take the time to learn where you went wrong.

The three full-length practice exams in this book each include 55 multiple-choice questions, three short-answer questions (including your choice of two prompts for the third question), one document-based question, and one long essay question (your choice from three prompts). You will have 55 minutes for the multiple choice questions, 40 minutes for the short answer questions, 60 minutes for the document based question, and 40 minutes for the long essay question. Before taking a practice exam, find a quiet place where you can work uninterrupted, and bring blank lined paper for the free-response questions. (The proctor will provide lined paper when you take the official exam.) Time yourself according to the time limit given at the beginning of each section. It's okay to take a short break between sections, but for the most accurate results, you should approximate real test conditions as much as possible.

As you take the practice exams, remember to pace yourself. Train yourself to be aware of the time you are spending on each problem. Try to be aware of the general types of questions you encounter, as well as being alert to certain strategies or approaches that help you to handle the various question types more effectively.

After taking a practice exam, be sure to read the detailed answer explanations that follow. These will help you identify areas that could use additional review. Even when you answered a question correctly, you can learn additional information by looking at the answer explanation.

Finally, it's important to approach the exam with the right attitude. You're going to get a great score because you've reviewed the material and learned the strategies in this book.

Good luck!

Practice Exam 1 Answer Grid

1. Ⓐ Ⓑ Ⓒ Ⓓ
2. Ⓐ Ⓑ Ⓒ Ⓓ
3. Ⓐ Ⓑ Ⓒ Ⓓ
4. Ⓐ Ⓑ Ⓒ Ⓓ
5. Ⓐ Ⓑ Ⓒ Ⓓ
6. Ⓐ Ⓑ Ⓒ Ⓓ
7. Ⓐ Ⓑ Ⓒ Ⓓ
8. Ⓐ Ⓑ Ⓒ Ⓓ
9. Ⓐ Ⓑ Ⓒ Ⓓ
10. Ⓐ Ⓑ Ⓒ Ⓓ
11. Ⓐ Ⓑ Ⓒ Ⓓ
12. Ⓐ Ⓑ Ⓒ Ⓓ
13. Ⓐ Ⓑ Ⓒ Ⓓ
14. Ⓐ Ⓑ Ⓒ Ⓓ

15. Ⓐ Ⓑ Ⓒ Ⓓ
16. Ⓐ Ⓑ Ⓒ Ⓓ
17. Ⓐ Ⓑ Ⓒ Ⓓ
18. Ⓐ Ⓑ Ⓒ Ⓓ
19. Ⓐ Ⓑ Ⓒ Ⓓ
20. Ⓐ Ⓑ Ⓒ Ⓓ
21. Ⓐ Ⓑ Ⓒ Ⓓ
22. Ⓐ Ⓑ Ⓒ Ⓓ
23. Ⓐ Ⓑ Ⓒ Ⓓ
24. Ⓐ Ⓑ Ⓒ Ⓓ
25. Ⓐ Ⓑ Ⓒ Ⓓ
26. Ⓐ Ⓑ Ⓒ Ⓓ
27. Ⓐ Ⓑ Ⓒ Ⓓ
28. Ⓐ Ⓑ Ⓒ Ⓓ

29. Ⓐ Ⓑ Ⓒ Ⓓ
30. Ⓐ Ⓑ Ⓒ Ⓓ
31. Ⓐ Ⓑ Ⓒ Ⓓ
32. Ⓐ Ⓑ Ⓒ Ⓓ
33. Ⓐ Ⓑ Ⓒ Ⓓ
34. Ⓐ Ⓑ Ⓒ Ⓓ
35. Ⓐ Ⓑ Ⓒ Ⓓ
36. Ⓐ Ⓑ Ⓒ Ⓓ
37. Ⓐ Ⓑ Ⓒ Ⓓ
38. Ⓐ Ⓑ Ⓒ Ⓓ
39. Ⓐ Ⓑ Ⓒ Ⓓ
40. Ⓐ Ⓑ Ⓒ Ⓓ
41. Ⓐ Ⓑ Ⓒ Ⓓ
42. Ⓐ Ⓑ Ⓒ Ⓓ

43. Ⓐ Ⓑ Ⓒ Ⓓ
44. Ⓐ Ⓑ Ⓒ Ⓓ
45. Ⓐ Ⓑ Ⓒ Ⓓ
46. Ⓐ Ⓑ Ⓒ Ⓓ
47. Ⓐ Ⓑ Ⓒ Ⓓ
48. Ⓐ Ⓑ Ⓒ Ⓓ
49. Ⓐ Ⓑ Ⓒ Ⓓ
50. Ⓐ Ⓑ Ⓒ Ⓓ
51. Ⓐ Ⓑ Ⓒ Ⓓ
52. Ⓐ Ⓑ Ⓒ Ⓓ
53. Ⓐ Ⓑ Ⓒ Ⓓ
54. Ⓐ Ⓑ Ⓒ Ⓓ
55. Ⓐ Ⓑ Ⓒ Ⓓ

SECTION I
Time—95 Minutes
58 Questions

Directions: Section I, Part A of this exam contains 55 multiple choice questions. The questions are organized into sets with corresponding historical sources. Each of the questions or incomplete statements is followed by four suggested answers or completions. Using both the provided source and your own historical knowledge, select the best answer choice.

Questions 1–3 refer to the passage below.

"Justinian created countless cities which did not exist before. And finding that the belief in God was . . . straying into errors . . . he brought it about that it stood on the firm foundation of a single faith. Moreover, finding laws obscure because they had become far more numerous than they should be, and in obvious confusion because they disagreed with each other. He preserved them [in the Legal Code of Emperor Justinian, A.D. 529] . . . by controlling their discrepancies with the greatest firmness."

Excerpt from *Buildings* by Procopius, Justinian's official court historian, circa 530 C.E.

1. Which of the following statements is true regarding religion under Justinian's rule?

   (A) The Roman Catholic Church split into Western and Eastern Orthodox branches.

   (B) Justinian encouraged a return to worshiping the gods and goddesses of the ancient Greek and Roman civilizations.

   (C) Justinian sought to limit the influence of Islam on his empire.

   (D) Justinian worked to convert his empire to Orthodox Christianity.

2. As emperor, Justinian based the principles of his law code most directly on

   (A) Hammurabi's Code

   (B) the Ten Commandments

   (C) the Roman Twelve Tables of Law

   (D) Islamic Sharia Law

3. Which of the following is true about the geography of the Byzantine Empire?

   (A) Justinian expanded the empire's territory to include nearly all of Italy and parts of Spain, North Africa, and Western Asia.

   (B) The empire's secluded geographic location was a detriment to its struggling economy and left it vulnerable to military attacks.

   (C) Even after Justinian's death, the empire continued to expand into both Western Europe and Asia.

   (D) At the time of Justinian's ascension to the throne, Byzantine territory included most of the Mediterranean Sea.

GO ON TO THE NEXT PAGE

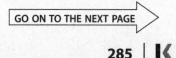

Questions 4–5 refer to the passage below.

"Oh Buddhas
Of unexcelled complete enlightenment
Bestow your invisible aid
Upon this hut I open
On the mountaintop"

Saichō, "Prayer on Mount Hiei," *Selected Writings*, circa 800 C.E.

4. Which of the following is most likely true about Saichō, a ninth-century Buddhist?

   (A) He worshiped natural objects like trees and mountains.

   (B) He strove to become Siddhartha Gautama, the Enlightened One.

   (C) He questioned his ability to reach nirvana.

   (D) He sought wisdom through contemplation and followed the Eightfold path.

5. Which of the following religions, in addition to Buddhism, has had the greatest impact on Japan through the centuries?

   (A) Daoism

   (B) Shinto

   (C) Christianity

   (D) Confucianism

GO ON TO THE NEXT PAGE

Questions 6–7 refer to the passage below on Daoism.

"The more prohibitions there are in the world,
The more sharp weapons the people have,
The more disorder is fomented in the family and state.
The more adroit and clever men are,
The more deceptive things are brought forth.
The more laws and ordinances are promulgated,
The more thieves and robbers there are."

Excerpt from Laozi's "Tao Te Ching," *Sources of Chinese Tradition*, 1999

6. Which of the following reflects the Daoist attitude toward war?

(A) It is better to submit to invaders than to engage in warfare.

(B) War should be used only for defensive purposes.

(C) War should be used as a tool to spread the beliefs of Daoism.

(D) Warriors should be revered as gods.

7. Based on the above excerpt, which of the following would a Daoist governor disagree with?

(A) Strict laws and punishments are needed to keep criminals in check.

(B) Stockpiling weaponry leads to civil strife.

(C) The more order a leader tries to impose, the more unstable society becomes.

(D) Economic control does not necessarily increase economic prosperity.

GO ON TO THE NEXT PAGE

 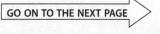

Questions 8–10 refer to the passage below.

"Hammurabi, the exalted prince, who feared God, to bring about the rule of righteousness in the land, to destroy the wicked and the evil-doers; so that the strong should not harm the weak; so that I should rule over the black-headed people like Shamash, and enlighten the land, to further the well-being of mankind.

Law 117. If any one fail to meet a claim for debt, and sell himself, his wife, his son, and daughter for money or give them away to forced labor: they shall work for three years in the house of the man who bought them . . .

Law 163. If a man marry a woman and she bear him no sons; if then this woman die, if the 'purchase price' which he had paid into the house of his father-in-law is repaid to him, her husband shall have no claim upon the dowry of this woman; it belongs to her father's house."

Excerpt from the Code of Hammurabi, circa 1800 B.C.E., translated by L.W. King

8. The excerpt from the Code of Hammurabi best illustrates which of the following features of slavery in ancient Mesopotamia?

(A) Slaves were generally an imported labor force made up of people captured from foreign lands.

(B) The majority of slaves were members of the society whose labor was sold to pay off debts.

(C) Slaves were often trained to provide services such as medical care and accounting to important families.

(D) Slaves were not allowed to marry or have children.

9. The excerpt from the Code of Hammurabi supports which of the following statements about Babylonian gender ideologies?

(A) Men and women enjoyed equal status in Babylonian society.

(B) Prostitutes were shunned and regarded on the lowest levels of society.

(C) Women usually received support from the men in their families in lieu of inheritance.

(D) Men could divorce their wives with little cause, but women had no grounds for divorce.

10. The introduction of the Code of Hammurabi provides support for which of the following transformations in ancient Mesopotamia?

(A) The transfer of authority from gods to humans

(B) The transition from an agrarian to a mercantile economy

(C) The transfer of political power from military leaders to wealthy landowners

(D) The transition of Babylon into a classless society

GO ON TO THE NEXT PAGE

Questions 11–12 refer to the passage below on Confucianism.

"7:15   The Master said, 'Having coarse rice to eat, water to drink, a bent arm for a pillow—joy lies in the midst of this as well. Wealth and honor that are not rightfully gained are to me as floating clouds.'

7:24   There were four things the Master taught: culture, conduct, loyalty, and trustworthiness.

9:4   Four things the Master eschewed: he had no preconceptions, no prejudices, no obduracy, and no egotism.

15:38   The Master said, 'In education there should be no class distinctions.'"

Excerpt from the Confucian *Analects*, circa 575 B.C.E

11. During the classical era, both Confucianism and Hinduism

   (A) officially included women in religious life by building convents as religious retreats

   (B) enforced patriarchal social patterns that limited women's rights and freedoms

   (C) were religions mainly dominated by male priests

   (D) spread widely and rapidly through trade networks

12. One of the primary differences between Confucianism and Hinduism is that, in Confucianism,

   (A) social hierarchy was largely determined by a person's education and work ethic

   (B) a person's class was determined at birth by which caste he or she was born into, making social mobility difficult

   (C) missionary work was important for spreading ideas to South Asia

   (D) emphasis was placed on the concept of reincarnation—the belief that living organisms continue eternally in cycles of birth, death, and rebirth

GO ON TO THE NEXT PAGE

 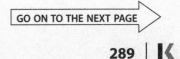

Questions 13–14 refer to the passage below.

"[Professor George Peter Murdock] suggests that there was an independent development of agriculture in the upper Niger region of the western Sudan between 5,000 and 4,000 B.C., at roughly the same period that agriculture was introduced into the lower Nile valley from southwest Asia. This African agriculture spread eastward across the Sudan and met in Nubia with the expanding Egyptian agricultural civilization before 3,000 B.C. It served too, Murdock submits, to stimulate a secondary agricultural complex in the Ethiopian highlands. In the last millenium B.C. Malaysian crops reached East Africa and, via the so-called Megalithic Cushites in that region, these spread westward along the northern fringe of the forest belt to West Africa. There they provided the basis for extensive population growth and the rise of despotic states, and for the beginnings of the Bantu diaspora from the modern Nigeria-Cameroons borderlands."

Philip H. Gulliver, *American Anthropologist*, 1960

13. One significant cause of both the Bantu and Polynesian migrations was

   (A) the need for groups of hunter-gatherers to follow herds of large animals

   (B) the development of double canoes and triangular sails which allowed for more efficient travel

   (C) forced exodus through active slave trade networks

   (D) population growth and the need for more resources

14. What would contradict George P. Murdock's hypothesis about Bantu migration?

   (A) Archaeological confirmation that the West African population increased after the introduction of Malaysian crops

   (B) The modern presence of Malaysian food crops in regions through which the Bantu traveled

   (C) The inability of Malaysian food crops to grow in equatorial Africa

   (D) Evidence showing that Malaysian food crops grow better in Africa than in Malaysia

GO ON TO THE NEXT PAGE

Questions 15–17 refer to the map of Africa below.

WEST AFRICAN TRADE ROUTES

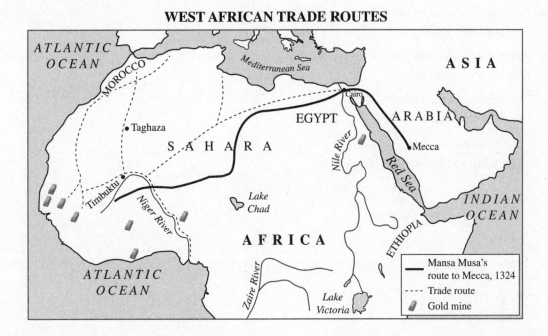

15. Historians often consider the year 600 C.E. to be a turning point in world history because by that point in history

    (A) the Axial Age had begun and two major religions, Buddhism and Islam, had been founded

    (B) several centuries of environmental degradation had resulted in severe weather patterns that year, including earthquakes and monsoons

    (C) the Roman Empire had collapsed and new political entities such as the Islamic Caliphates arose

    (D) the invention of the astrolabe and the lateen sail had allowed humans to engage in trade on the Atlantic and Pacific Oceans for the first time

16. Based on the map, which of the following conclusions can be made?

    (A) The expansion of trade networks and the spread of Islamic influence directly affected the development of the post-classical world.

    (B) Timbuktu and the Kingdoms of Mali and Ghana were the singular producers of gold in the world.

    (C) People moved throughout Western and Northern Africa to work in the gold trade.

    (D) Gold was traded freely between kingdoms.

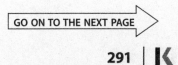

17. Mansa Musa's journey to Mecca

    (A) showed how the amount of gold he brought to Cairo deflated its value

    (B) exemplified the widespread conversion to Islam by African rulers

    (C) demonstrated the difficulty of travel through the Saharan desert

    (D) indicated his desire to abandon Timbuktu and build a new kingdom

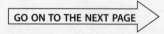
GO ON TO THE NEXT PAGE

Questions 18–21 refer to the passage below.

"Closed Country Edict of 1635

1. Japanese ships are strictly forbidden to leave for foreign countries.

2. No Japanese is permitted to go abroad. If there is anyone who attempts to do so secretly, he must be executed. The ship so involved must be impounded and its owner arrested, and the matter must be reported to the higher authority.

3. If any Japanese returns from overseas after residing there, he must be put to death.

4. If there is any place where the teachings of padres is practiced, the two of you must order a thorough investigation. . . .

7. If there are any Southern Barbarians who propagate the teachings of padres, or otherwise commit crimes, they may be incarcerated in the prison. . . .

9. No single trading city shall be permitted to purchase all the merchandise brought by foreign ships. . . .

11. After a list of merchandise brought by foreign ships is sent to Edo, as before you may order that commercial dealings may take place without waiting for a reply from Edo.

12. After settling the price, all white yarns [silks] brought by foreign ships shall be allocated to the five trading cities and other quarters as stipulated. . . .

15. The goods brought by foreign ships which remained unsold may not be deposited or accepted for deposit.

You are hereby required to act in accordance with the provisions set above. It is so ordered."

Excerpt from *Japan: A Documentary History*, translated and edited by D. J. Lu, 1997

18. All of the following statements are true about Japan from the 1600s to 1850 <u>except</u> that

    (A) foreign trade was restricted by the government

    (B) the shogun ruled the country

    (C) Christians were persecuted

    (D) the economy declined

19. The Tokugawa shogunate was remarkable in this period of world history because

    (A) in an era of increasing global interconnection, Japan successfully countered this trend

    (B) the shoguns deliberately imitated Chinese and Korean responses to Western pressure

    (C) Japan was the first East Asian country to adopt Western modes of production and warfare

    (D) its policies of agricultural and industrial expansion used wage labor rather than slavery or other forced systems

GO ON TO THE NEXT PAGE

20. The shoguns unified and pacified Japan after 1600 by

    (A) playing the Christian and Buddhist religious communities against each other

    (B) empowering the Emperor to intervene in cases of social injustice that threatened elite authority

    (C) balancing centralized control and local freedoms for the daimyo and samurai classes

    (D) giving peasants and merchants a new social status that reflected their contributions to the nation's prosperity

21. Revolts against the central government by the samurai and the peasants

    (A) occasionally occured in response to religious, political, and tax disputes

    (B) were a direct result of the embargo against Western trade goods and knowledge

    (C) were pacified by a system of state salaries

    (D) culminated in a violent civil war that eventually ended the Tokugawa period

GO ON TO THE NEXT PAGE

Questions 22–23 refer to the passage below.

"*Discourse on the Toquz-Oghuz Country and Its Towns*

East of it is the country of China; south of it, some parts of Tibet and the Qarluq (Khallukh); west of it, some parts of the Qirghiz; north of it, also the Qirghiz (?) extend along all the Toquz-Oghuz country. This country is the largest of the Turkish countries and original . . . the Toquz-Oghuz were the most numerous tribe. The kings of the whole of Turkestan in the days of old were from the Toquz-Oghuz. They are warlike people possessing great numbers of arms. In summer and winter they wander from place to place along the grazing grounds in the climates which (happen to be) the best. From their country comes much musk, as well as black, red, and striped foxes, furs of the grey squirrel, sable-marten, ermine, weasel . . . and yaks. The country has few amenities, and their commodities are things which we have enumerated, as well as sheep, cows, and horses. The country possesses innumerable streams. The wealthiest (of the Toquz-Oghuz?) are the Turks. The Tatar too are a race of the Toquz-Oghuz."

Excerpt from the *Hudūd al-'Alam*, circa 980 C.E.

22. From 600 to 1450 C.E., the Mongols, Turks, and Vikings were all examples of

    (A) peripheral peoples

    (B) nomadic cultures

    (C) large bureaucratic based governments

    (D) skilled horsemen

23. Which of the following best describes why Central Asia was the source of repeated nomadic incursions on Eurasian civilizations to the east, south, and west?

    (A) The Silk Road trade routes gave the nomads timely information on the military weaknesses of adjacent empires.

    (B) The Turks and Mongols desired the amenities of urban civilization, whether Chinese, Persian, or Islamic.

    (C) The nomadic peoples were mobile, used to raiding, and lived on the open steppes, which gave them access to the entire continent.

    (D) It was the expanding empires that actually pressured the nomadic lands, fenced in the pasturelands, and imposed heavy taxation.

GO ON TO THE NEXT PAGE

Questions 24–26 refer to the map below.

EXPANSION OF ISLAMIC WORLD BY 1500

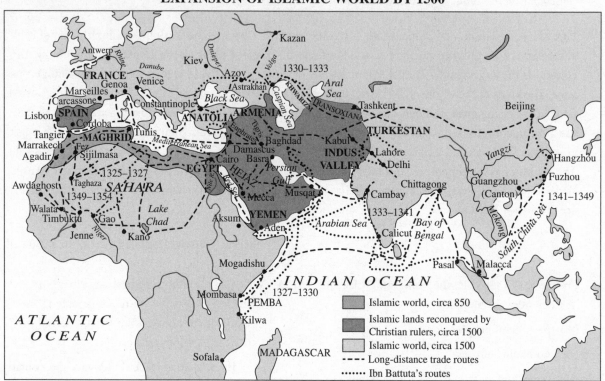

24. The term Dar al-Islam refers to

   (A) areas that share a common Muslim culture as a basis for society

   (B) lands that are enemies of the Muslim religion

   (C) communities that respect many religious influences, including Islam

   (D) conquered areas that refuse to convert to Islam

25. Which of the following factors was responsible for the rapid spread of Islam?

   (A) The rudimentary approach of Muslim armies

   (B) The strength of the Persian and Byzantine empires

   (C) The treatment of conquered peoples

   (D) The decline of Christian and Jewish populations

26. Which of the following was a lasting impact of the Islamic world?

   (A) The creation of a single, unified empire which lasted for many centuries

   (B) Technological and scientific advancements which were used by other cultures

   (C) A unique system of government which provided the foundation for future societies

   (D) Advancements in agriculture and livestock farming

GO ON TO THE NEXT PAGE

Questions 27–28 refer to the passage below.

"The poverty of the incapable, the distresses that come upon the imprudent, the starvation of the idle, and those shoulderings aside of the weak by the strong, which leave so many 'in shallows and in miseries,' are the decrees of a large, farseeing benevolence."

Herbert Spencer, *Social Statics*, 1851

27. The nineteenth-century ideology of Social Darwinism promoted the notion that

    (A) scientific processes could address all issues formerly only answered through religion

    (B) industrialization would lead to the eventual revolution of the working class, resulting in a natural reordering of society

    (C) the domination of Europeans over subject peoples was an inevitable result of innate superiority

    (D) a ruler had an obligation to protect the natural rights of his citizens

28. According to Herbert Spencer, providing government assistance to the poor

    (A) was one of the most important responsibilities of government

    (B) led to the development of a stronger society

    (C) was an inevitable requirement of diverse populations

    (D) hurt society in the long run by contradicting the natural order

GO ON TO THE NEXT PAGE

 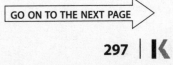

Questions 29–30 refer to the passage below.

"It is my humble opinion that this seizing of Oudh filled the minds of the sepoys with distrust and led them to plot against the Government. Agents . . . worked upon the feelings of the sepoys, telling them how treacherously the foreigners had behaved towards their king. They invented ten thousand lies and promises to persuade the soldiers to mutiny and turn against their masters, the English, with the object of restoring the Emperor of Delhi to the throne. They maintained that this was wholly within the army's powers if the soldiers would only act together and do as they were advised.

It chanced that about this time the Sirkar sent parties of men . . . for instruction in the use of the new rifle. These men performed the new drill for some time until a report got about . . . that the cartridges used for these new rifles were greased with the fat of cows and pigs.

The men from our regiment wrote to others in the regiment telling them of this, and there was soon excitement in every regiment. Some men pointed out that . . . nothing had ever been done by the Sirkar to insult their religion, but . . . [i]nterested parties were quick to point out that the great aim of the English was to turn us all into Christians, and they had therefore introduced the cartridge in order to bring this about, since both Muslims and Hindus would be defiled by using it."

Excerpt from Sita Ram's memoirs, "From Sepoy to Subedar," written in 1873

29. The Sepoy Mutiny was most similar to which of the following armed conflicts?

(A) The Boer War

(B) The Mexican Revolution

(C) The Bolshevik Revolution

(D) The Boxer Rebellion

30. The Sepoy Mutiny of 1857 had the effect of

(A) abolishing the East India Company and strengthening the Raj

(B) incorporating local princes into key political decisions

(C) legitimizing further colonial claims by the Dutch and Portuguese

(D) reorganizing the Indian military with Hindus, Muslims, and Europeans

GO ON TO THE NEXT PAGE

Questions 31–33 refer to the passage below.

"To the Lord Cardinal Firmanus:

My most reverend Father in Christ and most worshipful Lord. . . . Horrible news about the Turks was recently sent from Rascia [Serbia] as well as from Venice, and there was a pressing rumor that Constantinople had been destroyed, the Christian fleet lost, and Pera handed over to the Turks. This was so disturbing to the Emperor [Frederick III] and to his entire Court, that I wrote a long letter to our most holy lord [Pope Nicholas V] concerning this matter. Now happier news . . . or at least news that is not quite so harsh . . . has arrived. For it is said that the troops of our Lord have entered Constantinople and that the royal city has been defended, though some ships were lost. And so our minds are more at ease. The emperor has sent messengers to investigate the truth of the matter and we expect them [to return] any day. . . ."

Letter of Aeneas Silvius Piccolomini to Lord Cardinal Firmanus, 1453

31. What did the city of Constantinople most directly facilitate, during the centuries prior to 1453?

(A) Global trade and commerce

(B) The emergence of Protestantism

(C) The observance of Muslim beliefs

(D) The simplification of Roman laws

32. Women in the palace court of the Ottoman Empire most often wielded power by

(A) serving in administrative positions

(B) selecting the vizier

(C) influencing the sultan in private

(D) speaking in public on political matters

33. Which of the following was <u>not</u> a feature common to the Ottoman, Safavid, and Mughal Empires?

(A) Economic dependence on oil

(B) Artistic innovations and achievements

(C) Political support of Islam

(D) Utilization of firearms

GO ON TO THE NEXT PAGE

 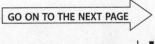

Questions 34–36 refer to the image below.

"America with those known parts in that unknowne worlde both people and manner of buildings" Map, with engraver Abraham Goos and cartographer John Speed, 1627

34. Which of the following did <u>not</u> directly promote commercial growth in the New World prior to 1492?

    (A) Incan road systems

    (B) Aztec cities

    (C) The Iroquois League

    (D) The Mayan solar calendar

35. All of the following crops were native to the New World, <u>except</u>

    (A) coffee

    (B) potatoes

    (C) manioc

    (D) maize

GO ON TO THE NEXT PAGE

36. The map most strongly suggests which of the following?

    (A) Patriarchy

    (B) The *encomienda* system

    (C) Imperialism

    (D) Globalization

GO ON TO THE NEXT PAGE

Questions 37–39 refer to the passage below.

"It appears from all this that the person of the king is sacred, and that to attack him in any way is sacrilege. God has the kings anointed by his prophets with the holy unction in like manner as he has bishops and altars anointed. . . . Without this absolute authority the king could neither do good nor repress evil. It is necessary that his power be such that no one can hope to escape him, and, finally, the only protection of individuals against the public authority should be their innocence. This conforms with the teaching of St. Paul: 'Wilt thou then not be afraid of the power? Do that which is good.'

. . . God is infinite, God is all. The prince, as prince, is not regarded as a private person: he is a public personage, all the state is in him; the will of all the people is included in his. As all perfection and all strength are united in God, so all the power of individuals is united in the person of the prince. What grandeur that a single man should embody so much!"

Excerpt from Jacques-Bénigne Bossuet's *Politics Drawn from the Very Words of Holy Scripture*, 1707

37. Between 1400 and 1750, the politics in Europe were trending toward

    (A) increasingly decentralized governments

    (B) democratic and republican forms of government

    (C) strong, centralized monarchies

    (D) diplomatic rather than military resolutions to conflict

38. A counter-example to Bossuet's assertions would be

    (A) the triumph of Parliament in England's Civil War

    (B) Peter the Great's modernization of the Russian state

    (C) Louis XIV's enormous expansion of the Palace of Versailles

    (D) the physical and mental disability of Charles V

39. In 1707, in what part of the world would one most likely hear a similar message?

    (A) At a Shinto shrine in Tokugawa, Japan

    (B) At a mosque in Safavid, Persia

    (C) At a Catholic church in Warsaw, in the Polish-Lithuanian commonwealth

    (D) At a Presbyterian kirk in Edinburgh, Scotland

GO ON TO THE NEXT PAGE

Questions 40–43 refer to the passage below.

"Freeman and slave, patrician and plebeian, lord and serf, guild-master and journeyman, in a word, oppressor and oppressed, stood in constant opposition to one another, carried on an uninterrupted, now hidden, now open fight, a fight that each time ended, either in a revolutionary reconstitution of society at large, or in the common ruin of the contending classes.

The modern bourgeois society that has sprouted from the ruins of feudal society has not done away with class antagonisms. It has but established new classes, new conditions of oppression, new forms of struggle in place of the old ones."

Karl Marx, *The Communist Manifesto*, 1848

40. Which of the following best represents a key idea of Karl Marx?

   (A) The formation of trade unions would alleviate the problems of the industrial workers.

   (B) The abuses of the capitalistic system would only be solved if the system were overthrown.

   (C) Moderate democratic reforms would bring greater equality to the working class.

   (D) Factory owners should give workers a guaranteed minimum wage and quality health insurance.

41. Based on the excerpt, an increase in labor division and specialization in a modern capitalistic system would likely result in

   (A) increased job satisfaction for skilled workers

   (B) a better-educated workforce

   (C) a lower quality of life for skilled workers

   (D) more freedom for skilled workers to choose better jobs

42. Which of the following individuals would likely be least oppressed, according to Marx?

   (A) The owner of a small family farm who does not employ any laborers

   (B) A highly skilled computer programmer who works for a software company

   (C) A factory worker who assembles small electronic components for a corporation

   (D) A union worker who has a high-wage job working for a large mining company

43. According to a Marxist theorist, what would be the most likely reason for a political revolution within a state?

   (A) A political corruption scandal involving the leader of a country

   (B) An cycle of inflation and deflation, leading to economic uncertainty

   (C) An increase in monopolization of private businesses

   (D) A significant increase in the amount of government regulation of business

GO ON TO THE NEXT PAGE

 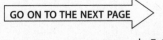

Questions 44–45 refer to the passage below.

". . . we are but a mixed species of aborigines and Spaniards. Americans by birth and Europeans by law, we find ourselves engaged in a dual conflict. . . . As our role has always been strictly passive and political existence nil, we find that our quest for liberty is now even more difficult of accomplishment; for we, having been placed in a state lower than slavery, had been robbed not only of our freedom but also of the right to exercise an active domestic tyranny . . . If a people, perverted by their training, succeed in achieving their liberty, they will soon lose it. . . . everyone should submit to their beneficent austerity; that proper morals, and not force, are the bases of law; and that to practice justice is to practice liberty. . . .

Nothing in our fundamental laws would have to be altered were we to adopt a legislative power similar to that held by the British Parliament. Like the North Americans, we have divided national representation into two chambers: that of Representatives and the Senate. . . . The creation of a hereditary senate would in no way be a violation of political equality. I do not solicit the establishment of a nobility, for as a celebrated republican has said, that would simultaneously destroy equality and liberty. What I propose is an office for which the candidates must prepare themselves, an office that demands great knowledge and the ability to acquire such knowledge."

Excerpt from Simón Bolívar's Message to the Congress of Angostura, 1819

44. In the second half of the nineteenth century, which of the following likely stemmed from colonization of Latin America?

(A) Hyperinflation

(B) Uneven distribution of wealth

(C) Agricultural exports

(D) Military control of government

45. The political visions of Bolívar and other Latin American liberators in the nineteenth century were not fully realized because

(A) the new nations failed to establish trade relations

(B) the *peninsulares* and Creoles fought for control

(C) Latin American Catholics opposed these ideologies

(D) the new nations lacked a democratic tradition

GO ON TO THE NEXT PAGE

Questions 46–47 refer to the passage below.

"The power, when it comes, will belong to the people of India, and it will be for them to decide to whom it placed in the entrusted. . . . Ever since its inception the Congress has kept itself meticulously free of the communal taint. It has thought always in terms of the whole nation and has acted accordingly. . . . I know how imperfect our Ahimsa is and how far away we are still from the ideal, but in Ahimsa there is no final failure or defeat. I have faith, therefore, that if, in spite of our shortcomings, the big thing does happen, it will be because God wanted to help us by crowning with success our silent, unremitting Sadhana for the last twenty-two years."

Excerpt from Mohandas Gandhi's "Quit India" speech, given in Bombay, 8 August 1942.

46. Gandhi's main approach to gaining Indian independence was

(A) using political action

(B) imposing economic sanctions on Britain

(C) combining Hindu and Islamic beliefs

(D) encouraging nonviolent civil disobedience

47. Which of these events most directly opposed Gandhi's vision of an independent India?

(A) The 1931 Round Table Conference

(B) The creation of India and Pakistan

(C) The Amritsar Massacre

(D) Nehru's post-independence reforms

GO ON TO THE NEXT PAGE

Questions 48–51 refer to the images below.

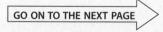
GO ON TO THE NEXT PAGE

48. Which of the following is a similarity between the Russian Revolution (1917) and the Chinese Revolution (1949)?

(A) Both replaced corrupt monarchies.

(B) Both involved a bloody civil war.

(C) Both appealed primarily to urban laborers.

(D) Both of their legacies lasted fewer than 25 years.

49. As Mao Zedong rose to power in China, he distanced himself from the Soviet Union by

(A) seeking to ease tensions between China and the United States

(B) supporting the North Vietnamese during the Vietnam Conflict

(C) denouncing Khrushchev's program of de-Stalinization

(D) allowing some market-based economic reforms in China

50. In the 1980s, both Communist China and the Soviet Union broke from their founders' intent by

(A) introducing capitalist reforms into their economies

(B) introducing democratic reforms into their governments

(C) relinquishing their ties to Fidel Castro in Cuba

(D) fighting against the mujahideen rebels in Afghanistan

51. Economically, the leaders of the Russian Revolution and the Chinese Revolution were similar in that both favored

(A) a national military-industrial complex

(B) five-year plans to restore devastated economies

(C) government control of heavy industries

(D) collectivization of farmland

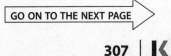

Questions 52–55 refer to the passage below.

"The world today now faces a great international crisis. . . . To be precise, one group is composed of countries which, having followed Imperialism, wish to hold . . . rights and interests they have conquered or acquired by the pursuit of Imperialism, . . . while the other group is composed of those countries which oppose the bearers of the Imperialist standard and wish to place all lands, material resources, and markets which have been monopolized at the disposal of all mankind. . . . This latter group aims at the reconstruction of the world upon the basis of international justice and the lofty ideal of co-existence so that the true foundation of a lasting peace may be laid. . . .

With people so disposed, Japan is only too willing to develop the natural wealth of Asia, open up its markets, and construct a new community without oppression or extortion. Japan sincerely believes that it is her duty to build a new Asiatic order in which the peoples of Asia will really enjoy freedom, independence, and peace. . . .

. . . when America strongly insists on her right to have a voice in some continent other than her own, and yet tries to close the American continents to any people but their own, is this not a most glaring inconsistency?"

Excerpt from "Some Questions for President Roosevelt" by Nagai Ryūtarō, 1939

52. Japan's expansionism in East and Southeast Asia in the 1930s was fueled by a desire to

   (A) acquire natural resources and new industrial markets

   (B) supplant the United States as a dominant industrial power

   (C) strengthen the growing influence of the League of Nations

   (D) assert Japan's newly-realized military power

53. The "glaring inconsistency" that Ryūtarō referred to in the excerpt refers to the inconsistent application of what American idea?

   (A) The Open Door Policy

   (B) Manifest Destiny

   (C) The Monroe Doctrine

   (D) The Roosevelt Corollary

54. In the 1930s, Japan and Nazi Germany were similar in all of the following regards <u>except</u>

   (A) both desired control of a vast empire

   (B) both sought systematic elimination of other races

   (C) both opposed Soviet Communism and its spread

   (D) both used the military to help their economies recover

55. Which event most directly influenced Japan's decision to invade French Indochina in 1941?

   (A) The creation of Manchukuo in 1932, made possible by the invasion of Manchuria

   (B) Attacks on central China, including the invasion of Beijing and Nanjing

   (C) France's early defeat in World War II

   (D) The oil embargo issued by the United States

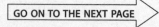

Directions: Section I, Part B of this exam consists of short answer questions. You must respond to Questions 1 and 2. For your final response, you must choose to answer EITHER Question 3 or Question 4. Use complete sentences; an outline or bulleted list alone is not acceptable.

1. Use the two passages below to answer all parts of the question that follows.

   Source 1

   "The new principles of construction are first distinctly and skillfully exemplified in the Abbey Church of St. Denis, located in the southern part of modern Paris, which dates from 1137 to 1141. And the origin of Gothic on mainland Europe, so far as existing monuments exhibit it, is now commonly traced to that building only. But the Abbey Church of Morienval, northeast of Paris, appears to anticipate, though in a halting manner, some of the principles that are carried out so remarkably in St. Denis. This church, a construction of the eleventh century, has an apse which dates from the end of the eleventh or the beginning of the twelfth century, and a rudimentary apsidal aisle whose vaults have diagonal ribs, pointed archivolts, and even rudely pointed transverse arches, though of these last arches one has no rib, while the other has a rudely adjusted and very heavy round-arched one. . . ."

   Charles Herbert Moore, *Development and Character of Gothic Architecture*, 1890

   Source 2

   "There is no doubt that a strong case exists for a theory of Norman* origins as providing the key to the beginnings of Gothic architecture. This appears particularly true when one tries to trace how rib vaulting started in the Île-de-France** area. The ambulatory of Morienval, often mentioned as showing the earliest rib vaults in the Paris region, does not deserve that distinction: the presence of slightly pointed arches, and a profile of ribs similar to that of the second period of vaulting at Saint-Etienne at Beauvais, are enough to prove that Morienval did not come first. Rib vaulting seems to have entered the Île-de-France from Normandy."

   *Normandy is located in northern France.
   **Île-de-France is the historic region where modern Paris is located.

   Jean Bony, *French Gothic Architecture of the Twelfth and Thirteenth Centuries*, 1983

   a) Identify ONE point of <u>agreement</u> between the authors about the origins or characteristics of Gothic architecture.

   b) Explain ONE point of <u>disagreement</u> between the authors about the origins or characteristics of Gothic architecture.

   c) Explain ONE way that the Gothic architecture described in the passages reflects other cultural developments.

GO ON TO THE NEXT PAGE

2. Use the image below to answer all parts of the question that follows.

Carving of Maitreya (future Buddha) featured in Singapore theme park Haw Par Villa, which was completed in 1937, photograph taken in 2006

a) Explain TWO <u>changes</u> between this statue's depiction of the Buddha/Buddhism and the original Buddha, Siddhartha Gautama.

b) Explain ONE <u>continuity</u> between Siddhartha Gautama's original teachings and the modern beliefs of Buddhism.

GO ON TO THE NEXT PAGE

Choose EITHER Question 3 or Question 4.

3. Answer all parts of the question that follows.

   a) Describe ONE reason that Mesopotamian city-states (3000 B.C.E. to 500 B.C.E.) were able to consolidate political power.

   b) Describe ONE <u>similarity</u> in the socio-political structure of Mesopotamian city-states and the city-state of Athens (700 B.C.E. to 300 B.C.E.).

   c) Explain ONE <u>difference</u> in the social or political structure of Mesopotamian city-states and the city-state of Athens.

4. Answer all parts of the question that follows.

   a) Describe ONE method used by leaders such as Mohandas Gandhi (India) and Kwame Nkrumah (Ghana) in their struggles for independence from Great Britain.

   b) Explain ONE <u>difference</u> in the social or political beliefs held by Mohandas Gandhi (India) and Mao Zedong (China).

   c) Explain ONE <u>similarity</u> in the social or political beliefs held by Mohandas Gandhi (India) and Mao Zedong (China).

GO ON TO THE NEXT PAGE

END OF SECTION I, PART B

SECTION II
Time—100 Minutes
2 Questions

Question 1: Document-Based Question
Suggested reading period: 15 minutes
Suggested writing time: 45 minutes

Directions: Question 1 is based on the accompanying documents. The documents have been edited for the purpose of this exercise.

In your response you should do the following.

- Present a thesis statement

- Develop and support a complex argument

- Utilize at least six of the accompanying documents

- Explain the significance of the author's point of view, purpose, historical context, and/or audience for at least four of the documents

- Situate the argument in its broader historical context

- Provide an example or additional piece of specific evidence

- Extend the argument by explaining the connections between the argument and a theme that is not the focus of the essay, or between the argument and a development in a different historical period, situation, era, or geographic location.

1. Analyze the processes associated with empire building in the Americas, Africa, and Asia from the early sixteenth century to the early twentieth century.

GO ON TO THE NEXT PAGE

Document 1

Source: Nzinga Mbemba (Afonso I), King of Kongo, letter to the King of Portugal, 1526

Sir, Your Highness should know that our Kingdom is being lost and it is necessary for you to act, since this is caused by the excessive freedom given to your agents and officials who come to our Kingdom to set up shops that sell goods that have been prohibited by us, and which are spread throughout our Kingdom to our vassals, whom we had in obedience, and who now do not comply because they have things in greater abundance than we ourselves; and it was with these things that we had them content and subjected under our control, so it is doing a great harm not only to the service of God, but the security and peace of our Kingdoms and State as well. . . .

That is why we beg of Your Highness to assist us by commanding your country's traders that they should not send either merchants or wares to Kongo. . . . Pray Our Lord in His mercy to have Your Highness under His guard and let you do forever the things of His service. I kiss your hands many times. . . .

From: *The Human Record: Sources of Global History,* vol. 1 (Boston: Houghton Mifflin, 2009), p. 433.

Document 2

Source: Drawing by native artist of Spanish and their native allies fighting the Aztecs, *General History of the Things of New Spain, 1585*

GO ON TO THE NEXT PAGE

Document 3

Source: Population estimates for Puerto Rico by ethnicity

Year	Europeans	Free Blacks	Mulattos*	Black Slaves	Natives
1530	10%	0%	0%	53.6%	36.4%
1600	55.6%	0%	16.6%	27.8%	
1775	40.4%	3.9%	46.7%	9%	
1795	38.4%	8.6%	34.5%	16%	2.5%
1815	47%	6.8%	36.9%	9.3%	
1860	51.5%	41.3%		7.3%	

*people of mixed race

From: "The Politics of Taíno Revivalism," Gabriel Haslip-Viera

Document 4

Source: François Bernier, physician, *An Account of India and the Great Moghul*, France, 1665

Your Majesty, you have seen the maps of Asia and how great is the extent of the empire of the Great Mogul,* which is commonly called India. . . .

There are more than an hundred rajahs, or sovereigns, dispersed through the whole empire; . . . amongst whom there are about fifteen or sixteen that are very rich and powerful; . . . each of them is able in a very short time to raise and bring into the field twenty-five thousand horses, and better troops than the Mogul's. . . .

The Mogul is obliged to keep these rajahs in his service for several reasons: first, because the militia of the rajahs is very good and because there are rajahs who can bring into the field above twenty-five thousand men; second, to make sure all of the rajahs pay tribute, and serve in the army when the Mogul requires it; third, the Mogul may choose to nourish jealousies among them to keep them from organizing against him. This last tactic is done so that they will fight with one another very frequently.

*Mughal emperor

http://www.fordham.edu/halsall/india/1655bernier.asp

 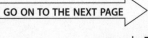

Document 5

Source: Harry Verelst, Governor of Bengal for Britain's East India Company, Letter to the company's Board of Directors in London, Delhi, India, 1769

The coming of the English to power in the Hindostan province of India occurred through a number of events distinguished by a series of fortunate and unforeseen occurrences; not the result of any fixed or connected plan. A colony of merchants influenced by principles of commerce, have acquired a political title and influence over the land, which in size, population, and revenue from trade may be compared to many of the most powerful states of Europe. . . . We see the increasing poverty of the country from the lack of circulation of money throughout. Since we have become governors here, however, the new policies we have made are designed to restore the equality of commerce, and the spirit of monopoly, promoted by the natives, shall be destroyed.

 GO ON TO THE NEXT PAGE

Document 6

> Source: Winston Churchill, excerpt from *The River War: An Account of the Reconquest of the Sudan* on the British-Sudanese Battle of Omdurman, 1899
>
> The moment was critical. It appeared to our cavalry commander that the Dervishes[*] would actually succeed, and their success would involve the total destruction of our corps of Camel cavalry. That could not, of course, be allowed. . . .
>
> But at the critical moment our gunboat arrived . . . and began suddenly to blaze and flame from Maxim [machine] guns, quick-firing guns, and rifles. The range was short; the effect tremendous. . . . The river slopes of the Kerreri Hills, crowded with the advancing thousands of enemy forces, sprang up into clouds of dust and splinters of rock. The charging Dervishes sank down in tangled heaps. Even the masses in their rear paused. It was too much fire even for those in the back of their formation. The approach of another gunboat completed their fear. Our Camel Corps, hurrying along the shore, slipped past the fatal point of interception, and found safety.
>
> [*]Sudanese fighters
>
> http://www.fordham.edu/halsall/mod/1898churchill-omdurman.asp

GO ON TO THE NEXT PAGE

Document 7

Source: Kisaburō Ohara, student, Keio University Japan, "A Humorous Diplomatic Atlas of Europe and Asia," 1904

English text reads in part: Black Octopus is the name newly given to Russia by a prominent Englishman. For the black octopus is so greedy that it stretches out its eight arms in all directions, and seizes everything that comes within its reach.

Norman B. Leventhal Map Center, https://collections.leventhalmap.org/search/commonwealth:9s161c15w

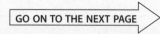

Question 2, Question 3, or Question 4: Long Essay Question

Suggested writing time: 40 minutes

Directions: Choose Question 2, Question 3, OR Question 4 to answer.

In your response you should do the following.

- Present a thesis statement
- Apply AP History Reasoning Skills as directed by the question
- Utilize specific examples of historical evidence to support the thesis, and explain relationships among the evidence.
- Extend the argument by explaining the connections between the argument and either: a development in a different historical period, situation, era, or geographic location; or a theme/approach to history that is not the focus of the essay.

2. Analyze the similarities and differences in the spread of Buddhism and the spread of Christianity between 600 B.C.E. and 600 C.E.

3. Analyze the similarities and differences in the spread of Christianity and the spread of Islam between 100 C.E. and 1450 C.E.

4. Analyze the similarities and differences in the spread of ideas/information before the end of World War I (1914–1918 C.E.) and after the end of World War I.

GO ON TO THE NEXT PAGE

END OF SECTION II

ANSWER KEY

Section I

1. D	15. C	29. D	43. C
2. C	16. A	30. A	44. B
3. A	17. B	31. A	45. D
4. D	18. D	32. C	46. D
5. B	19. A	33. A	47. B
6. B	20. C	34. D	48. B
7. A	21. A	35. A	49. C
8. B	22. A	36. C	50. A
9. C	23. C	37. C	51. C
10. A	24. A	38. A	52. A
11. B	25. C	39. B	53. C
12. A	26. B	40. B	54. B
13. D	27. C	41. C	55. C
14. C	28. D	42. A	

Section I, Part A Number Correct: _____

Section I, Part B (Short-Answer Questions) Points Earned: _____

Section II, Part A (Document-Based Question) Points Earned: _____

Section II, Part B (Long Essay Question) Points Earned: _____

Enter these results to see your 1–5 score and view detailed explanations by logging in at kaptest.com.

Haven't registered your book yet? Go to kaptest.com/booksonline to begin.

Practice Exam 2

Practice Exam 2 Answer Grid

1. Ⓐ Ⓑ Ⓒ Ⓓ   15. Ⓐ Ⓑ Ⓒ Ⓓ   29. Ⓐ Ⓑ Ⓒ Ⓓ   43. Ⓐ Ⓑ Ⓒ Ⓓ

2. Ⓐ Ⓑ Ⓒ Ⓓ   16. Ⓐ Ⓑ Ⓒ Ⓓ   30. Ⓐ Ⓑ Ⓒ Ⓓ   44. Ⓐ Ⓑ Ⓒ Ⓓ

3. Ⓐ Ⓑ Ⓒ Ⓓ   17. Ⓐ Ⓑ Ⓒ Ⓓ   31. Ⓐ Ⓑ Ⓒ Ⓓ   45. Ⓐ Ⓑ Ⓒ Ⓓ

4. Ⓐ Ⓑ Ⓒ Ⓓ   18. Ⓐ Ⓑ Ⓒ Ⓓ   32. Ⓐ Ⓑ Ⓒ Ⓓ   46. Ⓐ Ⓑ Ⓒ Ⓓ

5. Ⓐ Ⓑ Ⓒ Ⓓ   19. Ⓐ Ⓑ Ⓒ Ⓓ   33. Ⓐ Ⓑ Ⓒ Ⓓ   47. Ⓐ Ⓑ Ⓒ Ⓓ

6. Ⓐ Ⓑ Ⓒ Ⓓ   20. Ⓐ Ⓑ Ⓒ Ⓓ   34. Ⓐ Ⓑ Ⓒ Ⓓ   48. Ⓐ Ⓑ Ⓒ Ⓓ

7. Ⓐ Ⓑ Ⓒ Ⓓ   21. Ⓐ Ⓑ Ⓒ Ⓓ   35. Ⓐ Ⓑ Ⓒ Ⓓ   49. Ⓐ Ⓑ Ⓒ Ⓓ

8. Ⓐ Ⓑ Ⓒ Ⓓ   22. Ⓐ Ⓑ Ⓒ Ⓓ   36. Ⓐ Ⓑ Ⓒ Ⓓ   50. Ⓐ Ⓑ Ⓒ Ⓓ

9. Ⓐ Ⓑ Ⓒ Ⓓ   23. Ⓐ Ⓑ Ⓒ Ⓓ   37. Ⓐ Ⓑ Ⓒ Ⓓ   51. Ⓐ Ⓑ Ⓒ Ⓓ

10. Ⓐ Ⓑ Ⓒ Ⓓ   24. Ⓐ Ⓑ Ⓒ Ⓓ   38. Ⓐ Ⓑ Ⓒ Ⓓ   52. Ⓐ Ⓑ Ⓒ Ⓓ

11. Ⓐ Ⓑ Ⓒ Ⓓ   25. Ⓐ Ⓑ Ⓒ Ⓓ   39. Ⓐ Ⓑ Ⓒ Ⓓ   53. Ⓐ Ⓑ Ⓒ Ⓓ

12. Ⓐ Ⓑ Ⓒ Ⓓ   26. Ⓐ Ⓑ Ⓒ Ⓓ   40. Ⓐ Ⓑ Ⓒ Ⓓ   54. Ⓐ Ⓑ Ⓒ Ⓓ

13. Ⓐ Ⓑ Ⓒ Ⓓ   27. Ⓐ Ⓑ Ⓒ Ⓓ   41. Ⓐ Ⓑ Ⓒ Ⓓ   55. Ⓐ Ⓑ Ⓒ Ⓓ

14. Ⓐ Ⓑ Ⓒ Ⓓ   28. Ⓐ Ⓑ Ⓒ Ⓓ   42. Ⓐ Ⓑ Ⓒ Ⓓ

SECTION I
Time—95 Minutes
58 Questions

Directions: Section I, Part A of this exam contains 55 multiple choice questions. The questions are organized into sets with corresponding historical sources. Each of the questions or incomplete statements is followed by four suggested answers or completions. Using both the provided source and your own historical knowledge, select the best answer choice.

Questions 1–2 refer to the passage below.

"The city lacks ostentatious palaces, temples, or monuments. There's no obvious central seat of government or evidence of a king or queen. . . . Pottery and tools of copper and stone were standardized. Seals and weights suggest a system of tightly controlled trade."

"Mohenjo-daro," from a *National Geographic* article by John Roach

1. Which of the following is evidence of urban planning in Harappa and Mohenjo-daro?

   (A) A grid-like city layout with uniform housing

   (B) Pottery and decorative items

   (C) A writing system using approximately 400 symbols

   (D) Metal tools of bronze and copper

2. Based on the cited text, what archaeological find would provide the most new information on the culture of Mohenjo-daro?

   (A) A matching set of copper knives

   (B) A well-preserved public street

   (C) Part of the city drainage system

   (D) The tomb of a city official

GO ON TO THE NEXT PAGE

Questions 3–6 refer to the following map.

THE FERTILE CRESCENT

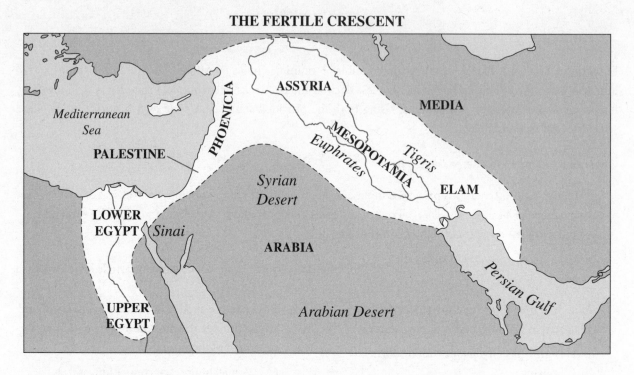

3. Which of the following was a motivation for the expansion of civilizations depicted on the map prior to 600 B.C.E.?

   (A) A desire for direct access to the Indian Ocean trade networks

   (B) The need for access to iron ore for use in agricultural and military technology

   (C) To obtain colonies in keeping with their mercantilist economic theory

   (D) To engage in missionary work

4. What effect did the annual flooding of the Nile have on ancient Egypt?

   (A) It frequently devastated the land around the river.

   (B) It prevented the construction of permanent structures.

   (C) It provided unusual agricultural advantages for the desert environment.

   (D) It prevented river-bound trading vessels from voyaging during the flooding.

GO ON TO THE NEXT PAGE

5. The civilization depicted in the map provided a land connection between

   (A) Africa and Europe

   (B) Europe and Asia

   (C) India and Asia

   (D) Africa and the Middle East

6. The Code of Hammurabi, developed in ancient Babylonia, was a result of

   (A) increasing social complexity in settled societies

   (B) the need for an agricultural almanac to better predict weather patterns

   (C) information gathered during an urban census

   (D) religious beliefs that were widely held at the time

GO ON TO THE NEXT PAGE

Questions 7–9 refer to the following excerpt.

"When walking, don't turn your head; when talking, don't open your mouth wide; when sitting, don't move your knees; when standing, don't rustle your skirts; when happy, don't exult with loud laughter; when angry, don't raise your voice. The inner and outer quarters are distinct; the sexes should be segregated. Don't peer over the outer wall or go beyond the outer courtyard. If you have to go outside, cover your face; if you peep outside, conceal yourself as much as possible. Do not be on familiar terms with men outside the family; have nothing to do with women of bad character. Establish your proper self so as to become a [true] human being.

Your father-in-law and mother-in-law are the heads of your husband's family. You must care for them as your own mother and father. Respectfully serve your father-in-law. Do not look at him directly [when he speaks to you], do not follow him around, and do not engage him in conversation. If he has an order for you, listen and obey."

Song Ruozhao, "Analects for Women," circa 700 C.E.

7. Which of the following reinforced traditional expectations of women's roles in China?

    (A) Chinese imperial expansion under Tang Empress Wu Zetian

    (B) The proliferation of Buddhist convents in China

    (C) The practice of foot binding during the Song dynasty

    (D) Ban Zhao's call for the education of Chinese girls

8. Under the Tang and Song dynasties

    (A) a revival of Confucian ideals occurred across many facets of society

    (B) class relations became increasingly egalitarian

    (C) the Confucian civil service system was discontinued

    (D) technological and farming advances both stagnated and eventually declined

9. Which of the following accurately describes foreign relations under the Tang and Song dynasties?

    (A) China established long-term military and governing dominance over Vietnam.

    (B) Japan avoided Chinese cultural influence, seeking to develop their own culture free from interference.

    (C) The Song dynasty had by far the most powerful military in East Asia.

    (D) New technological advancements facilitated the development of long-distance trade in the Indian Ocean and Persian Gulf.

GO ON TO THE NEXT PAGE

Questions 10–12 refer to the passage below.

"We must infer that all things are produced more plentifully and easily and of a better quality when one man does one thing which is natural to him and does it at the right time, and leaves other things."

Plato, *Republic Book II*, circa 380 B.C.E.

10. Which of the following characteristics <u>differs</u> from those displayed by all classical civilizations?

(A) Social stratification

(B) Trade

(C) An organized bureaucracy

(D) Democratic institutions

11. The government system that evolved in Rome after the Republic was

(A) a representative democracy

(B) a constitutional monarchy

(C) an autocratic empire

(D) a theocracy devoted to polythestic gods

12. According to the excerpt, Plato is advocating a society in which

(A) workers control the means of production

(B) citizens do the work they are best suited for

(C) citizens change their jobs freely

(D) all citizens perform the same function

GO ON TO THE NEXT PAGE

Questions 13–14 refer to the passage below.

"Thus the barbarians from beyond the seas, though their countries are truly distant, have come to audience bearing precious objects and presents.

The Emperor, approving of their loyalty and sincerity, has ordered us [Zheng] He and others at the head of several tens of thousands of officers and flag-troops to ascend [use] more than one hundred large ships to go and confer presents on them in order to make manifest the transforming power of the [imperial] virtue and to treat distant people with kindness."

Zheng He, Temple inscription, Fujian province, 1431 C.E.

13. Which of the following best explains why the Ming dynasty halted the voyages of Zheng He?

   (A) The Chinese had a difficult time competing with European technology

   (B) The Chinese had an unfavorable balance of trade

   (C) The voyages were expensive and the world beyond China was deemed of little value

   (D) Many of Zheng He's ships had been greatly damaged during his earlier expeditions

14. Ming China's withdrawal from ocean exploration most closely resembles

   (A) the decline of the Russian navy after the fall of the Soviet Union in 1991

   (B) Germany's liquidation of its African empire in 1918

   (C) the Islamic pullback from its advances into France in the 700s

   (D) the abandonment of the Viking settlements in North America around 1000

GO ON TO THE NEXT PAGE

Questions 15–16 refer to the following map.

BANTU MIGRATIONS

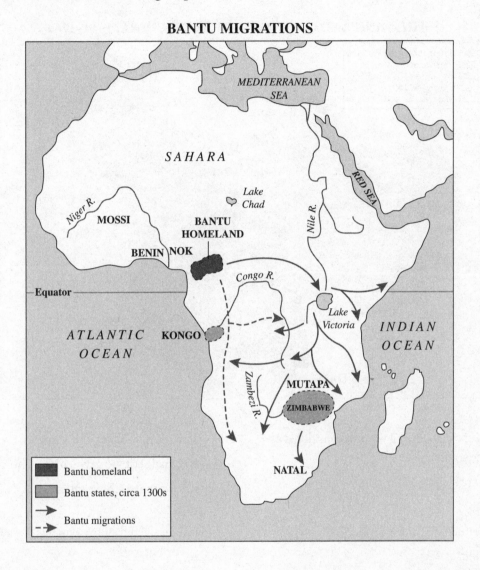

15. All of the following contributed to the Bantu Migration <u>except</u> for

    (A) animal domestication

    (B) population pressure

    (C) use of iron tools

    (D) cultivation of the banana

16. The impact of the Bantu Migration is most similar to which of the following?

    (A) The Polynesian Migrations

    (B) The Mongol conquest of Eurasia

    (C) The Indo-European Migrations (4000-1000 B.C.E.)

    (D) The African Diaspora

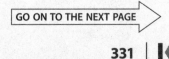

GO ON TO THE NEXT PAGE

Questions 17–19 refer to the following map.

THE MING AND QING DYNASTIES OF CHINA, 1644–1760

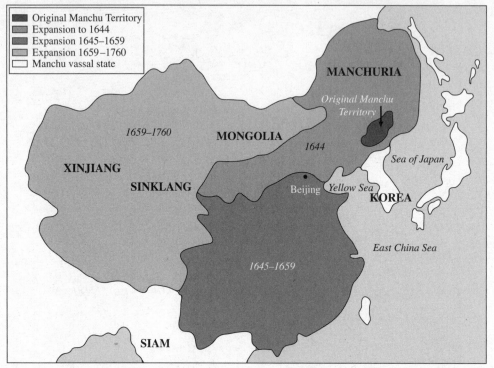

17. Which of the following was not considered a Chinese tributary state?

   (A) Korea

   (B) Tibet

   (C) Vietnam

   (D) India

18. Which of the following empires' tribute systems is most comparable to China's?

   (A) The Aztec Empire

   (B) The Roman Empire

   (C) Islamic Caliphate

   (D) None of the above

19. Under Kublai Khan, the Mongols

   (A) made tribute payments to China

   (B) occupied China and made it a Mongol tributary

   (C) received tribute payments from China's tributaries

   (D) relied on military strength rather than diplomacy

GO ON TO THE NEXT PAGE

Questions 20–23 refer to the following map.

SLAVE TRADE OUT OF AFRICA

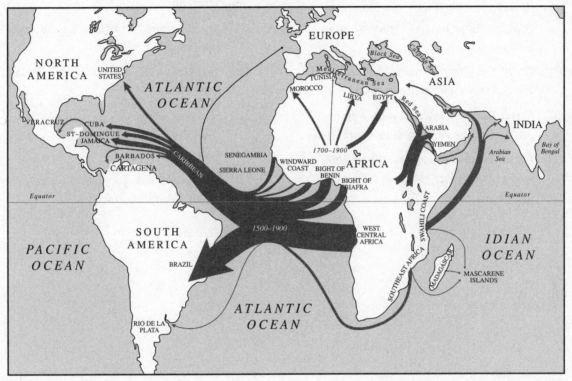

20. The forced migration of enslaved Africans to the Americas in the seventeenth and eighteenth centuries resulted in

    (A) a higher ratio of women to men in Western Africa

    (B) altered male-to-female ratios in Africa

    (C) a decline in the slave trade to Western Asia and the Mediterranean

    (D) lower agricultural yields in the Caribbean and Latin America

21. Why was the Atlantic trade in slaves from central Africa so much greater than the traditional Asian and north African slave trades?

    (A) The Atlantic trade supplied labor to new lands that were both available and suitable for plantation-style agriculture.

    (B) Slave life expectancy was approximately three times longer under traditional labor conditions in the Old World.

    (C) Sugar and cotton were discovered in the New World, leading to unprecedented demand for slave labor in the Americas.

    (D) Africa experienced a population explosion after about 1550, increasing the supply of potential slaves to European and Asian markets alike.

GO ON TO THE NEXT PAGE

22. The greatest number of slaves shipped west went to Brazil because

(A) slavery there continued long after other American societies had abolished the institution

(B) North and Central America had relatively few slave-owning European colonies

(C) Portugal's laws allowed slavery with no interference by royal or church authorities

(D) Brazil was the shortest sea voyage from west central Africa to a large area of cultivable land

23. Was African slavery the only form of coerced labor in South America during the seventeenth and eighteenth centuries?

(A) No, indentured servitude was the most common form of labor.

(B) Yes, African slavery was the only form of forced labor.

(C) No, many natives were enslaved or otherwise coerced in the encomienda or similar systems.

(D) It was, until Spain abolished slavery early in the eighteenth century.

GO ON TO THE NEXT PAGE

Questions 24–27 refer to the passage below.

"We stayed one night in this island [Mombasa], and then pursued our journey to Kulwa, which is a large town on the coast. The majority of its inhabitants are Zanj, jet-black in colour, and with tattoo marks on their faces. I was told by a merchant that the town of Sufala lies a fortnight's journey [south] from Kulwa and that gold dust is brought to Sufala from Yufi in the country of the Limis, which is a month's journey distant from it. Kulwa is a very fine and substantially built town, and all its buildings are of wood. Its inhabitants are constantly engaged in military expeditions, for their country is contiguous to the heathen Zanj.

The sultan at the time of my visit was Abu'l-Muzaffar Hasan, who was noted for his gifts and generosity. He used to devote the fifth part of the booty made on his expeditions to pious and charitable purposes, as is prescribed in the Koran, and I have seen him give the clothes off his back to a mendicant who asked him for them. When this liberal and virtuous sultan died, he was succeeded by his brother Dawud, who was at the opposite pole from him in this respect. Whenever a petitioner came to him, he would say, "He who gave is dead, and left nothing behind him to be given." Visitors would stay at his court for months on end, and finally he would make them some small gift, so that at last people gave up going to his gate."

Ibn Battuta, during his visit to the port city Kilwa in Eastern Africa, circa 1330 C.E.

24. According to the passage and your knowledge of world history, which of the following religions predominated in Eastern African cities such as Kilwa during the time period reflected in the passage?

   (A) Oduduwa

   (B) Christianity

   (C) Islam

   (D) Nyame

25. The following developments within East African society are supported by the passage except for

   (A) Islam spreading to African cities along trading networks

   (B) ports in Eastern Africa prospering as the trade of items, such as gold, increased

   (C) Arabic architecture integrating with indigenous East African culture

   (D) Bantu society migrating to Eastern Africa, bringing novel technologies

26. In the sixteenth century, why did the prosperous city described in the passage decline?

   (A) The Swahili mixture of African and Arabian culture weakened the city's cultural unity.

   (B) Portuguese explorers demolished many buildings.

   (C) Trade along the Indian Ocean routes diminished after the Silk Road was created.

   (D) Natural disasters such as volcanic eruptions eradicated the city's population.

27. Which of the following is true of trade in the Indian Ocean during the period 600 C.E. to 1450 C.E.?

   (A) Europeans played a dominant role in the Indian Ocean.

   (B) Due to nomadic invasions, economic activity slowed considerably.

   (C) Chinese merchants were the only major participants in the trade.

   (D) Trade flourished with a mix of East African, South Asian, and Middle Eastern merchants.

GO ON TO THE NEXT PAGE

Questions 28–30 refer to the passage below.

"Weapons and armor are a country's tools of violence. A warlike country, however huge and safe it may be, will end up declining and endangering its populace. Military force cannot be entirely eliminated nor used all the time. Teach people military arts when they are free from farming in order to equip them with a sense of military decorum and morale. Remember how Gou Jian, who paid respect to the fighting spirit of frogs, was able to achieve his supremacy, but Xu Yan, who disregarded military forces, lost his state. Why? Because Gou's troops were inspired and Xu was unprepared. Confucius said, 'Not teaching people how to fight is the same as discarding them.' Hence military might serves to benefit the realm. This is the gist of the art of war. . . .

Music should be played when a victory is gained; ritual should be established when the country is at peace. The ritual and music to be promulgated are rooted in Confucianism. Nothing is better than literature to spread manners and guide customs; nothing is better than schooling to propagate regulations and educate people. The Way is spread through culture; fame is gained through learning. Without visiting a deep ravine, one cannot understand how deep the earth is; without learning the arts, one cannot realize the source of wisdom. Just as the bamboos of the state of Wu cannot be made into arrows without feathers, so a clever man will not achieve any success without accumulating learning. Therefore, study halls and ritual halls should be built, books of various schools of thought should be widely read, and the six arts [propriety, music, archery, charioteering, writing, and mathematics] should be carefully studied."

Excerpt from Emperor Taizong's *Effective Government*, 648 C.E.

28. The following developments during the Tang dynasty contributed to the ideals outlined in the passage <u>except</u> for

(A) the origin of gunpowder

(B) the invention of printing

(C) the revival of trade

(D) the creation of steel

29. Which of the following was a consequence of the ideals outlined in the passage?

(A) The establishment of the scholar-gentry social class

(B) The development of Confucianism

(C) The construction of the Great Wall of China

(D) The popularization of the Mandate of Heaven

30. Which of the following places or empires had road systems similar to the Incan Empire and Tang dynasty?

(A) Athens and Sparta

(B) Moscow and Kiev

(C) Rome and Persia

(D) Egypt and Babylon

Questions 31–33 refer to the following image.

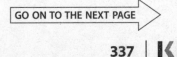

Mayan Dresden Codex, circa 1250 C.E.

31. The image most clearly reflects which aspect of Mayan civilization?

    (A) The complex system of hieroglyphics

    (B) The belief in the creator god Itzamna

    (C) The Mayan rulers' declarations of divine authority

    (D) The solar calendar

32. Which of the following is the most likely reason that Mayan civilization declined?

    (A) The weak military leadership of Hernán Cortés

    (B) Diseases imported from Europe

    (C) Natural disasters such as a volcanic eruption

    (D) Deforestation

33. Between 1450 C.E. and 1750 C.E., European interest in establishing colonies among the Aztec civilization was primarily motivated by

    (A) the need to escape the harsh European climate

    (B) its ability to spread democratic beliefs to a new poplutaions

    (C) the opportunity to make a large profit from cash crops

    (D) the ease of travel to the Americas

GO ON TO THE NEXT PAGE

Questions 34–36 refer to the passage below.

"When the Spanish crown entered into an alliance with France in 1795, it set off a series of developments that opened up economic and political distance between the Iberian countries and their American colonies. By siding with France, Spain pitted itself against England, the dominant sea power of the period."

"History of Latin America," *Encyclopaedia Britannica*

34. Dominant power in Latin America during the late 1700s and early 1800s lay in the hands of the

    (A) *peninsulares*

    (B) Creoles

    (C) middle class

    (D) mestizos

35. What was one of the major problems faced by governments of newly liberated Spanish colonies in the early nineteenth century?

    (A) Spanish rule had been incredibly popular.

    (B) The people had little experience in self-government.

    (C) They were dependent on agricultural products from Europe.

    (D) The departure of many Spanish-born citizens drastically reduced populations.

36. How did the Spanish alliance with France in 1795 C.E. create "economic and political distance" between Spain and its American colonies?

    (A) France took over administrative control of the colonies.

    (B) English propaganda sought to encourage revolution in the colonies.

    (C) English naval power disrupted communications between Europe and the colonies.

    (D) Spain tightened controls on commerce in the colonies.

GO ON TO THE NEXT PAGE

Questions 37–40 refer to the passage below.

"I was eleven years old when I went to work in the mill. They learnt me to knit. Well, I was so little that they had to build me a box to get up on to put the sock in the machine. I worked in the hosiery mill for a long time and, well, then we finally moved back to the country. But me and my sister Molly finally went back up there in 1910 and I went to work in the silk mill. Molly went to work in the hosiery mill. . . . We worked twelve hours a day for fifty cents. When paydays come around, I drawed three dollars. That was for six days, seventy-two hours. I remember I lacked fifty cents having enough to pay my board."

Excerpt from Victoria Byerly', *Hard Times Cotton Mill Girls*, 1986

37. Industrialization resulted in all of the following <u>except</u> for

(A) changes in working conditions

(B) the family unit serving as an economic unit

(C) greater opportunities for economic advancement

(D) cheaper manufactured goods

38. Which of the following aided in Great Britain's ability to industrialize?

(A) The enclosure movement creating additional small-farming opportunities

(B) An abundant supply of oil, which helped fuel industrialization

(C) Britain's economy being more regulated than other countries' economies

(D) A boom in railroad construction, which decreased transportation costs

39. Which of the following describes an early result of the European Industrial Revolution on other parts of the world?

(A) The beginning of the transatlantic slave trade

(B) Increased demand for commodities, such as cotton, rubber and palm oil

(C) A massive influx of migrants into Europe

(D) The partition of Africa by European imperial powers

40. All of the following describe conditions of urban neighborhoods during the Industrial Revolution <u>except</u> for

(A) they were often filled with severely overcrowded tenements

(B) inadequate municipal services created an atmosphere of sewage and pollution

(C) diseases such as smallpox, dysentery, cholera and tuberculosis proliferated

(D) most factory workers lived in fully-furnished, factory-owned apartment buildings

GO ON TO THE NEXT PAGE

Questions 41–44 refer to the passage below.

"It used to take ten days to get the twenty baskets of rubber—we were always in the forest to find the rubber vines, to go without food, and our women had to give up cultivating the fields and gardens. Then we starved. Leopards killed some of us while we were working away in the forest and others got lost or died from exposure and starvation. We begged the white man to leave us alone, saying we could get no more rubber, but the white men and their soldiers said: 'Go. You are only beasts yourselves, you are only nyama (meat).' We tried, always going further into the forest, and when we failed and our rubber was short, the soldiers came to our towns and killed us. Many were shot, some had their ears cut off; others were tied up with ropes round their necks and taken away."

Excerpt from Joseph Conrad's *Heart of Darkness*, 1899

41. The Berlin Conference of 1884–1885 C.E. resulted in the

(A) division of Africa among European powers

(B) creation of spheres of influence in China

(C) redrawing of the map of Europe

(D) colonization of India by the British

42. All of the following were causes of imperialism and colonialism in Africa <u>except</u> for

(A) medical advances allowing Europeans to enter Africa without fear of disease

(B) decreasing populations forcing European nations turn to Africa for outside labor

(C) steamships increasing European naval power, making navigation to Africa easier

(D) the invention of the machine gun allowing for easy European victories

43. During the nineteenth century, European powers maintained territorial acquisitions in Africa and Asia rather than pursuing new ventures in Latin America for all of the following reasons <u>except</u> for

(A) Latin America being too far geographically from Europe to be economically profitable

(B) European countries being overextended in Africa and Asia

(C) the U.S. claiming to defend the entire Western hemisphere against all outside intervention

(D) Latin Americans having shown themselves capable of resisting invasions

44. The "white men and their soldiers" would most likely describe the phrase "white man's burden," coined by English writer and poet Rudyard Kipling, as

(A) the struggle and toil of factory workers required during the Industrial Revolution

(B) the duty of European people to bring order and enlightenment to distant lands

(C) the responsibility of men to take care of their wives and children

(D) the guilt faced by Western civilizations for their role in creating systems of slavery

GO ON TO THE NEXT PAGE

Questions 45–47 refer to the passage below.

"Our relations with socialist countries, including the allies of the Warsaw Treaty Organization, entered a difficult critical, stage. . . . Perestroika, the development of democratization, [and] glasnost, confirmed the role of the Soviet Union as the leader in the process of socialist renewal. . . .

The European socialist countries found themselves in a powerful magnetic field of the economic growth and social well-being of the Western European states. . . . The constant comparing and contrasting of the two worlds, of their ways of life, production, intellectual cultures, entered our daily life thanks to the mass media, and there is no way around it. . . .

As a consequence, in a number of socialist countries, the process of rejection of the existing political institutions and the ideological values by the societies is already underway now."

Excerpt from Central Committee of the CPSU (Communist Party of the Soviet Union) to Alexander Yakovlev, "The Strategy of Relations with European Socialist Countries," 1989.

45. The terms glasnost and perestroika are most closely associated with which of the following leaders?

(A) Nikita Khrushchev

(B) Leonid Brezhnev

(C) Mikhail Gorbachev

(D) Boris Yeltsin

46. Which of the following world leaders was least likely to agree with the principles stated in the excerpt above?

(A) Fidel Castro of Cuba

(B) Lech Walesa of Poland

(C) Vaclav Havel of Czechoslovakia

(D) Margaret Thatcher of Great Britain

47. The policies of glasnost and perestroika contributed to the collapse of the Soviet Union by

(A) stabilizing the economy, allowing citizens to abandon Socialist theory

(B) exposing citizens to ethnic tensions that ultimately caused the U.S.S.R.'s division

(C) allowing citizens to voice dissent and undermine the Communist Party's power

(D) acquiescing to growing anti-Communist rhetoric coming from the United States

GO ON TO THE NEXT PAGE

 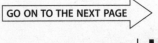

Questions 48–50 refer to the following image.

Japanese period print, 1861, courtesy of the United States Navy Institute

48. The scene above depicts a significant moment in Japanese history because it represents the

 (A) Japanese military's first defeat of a Western power

 (B) first mass migration of Americans to Japan

 (C) arrival of Japan's first Christian missionaries

 (D) end of an isolationist regime and the beginning of modernization

49. The industrial development of Japan in the Meiji Restoration most closely parallels the industrial development of which other nineteenth-century state?

 (A) The Ottoman Empire in the Tanzimat Era

 (B) Russia under the last Romanov tsars

 (C) China under the Qing emperors

 (D) Austria-Hungary under Emperor Franz Joseph

50. Japan's industrial and imperial development was
    <u>least</u> like those of Europe and the United States
    in the fact that

    (A) Japan's overseas empire focused on islands

    (B) continued industrial growth was motivated
        by militarism

    (C) Japan lacked its own supply of natural
        resources

    (D) railroads proved to be unnecessary in Japan

GO ON TO THE NEXT PAGE

Questions 51–52 refer to the passage below.

"The peace conditions imposed upon Germany are so hard, so humiliating, that even those who have the smallest expectation of a 'peace of justice' are bound to be deeply disappointed. . . .

The financial burden is so heavy that it is no exaggeration to say that Germany is reduced to economic bondage. The Germans will have to work hard and incessantly for foreign masters, without any chance of personal gain, or any prospect of regaining liberty or economic independence. . . .

These conditions will never give peace. All Germans must feel that they wish to shake off the heavy yoke imposed by the cajoling Entente, and we fear very much that that opportunity will soon present itself. For has not the Entente recognized in the proposed so-called 'League of Nations' the evident right to conquer and possess countries for economic and imperialistic purposes? Fettered and enslaved, Germany will always remain a menace to Europe."

Dutch *Algemeen Handelsblad* Editorial on the Treaty of Versailles, June 1919

51. The Treaty of Versailles did not forge a lasting peace after World War I because the

   (A) Russians would not agree to the terms of the treaty

   (B) treaty was influenced by Woodrow Wilson's Fourteen Points

   (C) Americans wished to punish the Germans for the war

   (D) Germans were forced to accept total blame and punishment for the war

52. After the Treaty of Versailles was signed, the most imminent threat to peace in Europe was

   (A) colonial independence in Africa and Asia

   (B) unrest among veterans returning from war

   (C) the lack of stable governments in war-torn nations

   (D) the Germans' inability to pay reparations

GO ON TO THE NEXT PAGE

Questions 53–55 refer to the two passages below.

"It is clear that we must find an African solution to our problems, and that this can only be found in African unity. Divided we are weak; united, Africa could become one of the greatest forces for good in the world.

Although most Africans are poor, our continent is potentially extremely rich. Our mineral resources, which are being exploited with foreign capital only to enrich foreign investors, range from gold and diamonds to uranium and petroleum. Our forests contain some of the finest woods to be grown anywhere. Our cash crops include cocoa, coffee, rubber, tobacco and cotton. As for power . . . Africa contains over 40% of the potential water power of the world, as compared with about 10% in Europe and 13% in North America. Yet so far, less than 1% has been developed. This is one of the reasons why we have in Africa the paradox of poverty in the midst of plenty, and scarcity in the midst of abundance."

Excerpt from Kwame Nkrumah's "I Speak of Freedom" speech, 1961

"A great part of Tanzania's land is fertile and gets sufficient rains. Our country can produce various crops for home consumption and for export. . . .

From now on we shall stand upright and walk forward on our feet rather than look at this problem upside down. Industries will come and money will come, but their foundation is the people and their hard work, especially in agriculture. This is the meaning of self-reliance."

Excerpt from Julius Nyerere's Arusha Declaration, 1967

53. What did both Nkrumah and Nyerere describe as necessary to sustaining independence in post-colonial Africa?

   (A) The utilization of Africa's abundant natural resources

   (B) An alliance of African countries and their former colonial powers

   (C) The development of a union of African countries

   (D) The rise of strong military leaders in Africa

54. The society that Nkrumah and Nyerere both desired for post-colonial Africa is most similar to

   (A) the Former Soviet Union after 1991

   (B) South America in the 1820s and 1830s

   (C) the Indian Subcontinent after 1947

   (D) the United States after the Revolutionary War

55. The following were causes of the challenges that sub-Saharan Africa faces today <u>except</u> for

   (A) political borders drawn by Europeans without regard to traditional African territories

   (B) loyalties divided between the capitalist West and the communist East during the Cold War

   (C) constant disagreement between the Organization of African Unity and the United Nations

   (D) frequent economic aid provided by the United States and Western Europe

GO ON TO THE NEXT PAGE

Directions: Section I, Part B of this exam consists of short answer questions. You must respond to Questions 1 and 2. For your final response, you must choose to answer EITHER Question 3 or Question 4. Use complete sentences; an outline or bulleted list alone is not acceptable.

1. Use the graph below to answer all parts of the question that follows.

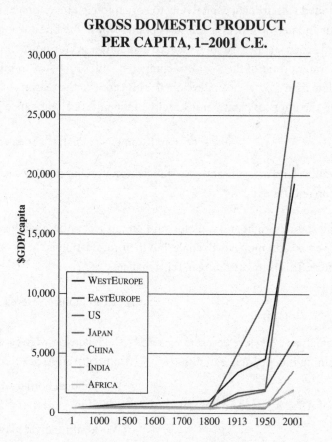

**GROSS DOMESTIC PRODUCT
PER CAPITA, 1–2001 C.E.**

Derek Thompson's "The Economic History of the Last 2,000 Years," *The Atlantic*, 2012.

a) Identify the <u>trends</u> demonstrated between 1450 and 2001 by TWO of the plot lines (Western Europe, Eastern Europe, United States, Japan, China, India, or Africa) in the graph above.

b) Explain at least one <u>historical event</u> that could have impacted the trends demonstrated by ONE of the graph's plot lines.

c) Explain at least one <u>historical event</u> that could have impacted the trends demonstrated by another ONE of the graph's plot lines.

GO ON TO THE NEXT PAGE

2. Use the passage below to answer all parts of the question that follows.

"As every individual, therefore, endeavours as much as he can both to employ his capital in the support of domestic industry, and so to direct that industry that its produce may be of the greatest value; every individual necessarily labours to render the annual revenue of the society as great as he can. He generally, indeed, neither intends to promote the public interest, nor knows how much he is promoting it. By preferring the support of domestic to that of foreign industry, he intends only his own security; and by directing that industry in such a manner as its produce may be of the greatest value, he intends only his own gain, and he is in this, as in many other cases, led by an invisible hand to promote an end which was no part of his intention."

Adam Smith, *The Wealth of Nations*, 1776

a) Describe ONE idea expressed by Karl Marx and Friedrich Engels in the *Communist Manifesto* (1848).

b) Explain a <u>similarity</u> between the ideas in the *Communist Manifesto* and world history events in the period after 1900 C.E.

c) Using Smith's description of the "invisible hand" in the passage above, explain a <u>difference</u> between how Adam Smith and Marx/Engels viewed the "invisible hand."

Choose EITHER Question 3 or Question 4.

3. Answer all parts of the question that follows.

a) Explain ONE <u>change</u> that occurred in Judaism during the period of Roman rule in the first and second centuries C.E.

b) Explain ONE area of <u>continuity</u> in Judaism during Roman rule in the first and second centuries C.E.

c) Identify a way in which Judaism influenced another world religion.

4. Answer all parts of the question that follows.

a) Identify ONE characteristic of trade relations between China and Europe in the seventeenth and eighteenth centuries C.E.

b) Explain ONE <u>change</u> that occurred in China as a result of contact with the British in the nineteenth century.

c) Explain ONE area of <u>continuity</u> in China during the period of British contacts in the nineteenth century.

GO ON TO THE NEXT PAGE

END OF SECTION I

**IF YOU FINISH BEFORE TIME IS CALLED,
YOU MAY CHECK YOUR WORK ON PART A.
DO NOT GO ON TO PART B UNTIL YOU ARE TOLD TO DO SO.**

SECTION II

Time—100 Minutes

2 Questions

Question 1: Document-Based Question
Suggested reading period: 15 minutes
Suggested writing time: 45 minutes

Directions: Question 1 is based on the accompanying documents. The documents have been edited for the purpose of this exercise.

Write your responses on the lined pages that follow the question.

In your response you should do the following.

- State a relevant thesis that directly addresses all parts of the question.

- Support the thesis or a relevant argument with evidence from all, or all but one, of the documents.

- Incorporate analysis of all, or all but one, of the documents into your argument.

- Focus your analysis of each document on at least one of the following: intended audience, purpose, historical context, and/or point of view.

- Support your argument with analysis of historical examples outside the documents.

- Connect historical phenomena relevant to your argument to broader events or processes.

- Synthesize the elements above into a persuasive essay that extends your argument, connects it to a different historical context, or accounts for contradictory evidence on the topic.

1. Analyze the economic and social effects of the Spanish conquest of the Americas.

GO ON TO THE NEXT PAGE

Document 1

Source: Hernán Cortés, Spanish conquistador, Letters from Mexico, August 12, 1521

On leaving my camp, I commanded Gonzalo de Sandoval to sail the brigantines (ships) in between the houses in the other quarter in which the Indians were resisting, so that we should have them surrounded, but not to attack until he saw that we were engaged. In this way they would have been surrounded and so hard pressed that they would have no place to move save over the bodies of their dead or along the rooftops. They no longer could find any arrow, javelins or stones with which to attack us; and our allies fighting with us were armed with swords and bucklers, and slaughtered so many of them on land and in the water that more than forty thousand were killed or taken that day.

Document 2

Source: Bernardino de Sahagún, a Franciscan friar who was instrumental in preserving information about Aztec culture, *General History of the Things of New Spain*, 1519 to 1521

After the previously mentioned hardships that befell the Spaniards in the year 1519, at the beginning of the year 1520 the epidemic of smallpox, measles, and pustules broke out so virulently that a vast number of people died throughout this New Spain. This pestilence began in the province of Chalco and lasted for sixty days. Among the Mexicans who fell victim to this pestilence was the lord Cuitlahuactzin, whom they had elected a little earlier. Many leaders, many veteran soldiers, and valiant men who were their defense in time of war, also died.

GO ON TO THE NEXT PAGE

Document 3

Source: Antonio Vázquez de Espinosa, a Spanish friar and missionary who sought to convert the Indians to Christianity, describes the silver mines of Potosí.

These Indians are sent out every year under a captain whom they choose in each village or tribe, for him to take them and oversee them for the year each had to serve; every year they have a new election, for as some go out, others come in. This works out very badly, with great losses and gaps in the quotas of Indians, the villages being depopulated; and this gives rise to great extortions and abuses on the part of the inspectors toward the poor Indians, ruining them and thus depriving the chief Indians of their property and carrying them off in chains because they do not fill out the mit'a assignment . . .

So huge is the wealth which has been taken out of this range since the year 1545, when it was discovered, up to the present year of 1628, which makes 83 years that they have been working and reducing its ores, and that merely from the registered mines, as appears from an examination of most of the account in the royal records, 326,000,000 pesos have been taken out.

Document 4

Source: Juan Ginés de Sepúlveda (1490–1573), a scholar and apologist for the Spanish treatment of the Indians in the Americas

Turning then to our topic, whether it is proper and just that those who are superior and who excel in nature, customs, and laws rule over their inferiors, you can easily understand . . . if you are familiar with the character and moral code of the two peoples, that it is with perfect right that the Spaniards exercise their domination over those barbarians of the New World and its adjacent islands. For in prudence, talent, and every kind of virtue and human sentiment they are as inferior to the Spaniards as children are to adults, or women to men, or the cruel and inhumane to the very gentle, or the excessively intemperate to the continent and moderate . . .

GO ON TO THE NEXT PAGE

Document 5

Source: Bartolomé de las Casas, Dominican friar, *A Short Account of the Destruction of the Indies*, 1542

As we have said, the island of Hispaniola was the first to witness the arrival of Europeans and the first to suffer the wholesale slaughter of its people and the devastation and depopulation of the land. It all began with the Europeans taking native women and children both as servants and to satisfy their own base appetites; then not content with what the local people offered them of their own free will (and all offered as much as they could spare), they started taking for themselves the food that natives contrived to produce by the sweat of their brows, (which was in all honesty little enough) . . . Some of them started to conceal food they had, others decided to send their women and children into hiding, and yet others took to the hills to get away from the brutal and ruthless cruelty that was being inflicted on them. . . .

Document 6

Source: Engraving by Flemish engraver Theodor de Bry taken from a sixteenth-century Dutch edition of *A Short Account of the Destruction of the Indies* by Bartolomé de las Casas

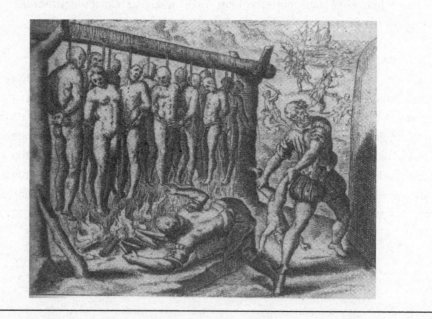

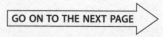

Document 7

Source: Ker Than, "Massive Population Drop Found for Native Americans, DNA Shows," *National Geographic News*, December 5, 2011

The number of Native Americans quickly shrank by roughly half following European contact about 500 years ago, according to a new genetic study.

The finding supports historical accounts that Europeans triggered a wave of disease, warfare, and enslavement in the New World that had devastating effects for indigenous populations across the Americas.

Using samples of ancient and modern mitochondrial DNA—which is passed down only from mothers to daughters—the researchers calculated a demographic history for American Indians.

Based on the data, the team estimates that the Native American population was at an all-time high about 5,000 years ago.

The population then reached a low point about 500 years ago—only a few years after Christopher Columbus arrived in the New World and before extensive European colonization began.

Study co-author Brendan O'Fallon, a population geneticist who conducted the research while at the University of Washington in Seattle, speculates that many of the early casualties may have been due to disease, which "would likely have traveled much faster than the European settlers themselves."

GO ON TO THE NEXT PAGE

Question 2, Question 3, or Question 4: Long Essay Question

Suggested writing time: 40 minutes

Directions: Choose Question 2, Question 3, OR Question 4 to answer.

In your response you should do the following.

- Present a thesis statement
- Apply AP History Reasoning Skills as directed by the question
- Utilize specific examples of historical evidence to support the thesis, and explain relationships among the evidence.
- Extend the argument by explaining the connections between the argument and either: a development in a different historical period, situation, era, or geographic location; or a theme/approach to history that is not the focus of the essay.

2. Analyze the continuities and changes in demography and the environment (for example, disease, population, new crops, and animals) in the Americas from 1450 C.E. to 1750 C.E.

3. Analyze the continuities and changes in demography and the environment (for example, disease, population, new crops, and animals) in sub-Saharan Africa from 1450 C.E. to 1750 C.E.

4. Analyze the global continuities and changes in demography and the environment (for example, disease, population, new crops, and animals) after 1900 C.E.

GO ON TO THE NEXT PAGE

END OF SECTION II

ANSWER KEY

Section I

1. A	15. A	29. A	43. A
2. D	16. A	30. C	44. B
3. B	17. D	31. A	45. C
4. C	18. D	32. C	46. A
5. D	19. B	33. C	47. C
6. A	20. B	34. A	48. D
7. C	21. A	35. B	49. B
8. A	22. D	36. C	50. C
9. D	23. C	37. B	51. D
10. D	24. C	38. D	52. C
11. C	25. D	39. B	53. A
12. B	26. B	40. D	54. D
13. C	27. D	41. A	55. C
14. A	28. C	42. B	

Section I, Part A Number Correct: _____

Section I, Part B (Short-Answer Questions) Points Earned: _____

Section II, Part A (Document-Based Question) Points Earned: _____

Section II, Part B (Long Essay Question) Points Earned: _____

Enter these results to see your 1–5 score and view detailed explanations by logging in at kaptest.com.

Haven't registered your book yet? Go to kaptest.com/booksonline to begin.

Practice Exam 3

Practice Exam 3 Answer Grid

1. Ⓐ Ⓑ Ⓒ Ⓓ
2. Ⓐ Ⓑ Ⓒ Ⓓ
3. Ⓐ Ⓑ Ⓒ Ⓓ
4. Ⓐ Ⓑ Ⓒ Ⓓ
5. Ⓐ Ⓑ Ⓒ Ⓓ
6. Ⓐ Ⓑ Ⓒ Ⓓ
7. Ⓐ Ⓑ Ⓒ Ⓓ
8. Ⓐ Ⓑ Ⓒ Ⓓ
9. Ⓐ Ⓑ Ⓒ Ⓓ
10. Ⓐ Ⓑ Ⓒ Ⓓ
11. Ⓐ Ⓑ Ⓒ Ⓓ
12. Ⓐ Ⓑ Ⓒ Ⓓ
13. Ⓐ Ⓑ Ⓒ Ⓓ
14. Ⓐ Ⓑ Ⓒ Ⓓ

15. Ⓐ Ⓑ Ⓒ Ⓓ
16. Ⓐ Ⓑ Ⓒ Ⓓ
17. Ⓐ Ⓑ Ⓒ Ⓓ
18. Ⓐ Ⓑ Ⓒ Ⓓ
19. Ⓐ Ⓑ Ⓒ Ⓓ
20. Ⓐ Ⓑ Ⓒ Ⓓ
21. Ⓐ Ⓑ Ⓒ Ⓓ
22. Ⓐ Ⓑ Ⓒ Ⓓ
23. Ⓐ Ⓑ Ⓒ Ⓓ
24. Ⓐ Ⓑ Ⓒ Ⓓ
25. Ⓐ Ⓑ Ⓒ Ⓓ
26. Ⓐ Ⓑ Ⓒ Ⓓ
27. Ⓐ Ⓑ Ⓒ Ⓓ
28. Ⓐ Ⓑ Ⓒ Ⓓ

29. Ⓐ Ⓑ Ⓒ Ⓓ
30. Ⓐ Ⓑ Ⓒ Ⓓ
31. Ⓐ Ⓑ Ⓒ Ⓓ
32. Ⓐ Ⓑ Ⓒ Ⓓ
33. Ⓐ Ⓑ Ⓒ Ⓓ
34. Ⓐ Ⓑ Ⓒ Ⓓ
35. Ⓐ Ⓑ Ⓒ Ⓓ
36. Ⓐ Ⓑ Ⓒ Ⓓ
37. Ⓐ Ⓑ Ⓒ Ⓓ
38. Ⓐ Ⓑ Ⓒ Ⓓ
39. Ⓐ Ⓑ Ⓒ Ⓓ
40. Ⓐ Ⓑ Ⓒ Ⓓ
41. Ⓐ Ⓑ Ⓒ Ⓓ
42. Ⓐ Ⓑ Ⓒ Ⓓ

43. Ⓐ Ⓑ Ⓒ Ⓓ
44. Ⓐ Ⓑ Ⓒ Ⓓ
45. Ⓐ Ⓑ Ⓒ Ⓓ
46. Ⓐ Ⓑ Ⓒ Ⓓ
47. Ⓐ Ⓑ Ⓒ Ⓓ
48. Ⓐ Ⓑ Ⓒ Ⓓ
49. Ⓐ Ⓑ Ⓒ Ⓓ
50. Ⓐ Ⓑ Ⓒ Ⓓ
51. Ⓐ Ⓑ Ⓒ Ⓓ
52. Ⓐ Ⓑ Ⓒ Ⓓ
53. Ⓐ Ⓑ Ⓒ Ⓓ
54. Ⓐ Ⓑ Ⓒ Ⓓ
55. Ⓐ Ⓑ Ⓒ Ⓓ

SECTION I
Time—95 Minutes
58 Questions

Directions: Each of the questions or incomplete statements below is followed by four suggested answers or completions. Select the one that is best in each case and then fill in the appropriate letter in the corresponding space on the answer sheet.

Directions: Section I, Part A of this exam contains 55 multiple choice questions. The questions are organized into sets with corresponding historical sources. Each of the questions or incomplete statements is followed by four suggested answers or completions. Using both the provided source and your own historical knowledge, select the best answer choice.

Questions 1–3 refer to the passage below.

"The Dynastic period of native Egyptian rulers is generally divided into 30 dynasties, following the Aegyptiaca of the Greco-Egyptian writer Manetho of Sebennytos (early 3rd century B.C.E.), excerpts of which are preserved in the works of later writers. Manetho apparently organized his dynasties by the capital cities from which they ruled, but several of his divisions also reflect political or dynastic changes—that is, changes of the party holding power. He gave the lengths of reign of kings or of entire dynasties and grouped the dynasties into several periods, but, because of textual corruption and a tendency toward inflation, Manetho's figures cannot be used to reconstruct chronology without supporting evidence and analysis."

"Ancient Egypt," *Encyclopedia Britannica*

1. Which of the following is true of both Mesopotamia and Egypt?

   (A) Both were organized into city-states.

   (B) Both were ruled by a military dictatorship.

   (C) Both used writing systems.

   (D) Both had monotheistic belief systems.

2. The surviving fragments of the Aegyptiaca provide modern historians with

   (A) a framework for organizing ancient Egyptian political history

   (B) an extremely precise chronology of Egyptian dynasties

   (C) a social history of everyday Egyptian life

   (D) a greater understanding of ancient Egyptian agriculture

3. Mesopotamian kings had all of the following in common with Egyptian pharaohs <u>except</u> that Mesopotamian kings

   (A) were the ultimate source of legal authority

   (B) were considered living gods

   (C) ordered massive construction projects

   (D) participated in religious rituals

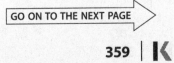
GO ON TO THE NEXT PAGE

Questions 4–6 refer to the passage below.

"'Everyone who calls on the name of the Lord will be saved.

How, then, can they call on the one they have not believed in? And how can they believe in the one of whom they have not heard?'"

Romans 10:13–14, NIV Bible translation

4. Buddhism and Christianity have which of the following in common?

(A) Belief in one god

(B) A hierarchal organization

(C) An emphasis on missionary activity

(D) De-emphasis on rituals

5. According to Buddhist tradition, prior to becoming a spiritual leader Siddhartha Gautama was

(A) a soldier

(B) a prince

(C) a farmer

(D) a carpenter

6. Paul, an early Christian leader, wrote the excerpt's questions in order to encourage

(A) missionary work

(B) acts of charity

(C) standardization of prayers

(D) construction of churches

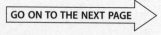
GO ON TO THE NEXT PAGE

Questions 7–9 refer to the following illustration.

INDIAN OCEAN TRADE ROUTES

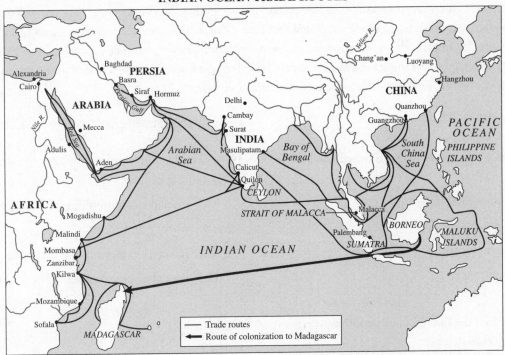

7. Which of the following had the most advanced naval technology in the period 600 C.E. to 1450 C.E.?

   (A) Western Europe

   (B) China

   (C) West Africa

   (D) India

8. Monsoon wind patterns in the Indian Ocean demonstrate an influence over

   (A) the intersection of human technological innovation and natural geography

   (B) the negative impact of weather on military campaigns in Asia

   (C) how humans overcame the difficulty of forming trade networks in the region

   (D) the superiority of sea trade compared to overland trade

9. The following goods were traded in the Indian Ocean <u>except</u> for

   (A) cocoa

   (B) slaves

   (C) gold

   (D) porcelain

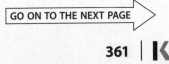

Questions 10–12 refer to the passage below.

"The function or purpose of art in Paleolithic life remains a subject of debate. Some scholars see the human and animal representations as evidence of the use of magical rites to ensure success in hunting or to guarantee fertility. Others have suggested that Paleolithic artists' accurate representations of animals' coats may be an early attempt to produce a seasonal notation system. Another viewpoint, disregarding utility altogether, sees the art of Paleolithic peoples solely as an outgrowth of a basic human need to creatively record and reproduce aspects of the surrounding world."

"Paleolithic Period," *Encyclopaedia Britannica*

10. Paleolithic society's religious beliefs can best be described as

(A) monotheistic

(B) polytheistic

(C) syncretistic

(D) animistic

11. Why does the function of Paleolithic art remain a subject of debate?

(A) Disagreement among written sources from the period

(B) Inadequate archaeological evidence from the period

(C) Uncertainty about ritual garments recovered from the period

(D) The inability to identify any of the figures visual art from the period

12. All of the following are features of Paleolithic culture <u>except</u> for

(A) nomadic communities

(B) use of primitive stone tools

(C) reliance on hunting and gathering

(D) the development of settled agriculture

Questions 13–15 refer to the following image.

Mughal painting depicting Mumtaz Mahal, circa 1700.

13. Which of the following was a significant consequence of constructing the painting shown above, along with the rest of the Taj Mahal?

   (A) An increase in land taxes, which further impoverished Indian peasants

   (B) A desire among artists to begin integrating Indian and Persian styles

   (C) An emergence of new gender attitudes, which encouraged Indian women to participate in politics

   (D) A migration of additional British commanders and soldiers to India

14. As the Ottomans dominated much of the Middle East and North Africa during the period 1450 C.E. to 1750 C.E., which of the following empires dominated South Asia?

   (A) Safavid

   (B) Delhi Sultanate

   (C) Manchu

   (D) Mughal

15. What did European countries use to economically expand their empires and share in the wealth that is depicted in this painting?

   (A) Deforestation

   (B) Soil Depletion

   (C) Joint-Stock Companies

   (D) Social Darwinism

GO ON TO THE NEXT PAGE

Questions 16-17 refer to the following map.

EARLY CIVILIZATIONS, CIRCA 3000 B.C.E.

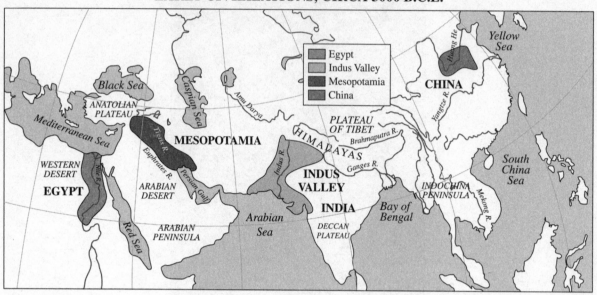

16. Why do historians know little about what led to the decline of the Indus Valley civilization?

    (A) This river valley civilization left no written records.

    (B) Its written records were destroyed by Mongol invaders.

    (C) Its writing system has never been deciphered.

    (D) It left written records which stop prior to its period of decline.

17. The shaded regions shown on the above map share all of the following characteristics <u>except</u> for

    (A) the development of written language

    (B) agricultural advances due to proximity to a river

    (C) discrete social classes

    (D) monotheistic religions

GO ON TO THE NEXT PAGE

Questions 18–20 refer to the following map.

TRADE ROUTES: THE SILK ROAD

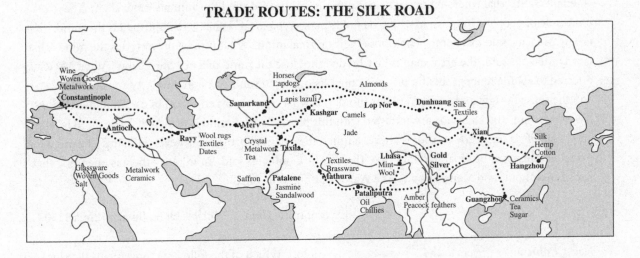

18. In the period 600 C.E. to 1450 C.E., Dunhuang, Kashgar, and Samarkand were examples of

    (A) oasis towns on the Silk Road

    (B) political capitals in East Africa

    (C) economic centers on the Mediterranean Sea

    (D) religious pilgrimage sites in South Asia

19. The concept of the Silk Road can best be described as

    (A) a cross-cultural exchange which enabled technological and political development

    (B) a system in which luxury goods were traded for other luxury goods

    (C) overland routes enabling population flow between East Asia and the Mediterranean

    (D) a system which eventually weakened the cities and kingdoms located along it

20. Which of these examples is most similar to transportation along the Silk Road?

    (A) The network of roads built across the Roman Empire

    (B) The Bantu migrations throughout sub-Saharan Africa

    (C) The use of Ancient Greek triremes on the Mediterranean Sea

    (D) The Arabs' and Berbers' use of camels to trade across the Sahara

GO ON TO THE NEXT PAGE

Questions 21–23 refer to the passage below.

"Mencius said, 'That wherein human beings differ from the birds and the animals is but slight. The multitude of people relinquish it, while the noble person retains it.' What is relinquished is the mind. That is why Mencius said that some people 'lose their original mind.' What is to be preserved is the mind. That is why Mencius said, 'the great man is he who does not lose the mind of a newborn babe.' [What Mencius referred to as] the four sprouts [of pity and compassion, shame and aversion, modesty and compliance, and the sense of right and wrong] are this mind. It is what Heaven has endowed in us. All human beings have this mind, and all minds are endowed with this principle. The mind is principle…The mind is one and principle is one. Perfect truth is always a unity; the essential principle is never a duality. The mind and principle can never be separated into two. That is why Confucius said, 'In my Way there is one thing that runs throughout,' and Mencius said, 'The Way is one and only one.'"

Excerpt from *Mind is Principle* by Lu Jiuyuan, circa 1150 C.E.

21. Neo-Confucianism refers to the

    (A) rejection of Confucian beliefs during the Yuan dynasty

    (B) blending of Buddhist and Confucian ideas

    (C) spread of Confucianism to Russia

    (D) use of Confucianism to monitor economic relations

22. Which of the following forms of art did not flourish in China during the years that Neo-Confucianism emerged?

    (A) Poetry

    (B) Ceramics

    (C) Wood carving

    (D) Landscape painting

23. Which of the following movements developed as Confucius's teachings were originally spreading in China, around 500 B.C.E.?

    (A) Animism

    (B) The Mandate of Heaven

    (C) Daoism

    (D) The Zhou

GO ON TO THE NEXT PAGE

Questions 24–26 refer to the passage below.

"War dominated much of Peter's reign. At first Peter attempted to secure the principality's southern borders against the Tatars and the Ottoman Turks. His campaign against a fort on the Sea of Azov failed initially, but after he created Russia's first navy, Peter was able to take the port of Azov in 1696. To continue the war with the Ottoman Empire, Peter traveled to Europe to seek allies. The first tsar to make such a trip, Peter visited Brandenburg, Holland, England, and the Holy Roman Empire during his so-called Grand Embassy. Peter learned a great deal and enlisted into his service hundreds of West European technical specialists. The embassy was cut short by the attempt to place Sofia on the throne instead of Peter, a revolt that was crushed by Peter's followers. As a result, Peter had hundreds of the participants tortured and killed, and he publicly displayed their bodies as a warning to others.

. . . Through his victories, Peter acquired a direct link with Western Europe. In celebration, Peter assumed the title of emperor as well as tsar, and Muscovy officially became the Russian Empire in 1721."

Excerpt from *Russia: A Country Study* by Glenn E. Curtis, 1991

24. The actions of Peter the Great, as described in the passage, most clearly exemplify which of the following?

    (A) Divine right of kings

    (B) Absolutism

    (C) Inflation

    (D) Nationalism

25. In addition to the military policies and political achievements outlined in the passage, all of the following were policies of Russia's Peter the Great <u>except</u> for

    (A) increased foreign trade

    (B) the introduction of Western styles of dress

    (C) improved technology

    (D) the use of Enlightenment ideas in the government

26. Which of the following developments occurred in Russia as a result of Peter the Great's reign?

    (A) Rulers became known as tsars

    (B) Protestants such as Huguenots emigrated

    (C) Aristocratic women further participated in society

    (D) Enlightenment ideals spread in the government

GO ON TO THE NEXT PAGE

Questions 27–30 refer to the passage below.

"During this period [the fifteenth century C.E.], the whole of the Swahili Coast enjoyed a revival of fortunes due to a combination of factors. The overland route to the east had been cut by the Mongols, leaving the sea route via the east African coast as the alternative. Several large trading fleets were sent by the Chinese to Africa, and an insatiable demand for eastern spices, particularly in Europe, helped put the city-states of the Swahili Coast, which acted as middlemen, back in the centre of international trade."

Excerpt from "The Wealth of Africa: The Swahili Coast," notes prepared
for educators by The British Museum

27. Both the ancient Greek city-states and the Swahili city-states

    (A) were economically reliant on wealth generated by sea trade

    (B) traded primarily on the Mediterranean Sea

    (C) frequently embarked on wars of conquest

    (D) were conquered by Alexander the Great during the third century B.C.E.

28. The final decline of the Swahili city-states can be attributed to

    (A) waning demand for eastern spices in Europe

    (B) government mismanagement of the wealth generated by trade

    (C) religious tension between local and foreign merchants

    (D) conquest by foreign powers

29. The excerpt mentions a "revival of fortunes" for the Swahili city-states in the fifteenth century. What event from the previous century most likely had the largest negative effect on the economic power of the city-states?

    (A) The beginning of the Hundred Years' War between England and France

    (B) The spread of the plague known as the Black Death

    (C) The Russian military victory over local Mongol forces near Moscow in 1380 C.E.

    (D) The Kalmar Union combining Sweden, Norway, and Denmark into one kingdom

30. What kind of effect did the monsoon winds, which blow from India to Africa from October to April, and from Africa to India from June to September, have on the rise of the Swahili city-states?

    (A) Minimal effect

    (B) Hurt, as they blew away from the African coast for months

    (C) Helped, as they made navigation more predictable for merchant vessels

    (D) Hurt, as they facilitated trade only with India

GO ON TO THE NEXT PAGE

Questions 31–32 refer to the passage below.

"Howbeit there is a most stately temple to be seen, the walls whereof are made of stone and lime; and a princely palace also built by a most excellent workman of Granada. Here are many shops of artificers, and merchants, and especially of such as weave linen and cotton cloth. And hither do the Barbarie merchants bring cloth of Europe. All the women of the region except maidservants go with their faces covered, and sell all necessary victuals. The inhabitants, & especially strangers there residing, are exceeding rich, insomuch that the king that now is, married both his daughters unto two rich merchants. Here are many wells, containing most sweet water; and so often as the river Niger overflows, they convey the water thereof by certain sluices into the town. Corn (sorghum), cattle, milk, and butter this region yields in great abundance: but salt is very scarce here; for it is brought hither by land from Tagaza, which is five hundred miles distant. When I myself was here, I saw one camel load of salt sold for 80 ducats. The rich king of Tombuto (Timbuktu) hath many plates and scepters of gold, some whereof weigh 1300 pounds; . . .
He hath always three thousand horsemen, and a great number of footmen that shoot poisoned arrows, attending upon him. . . . Here are great store of doctors, judges, priests and other learned men, that are bountifully maintained at the king's cost and charges. And hither are brought divers manuscripts or written books out of Barbarie, which are sold for more money than any other merchandise. . . ."

Leo Africanus, "Of the Kingdom of Tombuto," 1550 C.E.

31. All of the statements below refer to which em-
    pire in the period 1450 to 1750 C.E.?

    I. Lucrative trans-Saharan trade

    II. All emperors were Muslim

    III. Islamic scholarship at Timbuktu

    (A) Fatimid

    (B) Ottoman

    (C) Mughal

    (D) Songhai

32. The basis of Timbuktu's prosperity, as described
    in the passage, was

    (A) thriving trade between local Muslims and
        Christian pilgrims to the Holy Land

    (B) its favored location on regional trade routes

    (C) its early adoption of cloth spinning and
        weaving machinery

    (D) French and Portuguese traders staying
        there on their way to Morocco

GO ON TO THE NEXT PAGE

 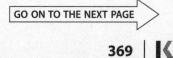

Questions 33–35 refer to the following quotation.

"All who have served Revolution have plowed the sea."

Simón Bolívar, circa 1830 C.E.

33. Simón Bolívar, Miguel Hidalgo, and José de San Martín are all examples of

(A) captains of industry

(B) Spanish viceroys

(C) leaders of slave revolts

(D) revolutionary leaders

34. Simón Bolívar was instrumental in liberating the following countries from European rule <u>except</u> for

(A) Venezuela

(B) Argentina

(C) Colombia

(D) Ecuador

35. The quote, attributed to Simón Bolívar near the end of his life, expresses his

(A) satisfaction at having achieved the impossible

(B) contempt for his fellow revolutionaries

(C) bitterness at the temporary success achieved

(D) realization that opposing Spanish authority was wrong

GO ON TO THE NEXT PAGE

Questions 36–39 refer to the passage below.

"*Proclamation of the Young Turks*

1. The basis for the Constitution will be respect for the predominance of the national will. One of the consequences of this principle will be to require without delay the responsibility of the minister before the Chamber, and, consequently, to consider the minister as having resigned, when he does not have a majority of the votes of the Chamber.

2. Provided that the number of senators does not exceed one-third the number of deputies, the Senate will be named as follows: one-third by the Sultan and two-thirds by the nation, and the term of senators will be of limited duration.

3. It will be demanded that all Ottoman subjects having completed their twentieth year, regardless of whether they possess property or fortune, shall have the right to vote. Those who have lost their civil rights will naturally be deprived of this right."

Excerpt from a proclamation made by the Young Turks, 1908

36. All of the following statements describe developments in the Ottoman Empire in the period 1750 C.E. to 1900 C.E. except that

    (A) Europeans were exempt from following Ottoman law

    (B) Tanzimat reformers were inspired by Enlightenment thought

    (C) the Young Turk Party promoted reforms

    (D) the Islamic leadership, or ulama, supported the liberal reforms

37. The chief source of Ottoman inflation during the sixteenth century was

    (A) uncontrolled spending by the nobles

    (B) widespread opium addiction

    (C) poor governmental tax-collecting policies

    (D) an influx of silver from the Americas

38. All of the following are examples of the Ottoman Empire's Mahmud II's reforms <u>except</u> for

    (A) creation of a new army instructed in European weaponry and tactics

    (B) forced disbandment and massacre of the Janissaries

    (C) strengthening of the ulama, the Islamic leadership

    (D) formation of a cabinet, called the Council of Ministers

39. Why do Ottoman historians call the period between 1718 C.E. and 1730 C.E. the Tulip Period?

    (A) During this time, the narcotic value of tulip poppies was discovered.

    (B) There was high demand for expensive tulip bulbs.

    (C) "Tulip" in Turkish translates to "changes."

    (D) The sultan Mahmud II wore a headdress shaped like a tulip.

GO ON TO THE NEXT PAGE

Questions 40–43 refer to the following passage.

"Without ignoring accomplishments, or casting a slur upon any of the graces which serve to adorn society, we must look deeper for the acquirements which serve to form our ideal of a perfect woman. The companion of man should be able thoroughly to sympathize with him—her intellect should be as well developed as his. We do not believe in the mental inequality of the sexes; we believe that the man and the woman have each a work to do, for which they are specially qualified, and in which they are called to excel. Though the work is not the same, it is equally noble, and demands an equal exercise of capacity."

Excerpt from *Godey's Lady's Book*, Vol. LIII, 1856

40. Which of the following accurately describes the changes for middle- and working-class European women during the Industrial Revolution?

(A) Both middle- and working-class women achieved the right to vote.

(B) Working-class women labored in factories, and middle-class women followed the cult of domesticity.

(C) Middle-class women were paid more than working-class women for similar jobs.

(D) Working-class women were not as affected by the Industrial Revolution as middle-class women.

41. During the Industrial Revolution, women typically earned

(A) just as much as men

(B) one-third to one-half as much as men

(C) ten percent of what men made

(D) nothing as their wages went straight to their father or husband

42. Which of the following statements about the Industrial Revolution during the nineteenth century is FALSE?

(A) Women and children made up the majority of the workforce.

(B) Worker satisfaction diminished as jobs became more repetitive and dangerous.

(C) It contributed to a dramatic restructuring of the family unit.

(D) It reduced differences between the social classes.

43. Which of the following correctly describes women during the Industrial Revolution?

(A) Unlike their male counterparts, women did not have access to labor saving devices.

(B) Middle-class women were supposed to remain confined to their domestic spheres.

(C) Most working-class women living in cities were employed by industries, particularly the textile industries.

(D) As women joined the workforce and earned their own wages, traditional family values were disrupted.

GO ON TO THE NEXT PAGE

Questions 44–45 refer to the following passage.

"Perestroika is an urgent necessity arising from the profound processes of development in our socialist society. This society is ripe for change. It has long been yearning for it. Any delay in beginning perestroika could have led to an exacerbated internal situation in the near future, which, to put it bluntly, would have been fraught with serious social, economic and political crises. . . .

In the latter half of the seventies—something happened that was at first sight inexplicable. The country began to lose momentum. Economic failures became more frequent. Difficulties began to accumulate and deteriorate, and unresolved problems to multiply. Elements of what we call stagnation and other phenomena alien to socialism began to appear in the life of society. A kind of 'braking mechanism' affecting social and economic development formed. And all this happened at a time when scientific and technological revolution opened up new prospects for economic and social progress."

Excerpt from Mikhail Gorbachev, *Perestroika: New Thinking for Our Country and the World*, 1987

44. During the mid 1980s, Mikhail Gorbachev attempted to revive the U.S.S.R. through all of the following <u>except</u> for

 (A) loosening censorship restrictions and permitting criticism of the government and the Communist Party

 (B) social reforms including increasing the rights of women and other minority groups

 (C) economic reforms such as reducing the size of the army and stabilization of the monetary system

 (D) democratization by allowing some choice of candidates for the national congress

45. After Mao Zedong's death, how did Deng Xiaoping save China from economic collapse?

 (A) China rejoined the world economy and allowed foreign investments.

 (B) Privatization of land became legal, increasing agricultural output.

 (C) Heavy subsidization of education created a more educated workforce.

 (D) Artificially inflating the yuan increased China's presence in global trade.

GO ON TO THE NEXT PAGE

 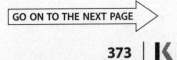

Questions 46–49 refer to the following passage.

"At the present moment in world history nearly every nation must choose between alternative ways of life. I believe that it must be the policy of the United States to support free peoples who are resisting attempted subjugation by armed minorities or by outside pressures."

Excerpt from the Truman Doctrine, 1947

46. Even though the Cuban Missile Crisis took place in Cuba, it was actually a conflict between which two nations?

    (A) Panama and the United States

    (B) Nicaragua and Guatemala

    (C) The Soviet Union and the United States

    (D) The Soviet Union and Italy

47. The Truman Doctrine was a U.S. policy stating that

    (A) the U.S. would help any nation wanting to repel the threat of Communism

    (B) the U.S. would help rebuild European economies after World War II

    (C) the U.S.-sponsored NATO (North Atlantic Treaty Organization) would fight against Soviet aggression

    (D) the U.S. supported a newly formed and independent Israel

48. The main purpose of Joseph Stalin's Five-Year Plan was to:

    (A) round up all political dissidents and sentence them to gulags

    (B) rapidly industrialize the U.S.S.R.

    (C) improve the quality of life of Soviet people

    (D) develop nuclear missile capabilities

49. African and Asian nationalist movements in the twentieth century were usually led by the

    (A) urban factory workers

    (B) aristocracy

    (C) peasantry

    (D) educated class

GO ON TO THE NEXT PAGE

Questions 50–51 refer to the following map.

THE BRITISH EMPIRE CIRCA, 1900

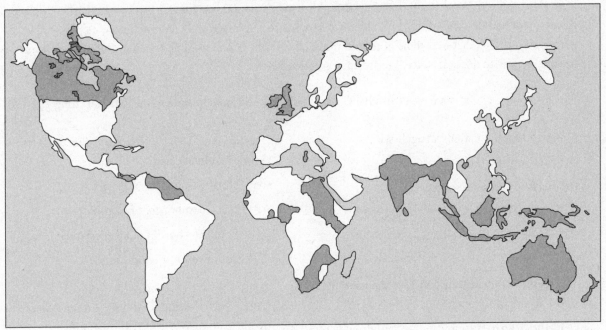

50. Which of the following conclusions can best be supported by this map of the British Empire in the nineteenth century?

   (A) Indian independence was achieved from Britain by the end of the 19th century.

   (B) British imperial power was declining in the 19th century.

   (C) British influence was limited to the Americas in the 19th century.

   (D) The British Empire had spread throughout the world in the 19th century.

51. Which of the following best describes British motivation to establish overseas colonies?

   (A) British manufacturing was dependent on raw materials produced overseas.

   (B) Britain sought new markets for its manufactured goods and technology.

   (C) Missionaries sought to convert colonized peoples to Christianity.

   (D) In the 19th century, European powers competed amongst each other for new overseas territory.

GO ON TO THE NEXT PAGE

 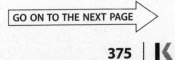

Questions 52–55 refer to the following passage.

"This alien government has ruined the country. In the beginning, all of us were taken by surprise. We were almost dazed. We thought that everything that the rulers did was for our good and that this English government had descended from the clouds to save us from internal and external invasions. Now we have perceived one fact, that the whole of this administration, which is carried on by a handful of Englishmen, is carried on with our assistance. We are all in inferior service."

Excerpt from Bal Gangadhar Tilak's address to the Indian National Congress, 1907

52. Many developing nations struggle with

(A) low fertility rates

(B) lack of natural resources

(C) no foreign aid

(D) a weak industrial base

53. Why is the Sepoy Mutiny considered a turning point in India's history?

(A) The British, suffering defeat, withdrew entirely from India.

(B) India was formally annexed under the direct rule of the Queen.

(C) Great Britain lost some of its holdings in India, including Delhi.

(D) England proclaimed to the rest of the world its moral superiority over the conquered India.

54. During World War I, where was the Western Front mainly located?

(A) Northeast border of France

(B) Northeast border of Germany

(C) Southeast border of Switzerland

(D) Southwest border of France

55. All of the following describe economic problems leading up to World War II <u>except</u> for

(A) the United States pursuance of isolationist policies

(B) Germany being forced to pay reparations for World War I

(C) imperialist rivalries between European countries

(D) the Great Depression's effect on the United States economy

GO ON TO THE NEXT PAGE

Directions: Section I, Part B of this exam consists of short answer questions. You must respond to Questions 1 and 2. For your final response, you must choose to answer EITHER Question 3 or Question 4. Use complete sentences; an outline or bulleted list alone is not acceptable.

1. Use the passage below to answer all parts of the question that follows.

   "The problems after the end of World War I might not have mattered if the new international organization established by the Peace of Paris, the League of Nations, had been able to keep a watchful eye on world affairs and settle disputes amicably. Almost from the start, the League proved a toothless tiger. A serious drawback was that three powerful nations had no part in it. Another of the League's major problems was that it had no means of enforcing its decisions, other than the imposition of ineffective economic sanctions. In the end, as the Japanese, Italians, and Germans were to discover, if a country chose to ignore the League's pronouncements, there was nothing the League could do about it.

   The settlements that brought the Great War to a close certainly did not make a second war inevitable. But they did leave important problems unresolved and a large reservoir of bitterness—certain recipes for future trouble. No wonder the great French general Marshal Foch called the Versailles settlement nothing more than a 'twenty-year cease-fire.'"

   Stewart Ross, *Causes and Consequences of the Second World War*, 1995

   a) Identify ONE <u>reason</u> Ross provides for World War II's causes.

   b) Explain the <u>evidence</u> Ross uses to support ONE of the reasons he provides for the causes of World War II.

   c) Explain ONE <u>additional factor</u> (not specifically mentioned in the passage) that contributed to the outbreak of World War II.

GO ON TO THE NEXT PAGE

 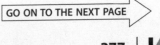

2. Use the image below to answer all parts of the question that follows.

The First Thanksgiving 1621, painted by Jean Leon Gerome Ferris in 1932

a) Identify ONE <u>similarity</u> between the impact of the Columbian Exchange on the Americas and its impact on Europe.

b) Explain ONE <u>difference</u> between the impact of the Columbian Exchange on the Americas and its impact on Europe.

c) Using the image, describe the artist's likely viewpoint about the Columbian Exchange.

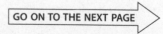
GO ON TO THE NEXT PAGE

Choose EITHER Question 3 or Question 4.

3. Answer all parts of the question that follows.

   a) Explain ONE cultural <u>change</u> that occurred in African societies as they encountered Arab travelers in the period 900–1300 C.E.

   b) Explain ONE economic <u>change</u> that occurred in African societies as they encountered Arab travelers in the period 900–1300 C.E.

   c) Explain ONE area of <u>continuity</u> in African societies as they encountered Arab travelers during the period 900–1300 C.E.

4. Answer all parts of the question that follows.

   a) Identify ONE <u>reason</u> that birth rates have been relatively low in developed nations in comparison with birth rates in developing nations since 1950.

   b) Explain ONE way in which worldwide demographic and/or economic trends since 1950 demonstrate <u>continuity</u> with the thinking of the English philosopher Thomas Malthus.

   c) Explain ONE way in which worldwide demographic and/or economic trends since 1950 demonstrate a <u>discontinuity</u> from the thinking of the English philosopher Thomas Malthus.

GO ON TO THE NEXT PAGE

 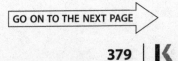

END OF SECTION I

**IF YOU FINISH BEFORE TIME IS CALLED,
YOU MAY CHECK YOUR WORK ON PART A.
DO NOT GO ON TO PART B UNTIL YOU ARE TOLD TO DO SO.**

SECTION II

Time—100 Minutes

2 Questions

Question 1: Document-Based Question

Suggested reading period: 15 minutes

Suggested writing time: 45 minutes

Directions: Question 1 is based on the accompanying documents. The documents have been edited for the purpose of this exercise.

Write your responses on the lined pages that follow the question.

In your response you should do the following.

- State a relevant thesis that directly addresses all parts of the question.

- Support the thesis or a relevant argument with evidence from all, or all but one, of the documents.

- Incorporate analysis of all, or all but one, of the documents into your argument.

- Focus your analysis of each document on at least one of the following: intended audience, purpose, historical context, and/or point of view.

- Support your argument with analysis of historical examples outside the documents.

- Connect historical phenomena relevant to your argument to broader events or processes.

- Synthesize the elements above into a persuasive essay that extends your argument, connects it to a different historical context, or accounts for contradictory evidence on the topic.

1. Analyze the roles of women under communist rule in the Soviet Union and the People's Republic of China.

GO ON TO THE NEXT PAGE

Document 1

Source: V. I. Lenin, leader of the Bolsheviks and instigator of Communist revolution in Russia, from articles in the official Soviet newspaper *Pravda*, 1920

The Soviet government was the first and only government in the world to abolish completely all the old, bourgeois, infamous laws which placed women in an inferior position compared with men and which granted privileges to men, as, for instance, in the sphere of marriage laws or in the sphere of the legal attitude to children. The Soviet government was the first and only government in the world which, as a government of the toilers, abolished all the privileges connected with property, which men retained in the family laws of all bourgeois republics, even the most democratic. The proletariat cannot achieve complete freedom, unless it achieves complete freedom for women.

Document 2

Source: Emma Goldman, an American anarchist deported to Russia in 1920, from her memoir *My Disillusionment in Russia*, 1923

. . . the rations were distributed at the Commissary, but one had to fetch them himself. One day, while waiting my turn in the long line, a peasant girl came in and asked for vinegar. "Vinegar! Who is it calls for such a luxury?" cried several women. It appeared that the girl was Zinoviev's servant. She spoke of him as her master, who worked very hard and was surely entitled to something extra. At once a storm of indignation broke loose. "Master! Is that what we made the Revolution for, or was it to do away with masters? Zinoviev is no more than we, and he is not entitled to more."

GO ON TO THE NEXT PAGE

Document 3

Source: Grigory Shegal, teacher at the Moscow Art Institute and artist, official government poster, 1931

Caption: Say goodbye to kitchen slavery! Let the new life begin!

Document 4

Source: Nadezhda Krupskaya, V. I. Lenin's wife and a leader within the Bolshevik Party, preface to Lenin's *The Emancipation of Women*, 1933

We in Russia no longer have the base, mean and infamous denial of rights to women or inequality of the sexes, that disgusting survival of feudalism and medievalism of the greedy bourgeoisie in every other country in the world without exception.

GO ON TO THE NEXT PAGE

Document 5

Source: Mao Zedong, Chairman of the Chinese Communist Party, excerpts from *The Selected Quotations of Mao Zedong* (known as the *Little Red Book*)

Introductory note to *Women Have Gone to the Labour Front*, 1955

In order to build a great socialist society it is of the utmost importance to arouse the broad masses of women to join in productive activity. Men and women must receive equal pay for equal work in production. Genuine equality between the sexes can only be realized in the process of the socialist transformation of society as a whole.

Document 6

Source: Poster used by the Chinese Communist Party (CCP), 1965

Caption: *Become a red seedling—Strike root, flower and bear seeds in the places the motherland needs it most!*

GO ON TO THE NEXT PAGE

Document 7

Source: Shao Dangdi, Chinese grandmother and insurance agent, comments quoted in the American magazine *The New Republic*, March 2004

After Liberation, women were made very equal. . . . The government promoted women's equality, but also it was necessary for family survival: you couldn't live on a single income. Now, you can. . . . Work units were required to maintain a rough gender balance in all departments and at all levels. . . . Now the workplace is so competitive. There are too many educated young people vying for too few positions, so employers pick the men first.

GO ON TO THE NEXT PAGE

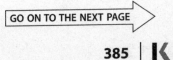

Question 2, Question 3, or Question 4: Long Essay Question

Suggested writing time: 40 minutes

Directions: Choose Question 2, Question 3, OR Question 4 to answer.

In your response you should do the following.

- Present a thesis statement
- Apply AP History Reasoning Skills as directed by the question
- Utilize specific examples of historical evidence to support the thesis, and explain relationships among the evidence.
- Extend the argument by explaining the connections between the argument and either: a development in a different historical period, situation, era, or geographic location; or a theme/approach to history that is not the focus of the essay.

2. Analyze the similarities and differences in the effect of religions on gender roles and social structures in American Indian societies and European societies prior to 1450 C.E.

3. Analyze the similarities and differences in the economic and political effects of the Hindu caste system and the Spanish American social structure from 1450 C.E. to 1750 C.E.

4. Analyze the continuities and changes in social structures due to the global economic transformations which occurred between 1750 C.E. and 1900 C.E.

GO ON TO THE NEXT PAGE

END OF SECTION II

ANSWER KEY

Section I

1. C	15. C	29. B	43. B
2. A	16. C	30. C	44. B
3. B	17. D	31. D	45. A
4. C	18. A	32. B	46. C
5. B	19. A	33. D	47. A
6. A	20. D	34. B	48. B
7. B	21. B	35. C	49. D
8. A	22. C	36. D	50. D
9. A	23. C	37. D	51. A
10. D	24. B	38. C	52. D
11. B	25. D	39. B	53. B
12. D	26. C	40. B	54. A
13. A	27. A	41. B	55. C
14. D	28. D	42. D	

Section I, Part A Number Correct: _____

Section I, Part B (Short-Answer Questions) Points Earned: _____

Section II, Part A (Document-Based Question) Points Earned: _____

Section II, Part B (Long Essay Question) Points Earned: _____

Enter these results to see your 1–5 score and view detailed explanations by logging in at kaptest.com.

Haven't registered your book yet? Go to kaptest.com/booksonline to begin.

Quiz Explanations

CHAPTER 3

Test What You Already Know

1. C

Stretching across modern-day Syria and through Iraq, the Tigris–Euphrates river system surrounds the areas once known as the Fertile Crescent. This river system allowed the Mesopotamian civilization to flourish. Therefore, **(C)** is correct. (A), (B), and (D) are all incorrect because they mismatch the rivers to their geographic areas, as shown in the map. The Nile River runs through Egypt, the Indus River runs through India and Pakistan, and the Huang He (Yellow) River is in China.

2. A

The Egyptian, Mesopotamian, and Indus Valley civilizations all had polytheistic religions, in which the supreme gods and goddesses controlled the forces of nature; a common characteristic for civilizations that relied on agriculture. The Chinese civilization, however, had a religion based on ancestor worship; there was no uniform system of religion. Because the question asked for a feature *common to all four* civilizations, **(A)** is the correct answer. All four of the civilizations thrived during the Bronze Age, generally considered to fall between 3000 B.C.E. and 1000 B.C.E. Further, archaeological evidence confirms that bronze was made and used in all four civilizations. Therefore, (B) is incorrect. Archaeologists have uncovered samples of writing in which pictures or symbols depicted specific concepts, including Egyptian hieroglyphics, Sumerian cuneiform, the Harappan Seals of the Indus Valley, and Chinese oracle bone inscriptions. Thus, (C) is incorrect. All four civilizations had varying degrees of social stratification. Generally, leaders and their advisers were at the top, followed by scholars, professionals, merchants, artisans, laborers, and the lower classes. (D) is incorrect.

3. D

The Nile River, noted for its dangerous rapids called "cataracts," was the backbone of the Ancient Egyptian civilization. Along with the Sahara Desert and the Mediterranean Sea, the Nile River provided an effective barrier against outside invaders due to its limited navigability. Therefore, **(D)** is the correct answer. The Huang He, although it deposited mineral-rich loess soil, often flooded violently and unpredictably, killing millions. The river is nicknamed

"China's Sorrow" for this very reason. Thus, (A) is incorrect. The Indus Valley Civilization's main cities were located far away from central India, the source of the Ganges; further, the Indus Valley Civilization developed largely in isolation from the rest of the Indian subcontinent. Therefore, (B) is incorrect. The map clearly shows the Tigris and Euphrates Rivers emptying into the Persian Gulf, which allowed easy access to Arabia, Persia, and beyond. Indeed, archaeological evidence confirms that Sumerian traders used riverboats and "gulf boats" to travel as far as the Indus Valley. Thus, (C) is incorrect.

4. D

Mohenjo-daro and Harappa were the most notable cities in the Indus Valley Civilization, centered in modern-day Pakistan and India. The ruins were discovered in the 1920s and are still being studied by archaeologists today. **(D)** is the correct answer. Some of the old oasis towns of the Silk Road, like Samarkand, are thriving cities today. Thus, (A) is incorrect. Athens and Sparta were the most dominant Ancient Greek city-states. Thus, (B) is incorrect. Many of the Mediterranean basin's port cities still thrive today, including Alexandria, Egypt. Therefore, (C) is incorrect.

5. A

The Harappan seals—metal and clay tiles featuring engraved images of animals and a script—remain undeciphered to this day. Linguists and archaeologists believe that translating these seals would help unlock the secrets of the Indus Valley Civilization. Therefore, **(A)** is correct. These cities are two of the earliest-known examples of urban planning and public sanitation. Therefore, (B) and (C) are incorrect. (D) is incorrect because the proximity of these cities to the Indus River not only provided the water needed to grow crops like wheat and cotton, but also provided a means to ship these goods elsewhere.

6. A

Both the Twelve Tables and Hammurabi's Code reflected the social structure of ancient societies, where a ruling elite occupied a privileged position above commoners. Thus, **(A)** is correct. While religious morality evolved alongside legal codes, they were not the primary motivation for social stratification. While the Roman Republic did, for a period, see its leadership bound by the rule of law, the first Babylonian empire was not a republic. Thus, (C) is incorrect. Both the Roman Republic and the first Babylonian empire were growing, internally stable bodies. They were not undergoing societal collapse; (D) is incorrect.

7. B

The Twelve Tables and Hammurabi's Code both embodied the idea that "the punishment should fit the crime." Indeed, the excerpts both display that more severe crimes were punishable by death. Further, both documents reference retaliation—the saying "an eye for an eye and a tooth for a tooth" originated in Hammurabi's Code. For these reasons, **(B)** is correct. Hammurabi expected his subjects to settle disputes through the Code itself, often using retaliation. Principles that are used in courtrooms today originated in the Twelve Tables. Therefore, (A) is incorrect. Both documents show that the wealthy paid fines for committing crimes that caused lower classes to be punished more severely. Thus, (C) is incorrect. Both legal codes made clear that a woman was to be subservient to her husband and to her home. (D) is incorrect.

8. B

Both of the excerpts reference the idea that "no one is above the law." Prior to the development of written legal codes, laws were arbitrary and the lower classes were often subjected to the abuses of the wealthy and powerful. By creating systems of uniform law that applied to everyone everywhere, the Twelve Tables and Hammurabi's Code both gave the lower classes rights that they had not had before; therefore, **(B)** is correct. (A) is incorrect because this statement only applies to the Twelve Tables; Hammurabi had vowed that anyone who changed, defiled, or destroyed his laws would be cursed. (C) is incorrect because only Republican Rome was ruled as a limited democracy, unlike Babylon, which was ruled by a king. (D) is incorrect because this statement only applies to Hammurabi's Code, which unified both Semitic and Sumerian ideas. The Twelve Tables were not intended to unify or change old customs.

9. A

In both Christianity and Buddhism, women could live the life of a nun. The Biblical excerpt illustrates the concept of becoming a nun. The Buddhist poem describes the transformation of a courtesan into a nun; for both, the aim is the same: seeking spiritual purity while being free from the traditional roles of wifehood and motherhood. For this reason, **(A)** is the correct answer. (B) is

incorrect because both religions considered women to be spiritual equals to men, despite socially delineated gender roles. (C) and (D) are both incorrect for a similar reason: the messages of both Christianity and Buddhism appealed to women. Both religions attracted female converts through their egalitarian ideals and their tales of holy men and holy women. Similarly, both Christian and Buddhist women were empowered to read spiritual texts (recall that Hindu women were not allowed to read the Vedas, and that Buddhism was created as an alternative to Hinduism).

10. D

As Christianity spread through the Mediterranean Basin, and as Buddhism spread through Asia, people started questioning the true nature of their respective founders. Consequently, different divisions of Christianity and Buddhism emerged, many of which are still practiced. For example, Nestorian Christians believed that Christ contained two distinct qualities, human and divine, rather than those two qualities being unified. Similarly, Theravada Buddhists consider the Buddha unique while Mahayana Buddhists believe he is merely one of many Buddhas. This similarity makes **(D)** the correct answer. (A) is incorrect because only Christianity is a religion of salvation; Christians believe that eternal life in Heaven is their ultimate goal, while Buddhists believe that nirvana, a state of perfect peace signified by breaking free from reincarnation, is their goal. (B) is incorrect because only Christianity are monotheistic while Buddhists feel that they can seek enlightenment without divine guidance. (C) is incorrect because it directly contradicts the correct answer; Buddhists do not see Buddha as both fully divine and fully human, and Christians only accepted this idea after the Council of Nicaea met in 325 C.E. and issued the Nicene Creed.

Test What You Learned

1. C

While currency as we know it today emerged in the Kingdom of Lydia (modern-day Turkey) around 600 B.C.E. with the creation of metal coins, paper currency was not developed until the seventh century C.E. under the Tang dynasty. Thus, **(C)** is correct. The rise of nomad confederations influenced the growth of trade along the Silk Road, as the Han dynasty sought to acquire horses that could put them on more equal footing with those ridden by the people on their periphery, and to separate potential nomadic allies in modern-day Mongolia and Tibet. Thus, (A) is incorrect. Knives and swords were known to exist as far back as 7000 B.C.E., but bronze smelting began around 2800 B.C.E., and iron metallurgy began in 1500 B.C.E. under the Hittites. Therefore, (B) is incorrect. Many of the earliest civilizations were built on trade; to keep accurate records, writing systems developed independently in many major civilizations. (D) is incorrect, as the earliest known example is cuneiform, the wedge-shaped writing of Mesopotamia.

2. D

The fall of the Western Roman Empire is only minimally due to foreign invasion, as the Romans had successfully fended off many such attacks in the past. Instead, the Roman Empire had been internally weakened ahead of the invasions. The breakdown of the tax and trade systems, political instability, the death of large numbers of the population due to disease, and the inability to recruit citizens to serve in the Legions leading to the hiring of Germanic mercenaries—all these factors weakened the Roman Empire enough for it to collapse when faced with a traditional challenge. Thus, **(D)** is correct. The Phoenicians were successively conquered by the Babylonians, Persians, and Macedonians. Finally, they and their colonies were absorbed by the Romans. Thus, (A) is incorrect. The exact cause of the downfall of the Minoans around 1450 C.E. is disputed, but is widely thought to be due to an earthquake, volcanic eruption, or other natural disaster. As these are natural causes and not internal problems, (B) is incorrect. The Gupta Empire suffered an invasion by the Huns, which fatally weakened it. This is the reverse of the Western Roman Empire. Thus, (C) is incorrect.

3. A

The Ancient World provided modern society with many valuable contributions in virtually every field. The idea of a direct democracy, in which people directly influence laws through voting and active participation, originated the sixth or fifth centuries B.C.E. in the Greek city-states. The very first democracy is a matter of speculation, but Athens, while its system came later in 508 or 507 B.C.E, is the most lasting and influential example. Since the question asked for an incorrect pairing, **(A)** is the correct answer. Rome was not a direct democracy but instead a republic. (B), (C), and (D) are all proper pairings. Paper as we know it was first manufactured in China between 179 B.C.E. and 105 C.E., and it quickly spread throughout the known world thereafter. Bronze, an alloy of copper and tin, was first smelted in Mesopotamia around 3000 B.C.E. Other civilizations perfected this powerful alloy to build tools and weapons in the following centuries. Because of the predictable flooding cycle of the Nile River, and a knowledge of astronomy, the Egyptians were able to create a 12-month, 30-day calendar with designated seasons based on the solar cycle.

4. D

Confucianism stressed the importance of harmony and order in relationships, focusing on five fundamental ones: ruler and subject, parent and child, husband and wife, siblings, and between friends. An alternate way to approach this question is to remember that Confucianism stresses the importance of filial piety as well as political stability. However, **(D)** refers to a religious relationship, and Confucianism is not considered a religion. (A), (B), and (C) are counted among the fundamental Confucian relationships.

5. D

In both Confucianism and Hinduism, scholars are highly regarded. Thus, **(D)** is correct. The highest caste in Hinduism is the Brahmin class, which consists of priests and scholars. Confucius taught that learning separated the inferior man from the superior man. Peasants were rarely educated and, in Hinduism, were part of the very lowest caste; (A) is incorrect. Artisans, while possibly educated, were part of the second-lowest caste, the Vaisyas, along with merchants and farmers. Therefore, (B) is incorrect. Government officials were part of the Kshatriyas, the second-highest caste, which included rulers, administrators, and warriors. Thus, (C) is incorrect.

6. D

Ashoka was an emperor of the Mauryan Dynasty (322–180 B.C.E.) in India who, after witnessing a bloody battle and feeling great sorrow and regret that the relatives of the dead would have to suffer, converted to Buddhism. Ashoka then issued a series of edicts that reference *dharma*. Thus, **(D)** is correct. Sikhism was founded in the fifteenth century C.E., well after the end of the Mauryan Dynasty; (A) is incorrect. Ashoka wanted to counteract the rising influence of the caste system, a key tenet of Hinduism; (B) is incorrect. Zoroastrians have long been minority in India, where they today belong to either the Parsi or Irani communities. (C) is incorrect.

7. C

In Ashoka's time, the Brahmin, the priestly and highest caste of Hinduism, was experiencing greater power. Buddhism was designed to reject the caste system, and by centralizing his government, Ashoka displaced the Brahmin in favor of a more egalitarian belief system. Therefore, **(C)** is correct. Ashoka converted to Buddhism after suffering the effects of a bloody war. He reinforced the Aryan reverence of cattle by prohibiting animal slaughter, leading to the modern Indian belief in the sanctity of the cow. Therefore, (A) is incorrect. Over thirty engraved tablets and columns have been found throughout South Asia; furthermore, Ashoka funded the construction of shrines called *stupas*, where Buddhist relics are kept. Thus, (B) is incorrect. The spread of Buddhism along the Silk Roads started when Ashoka sponsored missions to present-day Nepal, Pakistan, and Afghanistan. (D) is incorrect

8. B

After the fall of Rome, nomadic invasions continued, making it very difficult for the area to recover. As a result, a decentralized form of government developed that provided protection for its inhabitants. Thus, **(B)** is correct. Both Rome and the Han permanently lost political control of their respective empires; thus, (A) and (D) are incorrect. Rome's population decreased as a result of the spread of disease, rather than increasing as (C) indicates.

9. A

The Han dynasty was rife with dynastic intrigue, with many emperors deposed. Actual power often resided in whichever group had helped secure the throne for young puppet emperors. Thus, **(A)** is correct. While regencies could in theory provide stable government, they often exposed the dynasty to more infighting as different groups sought to install child emperors and rule through them; thus, (B) is incorrect. It cannot be inferred that the dynastic line was an unbroken patrilineal line, and the youth of so many emperors makes such an arrangement unlikely, eliminating (C). Religious beliefs and popular sentiments played no part in the installation of such young emperors; thus, (D) is incorrect.

10. C

The Yellow Turban Rebellion (184–205 C.E.) was a peasant revolt in Han China. Therefore, **(C)** is correct. Along with numerous other factors, such as political corruption and infighting at the highest levels of government, this rebellion contributed to the downfall of the Han dynasty. As the rebellion was confined strictly to opposing Han rule in China, (A), (B), and (D) are incorrect.

CHAPTER 4

Test What You Already Know

1. B

Both the Roman Empire and the Mongol Empire established periods of economic and political stability; **(B)** is correct. These periods, known as the *Pax Romana* and *Pax Mongolica*, enabled trade to flourish within a large zone of common administration. The Romans, at their maximum extent, ruled all of Europe save Germany and owned minimal territory in Asia. The Mongols never extended their control past Central Europe. Thus, (A) is incorrect. Both empires were primarily land-based powers; (C) is incorrect. While the Roman Empire spread Latin as a common language, leading to the rise of various daughter languages, like French, after the fall of Rome, the Mongols did not forcibly spread their own language throughout their empire. Therefore, (D) is incorrect.

2. D

Both the Turks and Mongols were nomads who originated from the Central Asian steppes, making **(D)** correct. Although the Mongols conquered Korea and made it into a semi-independent vassal, the Turks have never invaded Korea. The Mongols were not skilled administrators, often using local people to help them rule, which eliminates (B). While the Ottoman Turkish alphabet was based on Arabic, the Mongolian alphabet was not; therefore, (C) is incorrect.

3. B

The Mongol Empire was vast and did not long survive the death of Kublai Khan. Though they were skilled military conquerors, civil war resulted from political rivals fighting over the right to become the next Great Khan. Thus, **(B)** is correct and (C) is incorrect. The Mongols were largely tolerant of native religious beliefs among their conquests; thus, (A) is incorrect. While the Red Turbans overthrew the Yuan dynasty in China, the rest of the former Mongol Empire had fractured by that point into several states. These other states were largely unaffected by that revolt. Therefore, (D) is incorrect.

4. C

Consider both the key details of the sources and your own knowledge of West African kingdoms. Both sources refer to Mansa Musa's practice of Islam. The second source also notes his desire to further spread Islam throughout his kingdom. The other key detail concerns Mansa Musa's wealth: Source 1 references his "prodigal spending" to the extent that gold "depressed its value in Egypt." These details together indicate **(C)**.

5. D

As trade between regions increases, ideas and religions typically spread as well. Likewise, the spread of a religion or philosophy across cultures often leads to increased economic relations as well. In this specific question, as a result of the spread of Islam into West Africa, the volume of trade along the trans-Saharan trade routes increased. Relationships were established with Muslim merchants and those relationships led to more trade, making **(D)** correct. The other answer choices reflect the opposite of what tends to occur when cultures increase contact. West Africa's economy grew rather than slowed, as suggested by (A), and a more centralized form of government administered the growing economy, as in (B). Centralized governments often kept order in their kingdoms, and thus decreased internal conflict, eliminating (C).

6. B

During the Crusades, Western Europe's elites personally experienced the diverse luxury goods and literature of the Eastern Roman Empire and the Muslim caliphate. This, plus increased shipping capacity for troop movements, boosted the already-growing trade volumes with the eastern Mediterranean, and led to an increase in interaction with all the civilizations to the south and east of the European peninsula. Therefore, **(B)** is correct. While navigational technology improved in Europe due to the Crusades, (A) incorrectly credits Europe with full control of all the Muslim lands of Asia Minor, Syria, and Palestine. (C) misstates the reason for the Crusades' weakening of feudalism; it was not that peasants saw worse conditions elsewhere, it was that the knightly class loosened its hold on its landed estates by prolonged absences, war deaths, and sales to raise travel funds. The idea of (D), that the Crusades were a serious economic blow to Europe, goes too far; the expenses and losses of waging these unprofitable foreign wars were serious but not enough to cancel out, much less reverse, the improvements in farming and trade productivity that had taken place since the fall of Rome.

7. D

The Eastern Roman Empire had been fighting the Islamic armies for centuries, and had hoped the Western crusaders would join with them in a Christian coalition. But in 1204, in a climax to increasingly hostile relations following the Great Schism, crusaders sacked and took over the imperial capital of Constantinople. **(D)** is correct. The Byzantines recaptured the city, but afterwards they were both weakened in their resistance to Islamic pressure and intensely resentful of the Roman Catholic West. (A) distorts the Byzantine policy of negotiating with Muslim states to try to stabilize borders between wars; it falsely implies that the emperor fought with the Turks against the crusaders. Byzantium had a longtime interest in retaking its lost provinces in the Levant, but (B) mistakenly credits it with the temporary successes of the Latin armies in reasserting Christian rule in the Holy Lands. Thus, (B) is incorrect. The Great Schism between the Orthodox and Catholic Christian rites took place in 1054, before the Crusades. Therefore, (C) is incorrect.

8. C

The frequency of cultural transfers between hostile groups in this period reminds us that warfare and conquests in history have a strong economic basis. Victors who seized or defended a throne usually favored continued trade to increase the taxable wealth of their realms. The Mongols established the most extensive land empire in history in the thirteenth century C.E.; at its height, it reached from China to Eastern Europe. Therefore, **(C)** is correct. The ruling Mongol dynasties facilitated peaceful trade across all of Asia so that China and the Muslim world were in closer contact than usual during this period. For example, the Chinese learned from Islamic math and astronomy; the Muslims received Chinese innovations like block printing and gunpowder. (A) and (B) are correct, but only for a later period in world history; the question is limited to the time of the Crusades. While the Teutonic and other wars of conversion in the pagan Baltic regions were part of the crusade movement, any implication that Jewish religious culture became important to entirely Christian regions ignores the marginal role of Judaism in medieval European culture. Thus, (D) is incorrect.

9. A

(A) is correct because Zheng He made as many as seven long-distance sea voyages during his illustrious career serving the Ming dynasty in China, as illustrated by the dated arrows on the map. (B) is not validated by the map because it does not depict the Silk Route, and (C) and (D) are speculative statements that cannot be supported using the information presented in the map.

10. D

Confucian officials in the court of the Ming emperor believed that the voyages of Zheng He were too expressive and not worth the cost of investment, as the money could be better spent elsewhere in the realm. This is comparable to the downfall of the Mali Empire, as a series of kings that spent lavishly spurred internal unrest and the collapse of their empire. Thus, **(D)** is correct. The Mongol conquest of Song China took many decades and was a hard-fought conflict, which does not reflect either party weakened by excessive spending. Thus, (A) is incorrect. The rise of the Umayyad dynasty was the result of a militarily efficient and politically cohesive state, as it faced regional rivals that required care to defeat. Thus, (B) is incorrect. The 1204 C.E. sack of Constantinople primarily resulted from a sectarian religious conflict between Latin Christians and Roman Catholics. Therefore, (C) is incorrect.

Test What You Learned

1. C

These two religions came in contact along the trade routes of Central Asia; **(C)** is correct. Buddhism had spread to the region earlier from India along the Silk Road. Islam spread to Central Asia beginning in the eighth century C.E. and often overtook Buddhism as the dominant belief system. Although Islam was present in the Spanish and Balkan peninsulas, Buddhism had almost no presence in

Europe in this period except for reports from travelers to Asia. Thus, (A) and (D) are incorrect. Some Buddhist Indian traders may have interacted with Muslim merchant communities in the Red Sea and Egyptian regions, which border on East Africa, but that kind of casual contact is a less correct choice for a question that refers to the religions as major institutions. Therefore, (B) is incorrect.

2. D

The passage suggests that despite their considerable theological differences, Islam and Buddhism shared a social and cultural appeal to the worldly middle class of traders and businessmen, who could be found all across the Eurasian continent in the first millennium C.E. Thus, as **(D)** says, the two faiths' encounter when Islam drove east in the eighth century led to a long-drawn competition of sorts, in which Islam's more aggressive aspects gave it a popular advantage in many regions that had been largely Buddhist. (A) is more descriptive of a political or economic competition between long-established nations. Although Islam and Buddhism did affect each other, the exchanges were artistic and cultural, and the two faiths did not converge. (B) and (C) are incorrect.

3. B

Baghdad was a city along with the Silk Road, making **(B)** correct. The Mediterranean Sea, trans-Saharan routes, and Indian Ocean basin were common trade routes as well, but Baghdad was not located along any of them, making (A), (C), and (D) incorrect.

4. A

As the map of Baghdad includes water canals and land roads, trade in the Eastern Hemisphere occurred through land and water trade routes; thus, **(A)** is correct. Although disease pathogens, religious beliefs, and technologies did diffuse along trade routes, (B), (C) and (D) are incorrect because they are not supported by the map.

5. D

Baghdad trade was one destination along the Silk Road trade route. The Silk Road was not as significantly involved in the spread of Christianity as it was in the spread of Islam. Thus, **(D)** is correct. The bubonic plague and Chinese artwork such as porcelain did indeed spread along the Silk Road; therefore, (A) and (B) are incorrect. Travelers such as Marco Polo wrote as they migrated along the Silk Road. Thus, (C) is also incorrect.

6. B

Government support of industry did not take place until after the Industrial Revolution in the eighteenth and nineteenth centuries; thus, **(B)** is correct. Rather, commercial growth during the years 600 to 1450 C.E. was facilitated by the minting of coins (A), the establishment of trade organizations such as the Hanseatic League (C), and state-sponsored infrastructure projects, such as the construction of the Grand Canal in China (D).

7. C

The Red Turban Rebellion, an uprising of Chinese peasants upset over Mongol domination and high taxation, best reflects Voltaire's idea of a historical cycle where the elite are overthrown by an underclass that subsequently become the new elite. The Mongols had once been steppe nomads poor enough that they were forced to make clothes from the pelts of field mice. Now, even with the fragmentation of their empire, they ruled China under the banner of the Yuan dynasty. Zhu Yuanzhang, a peasant turned Red Turban, would overthrow them and become the first Ming emperor. Therefore, **(C)** is correct. The Kamakura Shogunate was established by Japanese nobles who took power from rival elites; thus, (A) is incorrect. The Ghana Empire arose organically from villages along a trade network; thus, (C) is incorrect. The Byzantine Empire arose from a political reorganization of the faltering Roman Empire, and can be seen as existing in continuity with it. Indeed, the Byzantines would refer to themselves as Romans. Thus, (D) is incorrect.

8. A

Temujin, better known as Genghis Khan, feared that the Mongol Empire he had founded would dissolve into civil war over the question of his successor, as had repeatedly happened with steppe nomad confederations in the past. To that end, prior to his death, he clearly outlined who would be the next Great Khan and arranged for an equitable division of territory to his other sons, so none of them would feel slighted. Therefore, **(A)** is correct. The Mongols did not adopt a unifying religion in Temujin's era; (B) is incorrect. Tang China had dissolved into rebellion centuries before the rise of the Mongols. Thus, (C) is incorrect. The *Pax Mongolica* did not represent an effort to avoid a succession crisis after Temujin's death, but rather was a result of Temujin's lifetime of conquest. Thus, (D) is incorrect.

9. B

The Tang dynasty reformed the civil service examination to allow for the entry of gentry and commoners, and dispensed with the recommendation requirement that had allowed Han dynasty aristocrats to consolidate power among their families. Thus, **(B)** is correct. The Song dynasty would favor the tribute system over a strong military. The Tang dynasty was overthrown, in part, because military governors were strong enough to ignore the emperor. Thus, (A) is incorrect. While upper-class women in Tang China had more rights than in most other dynasties, this was not a top-down reform intended to correct a fault that had led to both injustice and the downfall of the previous dynasty. Thus, (C) is incorrect. Buddhism was downplayed in favor of Neo-Confucianism, which itself was a reaction to the upsurge of popularity of Buddhism, seen in China as a foreign philosophy. (D) is incorrect.

10. D

The Mali and the Mongols lacked a policy of forcibly converting their subjects; thus, **(D)** is correct. The Mongols had no unifying religion throughout their empire. The Mali rulers supported Islam but allowed their subjects to follow other faiths. Trade flourished in both empires. Thus, (A) is incorrect. Both empires also collected taxes from conquered regions; (B) and (C) are incorrect. Mali famously defeated the Sosso at the landmark Battle of Kirina, allowing the Malians to absorb them and territories of the former Ghana Empire.

CHAPTER 5

Test What You Already Know

1. A

The Chinese economy was the world's largest in this period, but the country lacked domestic silver or gold resources. This had led to the earliest invention of paper money, but misuse of that currency resulted in an inflationary spiral in the Ming Dynasty in the late 1400s—just as Japan and then Spanish America discovered and exploited their large silver reserves. China stabilized its money by switching from paper to silver. This led to a great demand for silver over the next few centuries. Therefore, **(A)** is correct. As the map shows, although most New World silver seems to be exported to Europe, a large fraction of it was then traded further east, to China, for the luxury goods that could not be paid for with any other exchange. (B) is contradicted by the map: the world's largest sources of silver were the mines in Spanish Peru and Mexico. Although some silver passed through Ottoman lands and seas in the course of world trade, as in (C), the Silk Road routes were increasingly bypassed by European ships trading silver for Chinese goods directly by sea. Ironically, given its inflationary history with paper money, the Ming dynasty actually experienced serious inflation due to an excessive importation of silver. As high inflation does not strengthen any economy, (D) is incorrect.

2. B

The silver trade was a primary component in the first truly global trade system, so called because of the growing unification of the Eastern and Western hemispheres' economies after European expansion. **(B)** is correct. This is best illustrated by the small but significant trade route across the Pacific Ocean between Mexico, Peru, the Philippines, and China—the first to connect the New World with the eastern and western halves of the Old World. Spain did not modernize internally despite its huge reserves of precious metals from America. Rather, it continued subsidizing its elite landholding classes and paying cash for talented foreigners to conduct its trade, imperial administration, and imperial wars. Thus, (A) is incorrect. (C) mixes up its history: the Opium Wars were in the 1800s, and sought to balance the silver trade between England and China, not end it. It is true that, as silver became available in large quantities, gold declined somewhat in relative value as in (D); however, that had little to do with the expansion of the slave trade in this period, which was based on demand for plantation commodities paid for with manufactured goods.

3. B

Unlike Portugal, whose royal government financed all of its expeditions in the Indian Ocean, the relatively impoverished British rulers used joint-stock companies, in which prosperous investors—not the crown—funded the expeditions. Thus, **(B)** is correct. As Roe's letter says, this allowed the English captains to separate the idea of controlling monopoly territories (e.g., by setting up expensive fortified trading stations) from the concept of seeking the best markets and trading agreements with local powers. Other factors in England's rise were its generally stronger trading economy in the Atlantic and its successful competitions with France and the Netherlands, and Portugal's struggle with Spain and its increasing focus on its profitable empire in Brazil and Africa. (A) is out of period and region: the Opium Wars were in the 1800s and China was not primarily engaged in Indian Ocean trade. Although the Ottoman Empire had trading links to the Indian Ocean via its provinces on the Red Sea and Persian Gulf, it had never been the dominant naval or political power across the entire ocean basin as stated. Thus, (C) is incorrect. As noted, the Portuguese over time focused more on their Atlantic and African imperial holdings, but Portugal only abandoned its colonial ports at Goa in India and Macau in China in the late twentieth century. Thus, (D) is incorrect.

4. C

Ironically, given the close of Roe's letter, the British East India Company eventually did invest in "garrisons and land wars in India" in the eighteenth century. By the 1800s, this had led to a monopolistic business empire that ruled India as a private venture, supported indirectly by British military and legal institutions. General abuses of Indian sovereignty, culture, and privileges led to the "Mutiny" of the Company's native troops (Sepoys) in 1857, a bloody and bitter episode now called the "Rebellion" by Indian nationalists. Thus, **(C)** is correct. Although the Rebellion was unsuccessful in expelling the British, it did lead to the fall of the Company. The British government took over India as an imperial possession of Queen Victoria, and ruled there directly for another 90 years. The "Boston Tea Party," a 1773 riot against the Company's tea monopoly, contributed to the American Revolution but certainly didn't cause it. Thus, (A) is incorrect. (B) took place in conjunction with British expansion in India, and the two European empires in Asia engaged in border conflicts called "The Great Game," but Russia's interest in its southern neighbors was not dependent on the vulnerability of India. (D) is incorrect; Australia was initially set up as a penal colony after the American revolution eliminated North America as a place for transporting English criminals.

5. A

(A) is correct because though the Church was still quite powerful during the Renaissance, the growing power of merchant families and increasing interest in rediscovering the Greco-Roman past led to increasingly secular attitudes. New humanist philosophies depicted man as creative and rational, and the printing revolution supported a corresponding rise in literacy and interest in gaining knowledge. Therefore, (B) and (C) are incorrect. While attitudes were increasingly secular in outlook, stating that atheism become accepted by more and more Europeans goes too far. (D) is incorrect.

6. C

By supplying trade routes during the Crusades, Italy prospered immensely, making **(C)** correct. Additionally, contact with Eastern countries allowed for new ideas. (A) is not correct because Italy was a center of commerce. (B) is incorrect as the Protestant Reformation took place after the Renaissance. Lastly, political power in Italy was characterized by many competitive city states; thus, (D) is incorrect.

7. D

Europeans brought diseases such as measles and tuberculosis as they explored other regions, yet that is not depicted in the image. Therefore, **(D)** is correct. The horses and military apparel contained in the image demonstrate the transportation methods Spanish conquistadors used as they invaded; thus, (A) and (B) are incorrect. In the image, Cortés meets Xicotencatl, an indigenous leader who would ally with Cortés against Montezuma; there fore, (C) is incorrect.

8. B

In Aztec society, it was common for women to own property or involve themselves in religious traditions as priestesses, although these activities were uncommon in many other societies during that time period. Therefore, **(B)** is correct. Although the Aztec ruler did indeed claim that his rule was divinely inspired, because he himself had a divine origin, this assertion was relatively common, making (A) incorrect. Aztec society did incorporate slavery, and especially enslaved prisoners of war, and most Aztec commoners worked in agriculture, which makes (C) and (D) incorrect as well.

9. A

(A) is correct; both the Tokugawa Shogunate and the French government under Louis XIV created laws to manage timber resources. Both (B) and (D) are true; however, they did not occur during the period from 1450 to 1750 C.E. The Ottoman Empire did not try to reduce overfishing. Therefore, (C) is incorrect.

10. C

Following an earlier period where Christianity was seen as a useful tool in combating the influence of Buddhism, the Tokugawa shogunate began to perceive Christianity as a threat to its authority and began persecuting missionaries. Thus, **(C)** is correct. Japan colonized Korea during the twentieth century, after the reign of the Tokugawa shogunate; (A) is incorrect. The Tokugawa shoguns did severely limit European trade with Japan; however, not all overseas trade was stopped. Carefully controlled trade with China, Korea, Taiwan and some Dutch merchants was allowed. Therefore, (B) is incorrect. The Tokugawa shogunate ensured very limited contact between Japan and the outside world. Thus, (D) is incorrect.

Test What You Learned

1. A

The Byzantine Empire held Constantinople, a city which was heavily fortified and considered impregnable. The use of cannons, however, shifted the advantage to the side of the Ottomans, and Constantinople fell to the Turks. Thus, **(A)** is correct. (B) did occur at around the same time, but movable type did not aid the Turks militarily. The horse saddle had been around for many, many years prior to the fall of Constantinople. Thus, (C) is incorrect. Lateen sails allow ships to sail in any direction, regardless of wind. They were also invented around this time, but they were used to facilitate maritime exploration and oceanic trade routes. (D) is incorrect.

2. B

All three empires (Ottoman, Safavid, Mughal) were controlled by Muslim rulers. However, the Ottomans practiced the Sunni branch of Islam while the Safavids believed in the Shi'ite branch of Islam. Therefore, **(B)** is correct. The Ottoman and Safavid empires contained religious minorities, namely Christians and Jews. Thus, (A) is incorrect. As all three empires were both dominated by the military classes and experienced warfare during times of succession, (C) and (D) are incorrect.

3. D

(D) is correct; neither China nor Europe focused resources on reconnaissance in the Pacific Ocean during this period. The Indian Ocean region (India, the Middle East, and the coast of Africa) was explored by Chinese maritime reconnaissance voyages, especially under Ming Admiral Zheng He. Thus, (A) is incorrect. The Portuguese set up trading post empires in West Africa; (B) is incorrect. The Spanish colonized large territories in South America; (C) is incorrect.

4. D

Ming rulers were not afraid of Europeans. Rather, they believed China to be superior to the West, with nothing to gain from the rest of the world. Therefore, **(D)** is correct. Ming leaders feared the impacts technological innovation would have on social order; (A) is incorrect. Confucian officials did argue against commercial activity; (B) is incorrect. The surviving Yuan Mongols did raid western China, demanding attention and resources. Thus, (C) is incorrect.

5. B

In order to demonstrate the subjugation of the Han Chinese people, the invading Manchus of the Qing dynasty decreed that all Chinese men should shave their heads and adopt the queue hairstyle of the Manchu and other northern cultures. This most visible indignity aroused great resistance among the Chinese across all classes and regions. Thus, **(B)** is correct. However, the new style was enforced ruthlessly, becoming a common characteristic of Chinese men until the twentieth century. The other answers are incorrect: the Manchus did not attempt to restrict foreign trade (A), compel intermarriage between the cultures (C), or remove the Confucian bureaucracy it had inherited from the Ming dynasty (D). On the contrary, the Confucian bureaucracy of Ming China was preserved and used to administer the empire as efficiently as ever.

6. C

The Manchus' imposition of a distinctive hairstyle on the Chinese was in order to change their traditional appearance and make them look more like the conquering or elite culture. The closest event to this is the elimination of the turban (and robed clothing style) in favor of a fez hat (and more Western-cut clothes) by the Turkish elites of the Ottoman Empire, who wished to Westernize their empire's various Islamic subcultures. Thus, **(C)** is correct. As with the queue, the fez became identified with Turkish appearance so much that its later abandonment was as difficult and revolutionary as its initial adoption. What is different is that this decree was not due to a conquest but to an internal conflict on how to respond to outside pressure. (A), (B), and (D) are all instances of elites using

dress, appearance, and classification to separate and control, rather than integrate and unify, subordinate classes or hierarchies.

7. C

The early Spanish settlers in the Caribbean needed a large labor force to exploit the area's resources. Europeans saw the inhabitants of useful land as part of the land's value. No thought was given to transplanting Spanish peasants to a New World which had a thriving native population. Instead, under the *encomienda* system that had been used during the reconquest of Muslim territories in Spain, the King gave Spanish colonists the right to compel the labor of local native peoples in their newly developed mines and plantations. Therefore, **(C)** is correct. Although the result of this system, combined with introducing foreign diseases, was to decimate the native populations within a few decades, that was certainly not the purpose of *encomienda* but instead a result. Thus, (A) is incorrect. The slave trade from Africa resulted from the attrition of native labor; the Spanish had no ethical concerns about limiting its increase. Thus, (B) is incorrect. Finally, it should be clear that *encomienda*'s purpose was to exploit the Native Americans, not give them economic opportunities. Therefore, (D) is incorrect.

8. B

Past episodes in Spanish history of war, conquest, and economic development of neighboring areas greatly influenced Spanish colonialism in the Americas. The *encomienda* system was not made from whole cloth to solve the labor problem on newly settled Caribbean islands, but was adapted from an existing practice in Iberian feudal warfare. Therefore, **(B)** is correct. (A) and (C) both refer to slavery systems from the Old World that the Spanish would be aware of, but those systems depended on captive slave populations rather than the compulsory labor of existing local communities. (D) refers to a development in another part of the New World, when the Spanish conquered a large and organized state with an existing compulsory labor system imposed on its own people.

9. D

The Italian Renaissance (from the Latin word for "rebirth") was a period of social, political, and cultural learning and awareness that lasted from approximately from 1300 to 1600 C.E. During this time, wealthy families like the Medicis ruled city-states and funded artists like Leonardo da Vinci. The geography of Italy enabled its city-states to take advantage of trading routes in the Mediterranean; **(D)** is correct. Ideas and goods from Italy spread into Northern Europe, sparking the Northern Renaissance there; however, artists and writers from that region include Rembrandt, Jan van Eyck, and Erasmus; therefore, (A) is incorrect. The Protestant Reformation is one of the outcomes of the Northern Renaissance, not the Italian Renaissance, as it began in Germany with Martin Luther's *95 Theses* in 1517. Therefore, (B) is incorrect. The Enlightenment was a continuation of ideas that originated during the Italian and Northern Renaissances; however, it occurred in the eighteenth and nineteenth centuries—much later than the lives of da Vinci and the Medici family. Therefore, (C) is incorrect.

10. A

Art and literature reflected the developments of the Italian Renaissance, which was characterized by an appreciation for realism and nature, an interest in the human body and its beauty, and an emphasis on reason and logical thought. Therefore, **(A)** is correct. During the Italian Renaissance, artists and writers did not focus strictly on religious imagery and influences. Thus, (B) is incorrect. While much of the artwork was religious in nature, artists also worked to revive ancient classics from the Greek and Roman civilizations. Though it is counterintuitive, women did not gain any new rights or freedoms during the Italian Renaissance; thus, (C) is incorrect. The Italian Renaissance drew inspiration from Ancient Greece and Rome, as well as the Islamic world. (D) is incorrect.

CHAPTER 6

Test What You Already Know

1. B

Slave trading with Europeans began in coastal regions of Africa, causing previously established African trade routes to shift; **(B)** is correct. North Africa remained predominantly Islamic despite European imperialism, while sub-Saharan Africa largely Christianized in the twentieth century, well after the end of the transatlantic slave trade. Thus, (A) is incorrect. Also, the map suggests that relatively little slave trading occurred in regions of Northern Africa such as Egypt and Algeria. It also suggests that relatively

few slaves were sent to India and other Asian regions, and that relatively little slave trading occurred near Cape Colony in South Africa. Therefore, (C) and (D) are incorrect.

2. A

Although Islam did indeed spread throughout Africa during this time period, it had the least impact on the slave trade, making **(A)** correct. Influenced by Islamic and Asian technological developments, the Europeans improved ship design, utilized better navigation techniques, and produced goods such as gunpowder, which allowed them to more easily engage in global trade. Thus, (B) and (C) are incorrect. Once the Europeans established colonies in the Americas, they used slaves to provide labor in these regions. (D) is also incorrect.

3. B

Sugar was an especially labor intensive cash crop, meaning plantation owners required cheap labor. Their primary source of such labor was African slaves, who were transported to the Americas through the transatlantic slave trade. Therefore, **(B)** is correct. Industrialization began with the nineteenth century Industrial Revolution, postdating this map. Thus, (A) is incorrect. Although absolute monarchy was the primary political system in Europe during this period, it did not directly affect the economics of the slave trade. Therefore, (C) is incorrect. European countries of this time period adhered to mercantilist principles rather than laissez-faire capitalism; this meant that governments intervened in economic exchange by placing tariffs on goods from other countries and promoting industries within their countries, instead of allowing free market exchanges to occur. Thus, (D) is also incorrect.

4. C

Thomas Paine, the author of the popular pamphlet *Common Sense*, and other leaders of the American Revolution were inspired by Enlightenment philosophers—including Montesquieu, Locke, and Rousseau—to establish independence from England in the 1770s. These leaders were not primarily motivated by economic considerations. Therefore, **(C)** is correct. Charles Inglis, the Loyalist author of this passage, describes how the colonies' economic dependence on Great Britain should have otherwise deterred these leaders from embarking on such a risky revolution. (A) is incorrect; the Industrial Revolution did indeed begin in England, but it began in the 1780s, after the American Revolution had ended. Although the passage mentions metal, the American revolutionaries were not primarily motivated by a desire to improve the colonies' industries. Rather, more abstract ideas about natural rights and the social contract inspired them. Therefore, (B) is incorrect. (D) is also incorrect; it describes the Puritans' religious motivations to create their settlements in Massachusetts in the seventeenth century.

5. C

Although serfdom was no longer present in late eighteenth century France, many of the obligations and taxes of the feudal period continued to burden peasants up to the revolution. Thus, **(C)** is correct. Unlike the American Revolution, France's revolution was primarily an internal struggle resulting from dramatic social divisions and economic inequality. Thus, (A) is incorrect. While the wealthiest members of society were at the forefront of the American Revolution, the wealthy typically resisted the French Revolution, which was led primarily by the Third Estate. While a catch-all category for people who were not nobles or clergy, politically the Third Estate was primarily led by the *bourgeoisie*. Thus, (B) is incorrect. Enlightenment philosophers and ideals such as natural rights, the separation of powers, and the social contract inspired both revolutions. Therefore, (D) is incorrect.

6. A

The thirteen British colonies primarily provided England with their natural resources instead of growing their own industries. That model describes mercantilist principles; **(A)** is correct. Feudalism was a medieval social system which generally required peasants to serve vassals, who in turn served nobles. This does not describe the passage, so (B) is incorrect. Similarly, (C) is incorrect because monarchism is a political system, in which a monarch such as King George III of Great Britain rules over his people. Economic liberalism is a system which advocates for free trade and minimal government regulation of the economy, which contrasts with the limitations of mercantilist trade. Therefore, (D) is incorrect.

7. B

The Indian National Congress was a group of educated Indians formed with the permission of the British in the late nineteenth century. This group eventually helped to lead the nationalist movement in India under the leadership of Mohandas Gandhi. The Pan-African Congress first met in 1919 after World War I. It stressed African unity and

helped to create nationalist movements, which came to eventually defeat the European colonial powers. Therefore, **(B)** is correct, while (A), (B), and (D) are incorrect.

8. B

Toussaint L'Ouverture helped lead the Haitian revolution. Simón Bolívar led the establishment of Venezuela, Bolivia, Colombia, Ecuador, Peru and Panama as sovereign states, free of Spanish rule. Miguel Hidalgo y Costilla was a leader of the Mexican War of Independence. Therefore, **(B)** is correct. The Reconquista refers to a series of wars and battles between Christian Kingdoms and Muslim Moors for control of the Iberian Peninsula during the Middle Ages. Thus, (A) is incorrect. All three leaders advocated for the abolishment of slavery and predated the mid-eighteenth century development of communist ideology. (C) and (D) are incorrect.

9. D

Toussaint L'Ouverture led a successful slave revolt in Saint-Domingue, resulting in the independence of Haiti and abolition of slavery; **(D)** is correct and (C) incorrect. Prior to the revolt, France controlled Saint-Domingue, not the United States. Therefore, (A) is incorrect. Inspired by both Enlightenment ideals and the French Revolution, Haiti became the first democracy established in the Caribbean; (B) is incorrect.

10. A

The Sepoy Rebellion began after a rumor spread that gunpowder cartridges were made from cow and pig fat, which insulted Hindu and Muslim religious practices. In response, both Muslim and Hindu Indians rebelled cooperatively against British rule. Therefore, **(A)** is correct and (C) is incorrect. The Indian National Congress was instrumental in India's independence from Great Britain, but was formed after the Sepoy Rebellion; (B) is incorrect. After this war, the British East India Company no longer ruled India. Instead, the British crown ruled the subcontinent directly. Thus, (D) is incorrect.

Test What You Learned

1. C

John Locke argued that human beings have certain rights, such as the right to life, liberty and property. Thus, **(C)** is correct. Since governments exist in order to protect these rights, if they fail to do so, they can be overthrown and replaced. As John Locke argued for the separation of church and state, (A) is incorrect. He did not believe humans are born with innate knowledge of truths. Instead, Locke felt that humans learned by experience; (B) is incorrect. (D) refers to a government system of communism, which John Locke did not argue for.

2. C

During the Revolutionary War, American generals often employed the use of guerrilla warfare tactics, an unconventional military strategy. Therefore, **(C)** is correct. The Franco-American alliance did provide both moral and military support to the colonists; (A) is incorrect. The British army wasn't large enough to occupy enough North American territory, giving Americans a "home field" advantage. Thus, (B) is also incorrect. American patriotism united colonists in the cause for freedom, making (D) incorrect.

3. A

The Seven Years' War put Britain into massive debt. In order to pay off the debt, the English government imposed new taxes on its colonies. Additionally, Britain ended its policy of salutary neglect in favor of strict enforcement of parliamentary laws. Therefore, **(A)** is correct while (C) is incorrect. During the war, France lost North American territory, including Quebec, to the English; (B) is incorrect. Before the war, Native American tribes had good relations with French traders in the area. After the war, however, tensions between Native Americans and the English escalated, prompting conflicts such as Pontiac's War. Thus, (D) is incorrect.

4. A

This Renaissance-style building, called the Rokumeikan or "Deer Cry Hall," was built during the Meiji period and became a symbol of Japanese westernization, making **(A)** correct. The social and political changes during the Meiji period arose due to pressure on Japan to keep pace with Western influence and industrialization. European trading companies such as the British East India Company did not control any Japanese cities; therefore, (B) is incorrect. (C) is incorrect as the Tokugawa Shogunate used traditional Japanese architecture in constructing their palaces. The Showa era corresponds to the rule of Emperor Hirohito, who ruled from 1926 to 1989, which is long after the building pictured was built; therefore, (D) is incorrect.

5. B

Upon taking power, Emperor Meiji took an oath which declared, "We shall endeavour to raise the prestige and honor of our country by seeking knowledge throughout the world." After opening to Western influence, Japan sent its leaders abroad to learn about modern advances in military and manufacturing technology, making **(B)** correct. (A), (C), and (D) were all events and developments that did indeed occur during the Meiji restoration, which is the same era as the building's construction.

6. B

The 19th century saw contact and conflict between Western powers and East Asian empires which often turned violent, with the result of land ceded to Western powers, such as Britain. Emperor Meiji agreed to open trade not due to Commodore Perry's diplomatic tactics, but rather, the desire to avoid being forced into a trade relationship with the United States or worse, becoming a colony. Therefore, **(B)** is correct, and (A) is incorrect. Prior to Commodore Perry's arrival, Japan did not come into contact with or desire Western goods or technology, making (C) incorrect. (D) is incorrect as the shogun was overthrown in 1868 and replaced by the Emperor Meiji.

7. D

The Opium Wars most directly resulted in the weakening of Chinese sovereignty as it related to trade, as tariffs were removed and foreigners were granted special rights and privileges. Thus, **(D)** is correct. While the outbreak of the Taiping Rebellion resulted, in part, from the First Opium War, the rebellion was still ongoing when the Second Opium War broke out. Therefore, (A) is incorrect. The downfall of the shogunate and the restoration of the emperor describes the Meiji Restoration, which happened in Japan. Thus, (B) is incorrect. The Ottoman Empire adopted the French legal code and saw a soft takeover by the Young Turks; (C) is incorrect.

8. C

The Qing emperor declared that having a British diplomat come to his court to control trade with China would be unacceptable, or "contrary to all usage of my dynasty," matching **(C)**. He neither welcomed further foreign investment in his empire (A), nor stated that the British had any previous trading privileges that he would continue to uphold. The letter expressed polite gratitude to George III for sending an envoy so far, but did not reflect a submissive attitude. In fact, the closing statement encouraged George to embrace "perpetual submission to our Throne," reflective of the emperor's belief in China's superiority, so (D) is incorrect.

9. B

The Qing dynasty wanted very little commercial or cultural exchange with the outside world in the eighteenth century, continuing the isolationist policy of the previous Ming dynasty and matching **(B)**. Laissez-faire refers to totally unregulated trade, which does not fit with the emperor's resistance to opening trade with the British Empire, seen in the letter, so (A) is incorrect. China would not become a communist country until the post-imperial period, in 1949, eliminating (C). China was still a feudal empire at the time of the letter, so (D) is incorrect.

10. A

The French Revolution saw the internal revolt against a monarchy, the establishment of a republic, and eventually a failure of the initial revolution and rollback of its ideas. The Revolution of 1911, also called the Xinhai Revolution, likewise saw its gains rolled back as violence soon broke out and China descended into warlordism and civil war. Therefore, **(A)** is correct. The Paris Commune was a revolutionary socialist government. While one of Sun Yat-sen's Three Principles of the People was socialism, it was not as strident, and his revolution's Republic of China was not crushed by a large native army. Thus, (B) is incorrect. Sun Yat-sen took over his home country rather than fighting for independence from it. Thus, (C) is incorrect. The Young Turks installed a puppet sultan to rule through, while Sun Yat-sen and his fellow revolutionaries overthrew their own monarchy and established a republic.

CHAPTER 7

Test What You Already Know

1. B

Russia's rapid industrialization in the last decade of the nineteenth century resulted in poor living conditions

for the working class. This led to the organization of new socialist parties, such as the Marxist Social Democratic Party and the Social Revolutionaries. In January of 1905, socialist protesters, led by the priest Georgy Gapon, marched to the Winter Palace in St. Petersburg; **(B)** is correct. (A) and (D) are incorrect because the Tanzimat reform movement was a reformation period of the Ottoman Empire, and the Self-Strengthening Movement was a series of reforms during the Qing dynasty in China, both occurring in the nineteenth century. Although witnesses to the demonstration in the passage described the protestors as being "not our people," the protestors were socialist and not anti-nationalist, making (C) incorrect.

2. D

The Russian Revolution of 1905 directly ignited strikes and uprisings throughout the nation, but it also more generally spurred Russian revolutionary efforts to continue. Thus, **(D)** is correct. After the Revolution of 1905, the tsar did form the Duma in 1906; however, this legislative assembly disbanded during the later Revolution of 1917, making (A) incorrect. (B) is incorrect because tsarist rule continued in Russia until the Revolution of 1917, culminating in the execution of the tsar and his family in 1918. (C) is incorrect because socialism continued to grow as the primary revolutionary movement in Russia after 1905.

3. D

Gender equality became a key principle of communist social organization after the Chinese Cultural Revolution; **(D)** is correct. Women were often depicted in masculine clothing, with short hair and severe features, performing traditional male work. (A) is incorrect because the image was directed at Chinese youth, not Taiwanese dissidents. While Mao did transplant urban youth to rural areas in the "Down to the Countryside" movement, it is not depicted in this image; (B) is incorrect. Mao did not actively wish to imitate Russia's approach to communism, making (C) incorrect.

4. A

(A) is correct because the Cultural Revolution sought to destroy anything that could undermine communist ideals, which in Mao's view included art and literature from previous periods in Chinese history. (B) describes the aims of the Great Leap Forward, which achieved limited success; therefore, it is incorrect. The Cultural Revolution sought to eliminate political dissent and restore power to Mao and his allies, making (C) incorrect. The Cultural Revolution aimed to eliminate what were known as the "Four Olds"—old customs, old culture, old habits, and old ideas—not restore them; therefore, (D) is incorrect.

5. D

The United Nations was formed in 1945 as a result of World War II, making **(D)** correct. Fifty-one countries started the international organization, which was committed to maintaining international peace and security, developing friendly relations among nations, and promoting social progress. The Korean War began in 1950, after the United Nations had been well established, making (A) incorrect. The Cold War refers to the tension between the Eastern Bloc (the Soviet Union and satellite nations) and the Western Bloc (the United States and its Western European allies), and lasted approximately from the end of World War II until the collapse of the Soviet Union in 1991; (B) is incorrect. The international organization founded after World War I to promote peace was called the League of Nations, making (C) incorrect.

6. A

The League of Nations, the organization preceding the United Nations, was doomed to fail when the United States and Soviet Union, two of the most powerful countries at the time, refused to join; **(A)** is correct. (B) is incorrect because, while the Great Depression did negatively affect the global economy, the League of Nations was not involved in international commerce enough to be affected. The League of Nations had no force, making it powerless in military conflicts; (C) is incorrect. The global spread of communism did not become a significant issue until after World War II, when the League of Nations was replaced by the United Nations; therefore (D) is also incorrect.

7. C

While the charter does generally reference economic relations between countries, international trade is not an explicit purpose of the UN itself; therefore, **(C)** is correct. The UN charter outlines its mission of promoting personal freedoms in the form of human rights, (A), preventing military aggression through diplomacy, (B), and increasing "friendly relations among nations based on respect for the principle of equal rights and the self determination of peoples" (D).

8. D

In 1960, most Latin American countries had some form of dictatorship, and democracy, where it existed, was not complete or fully expressed. By 2000, almost all countries in the Western Hemisphere, with the notable exceptions of Cuba and Haiti, had a functioning democracy, making **(D)** correct. Cuba was the only Latin American country at this time to adopt a communist government, so (A) is incorrect. The majority of Latin American military dictatorships were overthrown in this period, making (B) incorrect. Most European colonial control in Latin America ended in the early 1800s; (C) is incorrect.

9. C

The socialist Sandinista National Liberation Front, with members known as Sandinistas, ruled Nicaragua after deposing Somoza in 1979, matching **(C)**. At this time Fidel Castro ran the communist nation of Cuba, and Honduras and Guatemala were subject to numerous government upheavals, eliminating (A), (B), and (D).

10. A

After establishing a communist regime in Cuba, Fidel Castro developed a diplomatic relationship with the Soviet Union, receiving financial and military support; **(A)** is correct. Neither Brazil nor Spain provided significant support to Cuba during this period, eliminating (B) and (D). During the height of the Cold War in the second half of the twentieth century, the United States opposed Cuban and Soviet efforts to aid socialist and communist uprisings in Latin America; (C) is incorrect.

Test What You Learned

1. B

During World War I, ships like the *H.M.S. Orvieto* accompanied Allied civilian ships in order to protect them against German U-boat attacks. The Germans attempted to interfere with supply shipments to Allied powers. Due to the defensive strength provided by armed convoys, Allied powers did not suffer the kind of food and supply shortages that Central powers did under the British naval blockade; therefore, **(B)** is correct. (A) is incorrect, as German U-boats did not succeed in sabotaging civilian supply shipments enough to impact Allied powers. Though the British Empire was large and spanned multiple continents, the map does not depict them, making

(C) incorrect. Ironclad ships were developed and first used by the British navy in 1861, long before the outbreak of World War I; (D) is incorrect.

2. C

The increased demand for raw materials during World War I led to an economic boon for countries like Chile, whose nitrate exports were used as an ingredient in gunpowder; **(C)** is correct. (A) is incorrect because, in comparison to other American wars, not many American men evaded the draft. Latin American countries were not directly involved in the fighting, making (B) incorrect. (D) is incorrect because Latin America exported raw materials, not luxury goods.

3. C

Many colonial territories relied on exporting one or two main products, leaving them vulnerable to fluctuations in the global market. Global demand for rubber, for example, dramatically decreased during the Depression, due in part to a dip in car tire manufacturing. This was disastrous for colonial economies, making **(C)** correct. Both (A) and (D) are incorrect as the Great Depression did not directly lead to independence or communist revolution. This occurred more after World War II, when imperial governments were weakened. (B) is incorrect because all global trade and manufacturing contracted, lessening the need for finished goods and raw materials alike.

4. B

In response to the global economic crisis spurred by the Great Depression, many countries adopted a policy of economic protectionism, which included raising tariffs in order to restrict imports; therefore, **(B)** is correct. The Global Depression resulted in political unrest and extremism for many countries, a rise in global unemployment, and the collapse of world financial centers; (A), (C), and (D) are incorrect.

5. C

The Russian Bolsheviks gained most of their support from working-class individuals living in the cities, not rural areas. On the other hand, China had an enormous peasant population that was sympathetic to communist policies like land redistribution; **(C)** is correct. (A), (B), and (D) are incorrect because these were all commonalities between the two communist revolutions. Both Russia and China struggled with how to communize societies that were mainly agricultural and pre-industrial, and accordingly, instituted Five-Year Plans; Russia and China were also similar in their totalitarian methods, as both imprisoned and even killed those who opposed their new regime.

6. A

The Sino-Soviet split was a rift that grew from approximately 1956 to 1960 and continued into the 1980s between the Soviet Union and China, the two biggest communist powers in the world at that time. Its origins lay in Nikita Khrushchev's denunciation of Stalin and grew to include larger differences in interpretation of communist ideology, dealings with the capitalist West, and communism around the world; **(A)** is correct. (B) is incorrect as the Soviet Union and China did not have, nor compete for, overseas colonies. Differences in ideology and overall national interests ran far deeper than the fractious relationship between Khrushchev and Mao, making (C) incorrect. (D) is incorrect because the détente between the United States and the Soviet Union was an outcome of the Sino-Soviet split, not a cause.

7. B

In the mid-1980s, Soviet leader Mikhail Gorbachev initiated policies that would ultimately lead to the dismantling of the U.S.S.R. *Glasnost*, or "openness," referred to a policy of cultural and intellectual freedom, leading to increased freedom for the press. *Perestroika*, or "restructuring," introduced some aspects of capitalism into the existing economic system; **(B)** is correct. (A), (C), and (D) are all incorrect as Mao, Stalin, and Castro all did not permit government transparency or freedom for their citizens.

8. A

(A) is correct, as the reunification of Germany was a result of the collapse, due to the loss of Soviet control of East Germany. (B) is incorrect because the costly invasion of Afghanistan proved disastrous for the already-stretched Soviet economy. The Solidarity movement in Poland was an anti-communist social movement which successfully overthrew the communist government in 1989. The Soviet Union therefore lost one of its most important satellite states, and many others in similar revolutions in 1989; (C) is incorrect. (D) is incorrect, as implementing the policies of *glasnost* and *perestroika* weakened the tight control the Soviet Union had held over its citizens.

9. B

Several Latin American countries struggled politically and economically through destabilizing regime changes in the twentieth century, but most moved politically toward representative democracy beginning in the 1980s; **(B)** is correct. Communism remains limited in the region, fundamentalist regimes have not come to power, and most totalitarian dictatorships have been deposed; therefore, (A), (C), and (D) are incorrect.

10. A

By liberalizing markets and encouraging foreign loans and investment, Chile was able to create a much stronger economy than many other Latin American dictatorships, making **(A)** correct. The regime under Augusto Pinochet was anti-communist, so (B) is incorrect. The Sandinista party was active in Nicaragua, not Chile, eliminating (C). Pinochet's staunch persecution of communists meant that Chile did not ally with the Soviet Union, making (D) incorrect.

References

CHAPTER 2

Document-Based Question

Document 4

Mintzuri, Hagop. *Istanbul Anilari 1897–1940*, translated by Silva Kuyumcuyan. Istanbul: Tarih Vakfi, 2002.

CHAPTER 3 (PERIODS 1 AND 2: UP TO 600 C.E.)

Test What You Learned (Post-Quiz)

Questions 1–3

Stokes Brown, Cynthia. "What is Civilization, Anyway?" *World History Connected*, 2009, http://worldhistoryconnected.press.illinois.edu/6.3/brown.html.

Questions 8–10

Silbergeld, Jerome, Erik Zürcher and others. "China." *Encyclopaedia Britannica, Inc.*, 2017, https://www.britannica.com/place/China/Dong-Eastern-Han.

CHAPTER 4

Test What You Already Know (Pre-Quiz)

Questions 6–8

Madden, Thomas F. The New Concise History of the Crusades. Rowman & Littlefield, 2005.

Test What You Learned (Post-Quiz)

Questions 1–2

Elverskog, Johan. *Buddhism and Islam on the Silk Road*. Philadelphia: University of Pennsylvania Press, 2010.

CHAPTER 5

Test What You Already Know (Pre-Quiz)

Questions 9–10

Lu, D. J. *Japan: A Documentary History*. London: Routledge, 1997.

Test What You Learned (Post-Quiz)

Questions 1–2

Marcus, Jacob. *The Jew in the Medieval World: A Sourcebook, 315-1791*. Cincinnati: Sinai Press, 1938.

Questions 5–6

Struve, L. A. *The Southern Ming, 1644–1662*. Yale University Press, 1984.

CHAPTER 7

Test What You Already Know (Pre-Quiz)

Questions 5–7

United Nations. Charter of the United Nations. 24 October 1945, 1 UNTS XVI, http://www.un.org/en/sections/un-charter/chapter-i/index.html.

Questions 8–10

Lockhart, James, Roger A. Kittleson, and David Bushnell. "History of Latin America." *Encyclopaedia Britannica, Inc.*, 2017, https://www.britannica.com/place/Latin-America.

Test What You Learned (Post-Quiz)

Questions 5–6

Zedong, Mao. "Outline for a Speech on the International Situation," December, 1959, *History and Public Policy Program Digital Archive*, http://digitalarchive.wilsoncenter.org/document/118893.

Questions 7–8

Lockhart, James, Roger A. Kittleson, and David Bushnell. "History of Latin America." *Encyclopaedia Britannica, Inc.*, 2017, https://www.britannica.com/place/Latin-America.

PRACTICE EXAM 1

Questions 6–7

de Bary, William Theodore and Irene Bloom, eds. *Sources of Chinese Tradition*. New York City: Columbia University Press, 1999.

Questions 13–14

Gulliver, Phillip H. *American Anthropologist* 62, no. 6 (1960): 900–903.

Questions 18–21

Lu, D. J. *Japan: A Documentary History*. London: Routledge, 1997.

Short-Answer Question 1: Source 2

Bony, Jean. *French Gothic Architecture of the 12th and 13th Centuries*. University of California Press, 1983.

Document-Based Question: Document 3

Haslip, Gabriel. "The politics of Taíno revivalism: The insignificance of Amerindian mtDNA in the population history of Puerto Ricans." *Centro Journal*, 2006.

PRACTICE EXAM 2

Questions 1–2

Roach, John. "Mohenjo Daro." *National Geographic*, 2017, http://www.nationalgeographic.com/archaeology-and-history/archaeology/mohenjo-daro/.

Questions 34–36

Lockhart, James, Roger A. Kittleson, and David Bushnell. "History of Latin America." *Encyclopaedia Britannica, Inc.*, 2017, https://www.britannica.com/place/Latin-America.

Questions 37–40

Byerly, Victoria. *Hard Times Cotton Mill Girls: Personal Histories of Womanhood and Poverty in the South.* IRL Press, 1986.

Questions 45–47

"Memorandum from the International Department of the Central Committee of the CPSU to Alexander Yakovlev," February, 1989. *History and Public Policy Program Digital Archive*, http://digitalarchive.wilsoncenter.org/document/112485.

Questions 53–55: Source 1

Nkrumah, Kwame. *I Speak of Freedom.* Zed Books, 1973.

PRACTICE EXAM 3

Questions 1–3

Samuel, Alan Edouard, Peter F. Dorman and others. "Ancient Egypt." *National Geographic*, 2017, https://www.britannica.com/place/ancient-Egypt.

Questions 10–12

"Paleolithic Period." *National Geographic*, 2017, https://www.britannica.com/event/Paleolithic-Period.

Questions 27–30

The Trustees of the British Museum. "The wealth of Africa: The Swahili Coast." *The British Museum*, 2010, https://www.britishmuseum.org/pdf/SwahiliCoast_TeachersNotes.pdf.

Questions 44–45

Gorbachev, Mikhail. *Perestroika: New Thinking for Our Country and the World.* HarperCollins, 1987.

Short-Answer Question 1

Ross, Stewart. *Second World War (Causes and Consequences).* Evans Brothers, 1995.

Document-Based Question: Document 2

Goldman, Emma. *My Disillusionment in Russia*. Doubleday, 1923.

Document-Based Question: Document 4

Lenin, Krupskaya. Preface. In *The Emancipation of Women*, written by V.I. Lenin. International Publishers, 1933.

Document-Based Question: Document 5

Zedong, Mao. *The Selected Quotations of Mao Zedong*. Kiefer Press, 2008.

Document-Based Question: Document 7

Dangdi, Shao. *The New Republic*. March 2004.